Holt MUSIC

TEACHER'S EDITION Grade 5

Eunice Boardman Meske
Professor of Music and Education
University of Wisconsin—Madison
Madison, Wisconsin

Barbara Andress
Professor of Music Education
Arizona State University
Tempe, Arizona

Mary P. Pautz
Assistant Professor of Music
 Education
University of Wisconsin—Milwaukee
Milwaukee, Wisconsin

Fred Willman
Professor of Music and Education
University of Missouri—St. Louis
St. Louis, Missouri

TEXAS EDUCATION AGENCY
Textbook Division

Readability Level Designation
State Textbook Adoption of <u>November 1988</u>
(To be filed in the Textbook Division no later than
5:00 p.m. on April 11, 1988)

Name of Publishing Company   HOLT, RINEHART AND WINSTON, INC.

Signed _Larry Hare_   SOUTHWEST REGIONAL MANAGER
                    (Name and Title of Company Official)

Name of Texas Depository   SOUTHWEST SCHOOL BOOK DEPOSITORY

Multiple List (Enter title & author)	Edition & Copyright	Name of Formula	Readability Level
HOLT MUSIC, Grade 5 Boardman and Andress	1988	Harris-Jacobson	4.6

Holt, Rinehart and Winston, Publishers
New York, Toronto, Mexico City, London, Sydney, Tokyo

Acknowledgments for previously copyrighted material
and credits for photographs and art begin on page 423.
ISBN 0-03-005303-X
7890 032 98765432

HOLT MUSIC

It's the leader of the band!

CONSIDER THE ADVANTAGES . . .

- **Dozens of the world's finest songs in each level—the songs your students want to sing!**

- **Exciting activities that enable students to interact with the music and acquire musical knowledge.**

- **Exceptionally motivating listening lessons that really get students involved in learning.**

- **Flexibly organized Teacher's Editions, rich with background information and no-nonsense teaching strategies.**

- **A wealth of supplementary materials that enhance, extend, and enrich.**

Music That Motivates

Every song in HOLT MUSIC builds on the natural enthusiasm that students have for singing, dancing—expressing themselves in creative ways! You'll find hundreds and hundreds of authentic songs that students really *want* to sing—songs with built-in appeal.

Choose from a rich variety of songs: contemporary, traditional, American and European folk, classical, holiday music, and more.

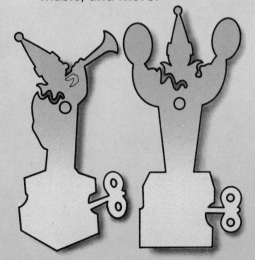

Just look at some of these favorites:

Galway Piper
Put On a Happy Face
Bicycle Built for Two
Edelweiss
I'd Like to Teach the World to Sing (In Perfect Harmony)
The Lion Sleeps Tonight
On the Road Again
Let There Be Peace on Earth
I Believe in Music
Anyone Can Move a Mountain

Lively, colorful photographs and illustrations provide the perfect visual accompaniment.

Music to Learn From

Songs throughout HOLT MUSIC develop note-reading skills and apply them as a basis for instrumental accompaniment and vocal exploration.

Each song provides a point of departure for creative involvement in learning.

Unique graphic devices that look like the music sounds introduce basic note-reading skills and reinforce concepts of melody and rhythm.

Music to Interact With

Engaging activities help students understand, relate to, and interact with music right from the start. These activities are more than entertaining—they're truly *instructive*, designed to strengthen and enhance musical understanding.

The Sea

Shore at Bas-Butin, Honfleur, c. 1886, by Georges Seurat. Oil on Canvas.
Musée des Beaux Arts, Tournai, Belgium.

Play the Soprano Ukulele

1. Learn to hold your ukulele.

2. Find these parts:

Tuning Pegs

Fingerboard
(on top of neck)

Frets

Strings

Neck
(below fingerboard)

Create a Light Show

Some of you will "paint" with colored lights.
Experiment with making different lines and shapes.
Will all of the lights be used all of the time?

Others will create music to match the movement of the lights.
Choose a different instrument for each colored light.

97

Speech to Song

Speaking and singing have many things in common.
Words may be spoken or sung.
Words express our feelings.
They can express excitement, happiness, sadness, or fright.
We use voice inflection when we speak.

Ba — na — nas for sale

We use exaggerated voice inflections when we sing.

Yes! We have no ba - na - nas,

Gestures help punctuate and emphasize our words.
Look at this storyboard.
What could these people be saying to each other?

Work with a partner.
Decide who the characters will be.
Play the roles of these two people.
Speak their conversation.
Perform the roles again by singing the conversation.

206

G C E A

4 3 2 1
String No.

Irresistible activities inspire singing, clapping, making up melodies and rhymes, and more—the true exhilaration of musical expression. Many activities involve poetry or related arts.

Short instrumental experiences begin at Kindergarten, employing readily available instruments.

Music Worth Listening To

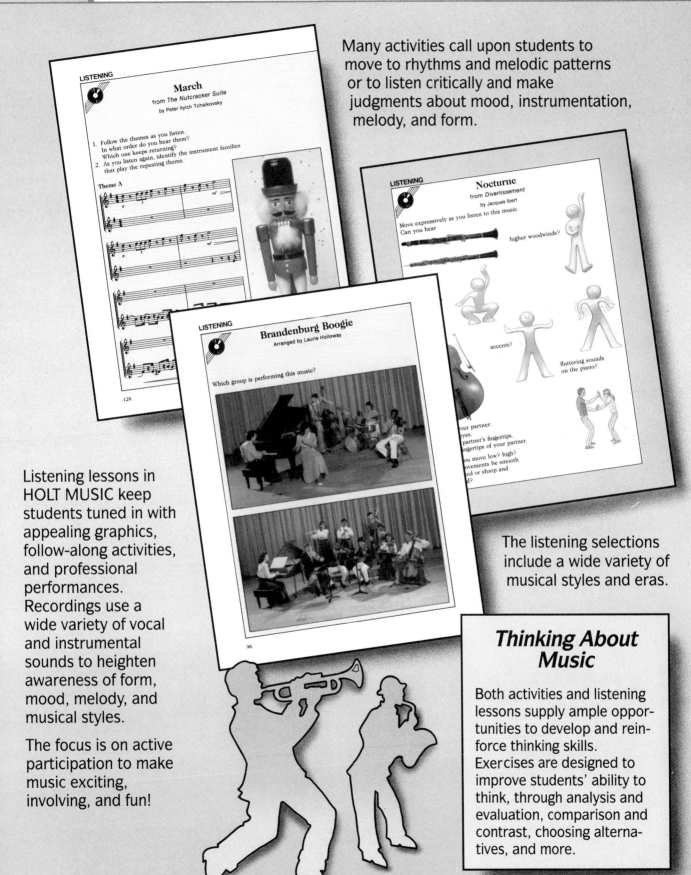

Many activities call upon students to move to rhythms and melodic patterns or to listen critically and make judgments about mood, instrumentation, melody, and form.

Listening lessons in HOLT MUSIC keep students tuned in with appealing graphics, follow-along activities, and professional performances. Recordings use a wide variety of vocal and instrumental sounds to heighten awareness of form, mood, melody, and musical styles.

The focus is on active participation to make music exciting, involving, and fun!

The listening selections include a wide variety of musical styles and eras.

Thinking About Music

Both activities and listening lessons supply ample opportunities to develop and reinforce thinking skills. Exercises are designed to improve students' ability to think, through analysis and evaluation, comparison and contrast, choosing alternatives, and more.

Music That's Realistic to Teach!

Whatever your musical background, you'll find all the backup help you need in HOLT MUSIC Teacher's Editions: concrete information, strategies you can rely on, and solid, flexible lesson plans with many optional suggestions. Every page is designed to bring musical understanding and appreciation within reach of all your students.

Each lesson begins with a clear objective and a complete list of program materials, including a detailed summary of recordings and the voices and instruments used.

A special logo signals when activity sheets are available for the lesson.

Each of the extension lessons in Unit 2 is cross-referenced to a core lesson.

"Introducing the Lesson" includes a simple-to-perform motivator that leads naturally into the lesson content.

"Developing the Lesson" gives step-by-step teaching suggestions to ensure that the lesson objective is met. Commentary and questions to the student are highlighted in boldface type.

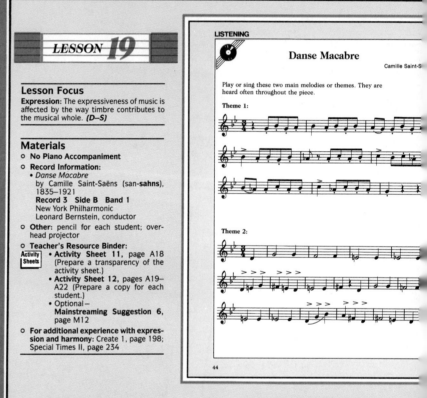

LESSON 19

Lesson Focus
Expression: The expressiveness of music is affected by the way timbre contributes to the musical whole. **(D–S)**

Materials
○ **No Piano Accompaniment**
○ **Record Information:**
- *Danse Macabre*
  by Camille Saint-Saëns (san-**sahns**), 1835–1921
  Record 3 Side B Band 1
  New York Philharmonic
  Leonard Bernstein, conductor
○ **Other:** pencil for each student; overhead projector
○ **Teacher's Resource Binder:**

Activity Sheets
- **Activity Sheet 11**, page A18 (Prepare a transparency of the activity sheet.)
- **Activity Sheet 12**, pages A19–A22 (Prepare a copy for each student.)
- Optional—
  Mainstreaming Suggestion 6, page M12
○ **For additional experience with expression and harmony:** Create 1, page 198; Special Times II, page 234

LISTENING

Danse Macabre

Camille Saint-S[...]

Play or sing these two main melodies or themes. They are heard often throughout the piece.

Theme 1:

Theme 2:

44

Introducing the Lesson

Ask the students to open their books to page 44. Familiarize the class with Themes 1 and 2 by playing them on the piano or by helping the students sing the themes.

Developing the Lesson

1. Review the instruments and families of the orchestra by displaying a transparency of Activity Sheet 11 (*Orchestra Seating Plan*). Draw the students' attention to the way the instruments are grouped by families within the orchestra seating plan. Recall the discussion in Lesson 18 regarding the reasons for orchestral family groupings.

2. Play the recording of *Danse Macabre*. **As you listen, how many instruments and orchestral**

families can you recognize? Discuss the in[...] struments that the students heard. Associat[...] them with the pictures shown on page 45.

3. Distribute copies of Activity Sheet 12 (*Dans[...] Macabre: A Musical Puzzle*). The compose[...] Camille Saint-Saëns, chose either individua[...] instruments or families of instruments to hel[...] him interpret this dance in music. Focus a[...] tention on the *Danse Macabre* "map" just dis[...] tributed. The map is divided into numbere[...] boxes. Within each box are "puzzle piece[...] that contain the names of instruments or o[...] chestral families. Explain to the students tha[...] as they hear each number spoken on the re[...] cording, they are to decide which instrumen[...] or instrument family is playing. They shoul[...] then mark the correct answer by circling th[...] puzzle piece. (For Box 12 they are to fill i[...] the name of the instrument being played.)

Freedom of choice is truly yours—lesson plans are designed for maximum flexibility. Each level is divided into two units. Unit 1, the core, contains 60 lessons for a minimum program. Unit 2 contains four chapters for reinforcement, enrichment, and special performances.

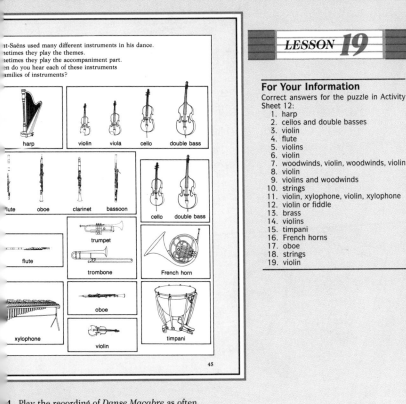

LESSON 19

For Your Information

Correct answers for the puzzle in Activity Sheet 12:

1. harp
2. cellos and double basses
3. violin
4. flute
5. violins
6. violin
7. woodwinds, violin, woodwinds, violin
8. violin
9. violins and woodwinds
10. strings
11. violin, xylophone, violin, xylophone
12. violin or fiddle
13. brass
14. violins
15. timpani
16. French horns
17. oboe
18. strings
19. violin

[instrument illustrations labeled: harp, violin, viola, cello, double bass, flute, oboe, clarinet, bassoon, cello, double bass, trumpet, trombone, French horn, flute, xylophone, oboe, violin, timpani]

45

4. Play the recording of *Danse Macabre* as often as needed for the students to complete the puzzle. After everyone has finished, read the correct answers and ask the students to correct any errors they may have made on their activity sheets.

Closing the Lesson OPTIONAL

Listen one last time to enjoy this dramatic composition. *Danse Macabre* is a symphonic poem that depicts Death playing the violin and skeletons dancing in a graveyard at midnight. It is a good example of the typically strong, expressive symphonic poems written in the Romantic style of the 19th century.

45

When a score is given in graphic notation in the pupil book, the music notation appears on the teacher's page.

''For Your Information'' provides a quick, convenient reference for background information about lesson contents.

A colored band designates the core pages. Optional steps are labeled with a logo.

''Closing the Lesson'' offers activities to apply what has been learned.

Special logos indicate when performance cassettes ⬚ and rehearsal cassettes ⬚ are available.

Music That's Manageable

The **Teacher's Resource Binder** makes classroom management uncommonly convenient. Blackline masters help teachers structure the course to match individual preferences.

Teachers who use the **Kodaly** approach will find creative teaching ideas and fun-filled student charts— all correlated to HOLT MUSIC.

The **Orff** activities will delight your class with chants, games, and lively instrumental arrangements.

The **Biography** series brings music personalities to life.

A complete set of **Evaluations** provides a comprehensive testing program for HOLT MUSIC.

Students who are especially interested in music or who are academically gifted will find plenty of challenges in the **Enrichment** ideas.

Students will love working with the call charts, games, puzzles, costume patterns, and other idea-packed **Activity Sheets**. These blackline masters are designed to supplement, extend, and enrich the basic lesson plans.

Mainstreaming activities ensure that involvement in music learning is an important part of every child's day.

Relating music to other areas of learning becomes a snap with **Curriculum Correlation** teaching suggestions and charts.

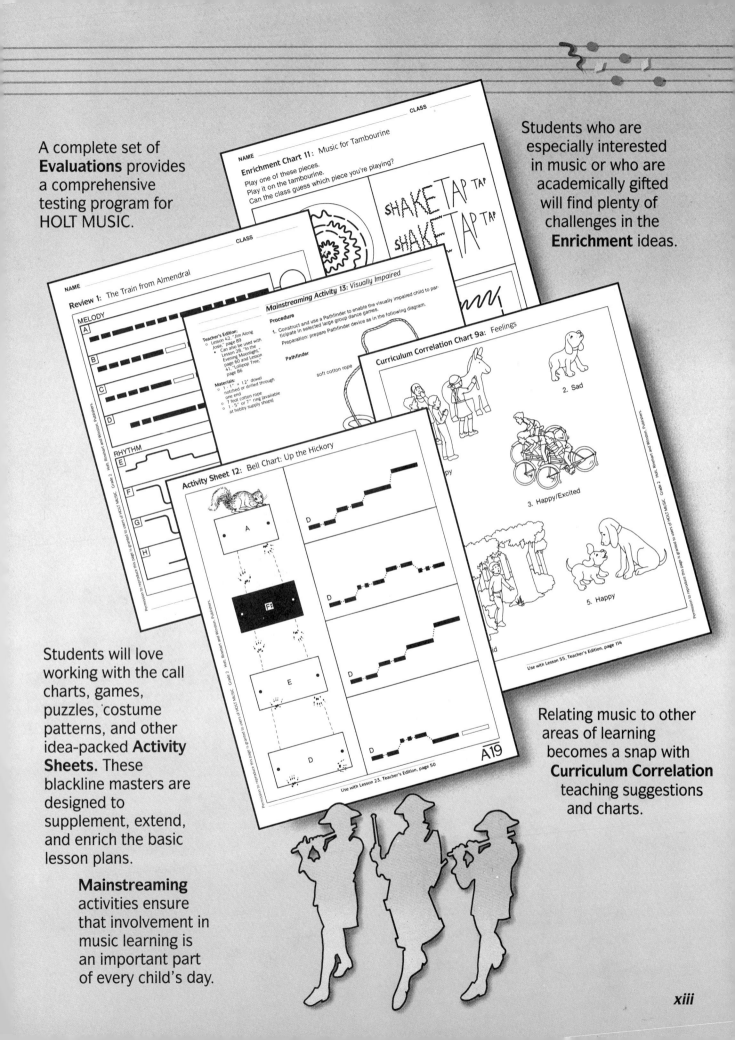

xiii

Music to Play

Recordings

A set of first-quality recordings serves a dual purpose: to give students a model for performance and to provide a valuable instrumental and vocal resource. Dual-track stereo allows separation of recorded voice and accompaniment. Recordings are digitally mastered.

A sturdy carrying case includes an index cross-referenced to lessons in the Teacher's Edition.

Song and listening selections appear in lesson order.

Extra Features!

Performance cassettes contain instrumental tracks specially edited for optimum sound in public performance.

Rehearsal cassettes for Grades 4–8 help students learn part songs by hearing each vocal part alone.

Supplementary Items

Wait Until You Hear This! music software uses songs from HOLT MUSIC to encourage active experimentation with musical elements. Students can rearrange phrases, alter rhythms, tempo, and timbre, and change key or mode to create new musical works. Three separate programs are available: Grades K–2, 3–5, and 6–8.

The *Holiday Song Book* includes lyrics and piano accompaniments for an additional 50 songs celebrating a year's worth of holidays — Mother's Day, Columbus Day, the Fourth of July, and more.

COMPONENTS CHART

	K	1	2	3	4	5	6	7	8
Pupil Book		✓	✓	✓	✓	✓	✓	✓	✓
Jumbo Book	✓	✓							
Teacher's Edition	✓	✓	✓	✓	✓	✓	✓	✓	✓
Recordings	✓	✓	✓	✓	✓	✓	✓	✓	✓
Teacher's Resource Binder	✓	✓	✓	✓	✓	✓	✓	✓	✓
Holiday Song Book	✓	✓	✓	✓	✓	✓	✓	✓	✓
Computer Software	✓	✓	✓	✓	✓	✓	✓	✓	✓
Performance Cassettes	✓	✓	✓	✓	✓	✓	✓	✓	✓
Rehearsal Cassettes				✓	✓	✓	✓	✓	✓

HOLT MUSIC offers you a total package for your classroom needs. A list of components is given in the chart at the left.

TABLE OF CONTENTS

CORE UNIT 1 *Music to Explore*...4

Meet the Authors .... **xxii**

Holt Music Field Test .... **xxiii**

A Guide to Holt Music .... **xxiv**

To the Classroom Teacher .... **xxv**

The Generative Approach to Music
  Learning .... **xxvi**

Scope and Sequence for Grade 5 ... **xxviii**

The First Quarter   6

LESSON 1 HARMONY 6
ON THE ROAD AGAIN

LESSON 2 HARMONY 8
HEY DUM DIDDELEY DUM

LESSON 3 HARMONY 10
MOCKIN' BIRD HILL

LESSON 4 HARMONY 12
Chords and Melody Go Hand in Hand
  (ACTIVITY)
SKIP TO MY LOU
OH, DEAR, WHAT CAN THE
  MATTER BE?

LESSON 5 HARMONY 14
ODE TO A WASHERWOMAN
Piano Quintet ("The Trout"), Fourth
  Movement *(LISTENING)*

LESSON 6 FORM 16
Theme and Variations *(ACTIVITY)*
Souvenir d'Amerique *(LISTENING)*
WADE IN THE WATER

LESSON 7 RHYTHM 18
MY AUNT CAME BACK

LESSON **8** RHYTHM **20**
BICYCLE BUILT FOR TWO
More About Rhythmic Relationships
    (ACTIVITY)

LESSON **9** RHYTHM **22**
MORNING COMES EARLY
THE TURTLE'S SONG—"I CAN WIN!"

LESSON **10** HARMONY **24**
SARAH THE WHALE
ON TOP OF OLD SMOKY

LESSON **11** HARMONY **26**
LA CUCARACHA
OLEANA

LESSON **12** HARMONY **28**
SIMPLE GIFTS
Variations on a Shaker Tune *(LISTENING)*

LESSON **13** EXPRESSION **30**
Moonlight *(ACTIVITY)*
Adagio for Percussion *(ACTIVITY)*
Moonlight Sonata, Adagio *(LISTENING)*

LESSON **14** EXPRESSION **34**
Make Musical Decisions *(ACTIVITY)*
BATTLE HYMN OF THE REPUBLIC

LESSON **15** EVALUATION 1 . . . . . . **36**
THERE'S WORK TO BE DONE
NO NEED TO HURRY

The Second Quarter **38**

LESSON **16** TIME AND PLACE **38**
MAYO NAFWA

LESSON **17** TIMBRE **40**
Sound Categories *(LISTENING)*

LESSON **18** TIMBRE **42**
THE MUSIC GOES 'ROUND AND
    AROUND

LESSON **19** EXPRESSION **44**
Danse Macabre *(LISTENING)*

LESSON **20** RHYTHM **46**
THERE'S A HOLE IN THE MIDDLE
    OF THE SEA

LESSON **21** DYNAMICS **48**
ANYONE CAN MOVE A MOUNTAIN

LESSON **22** EXPRESSION **50**
LIFT EVERY VOICE AND SING

LESSON **23** MELODY **52**
I BELIEVE

LESSON **24** MELODY **54**
Improvisation on Whole Tones *(ACTIVITY)*

LESSON **25** EXPRESSION **56**
Voiles *(LISTENING)*

LESSON **26** EXPRESSION **58**
The Sea *(ACTIVITY)*

LESSON **27** RHYTHM **60**
LORD, LORD, LORD

LESSON **28** RHYTHM **62**
I'D LIKE TO TEACH THE WORLD TO
    SING (IN PERFECT HARMONY)

LESSON **29** EXPRESSION **64**
SEVEN LIMERICKS

LESSON **30** EVALUATION 2 . . . . . . **66**
Shepherd's Hey *(LISTENING)*

The Third Quarter **68**

LESSON **31** RHYTHM **68**
TOEMBAI

LESSON **32** MELODY **70**
SPIDER ON THE FLOOR

LESSON **33** MELODY **72**
SWEET POTATOES

LESSON **34** HARMONY 74
EL YIVNE HA GALIL

LESSON **35** HARMONY 76
DOBBIN, DOBBIN

LESSON **36** HARMONY 78
A SMILE IS A FROWN UPSIDE DOWN

LESSON **37** RHYTHM 82
A Rhythm Challenge (ACTIVITY)
LIFE IN THE ARMY

LESSON **38** RHYTHM 84
YANKEE DOODLE BOY
Patriotic Polyrhythms (ACTIVITY)

LESSON **39** RHYTHM 86
FIFTY NIFTY UNITED STATES

LESSON **40** HARMONY 90
LOOK DOWN THAT LONESOME ROAD

LESSON **41** HARMONY 92
THE LION SLEEPS TONIGHT

LESSON **42** HARMONY 94
OLD HOUND DOG SALLY

LESSON **43** EXPRESSION 96
Brandenburg Boogie (LISTENING)
Create a Light Show (ACTIVITY)

LESSON **44** TIME AND PLACE 98
Brandenburg Concerto No. 2 in F
    Major, First Movement (LISTENING)

LESSON **45** EVALUATION 3 100
I BELIEVE IN MUSIC

The Fourth Quarter **102**

LESSON **46** RHYTHM 102
NORWEGIAN MOUNTAIN MARCH

LESSON **47** RHYTHM, MELODY . . .104
TURN THE GLASSES OVER

LESSON **48** RHYTHM, MELODY . . 106
GARDEN SONG
Allegretto from Symphony No. 7 (LISTENING)

LESSON **49** FORM 108
CATCH A FALLING STAR

LESSON **50** RHYTHM 110
SIM SA-LA-BIM
FORWARD-BACK! (ACTIVITY)
Rumanian Dance No. 5 from
    Rumanian Folk Dances (LISTENING)

LESSON **51** RHYTHM 112
GERAKINA

LESSON **52** MELODY 114
MAGIC PENNY

LESSON **53** MELODY 116
AMERICA, AMERICA
WHIPPOORWILL ROUND

LESSON **54** TIMBRE 118
Keyboard Instruments (ACTIVITY)
THE OLD PIANO ROLL BLUES

LESSON **55** MELODY 120
SOLOMON LEVI
Play a Keyboard Instrument (ACTIVITY)

LESSON **56** HARMONY 122
Play the Autoharp (ACTIVITY)
This Land Is Your Land (CHANT)
La Cucaracha (CHANT)

LESSON **57** HARMONY 124
OH SUSANNAH
ROCK ISLAND LINE

LESSON **58** EXPRESSION 126
Londonderry Air (LISTENING)
GALWAY PIPER

LESSON **59** TIMBRE, FORM 128
March, from Nutcracker Suite (LISTENING)

LESSON **60** EVALUATION 4 130
Learning a New Song (ACTIVITY)
WE SHALL OVERCOME

UNIT 2 More Music to Explore... 132

Perform Music   134

PERFORM 1   RHYTHM, FORM 134
MAORI STICK GAME

PERFORM 2   RHYTHM 136
I'M GOING CRAZY

PERFORM 3   RHYTHM 137
THE ZULU WARRIOR

PERFORM 4   EXPRESSION 138
SUNSHINE ON MY SHOULDERS

PERFORM 5   HARMONY 141
ALLELUIA

PERFORM 6   EXPRESSION 142
THE LONELY GOATHERD

PERFORM 7   HARMONY 145
PEACE OF THE RIVER

PERFORM 8   EXPRESSION 146
LET US SING TOGETHER

PERFORM 9   HARMONY 148
Play the Soprano Ukulele (ACTIVITY)
Learn to Strum on Open Strings (ACTIVITY)
Are You Sleeping (CHANT)
Row, Row, Row Your Boat (CHANT)
Three Blind Mice (CHANT)

PERFORM 10   HARMONY 150
Tune Your Ukulele (ACTIVITY)
GROUNDHOG
FOUND A PEANUT
YELLOW ROSE OF TEXAS

PERFORM 11   HARMONY 154
WHEN THE SAINTS GO MARCHING IN
STREETS OF LAREDO

PERFORM 12   HARMONY 156
SPANISH CAVALIER AND SOLOMON
   LEVI

PERFORM 13   HARMONY 158
Learn to Play a C Chord (ACTIVITY)
Three Blind Mice (CHANT)
THE BEE AND THE PUP

PERFORM 14   HARMONY 160
DEEP IN THE HEART OF TEXAS

PERFORM 15   MELODY 162
SOLDIER'S SONG

PERFORM 16   EXPRESSION 164
SING

PERFORM 17   HARMONY 166
THE INCHWORM

Describe Music 168

DESCRIBE 1 MELODY 168
PUT ON A HAPPY FACE

DESCRIBE 2 MELODY 170
JOHNNY'S MY BOY

DESCRIBE 3 FORM 172
Allegretto from Symphony No. 7 (LISTENING)

DESCRIBE 4 TIME AND PLACE 173
OLD DAN TUCKER

DESCRIBE 5 FORM 174
HAPPINESS

DESCRIBE 6 HARMONY 176
ONE BOTTLE OF POP

DESCRIBE 7 EXPRESSION 178
EDELWEISS

DESCRIBE 8 RHYTHM 180
St. Louis Polka (LISTENING)

DESCRIBE 9 RHYTHM 181
BLACK-EYED SUSIE

DESCRIBE 10 TIME AND PLACE ...182
TINA SINGU

DESCRIBE 11 EXPRESSION 184
Elfin Dance (LISTENING)

DESCRIBE 12 HARMONY........186
THIS LAND IS YOUR LAND

DESCRIBE 13 RHYTHM 188
Blue Rondo a la Turk (LISTENING)
A BLUE SONG

DESCRIBE 14 HARMONY.......190
THE LOST LADY FOUND

DESCRIBE 15 FORM 192
The Lost Lady Found from
    Lincolnshire Posy (LISTENING)

DESCRIBE 16 EXPRESSION 194
Hoe-Down from Rodeo (LISTENING)

DESCRIBE 17 FORM 196
OH, IT'S GREAT TO BE LIVIN' THIS
MORNING

Create Music 198

CREATE 1 HARMONY 198
PACHYCEPHALOSAURUS
Fossils from Carnival of the Animals
    (LISTENING)

CREATE 2 FORM 200
EVERY MORNING WHEN I WAKE UP

CREATE 3 HARMONY 201
GLEE REIGNS IN GALILEE

CREATE 4 FORM 202
Sky Singers (ACTIVITY)
The Dove from Noyes Fludde (LISTENING)
Symphony No. 6 ("Pastoral"), Second
    Movement (LISTENING)

CREATE 5 FORM 204
What Is Pink? (POEM)
Largo (ACTIVITY)
Autre Choral from En Habit de Cheval
    (LISTENING)

CREATE 6 EXPRESSION 206
Speech to Song (ACTIVITY)
Yes! We Have No Bananas (CHANT)
The Makings of an Opera (ACTIVITY)

CREATE 7 TIME AND PLACE 208
A LITTLE LOVE GOES A LONG WAY

CREATE 8 EXPRESSION 210
Kantan (MUSIC DRAMA)

CREATE 9 HARMONY 212
TZENA, TZENA

CREATE 10 EXPRESSION 214
Nocturne from Divertissement (LISTENING)

CREATE 11 EXPRESSION 215
FAREWELL MY OWN TRUE LOVE

CREATE 12 EXPRESSION 216
THE SLITHEREE DEE

CREATE 13 HARMONY 218
YES INDEED

Special Times 220

SPECIAL TIMES 1 HARMONY ... 220
EVER ONWARD!
A Nation's Strength (POEM)

SPECIAL TIMES 2 FORM 222
LITTLE LAMB

SPECIAL TIMES 3 EXPRESSION .. 224
On October (POEM)

SPECIAL TIMES 4 FORM 225
PUMPKIN SONG

SPECIAL TIMES 5 FORM 226
HAYRIDE

SPECIAL TIMES 6 HARMONY ... 228
HARVEST TIME

SPECIAL TIMES 7 TIME AND
PLACE 229
NOW THANK WE ALL OUR GOD

SPECIAL TIMES 8 HARMONY ... 230
PAT-A-PAN

SPECIAL TIMES 9 FORM 232
CHRISTMAS IS COMING

SPECIAL TIMES 10 RHYTHM ... 233
HERE WE COME A-WASSAILING

SPECIAL TIMES 11 EXPRESSION 234
Amahl and the Night Visitors (LISTENING)

SPECIAL TIMES 12 HARMONY .. 240
SILVER BELLS

SPECIAL TIMES 13 RHYTHM ... 242
I HAD A DREAM, DEAR

SPECIAL TIMES 14 MELODY ... 244
Sing a Valentine (ACTIVITY)
SOMEBODY WAITING

SPECIAL TIMES 15 EXPRESSION 246
YOU'RE A GRAND OLD FLAG

SPECIAL TIMES 16 MELODY ... 248
TALLIS'S CANON
HALELUYOH

SPECIAL TIMES 17 EXPRESSION 250
LET THERE BE PEACE ON EARTH
Tear Down the Walls (POEM)

Pupil's Glossary 252
Piano Accompaniments 254
Teacher's Glossary 421
Acknowledgments and Credits...... 423
Classified Index of Music, Art,
    and Poetry 426
Classified Index of Activities
    and Skills 429
Alphabetical Index of Music........ 431

Meet the Authors

Eunice Boardman Meske is Director of the School of Music and Professor of Music and Education at the University of Wisconsin, Madison. She works with university students in a ''lab school'' where she and her students teach grades K-8. Meske holds a Ph.D. from the University of Illinois.

EUNICE BOARDMAN MESKE

BARBARA ANDRESS

Barbara Andress is Professor in the School of Music at Arizona State University, Tempe. She received a B.A. and M.A. in education from Arizona State University. Andress has taught general music and instrumental music and for over twenty years was a district music supervisor.

Mary Pautz is Assistant Professor of Music Education at the University of Wisconsin, Milwaukee. In addition to teaching music education methods, she also teaches elementary music classes as part of a practicum for music majors. Pautz is a doctoral candidate at the University of Wisconsin, Madison.

MARY PAUTZ

FRED WILLMAN

Fred Willman is Professor of Music Education at the University of Missouri, St. Louis. Willman holds a Ph.D. from the University of North Dakota, Grand Forks. He has worked extensively in the development of computer software for use in music education.

Consultants

Nancy Archer
Forest Park Elementary School
Fort Wayne, Indiana

Joan Z. Fyfe
Jericho Public Schools
Jericho, New York

Jeanne Hook
Albuquerque Public Schools
Albuquerque, New Mexico

Danette Littleton
University of Tennessee at Chattanooga
Chattanooga, Tennessee

Barbara Reeder Lundquist
University of Washington
Seattle, Washington

Ollie McFarland
Detroit Public Schools
Detroit, Michigan

Faith Norwood
Harnett County School District
North Carolina

Linda K. Price
Richardson Independent School District
Richardson, Texas

Buryl Red
Composer and Arranger
New York, New York

Dawn L. Reynolds
District of Columbia Public Schools
Washington, D.C.

Morris Stevens
A.N. McCallum High School
Austin, Texas

Jack Noble White
Texas Boys Choir
Fort Worth, Texas

Contributing Writers

Hilary Apfelstadt
University of North Carolina at Greensboro
Greensboro, North Carolina

Pat and Tom Cuthbertson
Professional Writers
Santa Cruz, California

Louise Huberty
(*Special Kodaly Consultant*)
Milwaukee Public Schools
Milwaukee, Wisconsin

Susan Kenney
Brigham Young University
Salt Lake City, Utah

Janet Montgomery
Ithaca College
Ithaca, New York

Richard O'Hearn
Western Michigan University
Kalamazoo, Michigan

Diane Persellin
Trinity University
San Antonio, Texas

Arvida Steen
(*Special Orff Consultant*)
The Blake School
Minneapolis, Minnesota

Field Test Sites

While HOLT MUSIC was being developed, parts of the program were field tested by 25 teachers in 18 states. These teachers played a crucial role in the program's development. Their comments, suggestions, and classroom experiences helped HOLT MUSIC become the workable, exciting program it is. Our grateful appreciation goes to the following teachers who used our materials in their classrooms.

ARKANSAS
Judy Harkrader
Vilonia Elementary School
Vilonia

COLORADO
Nancylee Summerville
Hutchinson Elementary School
Lakewood

Robert Horsky
Goldrick Elementary School
Denver

Joan Tally
Eiber Elementary School
Lakewood

Germaine Johnson
University of Northern Colorado
   Laboratory School
Greeley

GEORGIA
Angela Tonsmeire
Cartersville Elementary School
Cartersville

Nancy Clayton
Norman Park Elementary School
Norman Park

INDIANA
Nancy Archer
Forest Park Elementary School
Fort Wayne

Elizabeth Staples
School #92
Indianapolis

Pat Gillooly
School #90
Indianapolis

KANSAS
Shelli Kadel
El Paso Elementary School
Derby

KENTUCKY
Patricia Weihe
Wright Elementary School
Shelbyville

MASSACHUSETTS
Marya Rusinak
Kennedy School
Brockton

MISSISSIPPI
Dottie Dudley
Crestwood Elementary School
Meridian

Mira Frances Hays
Forest Seperate School District
Forest

MISSOURI
Elizabeth Hutcherson
Parker Road Elementary School
Florissant

NEW JERSEY
Lorna Milbauer
North Cliff School
Englewood Cliffs

NEW YORK
Ruthetta S. Smikle
Hillary Park Academy
Buffalo

NORTH CAROLINA
Julie Young
Burgaw Elementary School
Burgaw

OKLAHOMA
Cindy Newell
Washington Irving Elementary School
Durant

OREGON
Larry Verdoorn
Hall Elementary School
Gresham

PENNSYLVANIA
Marianne Zimmerman
Steele School
Harrisburg

TENNESSEE
Sarah Davis
Powell Elementary School
Powell

WEST VIRGINIA
Eva Ledbetter
Cross Lanes Elementary School
Cross Lanes

WISCONSIN
Jill Kuespert Anderson
Lannon Elementary School
Lannon

A Guide To Holt Music

The HOLT MUSIC program can help you provide rich and enjoyable experiences for all of your students. The information given below will help you get acquainted with the Pupil Book, the Teacher's Edition, the Teacher's Resource Binder, and the Recordings.

Organization Of The Program

Each level of HOLT MUSIC is divided into two units. Unit 1, "Music to Explore," is the "core" unit. The core lessons are divided into four quarters, or chapters, of fifteen lessons each. Each quarter ends with an evaluation. If time for music class is limited, we suggest that you concentrate on the core, which provides a comprehensive program in itself.

Unit 2, "More Music to Explore," contains an additional four chapters for review, reinforcement, extension of core concepts, and seasonal music. Lessons in Unit 2 are cross-referenced in the Teacher's Edition to lessons in Unit 1. However, these cross-references are only suggestions; you will also be guided by the interests of your students and available class time.

Types Of Lessons In The Book

☐ **Song lessons**—Most lessons in the program are song-based lessons. Song lessons are identified by a gray band above and below the title. Usually both the music and the words are in the Pupil Book. However, in certain lessons only the words appear in the Pupil Book, and it is expected that students will learn the song by listening. Students are not expected to be able to read all of the musical notations that appear in their books. The lesson sequence is designed so that they will gradually acquire the skill to do so as they progress through the grades. For this reason it is strongly recommended that the core unit be followed in page order.

☐ **Listening lessons**—These lessons are built around a recording of a classical, folk, or contemporary work. Listening lessons featured in the Pupil Book are identified by a logo. Complete titles, composers, and performer credits are listed in the "Materials" section of the Teacher's Edition.

Many of the listening lessons have a chart or an illustration designed to help guide the children through the listening experience. In some lessons the recording includes "call numbers"—spoken numbers recorded over the music. The call numbers correspond to the numbers on the chart and help to focus attention on important features as the music continues.

☐ **Activities**—Many activity-based lessons are included in HOLT MUSIC. The type of activity in the Pupil Book is identified by a special logo: a quill pen and an ink bottle for creative activities, a

French horn for performance activities, and a human figure for activities involving movement.

The activity is always structured in some way; for example, a poem, a story, or a picture in the Pupil Book might serve as a focal point for creative exploration, or the students could be invited to explore certain sounds on instruments.

Using The Recordings

The recordings are essential teaching aids for HOLT MUSIC. The song recordings may be used in various ways: to help students learn words and melody if songs are beyond their current reading level; and to provide examples of appropriate tempo, diction, expression, and vocal tone quality. For teaching flexibility, song recordings have voices on one channel and instruments on the other. By turning the balance control completely to the right, you will hear instruments only. The grooves between all selections are locked.

Special Helps For The Teacher

☐ The **Scope and Sequence Chart,** page xxviii–3, summarizes concepts, terms, and skills covered in each grade level.

☐ The teacher's **Glossary,** page 421, gives definitions of musical terms used in the text.

☐ Complete **Classified and Alphabetical Indexes,** starting on page 426, provide a convenient way to locate songs, poems, listening lessons, and particular skills and concepts.

☐ Step-by-step **lesson plans** are provided for each page of the Pupil Book. The **Lesson Focus** indicates the concept to be studied and gives, in abbreviated form, an indication of the primary behavior and mode stressed. **P–I,** for example, means "perform" in the "ikonic mode." (See "The Generative Approach to Music Learning," page xxvi.)

☐ The **Teacher's Resource Binder** includes Activity Sheets, Biographies, Evaluations, and suggestions for Curriculum Correlation, Enrichment, Kodaly, Mainstreaming, and Orff. All binder materials are cross-referenced to lessons in the Teacher's Edition. This enables you to adapt or expand individual lessons to fit your special needs.

☐ **Instrumental accompaniments**—Most songs contain chord names for autoharp or guitar accompaniment, and many lesson plans include accompaniments for students to perform on classroom instruments. Piano accompaniments, provided in the back of the Teacher's Edition, are cross-referenced to each lesson plan. The piano score includes markers showing where a new line begins in the Pupil Book. The symbol $\overset{2}{\blacktriangledown}$ above the score, for example, indicates that the second line of music in the Pupil Book begins at this point.

To the Classroom Teacher

The classroom teacher's role in music education varies from school to school. Whatever the situation in your district, the classroom teacher is vital to the success of the total music program.

Many teachers approach music with mixed feelings: enthusiasm, apprehension, curiosity, or insecurity. These attitudes are influenced by the musical knowledge the teacher possesses, the memory of music in his or her own school experience, and by heavy demands on the teacher's time.

HOLT MUSIC welcomes the classroom teacher's participation. The suggestions that follow are provided with the hope that they will alleviate fears and encourage the teacher to enjoy and learn music with the students.

1 "I Don't Know How To Teach Music!"

Every classroom teacher can teach music with HOLT MUSIC—if he or she is willing to learn with the students and read through the lessons in the Teacher's Edition. The "generative" approach used in HOLT MUSIC can help the teacher learn along with the students.

Music presents a special challenge because of the need to occasionally demonstrate by singing, moving, or playing. HOLT MUSIC helps the teacher as much as possible with

- comprehensive, easily understood lesson plans
- quality demonstration recordings
- a teaching sequence that works
- appealing songs, listening lessons, and poetry
- activities that are fun for students to do

2 "There Isn't Time To Teach Music!"

The pressure for students to achieve in all curricular areas is intense. However, music can be interspersed throughout the school day. Sing a song to begin or end the day; create an instrumental accompaniment to enrich a story; share the music from the culture being highlighted in social studies.

The Curriculum Correlation section in the Teacher's Resource Binder provides many suggestions for integrating music into your day. To expand class time for music, set up music centers where small groups may work on their own.

However, a scheduled time devoted to music is just as important as time scheduled for other subjects. Just as reading throughout the day does not take the place of reading class, neither should the use of music throughout the day be considered sufficient. To achieve an understanding of music there must be a sequential course of study.

3 "I Don't Have Time To Hunt For Materials!"

The authors of HOLT MUSIC have gathered and organized all materials for you. You will find

- Complete lesson plans that include a lesson focus, an introduction, a development and a conclusion. Usually a lesson can be completed in 20 to 30 minutes.
- Integration of all types of activities—listening lessons, dances, creative experiences, and songs—within a lesson.
- Boldfaced dialogue in the lesson plans that may help you in presenting the lesson, especially if you are not familiar with musical concepts and terms.

4 "The Kids Will Laugh If I Sing!"

Students may need encouragement at first. However, young people will eventually sing if a positive atmosphere is created. Common teaching errors that hinder singing include

- expecting students to sing before they are ready (A new song must be heard several times before the students sing it.)
- expecting students to sing too loud

The students may laugh the first time they hear you sing. You are not alone: They are even more likely to laugh at a music specialist who has a trained voice! If you can laugh with the class and proceed with the song, the laughter is soon forgotten and the music enjoyed. Or if you prefer, you can rely on the recordings. By adjusting the balance on the stereo, the voice only may be heard; this is especially helpful in teaching a new song.

5 "What Will I Do With the Boys?"

There is nothing inherent in the genes of boys that causes them to have an aversion to music! Often they will be the most enthusiastic supporters. Expect all students to enjoy music; expect everyone to learn. You will find that an activity-based, hands-on experience in music will spark enthusiasm in both boys and girls. They will never tire of opportunities to play bells and autoharps, to use props such as streamers, wands, and balloons, or to work with the activity sheets provided in the Teacher's Resource Binder.

6 "I Can't Play the Piano!"

While playing the piano is helpful, it is not essential for teaching music. Instead, you can play the recordings or use autoharp accompaniments.

7 "I Remember How I Hated Music When I Was In School!"

Teachers who have had pleasant experiences with music are likely to approach music teaching with enthusiasm. Others, unfortunately, may have less pleasant memories. What was it in the experience that caused the bad feelings? You can prevent another generation from having unpleasant experiences by avoiding those stressful practices you recall.

The Generative Approach To Music Learning

HOLT MUSIC's generative approach is based on the recognition that

Learning begins with a "need to know." Real learning occurs only to the extent that the student willingly makes a commitment to the act of learning. Learning based on intrinsic "need to know" goals, which the learner personally identifies, is more permanent than learning based on extrinsic goals such as rewards or adult approval.

Learning leads to more learning. Once the student is personally committed to learning, each achievement is "generative"; it provides the foundation and the impetus for further learning.

Learning is future-oriented. The student who becomes enthralled with the learning process continues to seek opportunities to learn as long as each experience leads toward personal independence and self-actualization. Music learning thus approached allows the learner to become

- [ ] more deeply involved in the aesthetic experience
- [ ] aware of music as an avenue of one's own personal expression
- [ ] musically independent

The Generative Instructional Theory

The Generative Instructional Theory recognizes that music learning, whether formal or informal, involves four components. These components include

1. The musical concept to be learned. Musical understanding emerges gradually as the learner develops musical concepts, that is, principles or ways of categorizing musical sounds.

Concepts stressed in the generative approach include

- [ ] those related to musical elements
  - pitch (melody and harmony)
  - duration (rhythm and tempo) ■ dynamics
  - articulation ■ timbre (qualities of sound)
- [ ] those that reflect the way musical elements are organized into a complete musical statement that has ■ form ■ texture ■ an expressive nature ■ a cultural context (time and place)

The Scope and Sequence chart beginning on page xxviii gives the concepts covered in HOLT MUSIC.

2. A musical example that embodies the concept to be learned. Examples are selected for their musical value reflecting

- diverse musical heritages
- diverse times and places
- many forms of human emotion
- many different combinations of voices and instruments

3. A musical behavior through which the learner interacts with music, gradually developing essential musical concepts by

- performing music through singing and playing

- describing music through moving, visualizing, and verbalizing
- creating music through improvisation or composition

4. A conceptual mode that enables the learner to communicate understanding and move through three stages of conceptualization:

- [ ] **The enactive mode:** The learner begins to associate concept with example through observation, manipulation, and experimentation. Understanding is "acted-out" as the student interacts directly and nonverbally with the musical sound.
- [ ] **The ikonic mode:** The learner internalizes musical sound images that can be recalled even when the musical sound is absent. The learner demonstrates understanding through pictorial representations that "look like" the music sounds or with simple verbal imagery such as up-down, longer-shorter, or smooth-jerky.
- [ ] **The symbolic mode:** The learner builds on previous enactive and ikonic experiences until verbal and musical symbols gradually become associated with the sound.

The Lesson Focus

Lesson plans in HOLT MUSIC are built on the recognition that these four components must be present in order for learning to take place. The **Lesson Focus** for each plan identifies the concept, the behavior, and the conceptual mode. An example follows.

Lesson Focus
Melody: A series of pitches may move
up, down, or remain the same. *(P–I)*

- The **behavior** is identified at the end of the concept statement by the first letter.
  P Perform (singing/playing)
  D Describe (move/verbalize/visualize)
  C Create (improvise/compose)
- The **conceptual mode** at which it is expected that most students will be functioning in this lesson is identified by the second capital letter.
  E Enactive *I* Ikonic *S* Symbolic

Thus in the example given above, the designation *(P–I)* at the end of the concept statement indicates that the behavior stressed in the lesson is **Perform** and that the students will be primarily using the **Ikonic** mode in that lesson.

The Generative Approach To Music Reading

Lessons that help develop music-reading skills are an integral part of any learning sequence that leads toward musical independence. The generative approach to music reading used in HOLT MUSIC

- [ ] is based on a cyclic process that takes the learner through three stages corresponding to the three modes of conceptualization (See chart.)

- provides a lesson sequence that recognizes that a learner may be functioning at different stages of the cycle simultaneously—for example, a student might be reading simple rhythms from notation (symbolic stage) while associating melodies with ikons (ikonic stage) and learning harmonies aurally (enactive stage)
- presents each new skill in relation to the musical whole, rather than through pattern drill alone
- distinguishes between sight-reading (playing an instrument from notation) and sight-singing.

Reading Rhythm

The generative approach to reading rhythm

- recognizes that reading of rhythm depends on the perception of durational relationships
- is based on a two-dimensional approach
  - sensing durations within the melodic rhythm in relation to the underlying beat, and
  - sensing durations in the melodic rhythm in relation to the shortest sound within that rhythm

The **additive approach** described above is used because

- it is the rhythmic relationship to which the young person seems to respond most readily
- it allows the student to solve rhythmic problems by using addition rather than division
- it is the basis for rhythmic organization used in the music of many non-Western cultures, as well as in much of the popular music of today.

Reading Melody

The generative approach to reading melody

- begins with melodies based on major or minor modes because these are most familiar to the contemporary American child
- uses the body scale (see below) to help the beginning student internalize pitch relationships
- stresses the hearing and performing of melodies in relation to the underlying harmony
- makes use of scale numbers to describe tonal relationships because numbers

  - provide the learner with a way of internalizing and recalling melodic pitches in relation to a tonal center
  - build on a numerical concept that most children have when this stage is introduced
  - allow for meaningful transfer to the reading of staff notation
  - are commonly used to describe chord structure, thus helping the student to understand the relation of melody to harmony

---

Lessons that develop reading skills take the student through the three conceptual modes.

ENACTIVE MODE The student performs the rhythm of a melody and metric grouping by imitating what is heard.

IKONIC MODE The student associates rhythms with ikons that represent duration in relation to

- the shortest sound
- the beat and accent

As the student associates these ikons with sound patterns, vocabulary is introduced to describe

- sounds that make up the melodic rhythm (short, long, lo-ong)

short short long

short short long   lo-ong

- sounds in relation to the beat (shorter than, longer than)

shorter same   longer   lo-ong

- the accent (moves in twos, moves in threes)

moves in twos   moves in threes

SYMBOLIC MODE The process is completed as the child transfers the ability to read ikons to reading traditional music notation.

ENACTIVE MODE The student performs in response to melodies heard. During this stage the body scale is introduced, providing the child with another means of sensing and responding to pitch relationships.

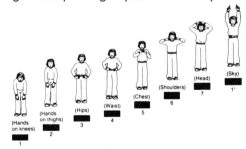

(Hands on knees) 1 (Hands on thighs) 2 (Hips) 3 (Waist) 4 (Chest) 5 (Shoulders) 6 (Head) 7 (Sky) 1'

IKONIC MODE The child first associates melodies with ikons that represent the up-down, step-skip relationship of pitches. Later, pitches are labeled with scale numbers to show their relationship to the tonal center.

1 2 3 1 1

SYMBOLIC MODE The student transfers the ability to read a new melody from scale numbers to staff notation.

1 2 3   1 5. 1

Scope and Sequence

As students grow in their understanding of musical concepts, they acquire skills for manipulating their own musical environments. Page numbers following each concept statement guide the teacher to lessons in HOLT MUSIC, Level 5, that focus on that concept. Boldfaced numbers represent lessons where that concept is dealt with as a primary focus of the lesson. Other numbers indicate

Concepts	Ikon	Musical Symbol
RHYTHM		
■ Music may be comparatively fast or slow, depending on the speed of the underlying pulse. *Pages:* **46–47**, 230–231		
■ Music may become faster or slower by changing the speed of the underlying pulse. *Pages:* 46–47, 48–49, 98–99, 170–171		
■ Music may move in relation to the underlying steady beat or shortest pulse. *Pages:* 6–7, 18–19, 24–25, 38–39, 46–47, 68–69, 82–83, 84–85, 102–103, 106–107, **136**, 148–149, 173, 180, **181**, 196–197, 218–219, 225, 242–243, 248–249		
■ A series of beats may be organized into regular or irregular groupings by stressing certain beats. *Pages:* 10–11, 18–19, **20–21, 22–23,** 24–25, 38–39, 46–47, 48–49, 92–93, **102–103, 110–111, 112–113, 134–135,** 156–157, 166–167, 172, 174–175, 182–183, **188–189,** 190–191, 229, 230–231, 233		
■ Individual sounds and silences within a rhythmic line may be longer than, shorter than, or the same as other sounds within the line. *Pages:* 20–21, 38–39, 60–61, 62–63, **68–69,** 78–81, **82–83, 84–85, 104–105, 106–107,** 108–109, 136, 168–169, **180,** 204–205, 244–245		
■ Individual sounds and silences within a rhythmic line may be longer than, shorter than, or the same as the underlying steady beat or shortest pulse. *Pages:* **18–19,** 22–23, 24–25, 36–37, **60–61, 62–63, 78–81, 86–89,** 100–101, **137,** 181, 182–183, 196–197, 198–199, 201, 208–209, 218–219, **233, 242–243**		
■ Accented sounds within a rhythmic line may sound with, before, or after the accented underlying beat. *Pages:* 84–85, 166–167, 174–175		
MELODY		
■ A series of pitches may move up, down, or remain the same. *Pages:* 10–11, 74–75, 102–103, 112–113, **120–121,** 200, 204–205, 225		
■ A series of pitches may move up or down by steps or skips. *Pages:* 8–9, 26–27, 28–29, 52–53, 54–55, **72–73,** 78–81, 92–93, 108–109, 116–117, 120–121, 166–167, 188–189, 198–199, 208–209, 212–213, 220–221, 229, 232, **244–245**		
■ Each pitch within a melody moves in relation to a home tone. *Pages:* 10–11, 26–27, 28–29, 46–47, **52–53, 70–71, 72–73,** 76–77, 82–83, **104–105, 106–107,** 110–111, **114–115, 116–117,** 141, 160–161, 173, 176–177, 181, 182–183, 190–191, 196–197, 208–209, 228, 244–245, **248–249**		
■ A series of pitches bounded by the octave "belong together," forming a tonal set. *Pages:* 14–15, 24–25, **52–53, 54–55,** 66–67, 68–69, **70–71,** 72–73, 94–95, **114–115, 116–117, 162–163, 170–171,** 198–199, 201, 220–221, 226–227, **248–249**		
■ A melody may be relatively high or low.		
■ Individual pitches, when compared to each other, may be higher, lower, or the same. *Pages:* 48–49, 78–81, 82–83, 114–115, 120–121, **168–169,** 176–177, 222–223		
TIMBRE		
■ The quality of a sound is determined by the sound source. *Pages:* **40–41, 42–43,** 66–67, 76–77, 84–85, 106–107, **118–119,** 172, 188–189, 202–203, 204–205		
■ The quality of a sound is affected by the material, shape, and size of the source. *Pages:* 20–21, **40–41, 42–43,** 198–199		
■ The quality of a sound is affected by the way the sound is produced. *Pages:* **42–43,** 110–111, 122–123, 124–125, 240–241		

lessons where the concept is dealt with, but not as the primary focus.

The skills list gives a sampling of representative behaviors for Level 5. Page numbers listed give only one example of a lesson where that skill is developed. For a comprehensive listing of skills, refer to the Classified Index of Activities and Skills, page 429.

Terms for Grade 5	Skills/Behaviors for Grade 5	
meter signature underlying beat or pulse tempo Adagio-Largo-Andante-Allegro-Presto fast-slow ritard syncopation rest shortest sound rhythm pattern triplet short-long	**Perform**	Sing and chant with emphasis on accurate rhythm. *18–19* Chant rhythms at varying tempos. *46–47* Learn to sing or play songs by reading ikonic or traditional notation while maintaining a steady beat. *Throughout*
	Describe	Compare and contrast syncopated rhythm patterns. *84–85* Identify the relationship between sounds that are included in the rhythm of the melody. *181* Compare and contrast symmetrical and asymmetrical rhythm patterns. *110–111* Add short sounds together to show the length of longer sounds within a rhythm. *20–21* Define the difference between duple and triple meter. *233* Use a rhythm ruler to show relationships of sounds within a rhythm to the beat or the shortest sound. *22–23*
	Create	Develop symmetrical and asymmetrical rhythm patterns. *112–113*
pitch range tone row melodic contour tonal center scale skip-step whole tone scale key signature high-low	**Perform**	Sing and play melodies from notation, using scale numbers. *Throughout* Play a melody on a keyboard by reading notation. *120–121* Use knowledge of melodic phrase and tonal center when learning to sing or play unfamiliar songs. *244–245*
	Describe	Identify scales and tonal centers by referring to the key signature. *70–71* Identify scales and tonal centers used as the basis of melodies by applying knowledge of scale numbers and letter names. *52–53*
	Create	Improvise original melodies using the whole tone scale. *54–55* Create a descant. *204–205*
voice woodwinds, such as bassoon, clarinet, oboe, flute strings, such as violin, viola, cello, bass brass, such as trombone, tuba, trumpet, French horn percussion, such as drums, cymbals	**Perform**	Play the autoharp using various strumming techniques to produce different tone qualities. *122–123*
	Describe	Catalogue instruments according to the way the sound is produced. *40–41* Associate the instruments of the orchestra with their pictures and sound. *42–43*

Concepts	Ikon	Musical Symbol	
■ The total sound is affected by the number and qualities of sounds occurring at the same time. *Pages:* 84–85, 94–95, 122–123, **128–129**, 136, 192–193, 225			
DYNAMICS ■ Music may be comparatively loud or soft. *Pages:* **48–49**, 204–205		*f* *p*	
■ Music may become louder or softer. *Pages:* **48–49**, 62–63, 84–85, 98–99			
ARTICULATION ■ A series of sounds may move from one to the next in either a smoothly connected or a detached manner. *Pages:* 48–49, 98–99, 242–243 ■ The quality of a sound is affected by the way the sound begins, continues, and ends. *Pages:* 186–187, 229			
HARMONY ■ Chords and melody may move simultaneously in relation to each other. *Pages:* **8–9, 10–11, 12–13, 14–15, 24–25, 26–27, 28–29,** 36–37, **74–75,** 76–77, 78–81, 82–83, **90–91, 92–93, 94–95,** 100–101, 102–103, **122–123, 124–125, 145, 148–149, 150–153, 154–155, 156–157, 158–159, 160–161,** 162–163, **176–177, 201, 212–213, 218–219, 220–221,** 233, **240–241** ■ A series of simultaneous sounds may alternate between activity and rest. *Pages:* 228 ■ Two or more pitches may be sounded simultaneously. *Pages:* 104–105, 112–113, 145, 160–161, **176–177, 186–187, 198–199,** 200, 220–221, 222–223, **230–231,** 240–241 ■ Two or more musical lines may occur simultaneously. *Pages:* **6–7,** 14–15, 68–69, 72–73, 74–75, **76–77, 78–81,** 84–85, 100–101, 108–109, 114–115, 116–117, 137, **141,** 148–149, 150–153, 156–157, 158–159, **166–167,** 170–171, 176–177, 182–183, 186–187, 188–189, 196–197, 198–199, 200, 208–209, 212–213, 220–221, 226–227, 228, 230–231, 232, 240–241, 248–249			
TEXTURE ■ Musical quality is affected by the distance between the musical lines. *Pages:* 74–75 ■ Musical quality is affected by the number of or degree of contrast between musical lines occurring simultaneously. *Pages:* 38–39, 78–81, 204–205, 229			
FORM ■ A musical whole begins, continues, and ends. *Pages:* 62–63 ■ A musical whole is a combination of smaller segments. *Pages:* **16–17,** 54–55, 76–77, 78–81, **108–109,** 114–115, 137, **196–197, 200,** 202–203, **204–205,** 220–221, **225** ■ A musical whole may be made up of same, varied, or contrasting segments. *Pages:* 12–13, 14–15, 16–17, 28–29, 36–37, 106–107, 120–121, **128–129, 134–135,** 156–157, 168–169, **172, 174–175,** 190–191, **192–193, 202–203, 222–223, 226–227** ■ A series of sounds may form a distinct musical idea within the musical whole. *Pages:* 186–187, **232** ■ A musical whole may include an introduction, interludes, and an ending segment. *Pages:* 28–29, 86–89, 92–93, 98–99, 100–101			
EXPRESSION ■ Musical elements are combined into a whole to express a musical or extramusical idea. *Pages:* **30–33, 34–35, 56–57, 58–59, 64–65, 96–97, 126–127, 142–144, 146–147, 164–165, 194–195, 210–211, 214, 215, 216–217, 234–239, 246–247, 250–251** ■ The expressiveness of music is affected by the way timbre, dynamics, articulation, rhythm, melody, harmony, form, tempo, and texture contribute to the musical whole. *Pages:* 16–17, 44–45, 50–51, 52–53, 98–99, **138–140, 178–179, 184–185, 206–207, 224**			
TIME & PLACE ■ The way musical elements are combined into a whole reflects the origin of the music. *Pages:* **98–99, 173, 182–183, 208–209** ■ A particular use of timbre, dynamics, articulation, rhythm, melody, harmony, and form reflects the origin of the musical whole. *Pages:* 16–17, **38–39,** 98–99, 186–187, **229**			

Terms for Grade 5		Skills/Behaviors for Grade 5	
keyboards, such as piano, harpsichord, player piano, electric piano, organ, synthesizer autoharp ukulele		**Create**	Invent a variety of tone colors on instruments to create unusual sound effects. *225*
loud-soft *piano-mezzopiano-mezzoforte-forte* crescendo-decrescendo		**Perform**	Sing and play with appropriate dynamic contrasts. *Throughout*
		Describe	Discuss variation in volume with knowledge of symbols for dynamic markings found in music scores. *48–49*
detached staccato sustained marcato slurred fermata legato		**Perform**	Sing a song, following the articulation as suggested by the expressive intent. *242–243*
		Describe	Identify symbols in music scores that indicate the manner in which sounds are to be articulated. *184–185*
chord ostinato chord symbols two-part harmony harmonic changes three-part harmony I-IV-V7 chords interval unison accompaniment root bass major minor descant modulation homophony polyphony echo canon round		**Perform**	Play chords on the ukulele. *148–149* Strum chords on the autoharp. *122–125* Perform a song with three-part vocal harmony. *8–9* Sing melodies in relation to an instrumental accompaniment. *Throughout* Sing a round, maintaining independent parts. *116–117* Sing a descant against the main melody. *226–227* Play an ostinato as a rhythmic and harmonic accompaniment. *76–77*
		Describe	Identify the chords needed to accompany a song. *10–11* Distinguish between I, IV, and V7 chords. *24–25* Discuss the difference between major and minor chords. *90–91*
		Create	Plan an instrumental accompaniment. *201* Create a vocal accompaniment in echo style. *218–219*
tutti solo		**Perform**	Play different rhythmic lines at the same time. *38–39*
		Describe	Discuss the difference between homophony and polyphony. *74–77*
		Create	Plan a composition that alternates between solo and tutti sections. *204–205*
suite Introduction, Interlude, march and Coda theme-variations movement phrase Refrain-Verse repeat question-answer *D.C. al Fine* **ABA ABACA AA'A"** *D.C. al Segno* **AA'BA** *Fine* opera rondo sonata section symphony theme concerto round first and second endings		**Perform**	Use knowledge of same, similar, and different phrases when learning to sing or play unfamiliar songs. *86–89*
		Describe	Demonstrate awareness of phrase structure by moving to different phrases within a song. *232* Identify ikons that show sequence of phrases and when sections are the same or different. *168–169* Identify different themes as they recur in long compositions. *128–129*
		Create	Organize a composition into several sections to create a rondo. *200*
mood dramatize aria recitative dance		**Perform**	Sing, play, and chant expressively to musical ideas. *Throughout*
		Describe	Discuss how the organization of musical elements affects the mood of a composition. *52–53* Develop a light show with colored light to reflect musical ideas heard in the composition. *96–97*
		Create	Improvise vocal and instrumental accompaniments to express ideas based on a painting. *58–59*
cowboy song play party waltz symphonic poem square dance impressionism folk song Polynesian stick game polka		**Perform**	Sing, play, clap, and chant to music that reflects different ethnic traditions. *38–39*
		Describe	Examine how accompaniment, rhythm, and melody may reflect a specific historical period. *98–99*

Unit 1

Unit Overview

Unit 1, *Music to Explore,* the "core" unit, presents basic musical concepts through enjoyable activites such as singing, moving, creating compositions and accompaniments, playing classroom instruments, and listening to a wide variety of recorded selections. The lessons in Unit 1 are most effective if taught in sequence.

The songs and listening activities in the First Quarter show the students how vocal harmonic accompaniments can be created, how musical form is defined by melodic and rhythmic similarities, and how a variety of musical elements work together to express extramusical ideas.

In the Second Quarter, the students learn to identify and categorize instruments. They are introduced to musical symbols, and they learn the

Music To Explore

concepts of dynamics and syncopation. They refine their performance skills, interpreting ideas through musical and extramusical activities.

The Third Quarter includes activities that focus on rhythm and chordal patterns. The students learn how to find the tonal center of songs by understanding the function of the key signature. They are introduced to the concepts of homophony and polyphony and continue to explore musical interpretation.

In the Fourth Quarter, the students consolidate their knowledge of rhythm patterns, tonal centers, and form. They become acquainted with irregular meters. The students learn to perform on keyboard instruments and the autoharp using both standard and innovative playing techniques to produce extramusical sound effects.

Lesson Focus

Harmony: Two or more musical lines may occur simultaneously. *(P–I)*

Materials

○ **Piano Accompaniment:** page 254
○ **Record Information:**
  • On the Road Again
  ▣ **Record 1   Side A   Band 1**
  Voices: children's choir
  Accompaniment: harmonica, pedal steel guitar, acoustic guitar, electric guitar, electric bass, piano, percussion
○ **Instrument:** hand drum
○ **Other:** overhead projector
○ **Teacher's Resource Binder:**

  | Activity Sheets |
  | • **Activity Sheet 1**, page A4 (Prepare a transparency from the activity sheet.) |
  • **Activity Sheet 2**, pages A5–A6 (Prepare harmony strips. See instructions on activity sheet.)
  • Optional—
  Biography 1, page B1
  Curriculum Correlation 1, page C2
  Mainstreaming Suggestion 1, page M6
○ **For additional experience with harmony:** Describe 12, page 186

The First Quarter

Chords not shown on pupil page

On the Road Again

Words and Music by Willie Nelson

Section A:

On the road a-gain,_____

Just can't wait to get on the   road a-gain._____

6

Introducing the Lesson

Welcome the students back to school by involving them in a "mixer" activity. Display the transparency prepared from Activity Sheet 1 (*If You Should Meet*). Tell the students that they are to walk around the room to the beat of your drum as you read the poem. They are to find the classmate nearest them and perform the rhythm pattern shown on the transparency in the manner described at the end of each verse. When the students understand what they are to do, read the poem while lightly tapping the drum in a steady beat. Play a two-measure interlude at the end of each verse so that the students can perform the appropriate actions.

Developing the Lesson

1. Play the recording of "On the Road Again." Many of the students may be familiar with this popular song. As they walk back to their seats, ask them to hum or sing along with the melody.

2. Ask the students to open their books to page 6. Guide them to follow the notation and words as they softly sing the song along with the recording.

3. Comment that one of the reasons this song is so well liked is the interesting harmony changes. Play the recording again; ask the students to raise their hands when they think they hear a change in the harmony. The most pronounced change is at the beginning of Measure 6. It should be easily recognized by the students.

4. Help the students learn to sing a harmony part for Section A that uses only four different pitches:

6

The life I love is mak-ing mu-sic with my friends,

and I can't wait to get on the road a - gain. ____

Section B:

On the road again,
Like a band of gypsies we go down the highway.
We're the best of friends,
Insisting that the world keep turning our way,
And our way is on the road again.

Repeat Section A.

Can you hear when the harmony changes in Section A?
Can you sing a harmony part?

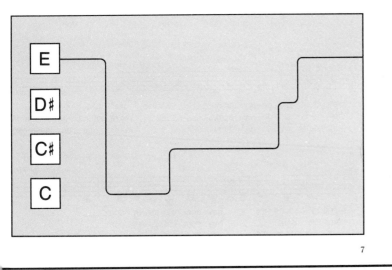

road... road...

music... a - gain.

Have the class listen to this part on the recording while they follow its contour on page 7.

Closing the Lesson

Provide a more graphic picture of the harmony part. Hand out several prepared copies of Activity Sheet 2 (*Harmony Strip*). (See activity sheet for instructions.) Small groups of students may gather around each copy and follow the contour as they practice this part. Divide the class into two groups, melody and harmony. Perform the song, singing Section A in harmony while continuing to sing Section B in unison.

On the Road Again
Words and Music by Willie Nelson

Section B

On the road a - gain, ____ Like a
band of gyp-sies we go down the high-way. ____
____ We're the best of friends, ____ In-
sist - ing that the world keep turn-ing our way, ____
____ and our way ____ is
(repeat Section A)

Lesson Focus

Harmony: Chords and melody may move simultaneously in relation to each other. *(P–I)*

Materials

- **Piano Accompaniment:** page 256
- **Record Information:**
  - Hey Dum Diddeley Dum
    Record 1   Side A   Band 2
    Voices: man, children's choir
    Accompaniment: flute, oboe, clarinet, bassoon, electric guitar, electric bass, electric piano, percussion
- **Teacher's Resource Binder:**
  - Optional—
    Kodaly Activity 11, page K17
    Mainstreaming Suggestion 2, page M6
- **For additional experience with harmony:** Perform 14, page 160; Describe 6, page 176

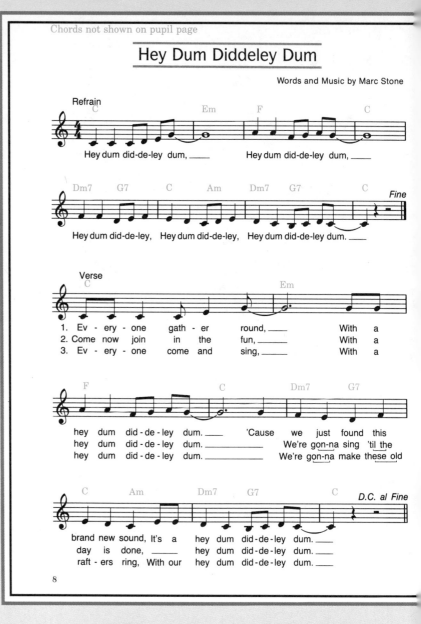

Chords not shown on pupil page

Hey Dum Diddeley Dum

Words and Music by Marc Stone

Introducing the Lesson

Introduce the idea of singing **root bass harmony.** Begin by reviewing the familiar round, "Are You Sleeping?" Sing it in unison. Tell the students to sustain the last pitch of the song. Identify this pitch as the tonal center (1). Ask the class to sing the entire song on that pitch. Divide the class into two groups. While one group continues to sing the drone, ask the other to sing the melody. Introduce the following root bass pattern for the students to sing as they follow your finger signals:

Using the same two groups, perform the song with this root bass pattern.

Developing the Lesson

1. Ask the students to open their books to page 8. **How much of this song can you learn to sing by following the notation?** Establish tonality in C. Ask the students to sing with scale numbers. Then listen to the recording.

2. When the students are familiar with the melody, help them add a vocal harmony part by following Harmony Part 1 on page 9. Warm up by asking the class to follow your finger signals again. Establish tonality in C. Signal them to sing "1–2–3–4–5." Call on a volunteer to sing the first line of the harmony part by following the numbers and the up-down direction of the words. If the class thinks the performer is correct they are to echo; if not, they should not sing. Proceed in this manner with other volunteers until the harmony part is performed correctly. Divide the class into two groups. Sing the refrain and Harmony Part 1 at the same time.

3. Challenge the class to learn Harmony Part 2. **Will you begin high or low?** (high) **Will the**

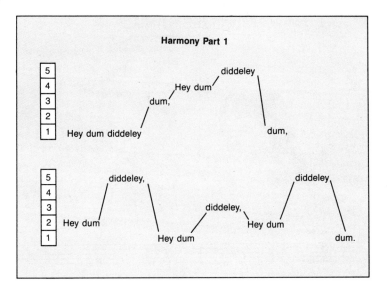

Harmony Part 1

```
5
4                    diddeley
3           Hey dum
2       dum,
1   Hey dum diddeley                          dum,
```

```
5       diddeley,                    diddeley
4
3                        diddeley,
2   Hey dum                          Hey dum
1           Hey dum                          dum.
```

Harmony Part 2

```
1'  Hey dum diddeley
7           dum,
6       Hey dum diddeley
5               dum,
4           Hey dum diddeley,
3               Hey dum diddeley,
2                   Hey dum diddeley
1                           dum.
```

For Your Information

Movement instructions:

Refrain: All stroll around room.

Verse 1: All come to middle, hands at sides, standing as close together as possible.

Refrain: All move outward and then stroll around.

Verse 2: Join hands to form chains. See how long each chain can become by the end of the verse.

Refrain: Break the chain. Return to strolling.

Verse 3: Form a large circle. Place hands on shoulders of individuals on either side. Begin to sway from side to side and continue until the end of the song.

pitches move up or down by steps or skips? (down by steps) Choose a volunteer to sing the part. The class should echo the part only after it has been sung correctly. Divide the class into three groups. Sing the melody and Harmony Parts 1 and 2 at the same time.

Closing the Lesson

When the students know the song, add movements. (See movement instructions in **For Your Information**.)

LESSON 3

Lesson Focus
Harmony: Chords and melody may move simultaneously in relation to each other. *(P–I)*

Materials
- **Piano Accompaniment:** page 258
- **Record Information:**
  - Hey Dum Diddeley Dum **(Record 1 Side A Band 2)**
  - Mockin' Bird Hill
  - **Record 1 Side A Band 3**
    Voices: solo child, children's choir
    Accompaniment: small show orchestra
- **Instruments:** resonator bells A, B, C♯, D, E, F♯, and G♯ in all available octaves; one bell mallet for each student
- **Other:** pencil for each student; overhead projector
- **Teacher's Resource Binder:**
  - **Activity Sheet 3,** page A7
    (Prepare a transparency or student copies of the activity sheet.)
- **For additional experience with harmony:** Create 9, page 212

Chords not shown on pupil page

Mockin' Bird Hill

Words and Music by Vaughn Horton

Verse

A   D

1. When the sun in the morn-in' peeps o-ver the hill,
2. Got a three-cor-nered plow and an a-cre to till,
3. When it's late in the eve-ning, I climb up the hill,

E7   A

And kiss-es the ros-es 'round my win-dow - sill;
And a mule that I bought for a ten-dol-lar bill;
And sur-vey all my king-dom while ev-ery-thing's still;

A   D

Then my heart fills with glad-ness when I hear the trill,
There's a tum-ble-down shack and a rust-y ole mill,
On-ly me and the sky and an ole whip-poor - will,

E7   A

Of the birds in the tree-tops on Mock-in' Bird Hill.
But it's my Home Sweet Home up on Mock-in' Bird Hill.
Sing-in' songs in the twi-light on Mock-in' Bird Hill.

10

TRO—© Copyright 1949 and renewed 1977 Cromwell Music, Inc., New York, NY. Reprinted in the United States by permission of The Richmond Organization.

Introducing the Lesson

Ask the students to open their books to page 8 and sing "Hey Dum Diddeley Dum" in three parts while you add a chordal accompaniment on the piano. Tell them to close their eyes and make up their own melodic ideas, using the word "doo," as you continue the accompaniment. Play the accompaniment several times as the students "sort out" the sounds they want to use.

Developing the Lesson

1. Ask the students to turn to page 10. Guide them to learn the song "Mockin' Bird Hill." Play the recording. On the first hearing they should softly tap the meter: "heavy–light–light." On the second hearing ask them to identify the end of each phrase (each phrase is 4 measures long). On the final hearing tell them to show the shape of the melody with

hand gestures. Invite them to sing the song without the recording.

2. Distribute all resonator bells having the pitches indicated on page 11 (one for each student). Form three groups with each representing one of the three chords: **A** (I), **D** (IV), and **E7** (V7). The D, E, and A bell players belong to two chord groups. The groups may play a bell accompaniment for the verse by following the chord sequence given at the bottom of page 11. **How long should each chord be played?** (for 3 beats) Show the students how to sustain the sound by tapping the bell lightly and rapidly.

3. Help the students understand that melody and harmony are closely related. Display Activity Sheet 3 (*Melody and Harmony*) as a transparency or distribute a copy to each stu-

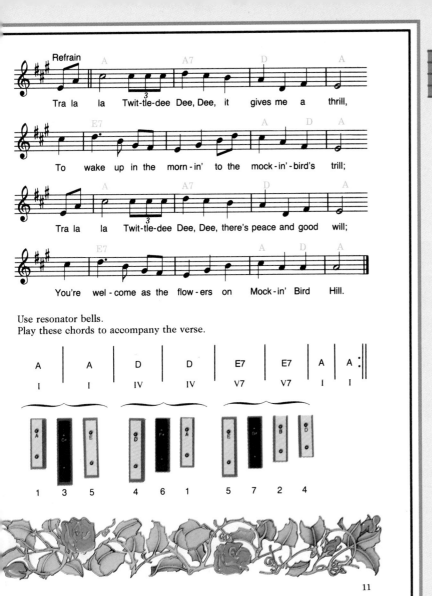

Refrain

| A | | A7 | | D | | A |

Tra la la Twit-tle-dee Dee, Dee, it gives me a thrill,

| E7 | | | | A | D | A |

To wake up in the morn-in' to the mock-in'-bird's trill;

| A | | A7 | | D | | A |

Tra la la Twit-tle-dee Dee, Dee, there's peace and good will;

| E7 | | | | A | D | A |

You're wel-come as the flow-ers on Mock-in' Bird Hill.

Use resonator bells.
Play these chords to accompany the verse.

| A | A | D | D | E7 | E7 | A | A |
| I | I | IV | IV | V7 | V7 | I | I |

1 3 5 4 6 1 5 7 2 4

11

---

dent. The melody is shown by scale numbers, with each box representing one measure. The students are to look at the scale numbers in each box and write the correct chord in the corresponding circle, using Roman numerals.

4. Ask nine students to form a row across the front of the room. Redistribute the resonator bells in this order: C♯, D, E, F♯, G♯, A′, B′, C♯′, and D′. **Be sure you know your scale numbers so that you will know when to play your bell.** (3, 4, 5, 6, 7, 1′, 2′, 3′, and 4′) The bell players are to strike the bells in the order shown on the activity sheet, not simultaneously as they did when they were playing chords. **What melody are we playing?** (verse of "Mockin' Bird Hill") Help the students realize that the melody consists almost entirely of pitches that outline one of the three chords. Ask the bell players to play the melody again in the correct rhythm.

Closing the Lesson

End the class by choosing a third group of bell players to perform the sustained chordal accompaniment (see Step 2) as the rest of the students sing the verse.

Lesson Focus

Harmony: Chords and melody may move simultaneously in relation to each other. *(P–I)*

Materials

○ **Piano Accompaniments:** page 260
○ **Record Information:**
  • Oh, Dear, What Can the Matter Be?
    Record 1   Side A   Band 4
    Voices: children's choir
    Accompaniment: harmonica, fiddle, mandolin, banjo, acoustic guitar, double bass
  • Skip to My Lou
    Record 1   Side A   Band 5
    Voices: children's choir
    Accompaniment: barrel organ, percussion
○ **Instruments:** resonator bells D, E♭, F, G, A♭, B♭, and C; bell mallets
○ **For additional experience with harmony:** Perform 7, page 145

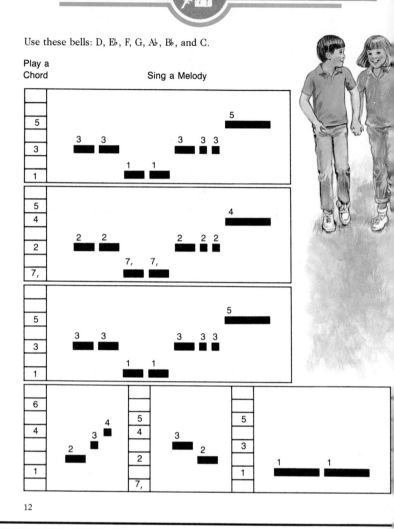

Chords and Melody Go Hand in Hand

Use these bells: D, E♭, F, G, A♭, B♭, and C.

Play a Chord

Sing a Melody

12

Introducing the Lesson

Ask the students to open their books to page 12 and read the title. **What do you suppose that means?** After they offer ideas, draw attention to the picture of chords and melody in the four boxes below the title. **What represents the chords?** (numbers stacked vertically at the beginning of each box) **What represents the melody?** (numbers shown in sequence) **What do you notice about the numbers that make up the chords and those that make up the melody?** (They are frequently the same.) **That is what the title means. Chords and melodies are as close together as your two hands!**

Explain to the students that in order to play the chords, they will need the resonator bells indicated at the top of the page. **Can you identify the letter name of the bell to be used for each scale number?** (Lowest scale number is 7,; lowest bell is D.)

Distribute as many bells and mallets as possible (one to each student if available). Instruct the students to play the chords. To sustain the sound, they must play lightly and rapidly. Sing the scale numbers while the students sustain the bell sound. **Can you recognize the song?** ("Skip to My Lou")

Developing the Lesson

1. The melody of "Oh, Dear, What Can the Matter Be?" goes hand in hand with the same chords used for "Skip to My Lou." **Can you locate the patterns that belong to each chord by studying the notation?** By comparing the chordal patterns with the song notation, help the students discover that the pitches of the melody outline the chords as follows:

   Measures 1–2: I Chord
   Measures 3–4: V7 Chord
   Measures 5–6: I Chord

Oh, Dear, What Can the Matter Be?

Traditional Folk Song

The I Chord   The IV Chord   The V7 Chord

E♭

Oh, dear, what can the mat - ter be?

B♭7

Oh, dear, what can the mat - ter be?

E♭

Oh, dear, what can the mat - ter be?

A♭   **B♭7**   **E♭**

My maid has gone to the fair. ———

13

Measure 7 (first 3 notes): IV Chord
           (last 3 notes): V7 Chord
Measure 8: I Chord

2. After the chord structure has been determined, ask the students to play the chords for
   each measure on the bells. To keep players
   together, count six pulses for each measure.

3. Ask the students to sing the song as they play
   the chordal accompaniment. **Listen carefully
   to the sounds of the chords. The pitches of
   your melody can usually be found there!**

Closing the Lesson

Suggest to the students that they create an **A B
A** form using the two songs they have learned.
With which will you begin? (Either could be chosen.) **Then what will you do?** (Sing the other
song.) **Are you finished with the form?** (No, they
must sing the first song again.)

Skip to My Lou
Traditional

E♭   **E♭**

Choose your part - ner, skip to my Lou,

B♭7   **B♭7**

Choose your part - ner, skip to my Lou,

E♭   **E♭**

Choose your part - ner, skip to my Lou,

A♭   **B♭7**   **E♭**

Skip to my Lou, my dar - ling.

LESSON 5

Lesson Focus

Harmony: Chords and melody may move simultaneously in relation to each other. *(P–S)*

Materials

- ○ **Piano Accompaniment:** page 261
- ○ **Record Information:**
  - Oh, Dear, What Can the Matter Be?
    (Record 1   Side A   Band 4)
  - Skip to My Lou
    (Record 1   Side A   Band 5)
  - Ode to a Washerwoman
    Record 1   Side A   Band 6
    Voices: children's choir
    Accompaniment: tin whistle, flute, cello, harp, concertina, percussion
- ○ *Piano Quintet* ("The Trout"), Fourth Movement (excerpt)
  by Franz Schubert (**shoo**-bert), 1797–1828
  Record 1   Side A   Band 7
  Miecyzslaw Horszowski, piano; members of the Budapest Quartet; Julius Levine, double bass
- ○ **Instruments:** resonator bells D, E♭, F, G, A♭, B♭, C, and E♭'; bell mallets
- ○ **Teacher's Resource Binder:**
  - Optional—
    Orff Activity 10, page O19

(continued on next page)

Ode to a Washerwoman

Traditional Folk Song

Here's a   wo-man, a   wo-man, a   good wash-er-wo-man, A
wo-man, a   wo-man, a   good wash-er-wo-man, A
wo-man, a   wo-man, a   good wash-er-wo-man. She
dan-ces   and   sings   as   she   wash-es   the   clothes.

Oh, Dear,
What Can the Matter Be?

Skip to My Lou

The Good Washerwoman

Plan an accompaniment for these songs.
Use the I, IV, and V7 chords.
Use these **pitches:** D, E♭, F, G, A♭, B♭, C, and E♭'.
Sing all three songs at the same time.

14

Introducing the Lesson

Review the two songs learned in the previous lesson (pages 12–13). Ask the students to identify the number of the chord used in each measure of "Oh, Dear, What Can the Matter Be?" Write them on the chalkboard:

| I | I | V7 | V7 | I | I | IV V7 | I ‖ |

Distribute resonator bells. Ask the students to play the chordal accompaniment as they sing the song. Suggest that they now play the same chordal accompaniment as they sing "Skip to My Lou." **Do you think it will work? Let's find out.** Play and sing the song. Discover that the same chord sequence is appropriate for this song as well. **Since both songs use the same chord sequence, we should be able to sing the songs at the same time!** Divide the class into two groups and perform the songs simultaneously. Play the

chords on the piano or choose some students to play them on bells.

Developing the Lesson

1. Ask the students to open their books to page 14. Explain that the chords for "Ode to a Washerwoman" are given above the staff in letter names. **E♭ is the I chord. What is the number of the A♭ chord?** Help the students name the pitches of the E♭ scale and number each pitch: E♭ (1), F (2), G (3), A♭ (4), B♭ (5). Agree that the A♭ chord is the IV chord; the B♭ chord is the V7 chord. As the students name the chords above each measure, write the number below the chords previously written on the chalkboard. The students will quickly discover that the chord sequence for this melody is the same as that used for the two songs they just sang.

14

LESSON 5

Piano Quintet ("The Trout")
Fourth Movement: Theme and Variations
by Franz Schubert

15

Materials (continued)
o **For additional experience with harmony and form:** Perform 12, page 156; Create 2, page 200

2. **You know the sound of the chord sequence. Do you think you can quickly learn the melody?** Turn the balance knob on the record player so that only the accompaniment to this song can be heard. Then play the recording as the students sing the melody.

3. When the students can sing this melody easily, perform all three songs as a rondo: **A B A C A B A.**

4. Challenge the class to perform "Ode to a Washerwoman" by singing all three songs at the same time. Divide the class into three groups and assign one song to each.

OPTIONAL

Closing the Lesson
Turn the students' attention to page 15. In the songs we've been singing, the chords and melody go hand in hand. This happens in music written for instruments as well. Play the recording of *Piano Quintet*, Fourth Movement (excerpt), as the students follow the melody and chords.

LESSON 6

Lesson Focus
Form: A musical whole is a combination of smaller segments. *(D–I)*

Materials
○ **Piano Accompaniment:** page 262
○ **Record Information:**
  • Wade in the Water
    Record 1   Side B   Band 1
    Voices: solo child, children's choir
    Accompaniment: tenor saxophone, trumpet, trombone, electric bass, electric organ, piano, percussion
  • *Wade in the Water*
    Record 1   Side B   Band 2
    Ramsey Lewis Trio
  • *Souvenir d'Amerique*
    by Henri Vieuxtemps (vyuh-**tahn**), 1820–1881
    Record 1   Side B   Band 3
    Soon-Ik Lee, violin
    Robert Marler, piano
○ **Teacher's Resource Binder:**
  • Optional—
    Curriculum Correlation 2, page C2
    Kodaly Activity 15, page K24
    Mainstreaming Suggestion 3, page M10
○ **For additional experience with form:** Create 4, page 202; Special Times 2, page 222

Theme and Variations

Look at these pictures.
What is the theme? How is it varied?

LISTENING

Souvenir d'Amerique
by Henri Vieuxtemps

Listen to this music.
What is its theme? How is it varied?

16

Introducing the Lesson   OPTIONAL

Ask the class to select from the three songs learned in Lessons 4 and 5 and create an **A B A** form. Using all three songs, review the form of a rondo (**A B A C A B A**).

Developing the Lesson

1. **There are other ways of organizing music besides the A B A and rondo forms. Can you think of any other forms that you studied last year?** Help the students recall theme and variations and canon. Discuss how the forms differ from each other. In a rondo there are three different themes. In theme and variations each section uses the same theme.

2. **I am going to play a recording for you.** Ask the students to listen carefully and be ready to answer these questions:

• Is this a serious or humorous composition?

• What song did the composer borrow for this composition?

• What form did the composer use?

3. Play only the introduction of *Souvenir d'Amerique*. **Could you answer any of the questions having heard this much?** (Sounds serious; no recognizable tune; cannot tell the form until the entire composition has been played.)

4. Play the entire composition and discuss the questions again. The students should decide the introduction was misleading and that this is a humorous composition. The composer based his composition on "Yankee Doodle." He used the theme and variations form. Share the title and information about the composition with the students (see **For Your Information**) and play the entire work once more.

Wade in the Water

Chords not shown on pupil page

Afro-American Melody

Wade ___ in the wa - ter, ___

Wade ___ in the wa - ter, chil - dren;

Wade ___ in the wa - ter,

God's goin' to trou - ble the wa - ter. ___ *Fine*

1. See that band all dressed in white, ___
2. See that band all dressed in red, ___

God's goin' to trou - ble the wa - ter. ___

1. The lead - er looks like the Is - rael - ite, ___
2. It looks like the band that ___ Mo - ses led, ___ *D.C. al Fine*

God's goin' to trou - ble the wa - ter. ___

17

For Your Information

Henri Vieuxtemps was a Belgian violin virtuoso. He visited America three times and expressed his love for this country in several works, including this humorous burlesque on "Yankee Doodle."

Form of *Souvenir d'Amerique*:

Introduction: Virtuosic violin solo

Theme: Violin plays "Yankee Doodle," which is comprised of a repeating A and B section; piano accompanies.

Variation 1: Violin plays theme with added notes in high register. During the repeat, violin plays plucked notes between bowed melody.

Variation 2: Violin plays theme; piano accompaniment is more active.

Variation 3: Piano plays theme; violin provides accompaniment.

Variation 4: Violin plays theme, heavily ornamented.

Variation 5: Violin softly plays theme with quiet piano accompaniment.

Variation 6: Piano plays Section A of theme with violin accompaniment. Violin plays Section B of theme with piano accompaniment.

Coda: Lengthy bravura equally shared by violin and piano.

---

5. Ask the students to look at the pictures on page 16. It shows a theme and variation. **What is the theme?** (egg) **How is the theme varied?** (fried, scrambled, decorated) **If the theme were "potato," what could some variations be?** (French fried, baked, planted, potato pancakes, etc.)

Closing the Lesson

Help the students learn to sing "Wade in the Water" on page 17. Ask them to listen to the recording as they follow the notation. **How could we vary this song?** (add instruments; change tempo, dynamics, rhythm, melody) Experiment with some of the changes the students suggest.

Play another recording of "Wade in the Water." **How many times can you recognize the theme?** (probably four) After its second appearance, the player varies the theme until it is difficult to

recognize. He returns to it in a simpler form, and then improvises on it again. Near the end of the piece, he returns to the theme once more. Play the recording again to give the students an opportunity to listen for the improvisation and to enjoy the sounds of the jazz trio.

17

Lesson Focus

Rhythm: Individual sounds and silences within a rhythmic line may be longer than, shorter than, or the same as the underlying shortest pulse. *(P–S)*

Materials

○ **Piano Accompaniment:** page 264
○ **Record Information:**
  • My Aunt Came Back
  Record 1   Side B   Band 4
  Voices: solo child, children's choir
  Accompaniment: recorder, hammered dulcimer, psaltery, shawm, barrel organ, shakuhachi, samisen, harp, electric guitar, electric bass, double bass, harpsichord, piano, percussion
○ **Other:** pencil for each student
○ **Teacher's Resource Binder:**
  [Activity Sheets] • **Activity Sheet 4,** page A8 (Prepare a copy for each student.)
  • Optional—
  Mainstreaming Suggestion 4, page M10
○ **For additional experience with harmony:** Create 13, page 218; Special Times 12, page 240

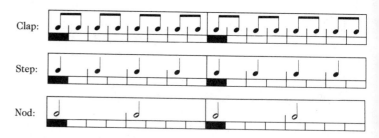

My Aunt Came Back

Traditional

How many things can you do at once?
Add one motion at a time.
How does each one move in relation to the others?

Clap:

Step:

Nod:

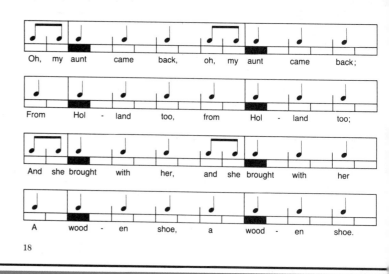

Read the rhythm of this chant in relation to the shortest sound.

Oh, my aunt came back, oh, my aunt came back;

From Hol - land too, from Hol - land too;

And she brought with her, and she brought with her

A wood - en shoe, a wood - en shoe.

18

Introducing the Lesson

How many different motions can you do at the same time? Can you pat your head while you rub your stomach? Ask the students to mirror your motions. Focus their attention on the information given at the top of page 18. **Can you clap a series of short sounds as you step beats that are each twice as long as the short sounds?** Invite the class to begin by clapping and then adding the steps. Finally, as they continue to clap and step, they should nod their heads on the first of every four short sounds.

Developing the Lesson

1. **"My Aunt Came Back" is a fun song with lots of motions that can be done at the same time.** Before they try them, have the students learn the rhythm of the melody. Guide them to read the first verse, displayed as a chant at the bottom of page 18. Help them determine the length of each note in relation to the underlying shortest sound.

2. When the students can perform the chant correctly, play the recording. As they listen they may add appropriate motions on the first and third beats of each measure, as shown by the rhythm for nodding at the top of the pupil page.

3. After hearing all the verses, most of the students will be able to sing the song without assistance. They may add the motions as they sing. Choose a small group of students to sing the leader's part.

4. Distribute copies of Activity Sheet 4 (*My Aunt Came Back*) and pencils to each student. **Can you make up your own verses about other people and cities, towns, or countries? How**

Leader **G** Group

Oh, my aunt came back, oh, my aunt came back

Leader **D7** Group

From Hol - land too, from Hol - land too;

Leader **D7** Group

And she brought with her, and she brought with her

Leader **G** Group

A wood - en shoe, a wood - en shoe.

1. *(Stamp your foot on the word "shoe," then keep stamping.)*

2. Oh, my aunt came back from Old Japan,
   And she brought with her a waving fan.
   (Wave fan and continue to stamp foot.)

3. . . . from Open Plain, . . . a walking cane.
   *(Hold cane and move both feet while continuing to wave
   fan and stamp foot.)*

4. . . . from near Kamloops, . . . some hula hoops.
   (Add hula-hoop movement.)

5. . . . from near Algiers, . . . some cutting shears.
   (Add cutting motion.)

6. . . . from the New York Fair, . . . a rocking chair.
   (Add rocking motion.)

7. . . . from Niagara Falls, . . . some Ping-Pong balls.
   (Move head to follow balls.)

19

will the rhythms change? Guide the students to write their own verses on one or both rhythm rulers on the activity sheet. They may use the example at the bottom of page 18 as a guide.

Closing the Lesson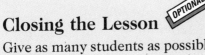

Give as many students as possible an opportunity to share their verses. Those sharing may sing the leader's part while the class echoes on the "group" part. Appropriate motions should be added. Invite the class to choose their favorite new verse. Add it to the original song as Verse 8. **Let's see how many motions we can continue doing throughout the song once they've been introduced.** Sing the song. Try to continue the motions from each previous verse until they can all be done simultaneously by the end of Verse 8.

LESSON 8

Lesson Focus

Rhythm: A series of beats may be organized into regular or irregular groupings by stressing certain beats. *(P–S)*

Materials

○ **Piano Accompaniment:** page 266
○ **Record Information:**
  • Bicycle Built for Two
    Record 1   Side B   Band 5
    Voices: children's choir
    Accompaniment: barrel organ, percussion
  • *Bicycle Built for Two*
    by Harry Dacre
    Record 1   Side B   Band 6
    Synthesized by Max. V. Matthews on a computer series for Bell Laboratories
○ **Instruments:** large hand drum or snare drum; brushes
○ **Teacher's Resource Binder:**
  • Optional—
    Curriculum Correlation 3, page C5
    Enrichment Activity 1, page E2
○ **For additional experience with rhythm:** Perform 2, page 136

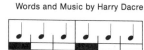

Bicycle Built for Two

Words and Music by Harry Dacre

In this song the ♩ is the shortest sound. Can you read the rhythm of the melody?

Dai - sy, Dai - sy, Give me your an-swer do. ____
I'm half cra - zy, All for the love of you. ____
It won't be a styl - ish mar - riage; ____
I can't af - ford a car - riage, ____
But you'll look sweet on a seat
of a bi - cy - cle built for two. ____

Listen to a second version of this song.
What do you notice?

20

Introducing the Lesson

Have you ever ridden a tandem bicycle? On a tandem bike the two riders must work together to pedal and balance. Explain that in the early 1900s, these bicycles were very popular. Play Band 1 of the recording "Bicycle Built for Two" as the students follow the notation on page 20.

Developing the Lesson

1. Ask the students to read the discussion at the top of page 20 and to look at the rhythm ruler. **Look at the song notation. What do the curved lines under some of the notes mean? Do you recall the purpose of these signs?** Before they answer guide the students' attention to the two rhythm rulers at the top of page 21. **Can you find the two ways to write the rhythm for the word "answer"?** (Tie two notes together or use one longer note.) **Will**

they sound the same or different? (the same) Explain that the sound for the word "do" can be shown only one way because the note lasts across the bar line and each measure must include its own notes.

2. Read the discussion at the bottom of page 21. Agree that the rhythm of "Bicycle Built for Two" will move in threes. The quarter note is the note that moves with the beat. Guide the students to complete the "rhythm equations" at the bottom of the page.

♩ = 1 beat

♩ = 2 beats

♩. = 3 beats

♩ + ♩ = 4 beats

♩. + ♩. = 6 beats

20

More About Rhythmic Relationships

The "musical plus sign": the tie.
Will these two patterns sound the same or different?

Give me your an - swer do. _____

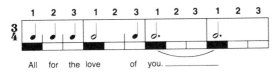

Give me your an - swer do. _____

The Meter Signature

3 ⟵ Look at the upper number.
        It tells how the beats are grouped.

4 ⟵ Look at the lower number.
        It identifies the note that moves with the beat.

Which note moves with the beat in
"Bicycle Built for Two"?

All   for   the   love   of   you. _____

How will each of these notes move in relation
to the beat? the shortest sound?

♩ = ?   ♩ = ?   ♩. = ?   ♩ + ♩ = ?   ♩. + ♩. = ?

21

For Your Information

Both the melody and accompaniment on Version 2 of the recording of "Bicycle Built for Two" were synthesized on a large computer at Bell Telephone Labs by Max V. Matthews. This recording is an early example of electronic music and somewhat primitive by today's standards.

3. Ask the students to use this information so that they can read the rhythm of the song, "Bicycle Built for Two." To help them sense the movement in threes, have one student play the beat with brushes on a drum. At the same time, the rest of the class taps the following pattern as they read the melodic rhythm:

Body:	Left knee	Right knee	Right knee
Drum:	Tap	Brush	Brush

4. When the students can perform the rhythm correctly, play the recording again. Focus their attention on the melodic contour. Invite the class to sing the song independently. When they are secure in their vocal performance, add the accompaniment performed during Step 3.

Closing the Lesson

Listen to a computer performance of this song. Explain that computers produce different kinds of sounds when different directions are given to them. By combining these directions in a new way, this early computer was made to sound like a voice and piano. Today's computers can make much more sophisticated vocal sounds, but this early example is still fun to hear.

LESSON 9

Lesson Focus

Rhythm: A series of beats may be organized into regular or irregular groupings by stressing certain beats. *(P–S)*

Materials

○ **Piano Accompaniments:** pages 265 and 268

○ **Record Information:**
  • Bicycle Built for Two
    (Record 1 Side B Band 5)
  • Morning Comes Early
    Record 2 Side A Band 1
    Voice: baritone
    Accompaniment: clarinet, trumpet, violin, bass, accordion
  • The Turtle's Song—"I Can Win!"
    Record 2 Side A Band 2
    Voices: children's choir
    Accompaniment: synthesizer, harp, piano, electric organ, celesta, percussion

○ **Teacher's Resource Binder:**
  | Evaluation | • Optional—
    Checkpoint 1, page EV1
    Curriculum Correlation 22, page C22
    Kodaly Activity 16, page K24

○ **For additional experience with rhythm:** Perform 1, page 134; Describe 9, page 181

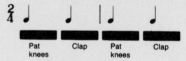

Introducing the Lesson

Review the meter signature information found on page 21. Ask the students to examine the meter signatures for "Morning Comes Early" and "The Turtle's Song–'I Can Win!' " on pages 22 and 23. Decide that the quarter note will move with the beat for both songs, because the lower number is the same in both meter signatures. In "Morning Comes Early" the beats will be grouped in twos because the upper number is a two. In the other song the beats will be grouped in fours.

Developing the Lesson

1. Draw attention to the patterns shown with the rhythm ruler at the top of page 22. Divide the class into three groups and challenge them to perform the patterns. Group 1 taps the shortest sound. Group 2 pats the beat on their knees. Group 3 chants the words in rhythm.

2. The students may then learn the melody by listening to the recording. When they know the song suggest that they add this pattern as they sing:

3. Draw the students' attention to the rhythm ruler for "The Turtle's Song–'I Can Win!' " on the bottom of page 22. Ask them to divide into groups as before (see Step 1) and chant the rhythm of this new song. **What will be different this time?** (The beats are grouped in fours.) **How will you show this?** (Stress the first sound in each measure.)

4. After the students have chanted the rhythm, play the recording. While they are listening, the entire class should lightly tap the beat in

1. Keep on mov-ing on though I know my steps are hea-vy and slow,
2. I can't wor-ry what some-one else is do-ing, I'll go my way,

One foot out and then one foot af-ter is the way that I go!
I know where I'm go-ing, and I will sure-ly get there some day;

Tho' they laugh to see me plod a-long and ask, "Why be - gin?"
Tho' they tease me and they taunt me I re - ply with a grin.

Just for me to start and keep go-ing, in a way is to win.

Let them laugh and let them de - ride — me,

Let them point their fin - gers and chide — me,

I know deep in - side me — I can win!

23

For Your Information

To interpret the Rhythm Ruler:
The lowest row of boxes shows the underlying beat. (These beats are to be stressed.) By counting the accented and unaccented beats, you can determine how the beats are grouped. One group of accented and unaccented beats equals a measure.

The middle row of boxes shows the shortest sound. These are accented pulses.

The top row shows a rhythm pattern. The boxes are of varying length, in relation to the underlying shortest sound. By comparing the length of the boxes in the top row with the boxes in the "shortest sound" row, you may determine the relative length of each sound within the rhythm pattern.

groups of fours. **Do you feel accents on any other beat besides the first beat of each set?** The students should recognize that the third beat is also stressed, although not as heavily as the first beat.

Let's create a "hand jive" pattern that will show both accents. Guide the students to create hand movements that accurately reflect each beat in sets of four: strong accent–no accent–weak accent–no accent. This might be done with motions such as: clap above head; hands apart; pat knees; hands apart. The students may add their movements to the song as they listen again.

5. Ask the students to listen again and think about the lyrics. Discuss their meaning. Emphasize that everyone is a "special person" and that even if one person may not always finish a race or some other task first, he or

she can be a winner in other ways. **Can you now sing the song without any help?**

Closing the Lesson

Sing "Bicycle Built for Two" (page 20) as students improvise "hand jives" in sets of three.

LESSON 10

Lesson Focus

Harmony: Chords and melody may move simultaneously in relation to each other. *(P–S)*

Materials

○ **Piano Accompaniments:** pages 270 and 271
○ **Record Information:**
  • Mockin' Bird Hill
    (Record 1 Side A Band 3)
  • Sarah the Whale
    Record 2 Side A Band 3
    Voices: children's choir
    Accompaniment: piccolo, clarinet, French horn, ukulele, double bass, accordion, piano, sound effects, percussion
  • On Top of Old Smoky
    Record 2 Side A Band 4
    Voice: children's choir
    Accompaniment: electric guitar, pedal steel guitar, double bass, percussion
○ **Instrument:** autoharp
○ **Other:** overhead projector
○ **Teacher's Resource Binder:**

| Activity Sheets | • **Activity Sheet 5,** page A9 (Prepare a transparency from the activity sheet.) |

  • Optional—
    Kodaly Activity 16, page K24

Sarah the Whale

Words by Tom Glazer   Music by Daniel D. Emmett

The melody of this song is based on three chords in the key of C.

Play the chords on the autoharp.
Strum once for each measure.
Listen carefully to the chords as you sing the melody on the word "loo."

24

Introducing the Lesson

Review "Mockin' Bird Hill" on page 10. Remind the students of their discoveries about how melody and harmony relate to each other.

Developing the Lesson

1. Ask the students to turn to pages 24 and 25. **Let's see if you can use your knowledge about how chords and melody go "hand in hand" to learn these songs. Before we study the melody, let's look at the rhythm of the two songs.** Help the students recall information learned during Lessons 7 through 9 on pages 18 to 23. Guide them to conclude that:

   • The quarter note moves with the beat in both songs.

   • "Sarah the Whale" moves in twos while "On Top of Old Smoky" moves in threes.

   • The melodic rhythm of "Sarah the Whale" frequently moves with the shortest sound (the eighth note).

   • The shortest sound in "On Top of Old Smoky" is the quarter note. The rhythm of this song often moves with longer sounds.

2. Ask the class to chant the words of "Sarah the Whale" in rhythm while one student taps the shortest sound.

3. Read the discussion at the top of page 24. Help the students replace the "?" beneath the chords with the appropriate letter. To do this, ask them to name and count the pitches of the C major scale (C D E F G A B C'; 1 2 3 4 5 6 7 1'). Conclude that I is C, IV is F, and V7 is G7.

4. Choose a student who can keep a steady beat

On Top of Old Smoky

Kentucky Folk Song

This melody is based on the same three chords used in "Sarah the Whale."

Can you decide when you should play each chord? You will need to name a chord for each box shown above the staff.

To choose a chord:
1. Look at the pitches used in the melody.
2. Compare them with the pitches used in the chords on page 24.
3. Choose the chord that includes important pitches from the melody.

Play the chords on the autoharp as you sing the song.

1. On top of Old Smok - y _____ All cov-ered with snow, _____
2. O court-ing's a plea - sure, _____ But part-ing's a grief, _____
3. A thief will but rob you _____ Of all that you save, _____
4. The grave will de - cay you _____ And turn you to dust, _____

I lost my true lov - er _____ By court - ing too slow.
And a false-heart-ed lov - er _____ Is worse than a thief. _____
But a false-heart-ed lov - er _____ Sends you to your grave. _____
But a false-heart-ed lov - er _____ You nev - er can trust. _____

25

LESSON 10

For Your Information

Chords to be added to boxes above "On Top of Old Smoky": C, F, C, C, G7, G7, and C.

---

to play the autoharp. Ask the class to listen and follow the notation in their books while the autoharp player performs the chord sequence to "Sarah the Whale." This sequence is given at the beginning of each staff. The player should perform each chord four times, on the beat.

5. As the accompanist plays the chord sequence a second time, challenge the class to sing the melody using the word "loo." Guide them to correct any errors they may make by singing the problem measures with scale numbers. Then sing the song again with the autoharp accompaniment.

6. Turn to page 25 and help the students learn the rhythm to "On Top of Old Smoky" by following the same process used in learning "Sarah the Whale."

7. Ask the students to determine the chords needed in "On Top of Old Smoky." Prepare a transparency of this page from Activity Sheet 5 (*On Top of Old Smoky*). Display it on the overhead projector. As the students give the name of each chord, write its name in the box above the staff. (See **For Your Information**.)

8. Follow the same process as outlined in Steps 4 and 5 to help the students learn to sing this melody with autoharp accompaniment.

Closing the Lesson

End the class by singing each song again, giving other students the opportunity to play the autoharp.

LESSON 11

Lesson Focus

Harmony: Chords and melody may move simultaneously in relation to each other. *(P–S)*

Materials

○ **Piano Accompaniments:** pages 263 and 272
○ **Record Information:**
  • La Cucaracha
    Record 2   Side A   Band 5
    Voices: children's choir
    Accompaniment: clarinet, trumpet, violin, accordion, double bass
  • Oleana
    Record 2   Side A   Band 6
    Voices: man, children's choir
    Accompaniment: string ensemble
○ **Instrument:** autoharp
○ **Other:** Prepare 20 3 × 5″ index cards. Write "Chordal Skips" on half of them and "Scale Steps" on the others.
○ **Teacher's Resource Binder:**
  Activity Sheets • **Activity Sheets 6a–c,** pages A10–A12 (Cut the chord cards apart. Write the name of the chord on the back of each card. To preserve the cards, which may be used many times, paste copies

(continued on next page)

La Cucaracha

Mexican Folk Song

Most songs of our culture move by patterns made up of:

Scale Steps

1 2 3 2 3 4 5

or

Chordal Skips

I Chord   IV   V   I

1 3 5   1 4 6   7, 2 5   1

Locate patterns in these songs that are made up of chordal skips. Which chords are used? Where does the melody move by steps?

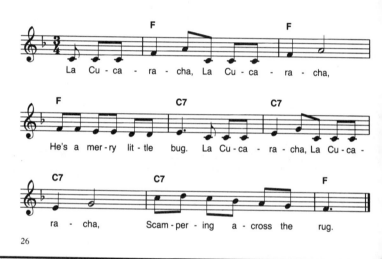

F   F

La Cu - ca - ra - cha, La Cu - ca - ra - cha,

F   C7   C7

He's a mer-ry lit-tle bug. La Cu-ca - ra - cha, La Cu-ca -

C7   C7   F

ra - cha,   Scam-per-ing a - cross the   rug.

26

Introducing the Lesson

Begin the class by challenging the students to a new game. Display the Chord Pattern cards prepared from Activity Sheet 6 (*Chord Patterns*). (See **Materials** for instructions.) Choose an autoharp player and a leader. The leader draws a card from your hand and tells the autoharp player what chord to play. This time play in the key of F. (I is F; IV is B♭; V7 is C7.) After the class has heard the chord, they should sing the pitches in the order shown on the card.

Developing the Lesson

1. Ask the students to turn to page 26. Draw attention to the information given at the top of the page. Distribute the Chord Pattern cards to some students. Give the rest of the students "Chordal Skips" and "Scale Steps" cards. (See **Materials** for instructions.)

Ask the class to look at "La Cucaracha." **Let's use our cards to show how each pattern moves in this song. Who has a card that describes whether the first pattern moves by chordal skips or by scale steps?** A student with the card "Chordal Skips" should come forward. Follow the same procedure until all patterns have been described and six students are holding cards in this order:

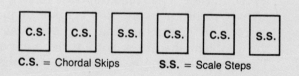

C.S. = Chordal Skips   **S.S.** = Scale Steps

2. **This song begins on low 5. 1 is in the first space.** Ask those students holding the Chord Pattern cards to compare them with the song notation for the patterns identified as chordal skips in Step 1.

Oleana

English Words by Beth Landis

Norwegian Folk Song

Chords not shown on pupil page

Refrain

O - le, O - le - an - a, O - le, O - le - an - a,

O - le, O - le, O - le, O - le, O - le, O - le - an - a. *Fine*

Verse

1. O that is where I'd like to be, There where the land is free;
2. The hens lay eggs as big as rocks, Roost-ers crow like eight-day clocks,
3. The sal - mon leap so high up there, Hold your ket - tle in the air;
4. O come and bring your fid - dle, Dance to the mid - dle,

D.C. al Fine

Wheat and corn they grow so high, The tas - sels dust - ing off the sky!
Roast - ed pigs run all a - bout With knives and forks stuck in their snouts!
They'll jump in, pull on the lid, And cook them-selves to look like squid!
O - le with his vi - o - lin Will help us make a mer - ry din!

27

LESSON *11*

Materials (*continued*)

on oak tag before cutting. You may also wish to laminate each card.)

- Optional—
Curriculum Correlation 4, page C7
Enrichment Activity 2, page E2
Kodaly Activity 17, page K27
Orff Activity 11, page O19

Are any of you holding a card that matches one of the chordal skip patterns used in this song? The chordal skip patterns should be replaced with the Chord Pattern cards as follows:

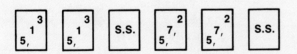

3. As one student plays the autoharp chords in the sequence shown at the beginning of each pattern, ask the class to sing the patterns shown on the Chord Pattern cards and "think" the patterns that move by scale steps.

4. Ask the class to sing the complete song, following the notation while the accompanist continues to play the autoharp.

OPTIONAL

Closing the Lesson

Follow the same procedure to learn the refrain of "Oleana." The cards should now be arranged in this order:

Replace the Chordal Skip cards with the following cards:

Discover that the verse is almost the same as the refrain. Sing the complete song.

27

LESSON 12

Lesson Focus

Harmony: Chords and melody may move simultaneously in relation to each other. *(P–S)*

Materials

○ **Piano Accompaniment:** page 274
○ **Record Information:**
  • Simple Gifts
    Record 2   Side A   Band 7
    Voices: mixed chorus (a cappella)
  • Variations on a Shaker Tune
    from *Appalachian Spring*
    by Aaron Copland, 1900–
    Record 2   Side A   Band 8
    The Boston Symphony Orchestra
    Aaron Copland, conductor
○ **Instruments:** autoharps
○ **Other:** Chord Pattern cards, prepared for Lesson 11 (page 26, from Activity Sheets 6a–c, *Chord Patterns*)
○ **Teacher's Resource Binder:**
  • Optional—
    Enrichment Activity 3, page E5
    Kodaly Activity 12, page K17

Chords not shown on pupil page

Simple Gifts

Shaker Song

Tune Up:

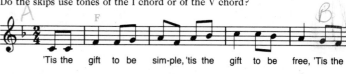

1   3   5   3   1   7,   2   5   2   7,   1

Most of this song moves by scale steps.
Find all the places that move by chordal skips.
Do the skips use tones of the I chord or of the V chord?

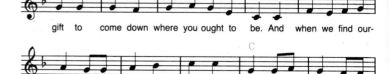

'Tis the   gift   to   be   sim-ple, 'tis the   gift   to   be   free, 'Tis the

gift   to   come down where you ought to   be. And   when we find our-

selves in the   place just   right, 'Twill   be   in the   val-ley of

love and de-light.   When   true   sim-pli-ci-ty   is   gained, To

bow and to   bend we   shan't be a-shamed. To   turn,   turn will

be   our de-light, Till by   turn-ing,   turn-ing we   come 'round   right.

28

Introducing the Lesson

Begin class by using the Chord Pattern cards introduced in Lesson 11 (page 26). (See **Materials.**) Divide the class into two teams, each with a leader and an autoharp player. The teams take turns. The leader draws a card from your hand and tells the autoharp player which chord to strum. The leader then conducts his or her team in performing the pattern on the card. Each correct pitch in the pattern counts for 1 point. Play the game in the key of F (I = F; IV = B♭; V = C; V7 = C7).

Developing the Lesson

1. Ask the class to follow the instructions at the top of page 28. Begin by locating the pitches that skip, using tones from the I and V7 chords:

Text	Chord
"Tis the gift"	I
"simple"	I
"ought to be,"	V
"And when"	I
"'Twill be"	V
"...light. When true"	I
"bend we"	I
"...shamed, To"	V
"To turn,"	I

Agree that most skips use tones that are included in the I chord.

2. Practice the "Tune Up" at the top of the page. Then challenge the class to sightsing the entire song, first with numbers then with words.

3. Discuss the origin of the song and the meaning of the words. (See **For Your Information.**)

28

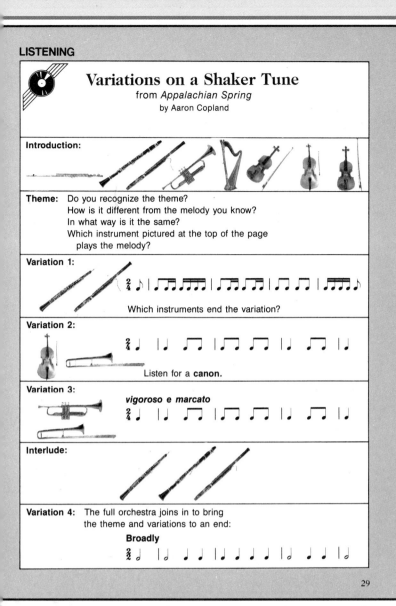

LISTENING

Variations on a Shaker Tune

from *Appalachian Spring*

by Aaron Copland

Introduction:

Theme: Do you recognize the theme?
How is it different from the melody you know?
In what way is it the same?
Which instrument pictured at the top of the page
plays the melody?

Variation 1:

$\frac{2}{4}$

Which instruments end the variation?

Variation 2:

$\frac{2}{4}$

Listen for a **canon.**

Variation 3:

vigoroso e marcato

$\frac{2}{4}$

Interlude:

Variation 4: The full orchestra joins in to bring
the theme and variations to an end:

Broadly

$\frac{2}{2}$

29

For Your Information

"Simple Gifts" is a Shaker song. The Shakers are a religious group, formed in New England during the 1700s. Their name comes from the custom of shaking and moving as part of their devotional exercises. Copland used this melody as part of his ballet *Appalachian Spring.*

Structure of "Variations on a Shaker Tune":

Introduction: Slow, wandering melody played by orchestra.

Theme: Clarinet introduces melody. Rhythm moves with four to the beat, instead of two as in "Simple Gifts."

Variation 1: Theme played as a duet between oboe and bassoon, later joined by clarinet.

Variation 2: Theme played by violas and trombone, with thicker orchestral accompaniment; theme then played in canon among the strings.
(Bridge)

Variation 3: Theme played as a vigorous duet between trumpet and trombone, followed by oboe, clarinet, and horns.
(Bridge)

Variation 4: Theme played by full orchestra.

4. Continue the lesson by listening to "Variations on a Shaker Tune." **Follow the examples and questions in your book as you listen to the first part of this composition. Raise your hand when you recognize the melody.** Play the introduction and first theme until the students indicate that they recognize the theme as the song they just learned.

Closing the Lesson

Play the complete recording. Tell the students to follow the guide in their books. **Can you tell when each variation comes to an end and another is about to begin?** After hearing the composition, discuss the statements and questions found on the pupil page.

Lesson Focus

Expression: Musical elements are combined into a whole to express a musical or extramusical idea. *(D–I)*

Materials

○ **No Piano Accompaniment**

○ **Record Information:**
  • *Moonlight Sonata*
    by Ludwig van Beethoven
    (**bay**-toe-vuhn), 1770–1827
    Record 2   Side B   Band 1
    Rudolf Serkin, pianist
  • *Moonlight Sonata*
    Record 2   Side B   Band 2
    Morton Gould, conductor

○ **Instruments:** large and small cymbals and triangles; various woodblocks, sticks, or other instruments of different sizes made of wood; mallets

○ **Other:** overhead projector

○ **Teacher's Resource Binder:**
  Activity Sheets • **Activity Sheet 7**, page A13 (Prepare a copy for each student.)
  • Optional—
    Biography 2, page B3
    Enrichment Activity 4, page E8

○ **For additional experience with expression:** Describe 11, page 184

Moonlight

Castle on the Rhine, 1857–59, by George Caleb Bingham. Oil on Canvas. Coe Kerr Gallery, New York.

30

Introducing the Lesson

Discuss the painting, *Castle on the Rhine*, by Bingham. **What aspect of the painting first draws your attention?** (Answers may vary. For most, it will be the moonlight streaming through the clouds and reflecting on the water.) **Is the feeling of this painting peaceful? agitated? exciting? amusing?** (Answers will again vary. Peaceful is probably most appropriate.) **How did the artist create this peaceful feeling?** (choice of colors, all muted tones; no strong contrasts; many curved rather than jagged lines; sailboats seem to be drifting; the lines in the water suggest calmness with few waves)

Developing the Lesson

1. Invite the students to perform music intended to elicit a calm, tranquil feeling. Encourage them to explore ways of controlling long sounds (see **For Your Information**) and of creating rhythmic patterns on three different instruments made of wood (high–medium–low, low–low–high, or low–high–low).

2. Hand out Activity Sheet 7 (*Adagio for Percussion*) and study the score. **How many short sounds will Group 2 play in relation to the longer sounds?** (anywhere from three to twelve) Remind the students that "adagio" means to play very slowly. Divide the class into three groups and read through the score. Use hand sounds such as snapping, clapping, or rubbing.

3. Ask the students to look at the instructions on page 31. Parts 1 and 3 will need ringing sounds at two different pitch levels (such as large and small cymbals or triangles). Part 2 will need three wood sounds, each at a different pitch level.

Adagio for Percussion

Play "Adagio for Percussion."

Part 1: Use high-pitched metal instruments to play long, ringing sounds.

Part 2: Play short sounds on wood instruments. Use low, middle, and high pitches.

Part 3: Use low-pitched metal instruments to play long, ringing sounds.

Follow the expressive markings as you perform.

31

For Your Information

Ways to control long sounds:
- Strike a cymbal. Stop the sound with the free hand.
- Hold two mallets in one hand. Place one mallet above the edge of the cymbal and the other below. Softly shake the mallets to produce a sound as long as desired.

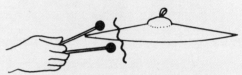

Structure of *Moonlight Sonata*, instrumental excerpt:
- Violins and violas play repeated patterns while double basses play low, sustained sounds.
- French horns enter, playing a single melodic line. String accompaniment continues.
- High strings play the melody. Lower strings echo the high strings. *Crescendos* and *decrescendos* are heard.
- This instrumentation continues as the melody ritards and then fades out to end the excerpt.

Distribute the instruments to three groups. Each group should consist of one player and several students who hold the instruments. They should stand close together so that the player can easily reach each instrument. The player should use two mallets, one in each hand.

4. When the players are sure of their parts, put them together to play "Adagio for Percussion." As they repeat their performance, draw their attention to the contrasts in dynamics that are marked in the score. **How will you respond to:**

   pp   very soft

   p   soft

   ⟨   gradually louder

   ⟩   gradually softer

   mf   medium loud

5. Choose another set of performers. **Will the music be the same?** (No, because each performer will choose different combinations of pitches, even though the rhythmic ideas will remain the same.)

6. Ask the students to turn to pages 32 and 33 and listen to *Moonlight Sonata.* Play the recording as the students follow the first part of the score. Help them realize that this composition is based on the same ideas as "Adagio for Percussion." Point out that short sounds are heard throughout the composition and that the melody is mostly made up of sustained, legato sounds.

7. Play the recording as the students follow the first part of the score in their books. **Listen to the first part again. Does the performer follow the dynamic markings in the score?** (yes)

LISTENING

Moonlight Sonata

First Movement: *Adagio*

by Ludwig van Beethoven

Listen to this music as it is performed on the piano.
Notice the short sounds in the accompaniment that are heard throughout the composition.
The melody is mostly made up of sustained, *legato* sounds.
After listening to the performance, can you decide what these words and symbols mean?

adagio sostenuto pp p mf

32

8. Compare the piano score with the "Adagio for Percussion." **How are they the same?** (Both have repeated short sounds and sustained parts in the bass and melodic line.) **different?** (Timbres are different—one has fixed pitches, while the other uses only high, medium, and low sounds.)

Closing the Lesson

Invite the students to listen to an orchestral version of the same composition. After hearing the composition, discuss why the different parts were heard more distinctly. (Because different timbres are playing the bass and melodic lines, each part is heard more easily.)

Listen to another performance of this composition. This time
it is played by full orchestra.
Why do you hear the different parts more distinctly?

33

Lesson Focus

Expression: Musical elements are combined into a whole to express a musical or extramusical idea. *(D–S)*

Materials

○ **Piano Accompaniment:** page 276

○ **Record Information:**
- *Battle Hymn of the Republic*
  Record 2   Side B   Band 4
  Mormon Tabernacle Choir
  Richard P. Condie, director
  Philadelphia Orchestra
  Eugene Ormandy, conductor
- *Battle Hymn of the Republic*
  Record 2   Side B   Band 5
  Pete Fountain Quartet
- Battle Hymn of the Republic
  Record 2   Side B   Band 3
  Voices: mixed chorus
  Accompaniment: brass quintet, drums

○ **Other:** pencils for several students

○ **Teacher's Resource Binder:**
- Optional—
  Kodaly Activities 5, 6, 9, pages K8, K14

○ **For additional experience with expression:** Special Times 3, page 224

Make Musical Decisions

Imagine music performed by robots.
How would it sound?
Imagine music performed by human beings.
How would it sound?
What would be the difference?

Chords not shown on pupil page

Battle Hymn of the Republic

Words by Julia Ward Howe

Music Attributed to William Steffe

Mine eyes have seen the glo - ry of the com - ing of the Lord;

He is tram-pling out the vin-tage where the grapes of wrath are stored;

34

Introducing the Lesson

Invite the students to discuss the pictures and ideas found on page 34. **How is a robot different from a human being?** (A robot is programmed to do certain tasks; it always does them the same way, and it cannot think up new ways to do them.) **Sometimes when we listen to recorded music we might think that a robot produced it because it sounds the same every time.** Discuss the fact that singers cannot be robots. They must make many decisions about how a song is to be sung. Ask the students what decisions must be made and list their ideas on the chalkboard. (dynamics, articulation, tempo, accompaniment, etc.)

Invite individuals to choose a song they have learned this year and make decisions about how it should be performed. Perform several songs following their suggestions.

Developing the Lesson

1. **Arrangers also make decisions about how to make their music interesting.** Ask the students what decisions they would make if they were the arranger for the song on this page. **Who would sing? What kind of accompaniment? What tempo?**

2. **Listen to two arrangements of "Battle Hymn of the Republic"** (Bands 4 and 5). Divide the class into teams of four students each and ask them to determine whether the arrangers of these two versions made the same or different decisions. Each team is to appoint a scribe to write down their answers on a blank sheet of paper. The paper should be divided into two columns: one column marked "Same," and one marked "Different." In the "Same" column, the scribe is to write anything the group

He hath loosed the fate-ful light-ning of his ter-ri-ble swift sword;

His truth is march-ing on.

Glo - ry, glo-ry, hal-le-lu - jah!

Glo - ry, glo-ry, hal-le-lu - jah!

Glo - ry, glo-ry, hal-le-lu - jah!

His truth is march-ing on.

35

For Your Information

Scoring for game:
If all teams have the same answer on their papers, each team will be awarded 100 points. If all but one team has the same answer, each team having that answer will score 200 points. If all but two teams have the same answer, each will score 300 points, and so on. A team having an answer that no one else has will be awarded the number of points equal to the number of groups multiplied by 100.

hears that is the same in both recordings. (For example, perhaps both pieces are played softly.) In the "Different" column, the note-keeper writes anything the group hears that is different in both recordings.

3. Play each recording of "Battle Hymn of the Republic" more than one time to allow the students time to compare, discuss, and write down their answers.

OPTIONAL

4. Ask a team to share one item under the "Same" column. Ask how many teams had that answer. Announce the scores. (See **For Your Information** for scoring procedure.) Continue to share from either column. If there is a disagreement, play the recording again to verify the answer.

Closing the Lesson

When the scores have been tallied, return to page 34. Listen to a third version of the song, performed by a brass ensemble and chorus. Invite the class to sing the melody after noticing the harmonizing parts that are included in this arrangement.

LESSON 15

Lesson Focus

Evaluation: Review concepts and skills studied in the First Quarter.

Materials

○ **Piano Accompaniment:** page 278

○ **Record Information:**
   • There's Work to Be Done/No Need to Hurry
   Record 3   Side A   Bands 1a–b
   Voices: children's choir
   Accompaniment: electric guitar, electric bass, penny whistle, steel drums, percussion

○ **Instruments:** autoharp; claves; guiro; bongos; maracas; resonator bells with pitches C, D, E, F, G, A, and B; seven mallets

○ **Other:** a pencil for each student

○ **Teacher's Resource Binder:**
   | Evaluation |
   • **Review 1**, pages Ev3–Ev4 (Prepare one copy of each page for each student.)
   • **Musical Progress Report 1**, page Ev5

Introducing the Lesson

Play Band 1a of "There's Work to be Done," through the first statement of this song. Invite the students to lightly tap the steady beat with one foot as they follow the music on page 36. Play the song again. This time tell the students to add the shortest sound by tapping with two fingers in the palm of the opposite hand.

Play the recording a third time, this time continuing through the first statement of "No Need to Hurry." **Are the beat and the shortest sound the same or different for this song?** (different)

Developing the Lesson

1. Distribute copies of Review 1 (*Hurry, Hurry*) and pencils to each student. Read each question with the students to be sure they understand the instructions. Give them a few minutes to answer Questions 1 and 2. Then play

Band 1b of the recording. Play it two or three times to give students ample time to identify each instrument when they answer Question 3. Play Band 1a again so that the students may answer Question 4A. Continue by playing Band 1b as the students answer Question 4B. Repeat each band as needed.

2. Collect the review sheets and pencils. Challenge the students to sing "There's Work to Be Done" as you add an accompaniment on the autoharp. They should sing first with scale numbers and then with words.

3. Follow the same procedure to help the students learn "No Need to Hurry."

4. Distribute the resonator bells to seven players. (See **Materials.**) Group them into the following chord sets: I, with pitches C, E, and G; V7, with pitches G, B, D, and F; and IV,

No Need to Hurry

Words and Music by Richard C. Berg

All right, I come now; all right, I come;

No need to hur - ry, no need to run.

It is too ear - ly; where is the sun?

I am so tired that I can - not run.

Create an **A B A form** by singing these two songs in the correct order.
Sing the two songs as partner songs.
Next add a percussion accompaniment.
Which pattern will you play on each instrument?

37

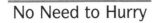

For Your Information

Recording information for "There's Work to Be Done/No Need to Hurry":
Band 1a — single melody
Band 1b — partner song
Answer for Review 1:

1. A.

B.

C.

2. A.

B.

3 3 3 5 1' 4 4 6 1'

5 5 5 7 2' 1' 1' 6 5

C. C G F
3. c. Maracas
   d. Claves
   b. Bongos
   a. Guiro
4. A. **A B A**
   B. a. b.

---

with pitches F, A, and C. Several students will be members of more than one chord group. Invite the players to add the chords as an accompaniment. They should play their bells on the beat at the appropriate time while the rest of the class sings the first song.

5. Draw attention to the question at the bottom of page 36. Guide the students to answer the question by asking them to compare the chords for "No Need to Hurry" with the sequence they just played. Conclude that the chord sequence for both songs is the same.

6. Read the first instruction on page 37 to the class. **How will you perform the songs to create the form A B A?** (Sing the first song, then the second, and finally return to the first.) Perform in this order as the students add the accompaniment.

7. **What will you need to do to follow the second instruction on page 37?** (Sing both songs at the same time.) **Will this sound all right?** (Yes, because both songs use the same chord accompaniment.)

Divide the class into two groups to sing the partner song version as you or a student add the autoharp accompaniment.

Closing the Lesson

Sing the songs again as a partner song while some students continue to add the chords on bells and others play the percussion parts shown at the bottom of page 37.

Use the information collected during this activity as well as other observations made during the First Quarter to complete a copy of *Musical Progress Report 1* for each student. This may be sent to parents as a report and/or filed.

LESSON 16

Lesson Focus

Time and Place: A particular use of timbre and rhythm reflects the origin of the musical whole. *(P–I)*

Materials

○ **No Piano Accompaniment**

○ **Record Information:**
  • West African Rhythm Complex
  Record 3   Side A   Band 2
  Ensemble: percussion
  • *Mayo Nafwa*
  Record 3   Side A   Band 3
  Voices: child solo; children's choir
  Accompaniment: percussion

○ **Instruments:** African gongs or cowbells; African rattles or maracas; low-pitched hand drum; high-pitched hand drum; other percussion instruments

○ **Other:** world map; overhead projector

○ **Teacher's Resource Binder:**

  Activity Sheets • **Activity Sheet 8**, page A14 (Prepare a transparency from the activity sheet. Cut in half along dotted line.)
  • Optional—
  Enrichment Activity 5, page E8
  Mainstreaming Suggestion 5, page M12

(continued on next page)

The Second Quarter

Chords not shown on pupil page

Mayo Nafwa

Bemba People
Zambia

Solo:
Ma - yo   na - fwa.   Ma - yo   na - fwa,   na-ma-ten-ge.

Solo:
Tu - mu - bi-ke kwi?   Tu - mu - bi-ke kwi?   na-ma-ten-ge.
Na - ko   ku mu-lu.   Na - ko   ku mu-lu,   na-ma-ten-ge.

38

Introducing the Lesson

Help the students locate West Africa on a world map. Listen to the recording of "West African Rhythm Complex." Explain that even though the rhythms seem complicated, they are not hard to perform. The sounds seem complex because there are many overlapping lines. This creates a thick texture.

Developing the Lesson

1. Display the upper half of the transparency prepared from Activity Sheet 8 (*Rhythm Score*). Establish the tempo of the shortest sound. Ask the students to pat their thighs while they repeatedly chant 1–2–3–4–5–6–7–8–9–10–11–12.

   As they continue to chant, help them perform each of the patterns, clapping on the first of each group of circled numbers.

2. When they can perform all the patterns, divide the class into five groups, named A to E. Beginning at a moderate tempo, the A group should perform the A pattern several times. Then add the B group performing the B pattern. Continue adding groups until the class can maintain all the patterns simultaneously. As they become familiar with the patterns, increase the tempo to create an exciting rhythm complex.

3. Overlay the bottom half of Activity Sheet 8 on the top half. Compare the traditional notation with the number system the class used when learning the patterns. Comment that the circles are like the "musical plus signs" used in Lesson 8 to show that short sounds are combined to make longer sounds.

4. **The rhythm complex we played is typical of accompaniments used in African music.** Play

38

Solo: All:
Ku - li a   ma-ko - zi.   Ku - li a   ma-ko - zi,   na-ma-ten-ge.

Solo: All:
Na - po   pa - nshi.   Na - po   pa - nshi,   na-ma-ten-ge.

Solo: All:
Pa - li   nye-le - le.   Pa - li   nye-le - le,   na-ma-ten-ge.

Solo: All:
Nan-dan   da yi-la na-ma-ten-ge.   Nan-dan   da yi-la na-ma-ten-ge.

Add these drum rhythms.

| 1 | 2 | 3 | 4 | 5 | 6 | 7 | 8 | 9 | 10 | 11 | 12 | 13 | 14 |

high drum: ↑   ↑   ↑   ↑   ↑   ↑   ↑
low drum: ↓   ↓   ↓   ↓   ↓   ↓   ↓   ↓   ↓

39

Materials (continued)
○ **For additional experience with time and place and rhythm:** Perform 3, page 137; Create 7, page 208

For Your Information
The eighth note is used throughout this lesson to represent the shortest sound. Each number from 1–12 used in Activity Sheet 8 (*Rhythm Score*) represents a single eighth note. When more than one number is circled, the combined numbers determine the note represented. (For example, two circled numbers equal a quarter note.)

Translation for "*Mayo Nafwa*":
The Bemba child has lost his mother. The singers ask what they can do to help the child.
Phonetic pronunciation for "*Mayo Nafwa*":
Mi-yo **nah**-fwa, **nah**-mah-**ten**-gay.
Too-moo-**bee**-kay-kwee, **nah**-mah-**ten**-gay.
Nah-kow koo moo-loo, **nah**-mah-**ten**-gay.
Koo-lee-**a mah**-koh-zee, **nah**-mah-**ten**-gay.
Nah-po **pahn**-gee, **nah**-mah-**ten**-gay.
Pah-lee **nyay**-lay-lay, **nah**-mah-**ten**-gay.
Nan-dan **dah** yee-lah, **nah**-mah-**ten**-gay.

the recording of "*Mayo Nafwa*" as the students follow the song notation on page 38. Draw attention to the accompaniment played on high and low drums, as shown on page 39.

Closing the Lesson

Help the students learn the song by singing the response parts with the voices on the recording. When they can confidently sing the song, add the high and low drum accompaniment.

LESSON *17*

Lesson Focus

Timbre: The quality of a sound is determined by the sound source.
Timbre: The quality of a sound is affected by the material, shape, and size of the source. *(D–S)*

Materials

○ **No Piano Accompaniment**
○ **Record Information:**
  • Sound Categories
  Record 3 Side A Band 4a–r
  See **For Your Information** for sequence of instruments.
○ **Other:** pencil for each student; "environmental soundmakers," such as pot lids, plastic or metal containers (with and without lids), jugs, bottles, pipes, large nails hung from string, rubber bands or thin wire over boxes, small bottles filled with dried beans or rice
○ **Teacher's Resource Binder:**
  [Activity Sheets] • **Activity Sheet 9,** page A15 (Prepare a copy of the activity sheet for each student.)
    • Optional—
    Enrichment Activity 6, page E11
○ **For additional experience with form and expression:** Create 6, page 206; Special Times 4, page 225

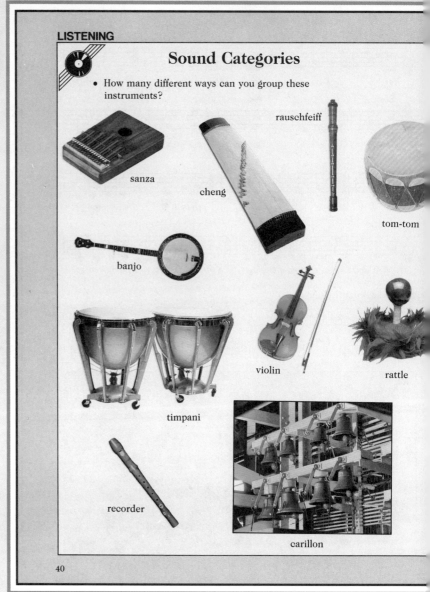

Sound Categories

• How many different ways can you group these instruments?

rauschfeiff

sanza

cheng

tom-tom

banjo

violin

rattle

timpani

recorder

carillon

40

Introducing the Lesson

Distribute a soundmaker to each student. (See **Materials**.) Ask them to produce a sound on each. **Can you group your instruments into "families"? Each family must have something in common.** Give the students time to form and name some families. As they share ideas, guide them to think about all the possible ways soundmakers could be grouped:
• the way the sound is produced (blowing, scraping, rattling)
• the material from which the soundmaker is made (wood, metal, plastic)
• the size and shape (big, little, square, round)

Developing the Lesson

1. Give each student a pencil and a copy of Activity Sheet 9 (*Sound Categories*). **Look at the instruments pictured on page 40 in your**

book. **They are from all over the world; some are old.** Ask the students to add these instruments to the categories they have already named. **Will you need to add new categories? new families?** Give the students time to write a category in the top row and family names in the second row of their activity sheet.

2. After a few minutes, invite the class to share ideas. Any method of categorization is valid as long as the class has a basis for the grouping. On the chalkboard write categories, families, and instrument names such as:

Category: How the sound is started			
Family			
PLUCK	SHAKE	STRIKE	BLOW
cheng	rattle	carillon	harmonica
sitar	tambourine	xylophone	recorder
banjo		tom-tom	clarinet
guitar		timpani	rauschfeiff
sanza		water drum	bagpipe
(violin)			

bagpipe

tambourine

harmonica

sitar

guitar

water drum

xylophone

clarinet

- How many ways could you group these instruments just by looking at them?
- Now listen to them! Will you group them the same way?

41

For Your Information

Sequence of instruments heard in "Sound Categories":

Band 4a: sanza
Band 4b: cheng
Band 4c: rauschfeiff
Band 4d: tom-tom
Band 4e: banjo
Band 4f: timpani
Band 4g: violin
Band 4h: ground rattles
Band 4i: recorder
Band 4j: carillon
Band 4k: bagpipes
Band 4l: tambourine
Band 4m: harmonica
Band 4n: sitar
Band 4o: guitar
Band 4p: xylophone
Band 4q: water drum
Band 4r: clarinet

For definitions of instruments as categorized by ethnomusicologists, see **Glossary**.

Category: Part of instrument that vibrates					
Family					
STRING	SKIN	REED	AIR COLUMN	METAL	WOOD
cheng	tom-tom	harmonica	recorder	sanza	rattle
sitar	water drum	clarinet		carillon	xylophone
banjo	timpani	rauschfeiff		tambourine	
guitar	(banjo)	bagpipe			
violin					

3. Ask the students to listen to the sound of each instrument. **Will you keep them in the same categories? Should you add other categories to your list?** Play the recording of "Sound Categories."

Closing the Lesson

The following chart categorizes and names the instruments shown on the pupil pages. These terms are used by ethnomusicologists, people who study the music of world cultures. (See

Teacher's Glossary for information on ethnic instruments included on these pages.)

MEMBRANOPHONES	AEROPHONES	IDIOPHONES	CHORDOPHONES
tom-tom	recorder	sanza	cheng
water drum	rauschfeiff	xylophone	sitar
tambourine	clarinet	rattle	banjo
timpani	bagpipe	carillon	violin
	harmonica	(tambourine)	guitar

Introduce these categories and names to the students.

LESSON 18

Lesson Focus

Timbre: The quality of a sound is determined by the sound source.
Timbre: The quality of a sound is affected by the material, shape, and size of the source.
Timbre: The quality of a sound is affected by the way the sound is produced. *(D–S)*

Materials

○ **Piano Accompaniment:** page 280
○ **Record Information:**
  • Variations on a Shaker Tune
    (Record 2   Side A   Band 8)
  • The Music Goes 'Round and Around
  Record 3   Side A   Bands 5a–e
    Voices: children's choir
    Accompaniment: See **For Your Information**
○ **Other:** pencil for each student
○ **Teacher's Resource Binder:**
  Activity Sheets • **Activity Sheet 10,** pages A16–A17 (Prepare two copies for each student.)
  • Optional—
    Kodaly Activity 8, page K11

Chords not shown on pupil page

The Music Goes 'Round and Around

Words by "Red" Hodgson

Music by Edward Farley and Michael Riley

I blow through here; ___ The mu-sic goes 'round and a-round.

Whoa-ho - ho-ho-ho - ho, and it comes up here. ___

I push the first valve down, The mu-sic goes down and a-round.

Whoa ho - ho - ho - ho, and it comes up here. ___

42

Introducing the Lesson

Review "Variations on a Shaker Tune" (page 29). **How many instruments that play the main theme can you identify?** Play the recording and discuss the instruments the students recognize. Remind them how they categorized instruments in Lesson 17 as aerophones, membranophones, idiophones, or chordophones. **Can you recall another set of categories that people often use to group orchestral instruments into families?** (woodwinds, brass, strings, percussion)

Developing the Lesson

1. Distribute two copies of Activity Sheet 10 (*The Music Goes 'Round and Around*) to each student. Help them identify the name of the first instrument. They should then write the name on the line marked "A" below the picture. **Can you decide whether it should be placed in the woodwind, brass, string, or percussion family? Put that answer on the line marked "B."** (See **Teacher's Glossary** for information regarding the definitions of each instrument family.)

   Follow this same procedure for the next four instrument pictures. Then give the students time to complete the remaining charts independently. After all have finished, discuss their answers.

2. **You've identified the instruments by how they look. Can you also identify them by how they sound?** Play the recording of "The Music Goes 'Round and Around." The students are to show the order in which the instruments are heard by writing a number in the circle inside each activity sheet box. (See **For Your Information.**) After listening to each band, pause and discuss the students' answers.

I push the mid-dle valve down, The mu-sic goes down a-round __ be-low, _

be - low, ____ be - low, __ Dee-dle-dee ho - ho ho.

Lis - ten to the ja - azz come out.

I push the oth-er valve down, The mu-sic goes 'round and a-round.

Whoa-ho - ho-ho - ho - ho and it comes out here.

43

LESSON 18

For Your Information

The recording of "The Music Goes 'Round and Around" has five bands as follows:

Band 5a: Song is sung; accompanied by piano, bass, and drums. •

Band 5b: Variation 1 — Woodwinds play melody, one at a time, then all at the end.

Band 5c: Variation 2 — Brass play melody, one at a time, then all at the end.

Band 5d: Variation 3 — Percussion play melody, then all at the end.

Band 5e: Variation 4 — Strings play melody.

3. Explain that the instruments that play each variation of this song belong to the same family. **Can you develop a definition for each?** (See **Teacher's Glossary.**)

4. **Open your books to page 42. Can you sing the song that was used as the theme for this instrumental composition?** Guide the students to sing the song without the recording. Turn the balance knob on the record player so that only the accompaniment to this song can be heard. Play the recorded accompaniment as the students sing the melody again.

Closing the Lesson

Ask the students to look at their activity sheets again. **We've organized the instruments into orchestral families. Can you decide to which of the ethnomusicological categories each belongs?**

Ask the students to write these answers on the "C" line below each picture. Discuss their answers. All brass and woodwinds are aerophones. All strings are chordophones. Membranophones include any percussion where a "membrane" vibrates, such as a drum or a tambourine. Other percussion are idiophones.

LESSON 19

Lesson Focus

Expression: The expressiveness of music is affected by the way timbre contributes to the musical whole. **(D–S)**

Materials

○ **No Piano Accompaniment**

○ **Record Information:**
  • *Danse Macabre*
    by Camille Saint-Saëns (san-**sahns**), 1835–1921
    Record 3   Side B   Band 1
    New York Philharmonic
    Leonard Bernstein, conductor
    David Nadien, violin

○ **Other:** pencil for each student; overhead projector

○ **Teacher's Resource Binder:**

Activity Sheets
  • **Activity Sheet 11**, page A18 (Prepare a transparency of the activity sheet.)
  • **Activity Sheet 12**, pages A19–A22 (Prepare a copy for each student.)
  • Optional—
    Mainstreaming Suggestion 6, page M12

○ **For additional experience with expression and harmony:** Create 1, page 198; Special Times II, page 234

LISTENING

Danse Macabre

Camille Saint-Saëns

Play or sing these two main melodies or themes. They are heard often throughout the piece.

Theme 1:

Theme 2:

44

Introducing the Lesson

Ask the students to open their books to page 44. Familiarize the class with Themes 1 and 2 by playing them on the piano or by helping the students sing the themes.

Developing the Lesson

1. Review the instruments and families of the orchestra by displaying a transparency of Activity Sheet 11 (*Orchestra Seating Plan*). Draw the students' attention to the way the instruments are grouped by families within the orchestra seating plan. Recall the discussion in Lesson 18 regarding the reasons for orchestral family groupings.

2. Play the recording of *Danse Macabre*. **As you listen, how many instruments and orchestral families can you recognize?** Discuss the instruments that the students heard. Associate them with the pictures shown on page 45.

3. Distribute copies of Activity Sheet 12 (*Danse Macabre: A Musical Puzzle*). The composer, Camille Saint-Saëns, chose either individual instruments or families of instruments to help him interpret this dance in music. Focus attention on the *Danse Macabre* "map" just distributed. The map is divided into numbered boxes. Within each box are "puzzle pieces" that contain the names of instruments or orchestral families. Explain to the students that as they hear each number spoken on the recording, they are to decide which instrument or instrument family is playing. They should then mark the correct answer by circling the puzzle piece. (For Box 12 they are to fill in the name of the instrument being played.)

44

Saint-Saëns used many different instruments in his dance.
Sometimes they play the themes.
Sometimes they play the accompaniment part.
When do you hear each of these instruments
or families of instruments?

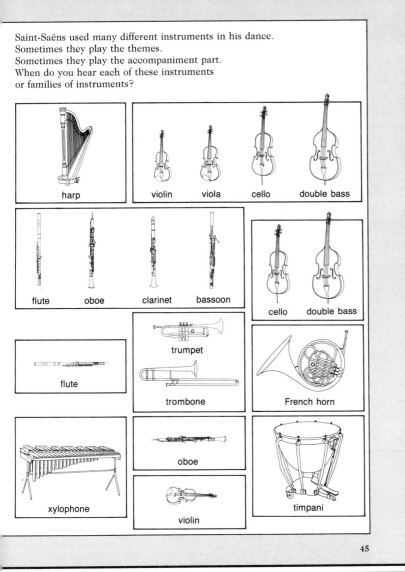

harp

violin   viola   cello   double bass

flute   oboe   clarinet   bassoon

cello   double bass

flute

trumpet

trombone

French horn

xylophone

oboe

violin

timpani

45

For Your Information

Correct answers for the puzzle in Activity
Sheet 12:
1. harp
2. cellos and double basses
3. violin
4. flute
5. violins
6. violin
7. woodwinds, violin, woodwinds, violin
8. violin
9. violins and woodwinds
10. strings
11. violin, xylophone, violin, xylophone
12. violin or fiddle
13. brass
14. violins
15. timpani
16. French horns
17. oboe
18. strings
19. violin

4. Play the recording of *Danse Macabre* as often
as needed for the students to complete the
puzzle. After everyone has finished, read the
correct answers and ask the students to correct any errors they may have made on their
activity sheets.

Closing the Lesson

Listen one last time to enjoy this dramatic composition. *Danse Macabre* is a symphonic poem
that depicts Death playing the violin and skeletons dancing in a graveyard at midnight. It is a
good example of the typically strong, expressive
symphonic poems written in the Romantic style
of the 19th century.

Lesson Focus

Rhythm: Music may be comparatively fast or slow, depending on the speed of the underlying pulse. *(P–I)*

Materials

o **Piano Accompaniment:** page 282
o **Record Information:**
  • There's a Hole in the Middle of the Sea
    Record 3   Side B   Band 2
    Voices: children's choir
    Accompaniment: synthesizer, sound effects, percussion
o **Instruments:** tambourine; autoharp
o **Other:** metronome
o **Teacher's Resource Binder:**
  • Optional—
    Curriculum Correlation 5, page C9
    Orff Activity 2, page O5

There's a Hole in the Middle of the Sea

Anonymous

1. There's a hole in the mid-dle of the sea,
   There's a hole in the mid-dle of the sea,
   There's a hole, _____ There's a hole,
   There's a hole in the mid-dle of the sea.

This is a cumulative song.
Keep adding words to each new verse.

2. There's a log in the hole in the middle of the sea.
3. There's a bump on the log in the hole in the middle of the sea.
4. There's a frog on the bump on the log in the hole in the middle of the sea.
5. There's a fly on the frog on the bump on the log in the hole in the middle of the sea.
6. There's a wing on the fly on the frog on the bump on the log in the hole in the middle of the sea.
7. There's a flea on the wing on the fly on the frog on the bump on the log in the hole in the middle of the sea.

46

Introducing the Lesson

Ask the students to turn to page 46 and learn the song "There's a Hole in the Middle of the Sea." Draw attention to the rhythm ruler at the top of the page. **Which note represents the shortest sound?** (sixteenth note) **How does it move in relation to the underlying beat?** (Four short sounds equals one beat.) Ask one student to set the tempo for the shortest sound by tapping a tambourine. The others may tap the beat on their knees. **Remember to tap one beat for every four short sounds.** Ask the class to read the words of the song in rhythm as they tap the beat.

Discuss how the melody moves. Notice that Phrase 2 is the same as Phrase 1, only one step higher. Phrase 3 outlines the I chord. Phrase 4 skips up from 5, to 5. It then moves downward to end the song on the tonal center. Play the autoharp as the class sings the song first on the syllable "loo," then with the words.

Developing the Lesson

1. Draw the students' attention to the instructions at the bottom of the page. **How slow will you need to sing the song at a *largo* tempo? How fast is *presto*?** Tell the students to follow the instructions on page 47 to help them decide the answers to these questions.

2. To determine the appropriate tempo for the song, begin by chanting the words in the top row marked "*Largo*." To set the tempo, chant each syllable at a steady, even speed that is comfortable without rushing the syllables. Tap on the accented beats. When the students are steadily chanting and tapping, tell them to "take the words inside" but to continue tapping the accented syllables. Each tap is one beat in a *largo* tempo. If a metronome is available, check the class's tempo against the metronome. Then invite them to sing the first verse of the song at that speed.

Sing all the verses of the song on page 46.
Begin at a *largo* tempo.
Can you sing the last verse *presto*?
To set your own tempo, try these ideas.

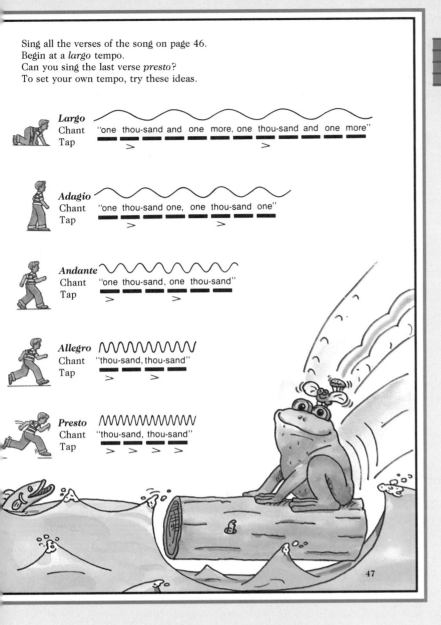

Largo
Chant   "one thou-sand and one more, one thou-sand and one more"
Tap

Adagio
Chant   "one thou-sand one, one thou-sand one"
Tap

Andante
Chant   "one thou-sand, one thou-sand"
Tap

Allegro
Chant   "thou-sand, thou-sand"
Tap

Presto
Chant   "thou-sand, thou-sand"
Tap

47

3. Use the same procedure for each of the other tempo terms: *Adagio, Andante, Allegro,* and *Presto.* Sing one verse at each tempo.

4. **There are more verses than tempo markings. At what tempo would you like to sing the last two verses?** Plan a tempo sequence for the entire song. Write the sequence on the chalkboard. Sing the complete song.

Closing the Lesson **OPTIONAL**

Listen to a recording of this song. Is it performed in the same sequence of tempos that we used? (Answers will vary depending on decisions the students made in Step 4.) Discover that the sixth verse begins *largo* and ends at *presto*. Explain that the tempo term meaning to change gradually from slow to fast is *accelerando.* The last verse is performed with a *ritardando,* which signifies that the song gradually slows down to the end.

Lesson Focus

Dynamics: Music may be comparatively loud or soft.
Dynamics: Music may become louder or softer. **(D–S)**

Materials

○ **Piano Accompaniment:** page 283
○ **Record Information:**
  • *Moonlight Sonata*
    (Record 2 Side B Band 1)
  • Anyone Can Move a Mountain
    Record 3 Side B Band 3
    Voices: children's choir
    Accompaniment: flute, alto flute, piano, electric piano, synthesizer, electric bass, percussion
○ **Teacher's Resource Binder:**
  | Evaluation | • Optional—
    Checkpoint 2, page Ev6
○ **For additional experience with melody:** Describe 1, page 168

Chords not shown on pupil page

Anyone Can Move a Mountain

Words and Music by Johnny Marks

Follow the **dynamic** and **tempo** instructions as you plan an expressive performance.

48

Introducing the Lesson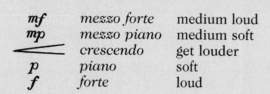

Ask the students to turn to pages 32–33. Play the recording of *Moonlight Sonata* as they follow the notation in their books. Review the meaning of the dynamic markings in the score.

Developing the Lesson

1. **Turn to page 48 in your books.** Guide the students to locate each dynamic marking in the song and define its meaning. Write their definitions on the chalkboard, along with the appropriate musical symbol and Italian term.

mf	*mezzo forte*	medium loud
mp	*mezzo piano*	medium soft
◁	*crescendo*	get louder
p	*piano*	soft
f	*forte*	loud

2. Play the recording of "Anyone Can Move a Mountain." **Do the performers of this song sing it as you expected?** Discuss the class's responses.

3. Discuss the meaning of the other expressive symbols found in the score:

‐	*tenuto*	(Begin each note with a slight stress.)
⌒	*legato*	(All notes connected by the curved line are sung in a smooth fashion.)
⌢	*fermata*	(Sustain the note longer than usual.)

4. Discuss the rhythm of the song. **How will the beats be grouped?** (in twos) **How does the rhythm of the melody usually move?** (with

1.
Just be-lieve it and you'll find it so. _____

2.
Just be-lieve it (just be-lieve it), just be-lieve it (just be-lieve it),

Rit.
And you'll find it so. _____

quarter notes, two to a beat) Focus attention on the triplet symbols. Play the recording again. **Tap the beat with your toe and lightly clap the short sound.** Help the students realize that when the triplets occur, relationships change from two quarter notes moving with the beat to three quarter notes.

Play the recording once again as the students practice shifting from two to three short sounds each time a triplet occurs.

5. Ask the students to examine the melodic contour. Discuss similarities and differences among the phrases:

- Phrases 1 and 2 are similar.
- Phrases 3 and 4 include four patterns, each similar in contour but a little higher than the previous one.
- Phrases 5 and 6 are like Phrases 1 and 2.
- Phrase 7 begins like Phrase 3.
- Phrase 8 begins with a melodic idea similar to the opening phrase.

Play the recording again as the students concentrate on the melody. **Can you now sing the song without the help of the recording?**

Closing the Lesson

When the students know the song, ask them to sing it, paying careful attention to the dynamic indications. **At what tempo should it be sung?** (Guide the students' attention to the term *andante* at the beginning of the song.)

Lesson Focus

Expression: The expressiveness of music is affected by the way tempo, articulation, and dynamics contribute to the musical whole. **(P–S)**

Materials

○ **Piano Accompaniment:** page 286

○ **Record Information:**
- The Music Goes 'Round and Around **(Record 3 Side A Bands 5a–e)**
- Lift Every Voice and Sing **Record 3 Side B Band 4** Voices: children's choir Accompaniment: organ, piano

○ **For additional experience with expression:** Perform 4, page 138; Special Times 15, page 246

Chords not shown on pupil page

Lift Every Voice and Sing

Words by James Weldon Johnson   Music by J. Rosamond Johnson

50

Introducing the Lesson

Review "The Music Goes 'Round and Around" on page 42. Using the method suggested in Lesson 21, ask the students to try singing the song at different tempos. Allow them to decide which they prefer. Follow a similar procedure as they make choices about dynamic markings for various parts of the song.

Developing the Lesson

1. Ask the students to turn to page 50. **What instructions have been given for the expressive performance of this song?** Ask the students to examine the score, identify each tempo and dynamic marking, and explain what information these markings convey regarding the performance of the song. If the students are unsure of some of the terms, refer them to the glossary in the back of their

books. Most students will be unfamiliar with the term *maestoso*. After looking up the term and discussing the students' ideas, play the recording. Help them sense that *maestoso* suggests a performance with a full vocal quality. Important words are slightly separated and stressed while at the same time sustained for their full length.

2. Examine the melody and discuss the form. Each phrase (except Phrase 6) is four measures long. Each should be performed as a single idea with no break. Draw attention to the similarities between Phrases 3–4 and 7–8.

3. Listen to the recording again. **Can you find ways that the melody supports the ideas of the words?** Observe that the meaning implied by "lift" is supported with many instances of rising melodic lines within most of the phrases. The words "rise," "high," and "sun"

ff a tempo   F   Dm   B♭   F   B♭   C   F

Fac-ing the   ris - ing   sun   Of our new   day   be -   gun,

G7   F   B♭   F

Let us march on   till vic - to - ry ____   is   won. ____

occur on the highest pitch of the melody. The idea of "marching on" is suggested by the steady, repetitive rhythm. Play the recording as needed until the students can perform the melody easily.

Closing the Lesson

End the class by reviewing favorite songs. Before singing each, call on volunteers to make suggestions regarding appropriate dynamic levels and tempos. Experiment with different ways of performing each song.

LESSON 23

Lesson Focus

Melody: Each pitch within a melody moves in relation to a home tone.
Melody: A series of pitches bounded by the octave "belong together," forming a tonal set. *(D–I)*

Materials

○ **Piano Accompaniment:** page 288
○ **Record Information:**
  • I Believe
    Record 3   Side B   Band 5
    Voices: children's choir
    Accompaniment: small show orchestra
○ **Instruments:** all available resonator bells, arranged in a single chromatic row; 8 bell mallets
○ **Other:** pencil for each student; overhead projector
○ **Teacher's Resource Binder:**
  Activity Sheets • **Activity Sheet 13**, page A23 (Prepare a transparency and student copies.)
  • Optional—
    Kodaly Activity 19, page K30
    Mainstreaming Suggestion 7, page M14
○ **For additional experience with expression:** Special Times 17, page 250

I Believe

Words and Music by Ervin Drake,
Irvin Graham, Jimmy Shirl, and Al Stillman

Learn to sing this song by following the notation.
As you sing, play the red notes on the bells.
Which bells will you need?

52

Introducing the Lesson

Ask the class to read the words of the song "I Believe," on page 52, as an expressive poem. Guide them to read the poem in the rhythm of the melody. Discuss the ideas expressed by the words. Help the class sense that each phrase is based on opposites: Out of something that seems bad, something good emerges. Invite the students to suggest personal experiences where something seemed bad and then something good happened.

Developing the Lesson

1. Remind the students of previous lessons where they explored ways of performing expressively by using appropriate dynamics, volume, and articulation. Suggest that expressiveness also results from the way the music is composed. Ask the students to look at the melodic contour of "I Believe" to see how it

supports the ideas of the poem. Focus their attention on the red notes. Help them discover that these notes move gradually upward by steps. **Why might this be a good melodic shape for the words of this song?** (It gradually builds to high 1′, just as the ideas of the poem gradually build to an important idea.)

2. Ask the class to follow the instructions on page 52 and learn the melody. **Which bells will you need?** If the students are not sure, refer to the staff at the top of the page. As the class calls out the names of the resonator bells, one student may select the bells from the bell box and distribute one (along with a mallet) to each of eight classmates.

3. When the correct bells have been selected, ask the eight students with bells and mallets to play their pitches in ascending order. Comment that the sound is that of the D major

For Your Information
Answers to Activity Sheet 13:

For Your Information
Answers to Activity Sheet 13:

1	2	3	4	5	6	7	1'
C	D	E	F	G	A	B	C
F	G	A	B♭	C	D	E	F
B♭	C	D	E♭	F	G	A	B♭
E♭	F	G	A♭	B♭	C	D	E♭

The whole- and half-step patterns on the bottom of the activity sheet are as follows:
W–W–H–W–W–W–H

some-one will come ____ to show the way. ____

I be - lieve, ____ I be - lieve.

way, ____ Then I know why I be - lieve! ____

53

scale. **We could say that this melody is based on the D major scale.** Explain that the song could be described as being in the key of D major because it uses the pitches of the D scale.

4. Challenge the class to sing the melody on the syllable "loo" by reading the notation through the first two measures of the first ending. At the same time, the appropriate bell player should play his or her bell whenever it occurs in the notation as marked in red. When the students are able to sing this portion of the melody, help them learn the remainder of the first ending and the second ending.

5. Discuss the fact that this song might be a little high for some students to sing. **If you wanted to perform it in a different key, could you figure out the bells that you would need? What would have to stay the same?** (The

pitches used would still have to make a major scale.) **Let's see if we can find a way to build a scale starting on a different pitch.** Distribute Activity Sheet 13 (*A Major Scale*) and a pencil to each student. Display a transparency of the activity sheet on the overhead projector. Help the class complete the activity sheet. (See **For Your Information**.)

Closing the Lesson

Return to the song "I Believe." Ask the students to sing it, using one of the scales they discovered when they completed Activity Sheet 13. **Which scales would make the song lower?** (the scales starting on C or B♭) **Which scales would make it higher?** (the scales starting on E♭ or F)

LESSON 24

Lesson Focus

Melody: A series of pitches bounded by the octave "belong together," forming a tonal set. *(C–I)*

Materials

○ **Instruments:** Provide a variety of barred instruments set up with pitches C, C♯, D, D♯, E, F, F♯, G, G♯, A, A♯, B, and C′; 13 bell mallets. (See **For Your Information.**)

○ **Other:** overhead projector

○ **Teacher's Resource Binder:**
  Activity Sheets • **Activity Sheet 14**, page A24 (Prepare a transparency of the activity sheet.)
  • Optional—
  Curriculum Correlation 6, page C9

○ **For additional experience with form:** Create 5, page 204

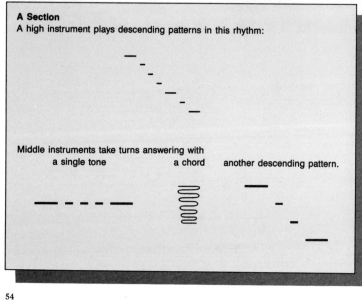

Improvisation on Whole Tones

Use **high** **middle** **low** mallet instruments.

Set up the instruments with these pitches:

C, D, E, F♯ (G♭), G♯ (A♭), and A♯ (B♭).

Improvise music using these ideas:

A Section
A high instrument plays descending patterns in this rhythm:

Middle instruments take turns answering with
a single tone   a chord   another descending pattern.

54

Introducing the Lesson

Ask thirteen students to form a row across the front of the room. Distribute the C chromatic scale resonator bells. (See **Materials** and **For Your Information.**) When the bells have been distributed, display Activity Sheet 14 (*What's in a Scale?*). Review the whole- and half-step sequence of the major scale introduced during Lesson 23 and shown at the top of this activity sheet.

Ask the thirteen students to arrange themselves to show the C major scale sequence. Students whose bells are not included should walk back one step, leaving an empty space to show whole steps. Ask the remaining eight students to play a C major scale from low to high.

Developing the Lesson

1. Ask the students who made up the major scale to play the melody written in scale numbers

at the bottom of the activity sheet as you point to each number. The students should identify the melody as "Twinkle, Twinkle, Little Star," although the rhythm is changed. Enjoy singing the song with the new words.

2. Draw the students' attention to the second scale shown at the top of the activity sheet. Ask the thirteen students to rearrange themselves to show this sequence. **What do you notice?** (all whole steps; only six pitches) **Will we need the same bells?** (Some will be different.) After the players have rearranged themselves, ask this group to play "Twinkle, Twinkle, Little Star." **What happened to the song?** (It sounds funny and strange, as though mistakes were being made.)

Explain that the scale on which a melody is based determines the way that melody is going to sound. **If we use a different scale, the**

B Section

A high instrument plays ascending *glissandi* by scraping a mallet across all resonator bells:

A low instrument answers with large skips:

C Section

A middle instrument improvises melody:

A low instrument accompanies with ascending long tones:

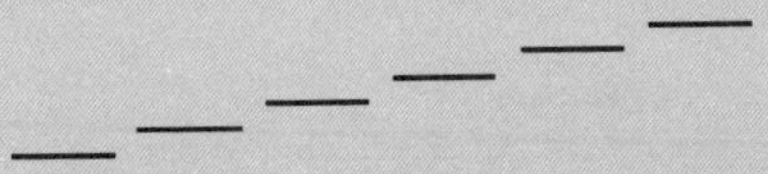

Combine the three sections in any order you like to make a complete composition.

55

For Your Information

Some sets of xylophones, metallophones, and glockenspiels are not chromatic and thus do not have all of the pitches required for the whole tone improvisation. If G♯(A♭) is not available, simply set the instruments up using the designated pitches that are available on that instrument.

sound will be different. **Could you come up with a name for this unusual scale?** Invite the students' suggestions and then give them the scale's name: **Whole Tone Scale.**

3. Ask the students to open their books to page 54 and follow the instructions to improvise a composition based on a whole tone scale. (See **For Your Information** for directions on how to set up instruments.) If possible, divide the class into several small groups. Each group is to create its own improvisation.

Closing the Lesson

Give groups time to plan their improvisations and to decide the order in which they will play the sections. It might be in a variety of sequences such as **A B A C, A A B C,** or **A B C A.** When each group has developed a composition, they may perform for the class.

LESSON 25

Lesson Focus

Expression: Musical elements are combined into a whole to express a musical or extramusical idea. *(D–E)*

Materials

○ **Record Information:**
   • Voiles, from *Preludes for Piano* by Claude Debussy (deh-byoo-**see**), 1862–1918
   Record 4   Side A   Band 1
   Robert Casadesus, pianist

○ **Instruments:** barred instruments set up for whole tone scale with pitches C, D, E, F♯, G♯, A♯, and C'; bell mallets

○ **Other:** watercolors, colored chalk, art paper, streamers, scarves, and pencils for individuals and groups of students

○ **For additional experience with expression:** Describe 16, page 194; Create 11, page 215

LISTENING

Voiles
by Claude Debussy

Listen to Debussy's composition on a whole-tone scale.
Does he use any ideas similar to the ones on page 54?
Here is part of the piano score. Try to follow it as you listen.
Can you tell when each of these sections is played?
Are any of the ideas repeated?

56

Introducing the Lesson

Invite the groups who performed "Whole Tone Improvisations" at the end of the previous lesson to perform their pieces again for the class.

Developing the Lesson

1. Claude Debussy, a famous composer, used many of the ideas you've explored when you were developing your improvisations on whole tone scales. He created a work for piano titled "Voiles," which might be translated as "Sails." Play the recording. Ask the students to identify parts of the music that used ideas similar to those in their improvisations.

OPTIONAL

2. Play the recording again and help the students follow the piano score on page 56. (See **For Your Information.**)

3. Discuss the ways in which Debussy's music suggests the idea of sails:
   • The whole tone scale is used. Because there is no half step between pitches, there is never a feeling of coming to rest. This suggests the movement of sailboats on the waves or light shimmering on the water.
   • The form adds to the indefinite feeling. The first musical idea repeats six times, each repeat slightly altered. The music never seems to pause. Phrase endings are blurred.
   • The rhythm is restless, with little repetition and no strong sense of an underlying beat.

4. **There are many other ways to describe the ideas suggested by the music "Voiles." Who could suggest one?** (Using just lines and shapes, draw a picture with a pencil, or create a seascape using chalk or watercolors. Write a poem. Create a dance. Move with streamers or scarves. Write an essay about what you

56

au Mouv¹

(comme un très léger glissando)

doucement en dehors

Voiles means "sails," as used on sailing ships. What kind of ship scene might Debussy have been suggesting?
What name would you give to your whole-tone composition?
Did you get ideas from Debussy's music that will help you improve yours?

57

For Your Information
Structure of "Voiles":
The composition begins with the patterns shown on the top of page 56. The music continues, using similar ideas for 22 measures, until single pitches rise by octaves.

The music proceeds with the segment that begins at the bottom of page 56 and continues on the top of page 57.

A skip from low to high signals the beginning of the next section shown on page 57. Patterns based on rising scale passages alternating with melodic fragments continue to the end of the composition.

hear.) List the choices on the chalkboard. **Listen to the music again. Decide how you would like to interpret the music.**

5. Indicate to the class where in the room each activity will be held. (Perhaps there is space at the back of the room for dancers, at a table for poets, for artists at their desks, and so on.) Remind the students that they are to listen to the music rather than talk as they proceed to plan their descriptions.

Closing the Lesson

Play the composition several times as groups complete their projects. Ask for volunteers to share their interpretations as the composition is played once again.

LESSON 26

Lesson Focus

Expression: Musical elements are combined into a whole to express a musical or extramusical idea. *(C–E)*

Materials

○ **Instruments:** barred instruments set up for whole tone scale with pitches C, D, E, F♯, G♯, A♯, and C′; bell mallets; autoharp (strings to be plucked at random)

○ **Teacher's Resource Binder:**
  • Optional—
    Curriculum Correlation 7, page C12
    Enrichment Activity 7, page E11

○ **For additional experience with expression:** Create 8, page 210; Create 12, page 216

 The Sea

Shore at Bas-Butin, Honfleur, c. 1886, by Georges Seurat. Oil on Canvas. Musée des Beaux-Arts, Tournai, Belgium.

The Muse: "I've never been able to understand how the sea came to be!"

The Muse

58

Introducing the Lesson

Recall the activities in Lesson 25 when the students created their own expressions of the ideas in "Voiles." Invite the students to discuss the painting on page 58 and compare its mood with that of "Voiles" and their own artistic efforts. **Is the mood similar?** (yes; calm, peaceful, and relaxing) Discuss the technique used by the artist to express his ideas. (See **For Your Information**.)

Developing the Lesson

1. After discussing the painting, guide the students to follow the instructions on page 59 to express a similar mood through words and music. Assign parts: a muse (someone who inspires artists), a conductor, players, and singers. The conductor and the players will need to decide what instruments to use and plan signals to show what sounds are to be

long or short, fast or slow, high or low, *legato* or *staccato*, and loud or soft.

2. The students may plan the composition as they proceed.
   • The muse begins.
   • The conductor then indicates to the players how they should perform in order to express in music "how the sea came to be."
   • To create a bridge from this section to the next, the conductor might have the players end with a *decrescendo* and resolve to a single, sustained pitch. That pitch may be continued to accompany the singers.
   • The singers begin by humming or singing on the syllable "loo." They may use the pitch with which the players ended or choose other pitches, creating chord clusters.
   • After the choral and instrumental accompaniments are established, individual singers take turns singing or speaking their idea

58

The Conductor

The Players

Conductor: Begin the music by signaling to the players. Conduct with hand motions to show how they should play . . .
- long or short sounds
- high or low
- fast or slow
- *legato* or *staccato*
- loud or soft

Decide how many people should play at the same time.

End this section by choosing a soft sound to be played while the singers answer the Muse.

The Singers

Singers: Sing your answers.
- Use many or few tones.
- Listen to others. Take turns: Enter when you think another singer has completed a song idea.

Conductor: Conduct an ending to the composition. Will it be loud? soft?

The Muse: Speak when all others are silent: "The sea . . . came to be!"

59

For Your Information
The painting, *Shore at Bas-Butin, Honfleur,* by Georges Seurat, uses a special technique called pointillism, which involves painting many dots rather than using brush strokes. This style allows for a clean-looking design and a luminous use of color.

LESSON 26

of "how the sea came to be" in a dramatic fashion, such as: "The sea rolled up from a vapor as steam. There were rocks and sand . . . no water on the land . . . the skies filled with clouds . . . the rains came."
- When the singers have completed their ideas, the conductor brings the performance to an end. The conductor might build a *crescendo* and then end abruptly or do just the opposite and direct a *decrescendo* that fades until no music is heard.
- The lone voice of the muse ends by saying, "The sea . . . came to be!"

Closing the Lesson

Perform "The Sea" several times. The students may take turns with the different roles. Encourage them to discuss how expressively the ideas were communicated in each performance.

LESSON 27

Lesson Focus

Rhythm: Individual sounds and silences within a rhythmic line may be longer than, shorter than, or the same as the underlying shortest pulse. *(P–S)*

Materials

○ **Piano Accompaniment:** page 290
○ **Record Information:**
 • Lord, Lord, Lord
 Record 4 Side A Band 2
 Voices: children's choir
 Accompaniment: piano, electric organ, acoustic guitar, electric guitar, electric bass, percussion
○ **Instruments:** tambourine, maracas; claves; cowbell with beater
○ **For additional experience with harmony:** Create 3, page 201

Chords not shown on pupil page

Lord, Lord, Lord

Arranged by Walter F. Anderson

Pattern 1

Pattern 2

Lord, Lord, Lord, you've sure been good to me.

I'm sing-ing Lord, Lord, Lord, you've sure been good to me.

Well it's Lord, Lord, Lord, you've sure been good to me.

For you've done what the world could not do.

Fine

60

Introducing the Lesson

Ask the class to examine the rhythm rulers shown at the top of page 60. Review how to interpret the ruler. (See **For Your Information,** page 23.) **In what ways are the two rulers the same?** (Both move in fours. Both have the same number of long and short notes.) **What is different about them?** (the order of the long-short notes and the placement of the accent)

Divide the class into three groups. Group 1 is to pat the beat on their knees. Group 2 is to tap the shortest sound with their hands. Group 3 is to chant the rhythm pattern by saying "ch." **Be sure you stress the accented notes.** (The accent above the ruler indicates that the note should be stressed.) After the students have performed the patterns, guide them to see that in Pattern 1 the accent for each group falls on the same beat. In Pattern 2, the accent in the rhythm pattern occurs after the accented beat. **When accents occur**

at a different time than the accent of the underlying beat, the rhythm pattern is "syncopated."

Developing the Lesson

1. **Look at the song notation. Where do you find examples of syncopation?** Help the class locate the examples of syncopation above the words "hun-gry, you've" and "done what the."

2. With the class still organized into the groups identified in **Introducing the Lesson,** help the students perform the rhythm of the entire melody. After practicing by chanting "ch," ask all the groups to read the words in rhythm while patting the underlying beat.

3. Help the students learn the melody by listening to the recording. When they can sing it with confidence, call attention to the accom-

60

paniment parts found at the bottom of pupil page 61. **Are any of these parts syncopated?** (the claves pattern) The entire class should practice tapping each part as one or more students play the instrument indicated. Continue adding parts until all are being used to accompany the song.

Closing the Lesson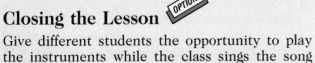

Give different students the opportunity to play the instruments while the class sings the song one last time to end the class period.

Lesson Focus

Rhythm: Individual sounds and silences within a rhythmic line may be longer than, shorter than, or the same as the underlying shortest pulse. *(D–S)*

Materials

o **Piano Accompaniment:** page 292
o **Record Information:**
  • Lord, Lord, Lord
    (Record 4   Side A   Band 2)
  • I'd Like to Teach the World to Sing
  ⊡ **Record 4   Side A   Band 3**
    Voices: children's choir
    Accompaniment: flugel horn, acoustic guitar, electric guitar, piano, electric bass, percussion
o **Instruments:** claves
o **Other:** pencil for each student
o **Teacher's Resource Binder:**

  Activity Sheets • **Activity Sheet 15,** page A25 (Prepare a copy of the activity sheet for each student.)

o **For additional experience with form:** Describe 5, page 174

Chords not shown on pupil page

I'd Like to Teach the World to Sing (In Perfect Harmony)

Words and Music by B. Backer, B. Davis, R. Cook, and R. Greenaway

I'd   like to build the world ____ a home and fur-nish it with love, ____

Grow   ap-ple trees and hon-ey bees and snow-white tur-tle doves. ____

I'd   like to teach the world ____ to sing in   per-fect har-mo-ny, ____

I'd   like to hold it   in my arms and   keep it com-pa-ny. ____

I'd   like to see the world ____ for once all stand-ing hand in hand, ____

Fine

And hear them ech-o through ____ the hills for peace through-out the land. ____

62

Introducing the Lesson

Review "Lord, Lord, Lord," page 60, choosing some students to add the accompaniment patterns shown at the bottom of page 61.

Distribute copies of Activity Sheet 15 (*Rhythm Ruler*) and pencils. Ask the students to write the accompaniment patterns on the activity sheet to show the relationship of each note to the underlying shortest sound. Identify the claves rhythm as syncopated.

Developing the Lesson

1. Ask the students to look at the song on pages 62 and 63. **Can you find any examples of syncopation?** ("ap-ple", "hon-ey", "tur-tle", "in my", "ech-o")

2. **Listen to the recording and tap the steady beat.** The class should listen carefully to the rhythm of the melody. **Can you hear other syncopated patterns?** Play the recording again. Some students may sense that there are many places where syncopation occurs.

3. Draw attention to the first phrase of the song. Focus on the places where the accents of the pattern occur before the accent of the beat. **Practice the pattern. What might help us know that this pattern is syncopated?** Help the students realize that the long sound resulting from a tie creates syncopation when it begins before or after the accented beat.

4. Play the recording again. The students may softly tap the rhythm of the melody as they listen and follow the notation.

5. **Did you have trouble following the music from the beginning to the end?** Some students may say "yes." **What signs must you**

That's the song I hear, ____ Let the world sing to-day, ____

A song of peace that ech-oes on _ and nev-er goes a-way. ____

Put your hand in my hand; Let's be-gin to-day.

D.S. al Fine

Put your hand in my hand; Help me find the way. I'd

observe? Review the meaning of *D.S. al Fine* and 𝄋. Help the students recall that *D.S. al Fine* means "go back to the sign and sing to the end" (which is indicated by *Fine*).

Play the recording again so that the students can follow the music from beginning to end.

6. **Can you sing the song?** Inform the students that they should be able to perform it independently, without help from the recording. When they can sing the melody accurately, they may sing with the recorded accompaniment. (Adjust the balance so that only the accompaniment is heard.)

Closing the Lesson

Return to the activity sheet used in **Introducing the Lesson.** Each student may write a rhythm pattern to be used as an accompaniment to "I'd

Like to Teach the World to Sing." They must write it in notation on the last rhythm ruler shown on the activity sheet.

When patterns have been devised, select some to be performed by the people who wrote them while the remainder of the class sings the song.

Lesson Focus

Expression: Musical elements are combined into a whole to express a musical or extramusical idea. **(P–S)**

Materials

○ **Piano Accompaniment:** page 295

○ **Record Information:**
  • Seven Limericks
    Record 4   Side A   Band 4
    Voices: children's choir
    Accompaniment: piano, percussion

○ **Instruments:** chromatic set of resonator bells with pitches D, E♭, E, F, F♯, G, A♭, A, B♭, B, C, and D′; triangles; tambourines; maracas; woodblocks; castanets; cymbals; drums; mallets

○ **Other:** overhead projector

○ **Teacher's Resource Binder:**
  Activity Sheets • **Activity Sheet 16,** pages A26–A27 (Prepare transparencies of the activity sheets.)

Introducing the Lesson

Ask the students to examine the title of the song "Seven Limericks" on page 64. What do you think a limerick is? The students may get clues by reading through the text and enjoying the humor. Conclude that a limerick is a nonsense poem usually consisting of five lines. The first, second, and fifth lines rhyme with each other, and the third and fourth lines rhyme with each other.

Developing the Lesson

1. Distribute the following bells and a mallet to nine students: D, E, F♯, G, A, B♭, B, C, and D′. Each student must identify the note on the staff that belongs to their bell. Challenge them to perform the melody of the first verse as in a handbell choir, with each person playing his or her bell at the correct time. The remainder of the class should softly count the steady beat

(in threes) in a moderate tempo as the bell players practice. When the students can play the melody without error, ask the class to sing the first verse.

2. Ask the students to follow the notation as they listen to the entire piece. **Listen for changes that occur in the music.** Help them recognize that the melody of Verses 3 and 4 are a half-step higher than all other verses.

3. While playing the recording again, display Activity Sheet 16 (*Limericks Accompaniment*). Ask the students to identify the instruments and rhythmic patterns that are heard in each verse and the interlude between each verse.

   Verse 1: bells *(mf)*

   Verse 2: bells, tambourine, maracas *(mf)*

   Verse 3: bells and triangle *(mp)*

When it grew out of sight, she ex-claimed in a fright,
For he said, "To eat mice is not pro-per or nice," _

"Oh! Fare-well to the end of my nose!" _____
_ That am-i-ca-ble man of Dum-bree.

5. There was an old per-son of Ware, _____
6. There was a young la-dy of Bute, _____
7. There was an old man who, when lit-tle, _____

Who rode on the back of a bear; _____
Who played on a sil-ver gilt flute; _____
Fell ca-su-al-ly in-to a ket-tle; _____

When they asked, "Does it trot?" He said, "Cer-tain-ly not!
_ She played sev-er-al jigs to her un-cle's white pigs;
_ But grow-ing too stout he could nev-er get out,

5.,6.
He's a Mop-pi-si-kon Flopp-si-kin bear!" _____
That a-mus-ing _ young la-dy of Bute. _____

7.
So he passed all his life in that ket-tle! _____

65

For Your Information
Form of "Seven Limericks":
Intro
a–a–b–c (two verses), with an interlude after each section
a–a–b–c (two verses one half–step higher), with an interlude after each section
a–a–b–c (two verses in the original key), with an interlude after each section
a–a–b–c (one verse in the original key), followed by a short coda

---

Verse 4: woodblock and castanets *(p)*

Verse 5: cymbals and drums *(mf)*

Verse 6: bells, woodblock, castanets, cymbals, drums *(f)*

Verse 7: all instruments *(f)*

4. Discuss the tambourine notation. Observe that the fourth note indicates a roll. Ask the students to follow the instrumental parts and to locate the roll and the accent marks. Help them determine where each occurs.

5. Review the following dynamic markings:

   p   mp   mf   f

   Ask the students to determine the dynamic level used for each verse. (The answers are provided at the end of Step 3.)

6. Invite the students to sing the song with the recording. Help them realize that they will need to adjust their singing to fit with the dynamic changes that occur in the instrumental parts.

7. Divide the class into nine groups, one group for each of the instrumental parts used with the accompaniment. If possible, each group member should have his or her own instrument. If not enough are available, the students should take turns playing while others lightly clap the rhythm pattern. Each group should practice their part until they can play it accurately all the way through.

Closing the Lesson
Choose one player from each of the groups to play the accompaniment while the rest of the class sings the complete song.

LESSON 30

Lesson Focus
Evaluation: Review concepts and skills studied in the Second Quarter.

Materials
- ○ **No Piano Accompaniment**
- ○ **Record Information:**
  - *Shepherd's Hey*
    by Percy Grainger (1882–1961)
    Record 4 Side A Band 5
    The Cleveland Winds
    Frederick Fennell, conductor
- ○ **Other:** a pencil for each student
- ○ **Teacher's Resource Binder:**

  Evaluation   • **Review 2**, pages Ev8–Ev9
    (Prepare one copy of each page
    for each student.)
  - **Musical Progress Report 2,**
    page Ev10

Introducing the Lesson   OPTIONAL
Establish a tonality in E♭. Write the following scale patterns on the chalkboard and ask the students to sing them as you point to the numbers in sequence.

- 1–2–3–4–5–6–7–1'
- 1–3–5–3–1–5,–1
- 3–4–5–3–4–5–6–5
- 5–5,–1

Developing the Lesson
1. Ask the students to turn to page 66 and learn to sing each of the three musical ideas. After the students have learned the three melodies, divide the class into three groups. Assign each group one of the patterns. Listen to the recording of *Shepherd's Hey.* **Raise your hand each time you hear your idea played.**

2. Distribute copies of Review 2 (*Shepherd's Hey*) and a pencil to each student. Give the students time to complete the test. They will need to hear the recording of *Shepherd's Hey* several times to determine which instruments are used.

Closing the Lesson
Discuss the correct answers. Replay the recording so that the students can confirm that all the instruments shown on page 67 are heard at some time during the piece.

Use the information collected during this activity as well as other observations made during the Second Quarter to complete a copy of *Musical Progress Report 2* for each student. This may be sent to parents as a report and/or retained in your files.

The instruments shown here are heard in *Shepherd's Hey.*
To which family does each belong?

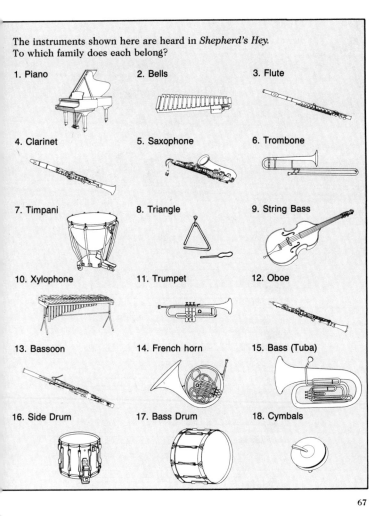

1. Piano
2. Bells
3. Flute
4. Clarinet
5. Saxophone
6. Trombone
7. Timpani
8. Triangle
9. String Bass
10. Xylophone
11. Trumpet
12. Oboe
13. Bassoon
14. French horn
15. Bass (Tuba)
16. Side Drum
17. Bass Drum
18. Cymbals

67

For Your Information

Answers for Review 2:

1.

2.

5 3 4 3 4 | 3 5 2 | 3 4 5 4 3 4 | 5 6 7 1'

3. **Brass:** trombone, trumpet, French horn, bass (tuba)
   Woodwind: flute, clarinet, saxophone, oboe, bassoon
   String: string bass
   Percussion: piano, bells, timpani, triangle, xylophone, side drum, bass drum, cymbals
4. **Aerophones:** trombone, trumpet, French horn, bass (tuba), flute, clarinet, saxophone, oboe, bassoon
   Chordophones: string bass
   Membranophones: timpani, side drum
   Idiophones: bells, triangle, xylophone, cymbals
5. Call 1: *allegro p* or *mp*

   Call 2: *accelerando f*

   Call 3: *presto ff*

LESSON 31

Lesson Focus

Rhythm: Individual sounds and silences within a rhythmic line may be longer than, shorter than, or the same as other sounds within the line. *(P–I)*

Materials

○ **No Piano Accompaniment**

○ **Record Information:**
  • Toembaï
  Record 4   Side A   Band 6
  Voices: children's choir
  Accompaniment: percussion

○ **Instrument:** autoharp

○ **Other:** 5 round containers (such as ice-cream or fast-food cartons); cover the tubs with contact paper. Prepare five 4 × 4″ cards, with letters "M," "U," "S," "I," and "C" placed separately on each. See further instructions on Activity Sheet 17.

○ **Teacher's Resource Binder:**
  Activity Sheets • **Activity Sheet 17,** page A28 (See instructions on the activity sheet.)
  • Optional—
  Kodaly Activity 4, page K5
  Orff Activity 5, page O9

○ **For additional experience with harmony:** Special Times 6, page 228

The Third Quarter

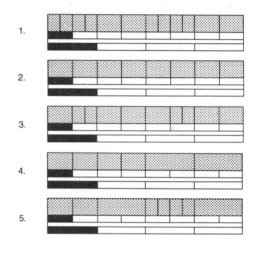

Toembaï

Israeli Round

1.
2.
3.
4.
5.

68

Introducing the Lesson

What T.V. game shows do you like to watch? (Answers will vary.) **We're going to have a game show today just like one of those on T.V., except you won't win a new car or lots of money. Let's practice before we start the game.**

Ask the students to turn to page 68. While one student taps the shortest sound and another student keeps the beat, direct the class to practice reading each of the patterns shown at the bottom of the page.

Developing the Lesson

1. **We're ready to start the game.** Set out the five rhythm cards prepared from Activity Sheet 17 (*Challenge*). (See **Materials.**) The students should recognize that these are the patterns they just performed. **Can you perform all five without losing a beat between patterns?**

2. Tell the students to keep repeating the rhythm of the patterns without stopping in between them. **I'm going to do something with these tubs while you chant.** (See **Materials.**) **Don't pay any attention to me! Your task is to keep chanting no matter what I do.**

3. As the students continue the chant a second time, cover Card 1 with a tub. As they continue a third time, tap the tub to indicate that they must continue to chant that pattern even if they cannot see it. Cover Card 2 with another tub. Continue until all the cards are covered.

4. As the class continues chanting, place the cards spelling "M–U–S–I–C" on top of the tubs. (See **Materials.**) Direct the class to stop. **Who can tell me what is under the "S"? the "C"?** After a student has chanted the specified pattern, remove the tub to verify the answer.

Which of the patterns shown on page 68 can you
find in this song?
Tap the shortest sound at an *andante* tempo.
Chant the rhythm of the melody on the word "too."

Fast, with marked rhythm

1.　　　　　　　　　　　　　　　to line 2

Toem-baï, toem-baï, toem-baï, toem-baï, toem-baï, toem-baï, toem-baï.

2.　　　　　　　　　　　　　　　to line 3

Tra - la - la,　la-la-la-la-la,　la - la - la - la - la - la.

3.

Tra - la-la-la - la,　la - la-la-la - la,　la - la - la - la - la - la.

Learn the melody.
Tune up by singing this scale:

Tune up:

Is the song based on a major or a minor scale?
When you know the melody, sing it at an *allegro* tempo.

69

After all patterns have been revealed, mix
them up and repeat the activity. Announce
that this is a very special T.V. game: Everyone
is a winner!

5. **Look at your books again.** Play the song on
page 69. **Can you hear any of the patterns
you've chanted?** Play the recording. Help the
students locate each pattern:

- Measure 1 is Pattern 2.
- Measures 2, 4, and 6 all use Pattern 4.
- Measure 3 is Pattern 5.
- Measure 5 is Pattern 3.

(Pattern 1 is not used.)

6. Ask the students to follow the instructions at
the bottom of the page. Decide that the song
is in E minor. After tuning up on the E minor
scale, challenge the students to sing the melody on the syllable "lah." Play the recording.

Closing the Lesson

When the students know the melody well, divide
the class into three groups and sing the song as
a round. This may occur on another day, after
the song has been sung several times.

LESSON 32

Lesson Focus

Melody: Each pitch within a melody moves in relation to a home tone.
Melody: A series of pitches bounded by the octave "belong together," forming a tonal set. *(D–S)*

Materials

- **Piano Accompaniment:** page 298
- **Record Information:**
  - Sarah the Whale
    (Record 2 Side A Band 3)
  - Spider on the Floor
    Record 4 Side A Band 7
    Voices: child solo
    Accompaniment: transverse flute, bassoon, French horn, synthesizer, harpsichord, lute, viola da gamba
- **Instruments:** complete set of chromatic resonator bells; bell mallets
- **Other:** overhead projector; pencil for each student
- **Teacher's Resource Binder:**
  Activity Sheets
  - **Activity Sheets 18–19,** pages A29–A30 (Prepare transparencies and a copy for each student.)
  - Optional—
    Curriculum Correlation 8, page C12
- **For additional experience with melody:** Perform 15, page 162; Special Times 16, page 248

Chords not shown on pupil page

Spider on the Floor

Words and Music by Bill Russell

Verse 1

There's a spi-der on the floor, on the floor.

There's a spi-der on the floor, on the floor.

Who could ask for an-y more than a spi-der on the floor.

There's a spi-der on the floor, on the floor.

Sing each new verse a little higher than the one before it.
The key and the first few pitches are shown for each verse.
Sing the remainder of each verse in that new key,
using the melody for Verse 1.

Verse 2

2. Now the spider's on my leg, on my leg.
   Oh the spider's on my leg, on my leg.
   Oh he's really, really big, this old spider on my leg.
   There's a spider on my leg, on my leg.

70

Introducing the Lesson

Review "Sarah the Whale" (page 24). Ask the class to hum the tonal center, which is the last pitch of the melody. **How good is your tonal memory?** Challenge the class to sing the song again, with their books closed. **Begin while sitting down. The first time you sing the tonal center, stand up. Remain standing until you sing it again.** (Repeated pitches don't count.) The students should move only on the low l (C) at the beginning and end of the song ("Fris-" and "-er").

Remind the students that every scale has two tonal centers, low and high "l." **This time, change position each time you hear either tonal center.** The students should change position on "Fris-," "pail," "tea," and "-er." (This is tricky but fun.)

Developing the Lesson

1. **You did well hearing the home tone of a familiar song. Listen to an unfamiliar song.**

When the music ends, hum the tonal center. Play Verse 1 of the recording "Spider on the Floor." The class should hum the final pitch (D) of the song.

2. **Keep that tonal center "in your head" as you hear the entire song.** Play the complete recording. **Raise your hand each time you hear the tonal center.** For Verse 1 they should raise their hands on "spider" and "the" (Phrase 1), "on" (Phrase 2), "floor" (end of Phrase 3), and "floor" (end of Phrase 4).

Listen to the entire recording, with a puzzled look as the tonal center shifts with each verse. **What happened?** (The students' answers may vary.) Agree that the tonal center kept changing, moving up with each verse.

3. **You can *hear* tonal centers. Can you find the tonal center by looking?** Distribute Activity Sheets 18 and 19 (*Locate Tonal Centers:*

Verse 3

3. Now the spider's on my stomach, on my stomach.
Oh, the spider's on my stomach, on my stomach.
Oh, he's just a dumb old lummok, this old spider on my stomach.
There's a spider on my stomach, on my stomach.

Verse 4

4. Now the spider's on my neck, on my neck.
Oh, the spider's on my neck, on my neck.
Oh, I'm gonna be a wreck, I've got a spider on my neck.
There's a spider on my neck, on my neck.

Verse 5

5. Now the spider's on my face, on my face.
Oh, the spider's on my face, on my face.
Oh, what a big disgrace, I've got a spider on my face.
There's a spider on my face, on my face.

Verse 6

6. Now the spider's on my head, on my head.
Oh, the spider's on my head, on my head.
Oh, I wish that I were dead, I've got a spider on my head.
There's a spider on my head, on my head.

Spoken: But he jumps off. . . . .

Repeat Verse 1 on this key:

71

Sharps and *Locate Tonal Centers: Flats*) and a pencil to each student. If multiple sets of resonator bells are available, organize the class into two groups, with each half working on each activity sheet. If they are not available, display transparencies of the sheets and complete the activity together. Individuals may take turns locating the bells and calling out the letter names.

4. When the activity sheets are completed, share information. Help the students develop rules for locating the tonal center as it applies to each kind of key signature.

For key signatures with flats, find the last flat to the right. Count down four steps. The note you have reached is the tonal center. For key signatures with sharps, find the last sharp to the right. This time count down seven steps to find the tonal center.

Closing the Lesson

Ask the students to look at the notation for "Spider on the Floor" on page 70. **Look at the key signature. In what key is Verse 1?** (D) While the class sings Verse 1, a student may play the D bell each time the tonal center occurs in the melody. Follow the same procedure for each verse. (The order of keys is D, E♭, E, F, G, A♭, and C.) End the class by singing the entire song without stopping. **Remember to change the key as each new verse begins.** The students will enjoy performing with the recording.

Collect the students' activity sheets so that they can be used again in subsequent lessons.

Lesson Focus

Melody: A series of pitches may move up or down by steps or skips.
Melody: Each pitch within a melody moves in relation to a home tone. *(P–S)*

Materials

○ **Piano Accompaniment:** page 303
○ **Record Information:**
  • Spider on the Floor
    (Record 4 Side A Band 7)
  • Sweet Potatoes
  ▭ **Record 4 Side A Band 8**
    Voices: children's choir
    Accompaniment: banjo, two guitars, percussion
○ **Instruments:** multiple sets of chromatic resonator bells; bell mallets
○ **Other:** copies of Activity Sheets 18 and 19 prepared for Lesson 32; a pencil for each student
○ **Teacher's Resource Binder:**
  [Activity Sheets] • **Activity Sheet 20,** page A31
    (Prepare a copy of the activity sheet for each student.)
  • Optional—
    Mainstreaming Suggestion 8, page M14
    Orff Activity 12d, page O30

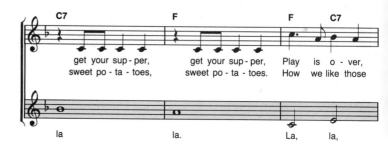

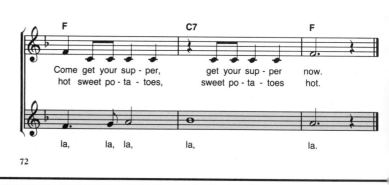

72

Introducing the Lesson

Begin class by reviewing "Spider on the Floor" on page 70. Write this pattern on the chalkboard:

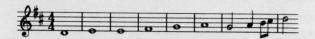

Invite a student to locate the needed resonator bells and play the pattern for the class. Discover that the pattern uses all the pitches of the D scale. One student may play it as an accompaniment as the class sings Verse 1.

Distribute the students' copies of Activity Sheets 18 and 19, which were completed during Lesson 32, Activity Sheet 20 (*Staffs*), and a pencil to each student. Ask them to choose one of the verses of the song, study the key signature, and determine the tonal center. **Write the accompaniment pattern for your chosen verse on the staff. You can check your copies of Activity Sheets 18 and 19 to be sure you know which pitches to use.**

After the students have finished the accompaniment, invite volunteers to play the patterns they have written while the class sings that verse in the appropriate key.

Developing the Lesson

1. **Turn to page 72. In what key is this song written?** (F) Establish the key and help the students learn to sing the melody, which is the upper part of each pair of staffs.

2. **What bells will we need if we want to play the harmonizing part on the lower staff?** As the class names the pitches (C, E, F, G, A, and B♭), one student may locate the bells and then play the part as the class sings. Divide the class into two groups and learn to sing the song in harmony.

Accompaniments:

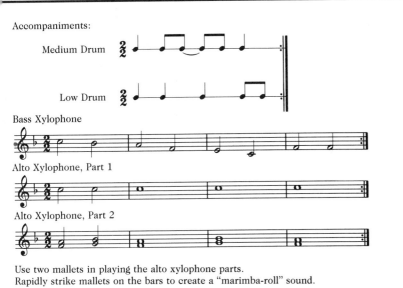

Use two mallets in playing the alto xylophone parts.
Rapidly strike mallets on the bars to create a "marimba-roll" sound.

73

For Your Information

Tints on part music throughout HOLT MU-
SIC assist the student who is inexperienced
in reading music from multiple staffs.

3. On the chalkboard, write one of the key signatures shown below:

**Who can establish the tonality by playing the
tonal center for this song?** After the correct
bell has been located (G or E♭), sing in this
new key. Write other key signatures on the
chalkboard and follow the same procedure.

Closing the Lesson

Choose individuals to practice the accompaniment parts on page 73. Add these parts as the
class sings in harmony.

73

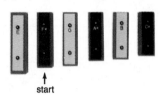

LESSON 34

Lesson Focus

Harmony: Chords and melody may move simultaneously in relation to each other. *(D–I)*

Materials

o **No Piano Accompaniment**

o **Record Information:**
  • *El Yivne Ha Galil*
  Record 4   Side B   Band 1
  Voices: children's choir
  Accompaniment: clarinet, trumpet, trombone, tuba, violin, double bass, cimbalom, mandolin, percussion

o **Instruments:** resonator bells E, F♯, G, A♯, B, and C♯; bell mallets; tambourine; finger cymbals

o **Other:** overhead projector

o **Teacher's Resource Binder:**
  • Optional—
  Orff Activity 3, page O8

o **For additional experience with expression:** Perform 6, page 142

El Yivne Ha Galil

Hassidic Folk Tune

Play these bells to help you learn the melody:

El   yi-v'-ne ha-ga-lil. ___   El   yi-v'-ne ha-ga-lil.

El   yi-v'-ne ha-ga-lil. ___   El   yi-v'-ne ha-ga-lil.

Ba-ruch yi-v'-ne ha-ga-lil.   Ba-ruch - yiv' ne ha-ga-lil.

Ba-ruch yi-v'-ne ha-ga-lil.   Ba-ruch - yiv' ne ha-ga-lil.

74

Introducing the Lesson

Play the recording of *"El Yivne Ha Galil."* **When do the voices sing in unison? When are they producing harmony?** (See **For Your Information.**) Draw the students' attention to the design at the top of page 75. **This shows the patterns you heard when the voices were singing in harmony. How does the harmony move in relation to the melody?** (They are parallel; that is, they are always the same distance apart.)

Developing the Lesson

1. Play the recording again as the students lightly tap the rhythm of the melody. Practice chanting the Hebrew words in rhythm. (See **For Your Information** for phonetic pronunciation.)

2. Ask one student to locate the bells shown at the top of page 74 and play them in order from low to high. **Does this sound like part of a major scale?** (no) Comment that songs from this part of the world are frequently based on scales that are different from the major and minor scales we hear most often. Ask the bell player to play the first measure. Then ask the class to sing that pattern. Learn other patterns the same way. Invite the students to sing the song with the recording.

3. When the class is confident of the melody, invite some of them to sing the harmony part shown on page 75. **How far above the melody is the harmony part?** (a third) Explain that when the accompanying part moves with the melody, as in this song, the harmony is described as **homophony**. Add the finger cymbal and tambourine parts shown on the bottom of page 75.

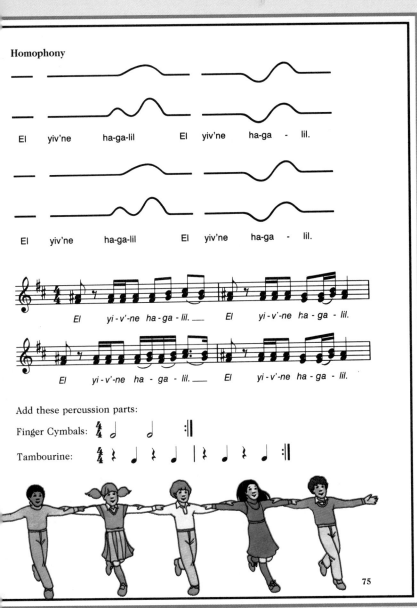

Homophony

El   yiv'ne   ha-ga-lil   El   yiv'ne   ha-ga - lil.

El   yiv'ne   ha-ga-lil   El   yiv'ne   ha-ga - lil.

El   yi-v'-ne ha-ga - lil. ___   El   yi-v'-ne ha-ga - lil.

El   yi-v'-ne ha-ga - lil. ___   El   yi-v'-ne ha-ga - lil.

Add these percussion parts:

Finger Cymbals:

Tambourine:

75

LESSON 34

For Your Information
This song was adopted by early Palestinian pioneers as their national folk dance (the Hora).

The text translates: "God will build up Galilee. The blessed one will build up Galilee."

Phonetic pronunciation of "*El Yivne Ha Galil*":
El **yeev**-nuh **hah**-gah-leel.
Bah-**rukh** **yeev**-nuh **hah**-gah-leel.

Form of "*El Yivne Ha Galil*":
1. Introduction
2. Melody in unison
3. Melody and harmony; finger cymbals
4. Melody and harmony with tambourine
5. Melody only

Closing the Lesson   OPTIONAL

Teach the class the following dance called the **Hora. Perform it with the recording of** "*El Yivne Ha Galil.*"
- Formation: All stand in a circle facing the center with arms overlapped.
- Measure 1
   Beat 1: Step to left with left foot.
   Beat 3: Cross right foot behind; step on right foot.
- Measure 2
   Beat 1: Step to left with left foot.
   Beat 3: Hop on left foot; swing right foot across in front.
- Measure 3
   Beat 1: Step to right with right foot.
   Beat 3: Hop on right foot; swing left foot across in front.
- Repeat the three-measure pattern throughout the song.

Lesson Focus

Harmony: Two or more musical lines may occur simultaneously. *(P–S)*

Materials

- ○ **Piano Accompaniment:** page 304
- ○ **Record Information:**
  - • Dobbin, Dobbin
    Record 4   Side B   Band 2
    Voices: children's choir
    Accompaniment: clarinet, trumpet, violin, accordion, double bass, percussion
- ○ **Instruments:** autoharp; bass xylophone; mallets; woodblock; coconut shells (or Styrofoam cups)
- ○ **Other:** Activity Sheets 6a–c, prepared for Lesson 11
- ○ **For additional experience with harmony:** Perform 17, page 166; Special Times 1, page 220

Dobbin, Dobbin

Dutch Tune

Polyphony results when two or more different melodies are heard at the same time.

Verse

1. Dob - bin, Dob - bin   on   your way,   We've been to-geth-er For
2. Dob - bin, Dob - bin   don't you stop,   Just   let your feet _ go

man - y   a   day, So   let your   tail   go   swish   as   the
clip - pe - ty   clop and   let your   tail   go   swish   as   the

wheels go   'round,   Gid - dy - ap!   We're   home - ward bound.
wheels go   'round,   Gid - dy - ap!   We're   home - ward bound.

76

Introducing the Lesson

Play the Chord Pattern Game introduced during Lesson 11, page 26. (See **Materials**.) Sing the patterns in the key of F. One student may play the appropriate autoharp chord to help the singers stay "in tune." After the students have sung several of the cards, add a new dimension. Display a card. After one team sings the pattern, choose a student to draw the pattern on the chalkboard, using notes on a staff.

Developing the Lesson

1. Ask the students to turn to page 76 and scan the notation of the verse to identify patterns that outline the I or V7 chords. They should discover that each measure uses notes from one or the other of these chords. Challenge the students to sing the melody while someone adds the autoharp accompaniment.

2. Draw attention to the three pitches that begin each phrase of the refrain of "Dobbin, Dobbin" on page 77. Note the symbol in front of the second pitch (B). Explain that this is a "natural" sign. It tells us to sing B instead of the B♭ as indicated by the key signature. Play the pattern as written. Then play it again using B♭. Ask the students to sing each pattern. After they practice these pickup notes, ask the students to sing the refrain, noting that this melody also outlines the same chords as found in the verse.

3. Play the recording. Focus attention on the accompaniment played by the bass guitar. **This ostinato is notated in your book at the bottom of page 77.** Play the recording again as the students follow the notation.

4. One student may play the ostinato on the bass xylophone. Others may add the woodblock

Refrain — F — C7
I like to take a horse and bug-gy

C7 — F
When I go trav-'ling to the town.

F — C7
I like to hear old Dob-bin's clip - clop.

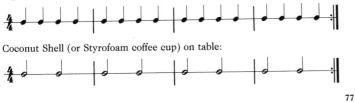

C7 — F
I like to feel the wheels go 'round. ___

Can the verse and refrain be sung as a partner song?
Look at the music. What will help you decide?

Play this **ostinato** on the Bass Xylophone:

1   5,   2   5,

7,   1

High-pitched Woodblock:

Coconut Shell (or Styrofoam coffee cup) on table:

77

and coconut-shell parts while the class sings
the song. Some may enjoy singing the xylophone part (using numbers) as a vocal ostinato.

5. **In the middle of the recording you heard the
   verse and refrain sung together. Why do you
   think these song parts fit?** (They are based
   on the same chord sequence.) **Polyphony** occurs when two (or more) independent melodies are performed at the same time.

Closing the Lesson

Divide the class in half and practice singing the
verse and refrain together. Then sing the song
with the recorded accompaniment as follows:
• Verse 1–Refrain–Verse 2–Refrain
• Verse 1 and Refrain together
• Verse 2 and Refrain together
• Verse 1–Refrain–Verse 2–Refrain

77

Lesson Focus
Harmony: Two or more musical lines may occur simultaneously. *(P–S)*

Materials
- **Piano Accompaniment:** page 305
- **Record Information:**
  - *El Yiv'ne Ha Galil*
    (Record 4   Side B   Band 1)
  - Dobbin, Dobbin
    (Record 4   Side B   Band 2)
  - A Smile Is a Frown Upside Down
  - **Record 4   Side B   Bands 3a-b**
    Voices: child solos, man, woman, children's choir
    Accompaniment: electric guitar, electric bass, penny whistle, steel drums, percussion
- **Instruments:** maracas; claves; bongos
- **Teacher's Resource Binder:**
  - Optional—
  Curriculum Correlation 9, page C13
  Mainstreaming Suggestion 9, page M17
- **For additional experience with harmony and melody:** Perform 5, page 141; Describe 2, page 170

A Smile Is a Frown Upside Down

Words and Music by Fred Willman

Moderate Calypso tempo

Section 1

A smile is a frown up-side down,

A smile is a frown up-side down,

So when you are smil-ing, you can't frown,

You'll have a great new day.

78

Introducing the Lesson
Review "*El Yivne Ha Galil*" and "Dobbin, Dobbin" on pages 74 and 76. **When were we creating homophony?** (when we added harmony to the first song) **polyphony?** (when we sang the verse and refrain of "Dobbin, Dobbin" at the same time)

Developing the Lesson
1. Listen to Band 3a of "A Smile Is a Frown Upside Down" as the students follow the music on pages 78–80 in their books. **How many sections make up the song?** (five) Guide the students to compare the five sections. Begin by examining the rhythm. Help the students discover that Section 4 usually moves with the beat. Section 3 moves with tones that are twice as long as the beat. Section 1 includes syncopated patterns.

2. Study the melody and harmony. Help the students discover that each section has the same chord sequence. Notice that many measures in Section 1 outline chords, as in "Dobbin, Dobbin." The melody for Section 2 is similar to Section 1. Section 3 begins with upward skips. Section 4 begins with a downward stepping movement. The end of Section 5 is similar to that of Section 1.

3. Play the chordal accompaniment as the students practice singing each section.

4. Ask the students to listen to Band 3b of "A Smile Is a Frown Upside Down." **How is the vocal harmony created in this version?** (by singing two, three, four, or five of the melodies at the same time) **Which of these melodies can be sung together?** (all of them) **Why?** (Each melody contains the same number of measures and the same chord sequence.) **Is**

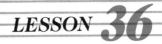

Section 2

Section 3

79

the result homophony or polyphony? (polyphony) Why? (Each part is an independent melody.)

5. Divide the class into two groups and sing the song as shown in the upper two rows of the chart on page 81. **Is this the same as singing a round?** (no, because the second group stops before singing all five of the melodies)

6. When the students can easily sing the song in two parts, try singing in three, four, or five parts as shown in the chart. The students may also experiment with other ways to combine the melodies.

Closing the Lesson

Choose a few students to add the percussion parts shown on the bottom of page 81.

LESSON 36

Section 4

mf F   Gm   C7   F

Let your friends all know you care. Make them hap-py, do you dare?

F   B♭   C7   F

When you smile they'll try it too, So let it start with you.

Section 5

F   Gm

So smile, smile, turn it a - round,

C7   F

So smile and you won't frown,

F   B♭

You'll see the world in a dif - ferent way,

C7   *f* F

You'll have a great new day.

80

Sing several of the sections together.
How many groups will you use?

Group 1	Section 1	Section 2	Section 3	Section 4	Section 5
Group 2		Section 1	Section 2	Section 3	Section 4
Group 3			Section 1	Section 2	Section 3
Group 4				Section 1	Section 2
Group 5					Section 1

Why do the melodies fit together?
Can you think of other ways to combine them?

Add these **percussion** parts:

Maracas:

Claves:

Bongos: High / Low

81

LESSON 37

Lesson Focus

Rhythm: Individual sounds and silences within a rhythmic line may be longer than, shorter than, or the same as other sounds within the line. **(D–S)**

Materials

○ **Piano Accompaniment:** page 310
○ **Record Information:**
  • Life in the Army
    Record 4   Side B   Band 4
    Accompaniment: trumpet, French horn, trombone, tuba
○ **Instrument:** autoharp
○ **Other:** 5 round containers; materials prepared for Lesson 31
○ **Teacher's Resource Binder:**
  | Activity Sheets | • **Activity Sheet 21,** page A32 (See instructions on the activity sheet.) |

  • Optional—
    Kodaly Activities 2, 9, pages K2, K14
○ **For additional experience with rhythm:** Special Times 13, page 242

Introducing the Lesson

Play the Challenge game introduced during Lesson 31. When the students can perform the rhythm patterns, set out five new rhythm cards prepared from Activity Sheet 21 (*Challenge 2*) in the order shown on page 82. Guide the students to notice that some include a "pickup." That is, the first note of the rhythm pattern begins one short sound before the first accented beat of the measure. Explain that they will need to "think" seven short sounds and then be ready to start chanting on the eighth short sound. Count "1–2–3–4–5–6–7–8." The class should begin as you count "8," reading each pattern with the sound "ch" or "doo." Challenge them to perform all five patterns without losing a beat between them.

Developing the Lesson

1. Continue to play the game as in Lesson 31. Cover different patterns with the tubs. This

time, cover them at random. Remind the class that they must chant each pattern even though it is hidden.

2. As the class continues to chant, place the cards prepared from Lesson 31 on top of the tubs. As before, challenge the students to demonstrate their rhythmic memory by chanting the specified pattern.

3. Direct attention to the rhythm patterns on page 82. The students will realize that these are the patterns they have been chanting. **Can you match each rhythm pattern with the notated patterns?** (See **For Your Information**.)

4. Help the students locate the rhythms in "Life in the Army" on page 83. (See **For Your Information**.) Chant the song with words. **Is it likely that soldiers might sing this song when they're on their marching drills in training?**

OPTIONAL

82

Life in the Army

Traditional

Vigorously

1. The bis-cuits in the ar-my they say are might-y fine,
2. The cof-fee in the ar-my they say is might-y fine,
3. The chick-en in the ar-my they say is might-y fine,

But one rolled off the ta-ble and killed a friend of mine,
It looks like mud and wa-ter and tastes like i - o - dine,
But once two drum-sticks got up and start-ed beat-ing time,

Oh, I have had e - nough of ar - my life,

Gee Ma, I wan - na go, Hey Ma, I got to go,

Gee Ma, I wan - na go home.

83

For Your Information

Correct answers for matching patterns on page 82:
1. C
2. A
3. D
4. E
5. B

Correct answers for matching patterns on page 82 to song on page 83:
A. Measures 1 and 3 (with pickup)
B. Measure 6
C. Measures 2 and 4 (with pickup)
D. Measure 5
E. Measures 7, 8, and 9

(Yes, the rhythm would help keep them in step. The lyrics make fun of army life.)

Closing the Lesson

In what key is this song? (G) Call on a student to play this chord sequence on the autoharp: G–G–G–G–D7–D7–D7–D7–G–G–G–G. **Why will this be a good introduction?** (It sets the meter in fours. It sets the tempo. It gives the sound of the I chord from which the starting pitch can be determined.) After the students have worked out the melody and noticed that it frequently uses tones from either the I or V7 chord, they may sing the entire song as a different student accompanies each verse.

Encourage the students to create new verses, such as "The money in the army they say is mighty fine, They give you fifty dollars and take back forty-nine. . . ."

LESSON 38

Lesson Focus

Rhythm: Individual sounds and silences within a rhythmic line may be longer than, shorter than, or the same as other sounds within the line. *(D–S)*

Materials

- ○ **Piano Accompaniment:** page 308
- ○ **Record Information**
  - Yankee Doodle Boy
    Record 4 Side B Band 5
    Voice: child's voice
    Accompaniment: brass ensemble, piccolo, percussion
- ○ **Instruments:** three percussion instruments with different timbres, such as cymbals, woodblocks, and guiros
- ○ **Other:** overhead projector
- ○ **Teacher's Resource Binder:**
  - **Activity Sheet 22**, page A33 (Prepare the activity sheet as a transparency.)
  - Optional—
    Kodaly Activity 7, page K11
- ○ **For additional experience with time and place and harmony:** Describe 10, page 182; Describe 14, page 190

Yankee Doodle Boy

Words and Music by George M. Cohan

I'm a Yan-kee Doo-dle Dan - dy,
A Yan - kee Doo-dle, do or die;___
A real live neph-ew of my Un - cle Sam,
Born on the Fourth of Ju - ly.___
I've got a Yan-kee Doo-dle sweet - heart,

84

Introducing the Lesson

Play the recording of "Yankee Doodle Boy" as the students enter the room. Indicate that they should move to their seats in a way that reflects the style of the music. Write the words "Waltz," "March," and "Polka" on the chalkboard. **Which word describes the music you just heard?** (march) **Why do you think it is a march and not a waltz?** (It is a march because it moves in twos. Waltzes move in threes.)

Developing the Lesson

1. Display Activity Sheet 22 (*Yankee Doodle Rhythms*) as a transparency. Establish the beat in twos and guide the students to perform Chants 1 and 2.

2. Divide the class into two groups and perform Chants 1 and 2 simultaneously. Perform again. Ask the groups to clap the patterns while stepping the beat.

3. Ask the students to look at "Yankee Doodle Boy" on page 84. **Can you find the first pattern you chanted?** (Phrases 1 and 2) **Where is the syncopated rhythm of "un-e-ven, un-e-ven"?** ("Born on the," "Fourth of Ju-," and "I am a") Play the recording as the students tap the rhythm of the melody.

4. **Before we learn the melody, tell me what you see that will help in learning this song.** (Phrases 1–2 and 5–6 are almost the same. Phrase 7 is from "Yankee Doodle.") Play the recording again. Then challenge the students to sing the song without assistance.

5. Follow the suggestions on page 85 and perform "Patriotic Polyrhythms." Group 1 begins with a "pickup" before Group 2 enters.

84

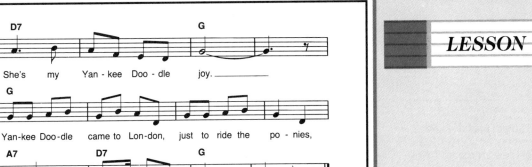

She's my Yan - kee Doo - dle joy. _____

Yan-kee Doo-dle came to Lon-don, just to ride the po - nies,

I am a Yan - kee Doo - dle boy. _____

Patriotic Polyrhythms

Clap the rhythm patterns of the words for these two songs:
"America" "America, the Beautiful"
Form two groups.
Clap the patterns of both songs at the same time.
Be sure to accent the first beat in each measure.

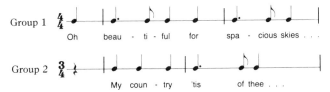

Group 1 4/4
Oh beau - ti - ful for spa - cious skies . . .

Group 2 3/4
My coun - try 'tis of thee . . .

How do the rhythm patterns compare with each other?
Do the accents fall on the same beat for both songs?
Do the songs end at different times? same time?
Perform again using two different timbres,
such as the sound of sticks or drums.
What effect does the use of two different timbres have on
the performance?

85

6. **You just performed "Patriotic Polyrhythms." Can you define polyrhythm?** (two contrasting rhythms, which may or may not be in different meters, sounded simultaneously) Discuss the relationships between the rhythms. Notice that:

   - Uneven rhythm patterns of one song often occur simultaneously with even patterns of the second song.

   - Accented first beats usually fall at different times. (Some students may notice that the accents come together every thirteenth beat.) The songs end at different times because "America the Beautiful" is longer than "America."

7. Divide the class into three groups. While groups 1 and 2 perform "Patriotic Polyrhythms," Group 3 will clap the rhythm of "Yankee Doodle Boy."

Closing the Lesson

Perform the three-part chant as a percussion piece. Discuss the effect of using contrasting timbres. (Each rhythm is more distinct and can be heard more clearly.)

Lesson Focus

Rhythm: Individual sounds and silences within a rhythmic line may be longer than, shorter than, or the same as the underlying shortest pulse. *(P–S)*

Materials

o **Piano Accompaniment:** page 311
o **Record Information:**
  • Fifty Nifty United States
  ▱ **Record 4   Side B   Band 6**
  Voices: child solos, children's choir
  Accompaniment: small show orchestra
o **Other:** overhead projector
o **Teacher's Resource Binder:**

| Activity Sheets | • **Activity Sheet 23,** page A34 (Prepare a transparency of the activity sheet and make two flashcards of each pattern.) |
| Evaluation | • Optional— **Checkpoint 3,** page Ev11 |

Fifty Nifty United States

Words and Music by Ray Charles

Section A

Fif - ty nif - ty U - nit - ed States from

thir - teen o - rig - i - nal col - o - nies,

Fif - ty nif - ty stars in the flag that

bil - lows so beau - ti - f'ly in ____ the breeze.

Each in - di - vid - u - al state

con - trib - utes a qual - i - ty that is great.

86

Introducing the Lesson

Display Activity Sheet 23 (*Rhythm Patterns*) as a transparency. Establish the shortest sound (eighth note) by chanting "Short–short–short–short, 1–2, start now." Point to the various patterns at random. Have the class chant each pattern using a neutral syllable such as "choo."

Developing the Lesson

1. **We are going to play a game called "Rhythm Pattern Upset."** Distribute the flashcards prepared from the activity sheet.

   If I give you a flashcard, can you practice it by yourself? Do not show anyone else your pattern. Two copies of each rhythm pattern have been made so that two students will have the same pattern. Give one flashcard to each student. Give them time to practice their rhythm pattern.

2. Explain the game. (See **For Your Information.**) Choose a student to go to the center. Take that student's place (and flashcard) in the circle. Set the shortest sounds before each rhythm pattern is chanted. Play the game as long as desired.

3. Collect all of the rhythm cards as the students return to their desks. Then ask the students to open their books to page 86. **The patterns you performed all belong to this song. Can you chant them in the order that they appear in the notation as shown on pages 86 to 89?** After the students have read the words in rhythm, ask them to listen to the recording a number of times until they can perform the melody for Section A.

4. When the students can perform Section A, draw attention to the words for Section B,

Each in-di-vid-u-al state de-serves a bow, Let's sa-lute them now!

Fif-ty nif-ty U-ni-ted States from thir-teen o-rig-i-nal col-o-nies,

Shout 'em, scout 'em, Tell all a-bout 'em,

One by one, 'til we've gi-ven a day to

87

For Your Information

Instructions for "Rhythm Pattern Upset": This game is an adaptation of "Fruit Basket Upset." The class forms a circle while one student stands in the center. Each member of the circle has a Rhythm Pattern flashcard. (See **Materials.**) The student standing in the center chants a rhythm pattern from the transparency. Those in the circle who are holding that rhythm on their flashcards try to exchange places with each other. The object of the game is for the student in the center to try to take one of those places in the circle. The student who is left without a place then moves to the center and is the chanter for the next rhythm. If the students in the circle exchange places before the student in the center finds the spot, he or she remains in the center and chants another rhythm. Twice during the entire game, the student in the center may choose to say "Rhythm Pattern Upset" instead of chanting a pattern. When that happens each person in the circle must exchange places with whoever has a matching flashcard. The student in the center tries to take one of the places. The displaced student goes to the center.

which list all of the states in alphabetical order. Suggest that the students lightly tap the rhythm of the melody as they listen to this section. When they can perform it, help them learn the coda.

Perform the entire song after making sure the students understand how to follow the instructions "D.S." (return to the sign) just before the coda on page 89. Explain that the students are to sing to the measure where ⊕ (indicating "to coda") occurs and then skip to that section to finish the song.

Closing the Lesson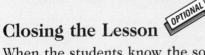

When the students know the song well, create a new interlude. It could occur in place of Section B or after the repetition of Section A before proceeding to the coda. Teach the following chant to the students:

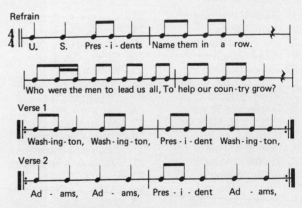

Perform as follows:
- Everyone chants the refrain.
- Student 1 answers with Verse 1.
- The class repeats Verse 1 and the refrain.
- Student 2 adds Verse 2.
- The class repeats Verse 2, 1, and the refrain.

Continue as long as desired. The list of presidents can be found on page 88.

87

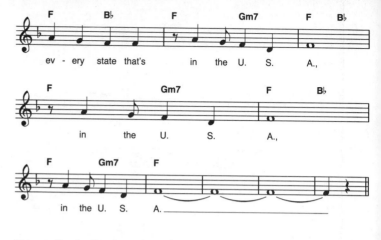

ev - ery state that's in the U. S. A.,

in the U. S. A.,

in the U. S. A.

Listen to Section B to learn the melody:

Alabama, Alaska, Arizona, Arkansas,

California, Colorado, Connecticut,

Delaware, Florida, Georgia, Hawaii, Idaho, Illinois,

Indiana, Iowa, Kansas, Kentucky,

Louisiana, Maine, Maryland, Massachusetts, Michigan,

Minnesota, Mississippi, Missouri, Montana,

Nebraska, Nevada, New Hampshire, New Jersey,

New Mexico, New York, North Carolina, North Dakota,

Ohio, Oklahoma, Oregon, Pennsylvania, Rhode Island,

South Carolina, South Dakota, Tennessee, Texas,

Utah, Vermont, Virginia, Washington, West Virginia,

Wisconsin, Wyoming.

88

1. George Washington
2. John Adams
3. Thomas Jefferson
4. James Madison
5. James Monroe
6. John Quincy Adams
7. Andrew Jackson
8. Martin Van Buren
9. William H. Harrison
10. John Tyler
11. James K. Polk
12. Zachary Taylor
13. Millard Fillmore
14. Franklin Pierce
15. James Buchanan
16. Abraham Lincoln
17. Andrew Johnson
18. Ulysses S. Grant
19. Rutherford B. Hayes
20. James A. Garfield

21. Chester A. Arthur
22. Grover Cleveland
23. Benjamin Harrison
24. Grover Cleveland
25. William McKinley
26. Theodore Roosevelt
27. William H. Taft
28. Woodrow Wilson
29. Warren Harding
30. Calvin Coolidge
31. Herbert C. Hoover
32. Franklin D. Roosevelt
33. Harry S. Truman
34. Dwight D. Eisenhower
35. John F. Kennedy
36. Lyndon B. Johnson
37. Richard M. Nixon
38. Gerald R. Ford
39. Jimmy Carter
40. Ronald Reagan

Fifty Nifty United States
Words and Music by Ray Charles

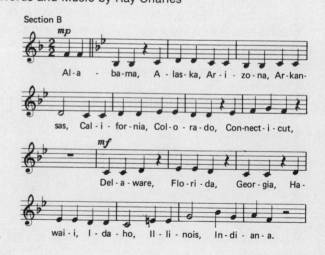

Section B

Al - a - bama, A - las - ka, Ar - i - zo - na, Ar - kan -

sas, Cal - i - for - nia, Col - o - ra - do, Con - nect - i - cut,

Del - a - ware, Flo - ri - da, Geor - gia, Ha -

wai - i, I - da - ho, Il - li - nois, In - di - an - a.

Slowly

mf F   Gm   Dm   F

North,   South,   East,   West,

C   (Ad lib)

In our cool,   con - sid - ered,   ob - jec - tive,   un -

C   3

prej - u - diced   o - pin - ion,   (*)

ff   C7   G   C7   D.S. Coda   F   B♭

(*) _____ is the   best   of   the   add   up   to   U.

C7   *ritard.*   *ff* F

S.   A! _____

* Insert the name of your favorite state.

89

I - o - wa, Kan - sas, Ken - tuck - y, Lou - i - si -

an - a, Maine, Mar - y - land, Mas - sa - chu - setts, Mich - i - gan.

f

Min - ne - so - ta, Mis - sis - sip - pi, Mis - sou - ri, Mon -

tan - a,   Ne - bras - ka.   Ne - vad - a.

f (Chant)

New Hamp - shire, New   Jer - sey, New Mex - i - co,

New York,   North Car - o - li - na,

North Da - ko - ta,   O - hi - o!

mf (Sing)

Ok - la - ho - ma, Or - e - gon, Penn - syl - va - nia,

Rhode Is - land, South Ca - ro - li - na, South Da - ko - ta,

f

Ten - nes - see,   Tex - as.   U - tah, Ver -

mont,   Vir - gin - ia,   Wash - ing - ton,

West Vir - gin - ia, Wis - con - sin, Wy - o - ming.

LESSON 40

Lesson Focus

Harmony: Chords and melody may move simultaneously in relation to each other. *(D–I)*

Materials

- **Piano Accompaniment:** page 320
- **Record Information:**
  - Look Down That Lonesome Road
    Record 4   Side B   Band 7
    Voice: man
    Accompaniment: English horn, guitars
- **Instruments:** autoharps
- **Other:** three different-colored crayons; a pencil for each student
- **Teacher's Resource Binder:**

  [Activity Sheets] • **Activity Sheet 24–25**, pages A35–A36 (Prepare a copy of the activity sheets for each student.)

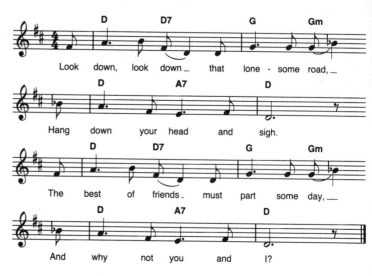

Look Down That Lonesome Road

Traditional

Look down, look down _ that lone - some road, _

Hang down your head and sigh.

The best of friends _ must part some day, _

And why not you and I?

90

Introducing the Lesson

Distribute Activity Sheets 24 and 25 (*Same or Different* and *Chord Bingo*), a pencil, and three crayons to each student. **Today we're going to play "Chord Bingo." First you must answer the questions on Activity Sheet 30. I will strum twice on the autoharp. Listen carefully. Is the second chord the same as or different from the first?** Play the G major chord on the autoharp, slowly strumming the strings from low to high. Then strum the G7 chord. **Circle the correct answer for Question 1 on your activity sheet.** Follow the same procedure for Question 2. Strum the G major chord, followed by the G minor chord. For Question 3, play G7, then the G minor chord.

Developing the Lesson

1. Invite the students to play "Chord Bingo" on Activity Sheet 25 so that they can compare the chords they just heard. Hold down the G chord button and pluck each string named in Column 1 of the activity sheet, beginning with the lowest pitch. Show how some of the strings will make a clear sound when plucked. Others will be silent or just make a "thud." Call out the letter name of the string you are plucking. If it makes a clear sound, it belongs to the G chord and the class should color in that box in Column 1 with one of their crayons. After all pitches listed in the column have been plucked, call out the correct pitches: G, B, and D. Students who marked the boxes correctly may shout "Bingo."

2. Hold down the G7 chord and repeat the process. The students should use a different crayon. Correct pitches are G, B, D, and F. Pluck strings a third time as you hold down the G minor chord. Correct pitches are G, B♭, and D.

90

Follow the chords shown above the staffs on page 90.
Touch the chords on this practice autoharp
as you sing.

D	G Min.	A7	D Min.	E7	A Min.	D7
E♭	F7	B♭	C7	F	G7	C	G

91

3. Tell the class to compare the pictures they made of the G major and G7 chords and then turn back to Activity Sheet 24 and answer Box 4 questions. Next, tell the students to compare the G major and G minor chord pictures and answer Box 5 questions. Finally, they should compare all three chords and answer the question in Box 6.

Closing the Lesson

Play the recording of "Look Down That Lonesome Road" with books closed. **Can you identify the kind of chords used in the accompaniment?** Write the lyrics on the chalkboard. Play the recording several times as the students tell you which chord they think they hear. Write "M" (for major), "7" (for 7th), or "m" (for minor) above the appropriate words. The students may open their books to page 90 to check their answers.

Ask the class to sing the song and learn the autoharp accompaniment. Some may practice on the chart on page 91 while others play autoharps, singing as they rehearse.

LESSON 41

Lesson Focus
Harmony: Chords and melody may move simultaneously in relation to each other. *(P–I)*

Materials
- ○ **Piano Accompaniment:** page 318
- ○ **Record Information:**
  - My Aunt Came Back
    (Record 1   Side B   Band 4)
  - The Lion Sleeps Tonight
    Record 4   Side B   Band 8
    Voices: children's choir
    Accompaniment: soprano saxophone, pan pipes, banjo, electric guitar, percussion
- ○ **Instruments:** autoharps
- ○ **Teacher's Resource Binder:**
  - Optional —
    Mainstreaming Suggestion 10, page M18

Introducing the Lesson

Sing the song "My Aunt Came Back" (page 18). The harmony of the song consists of two chords, G and D7. Ask the students to maintain the beat by patting their legs when hearing the G chord and softly clapping their hands when the harmony changes to D7. **Here's one clue: The song begins and ends with the G chord.** Make several autoharps available so that individuals may accompany the song as the class sings and moves.

Developing the Lesson

1. Introduce "The Lion Sleeps Tonight" on page 92. Help the class learn the song by focusing first on the refrain. **Will you be able to learn this easily?** (Yes, because it always moves with the short sounds, except for the last note. The melody moves by steps, using only three pitches.) One student may play the B–C–B–A pattern while the class sings.

2. Focus next on the verse. Practice tapping the rhythm. Help the students sense the change caused by the triplet. Practice tapping two sounds to a beat, then three sounds. **Can you sing the melody as I play the autoharp?** Note that it usually moves by steps. Finally, sing the introduction, which is similar to the verse.

3. When the students are familiar with the song, direct their attention to the discussion on page 93. By looking at the chord chart, the students should conclude that B is in the G chord, C is in the C chord, and A is in the D7 chord. In response to the first question below the chart, agree that the chord sequence G–C–G–D7 must be performed four times for each verse and refrain. (The repeat signs indicate that each section is to be sung twice.) In answer to the last question, discover that the sequence G–C–G occurs during the introduction and coda.

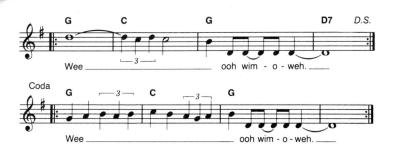

Wee ___ ooh wim - o - weh. ___

Coda

Wee ___ ooh wim - o - weh. ___

Sing these pitches:

$\frac{4}{4}$ B - - | - C' - - | - B - - | - A :‖

In which chords are these pitches found?

G Chord	D7 Chord	C Chord
D'		
	C'	C'
B		
	A	
G		G
	F♯	
		E
	D	
		C

How many times will you perform this chord sequence?
  G   C   G   D7

Sing the harmony part each time it appears.

When will you perform this sequence?
  G   C   G

93

4. Divide the class into two groups. One group sings the melody while the other sings the pitches B–C–B–A each time the chord sequence G–C–G–D7 is performed in the song. Discover that these pitches provide harmony during the verse. During the refrain both groups are singing the same melody. Only the rhythm is different.

Closing the Lesson

Distribute as many autoharps as are available. Give the students the opportunity to play the chordal accompaniment while the class sings.

LESSON 42

Lesson Focus

Harmony: Chords and melody may move simultaneously in relation to each other. *(P–I)*

Materials

○ **Piano Accompaniment:** page 320
○ **Record Information:**
  • Mockin' Bird Hill
  (Record 1 Side A Band 3)
  • Old Hound Dog Sally
  Record 5 Side A Band 1
  Voices: children's choir
  Accompaniment: hammer dulcimer, mountain dulcimer, psaltery, Jew's harp, acoustic guitar, double bass, fiddle sticks
○ **Instruments:** bass and alto xylophones; alto and soprano metallophones; soprano glockenspiel (or substitute available instruments)
○ **Other:** overhead projector
○ **For additional experience with time and place:** Describe 4, page 173

Old Hound Dog Sally

Southern Folk Song
Adapted by Sharon Falk

1. Way down yon-der in the green, green val-ley. Hey did-dle-i - ay.

I took my old hound dog named Sal-ly. Hey did-dle-i - ay.

I turned old hound dog Sal-ly loose. Hey did-dle-i - ay.

To catch the fox that stole our gray goose. Hey did-dle-i - ay.

2. Fox he run till he come to the "holler." Hey diddle-i-ay.
   Me and Sally up and "foller." Hey diddle-i-ay.
   Old hound dog Sally smelled the ground. Hey diddle-i-ay.
   But the fox was nowhere to be found. Hey diddle-i-ay.

3. We searched all day and we searched all night. Hey diddle-i-ay.
   But the fox he was nowhere in sight. Hey diddle-i-ay.
   The fox was hiding in his den. Hey diddle-i-ay.
   So me and Sally went home again. Hey diddle-i-ay.

94

Introducing the Lesson

Ask the students to sing "Mockin' Bird Hill" on page 10. Learn a circle dance that involves a clogging step. (See **For Your Information.**)

Developing the Lesson

1. **Open your books to page 94 and learn to sing "Old Hound Dog Sally."** In what key is this song written? Recall the rule developed for locating key signatures and conclude that it is in G. **What will help you perform the first measure of the melody?** (It uses only tones of the G chord.) Establish the tonality and ask the class to sing the first phrase with scale numbers, starting on low 5. Challenge the class to sight-read the entire song.

2. Ask the students to look at the instrumental parts on page 95. All parts are written on the staff except for the alto metallophone part. (Another instrument may be substituted.) Only the chord symbols are indicated for this instrument. The students' task will be to determine which pitches the metallophone players should play. On the chalkboard, write the following pitches as whole-note chords:

Alto Metallophone

Two students may play the instrument together, dividing the part. Player 1 plays the lowest pitch of each chord, while Player 2 plays the two upper pitches. Accompany the song with the chords on the metallophone.

Closing the Lesson

Individuals may learn as many instrumental parts as time allows. Combine them to provide

94

Xylophone

ylophone

Metallophone

no Metallophone

no Glockenspiel

m a circle dance to "Mockin' Bird Hill."

ree-beat patterns.

Move counterclockwise while clogging. **1** Left foot
2 Right heel knock on floor. **3** Left foot hop. Repeat
starting on the right foot.

n Face a partner. **1–2** Clap own hands twice. **3** Clap
r's left hand. **1–2** Clap own hands twice. **3** Clap part-
ight hand. Repeat through refrain.

95

For Your Information
Instructions for circle dance:

Formation: Partners form a circle that moves in a counterclockwise motion.

Verse: Dancers perform a clogging step. Each pattern takes three beats:
Left foot step–right heel knock on floor– left foot hop;
Right foot step–left heel knock on floor– right foot hop

Refrain: Dancers face partners and per- form clapping pattern, also in threes:
Beats 1–2: Clap own hands twice.
Beat 3: Clap partner's left hand.
Beats 1–2: Clap own hands twice.
Beat 3: Clap partner's right hand.
Repeat for the complete song.

an accompaniment for the song. You may wish to return to this song at another time and add other parts until the ensemble is complete.

LESSON 43

Lesson Focus

Expression: Musical elements are combined into a whole to express a musical or extramusical idea. *(C–E)*

Materials

- ○ **No Piano Accompaniment**
- ○ **Record Information:**
  - *Brandenburg Boogie*
    Arranged by Laurie Holloway
    Record 5 Side A Band 2
    Laurie Holloway, piano
    Stéphane Grappelli, violin
- ○ **Instruments:** autoharps; available resonator bells; non-pitched percussion instruments (such as woodblocks, maracas, tambourines, triangles, and finger cymbals)
- ○ **Other:** three (or more) flashlights; colored cellophane paper; projection screen (if available)
- ○ **Teacher's Resource Binder:**
  - Optional—
    Enrichment Activity 8, page E11
- ○ **For additional experience with expression:** Describe 7, page 178; Create 10, page 214

Brandenburg Boogie

Arranged by Laurie Holloway

Which group is performing this music?

96

Introducing the Lesson

Many people are fascinated by light shows. Every Fourth of July, crowds gather to watch fireworks. Rock groups use lighting displays, as do T.V. shows and commercials. Why are lights used so often? (for interest, for excitement, to create a beautiful sight) **Today we are going to create a light show of our own.**

Show the students the prepared flashlights. (See **For Your Information.**) Before you play the recording, ask the class to think about how they might use the flashlights to describe the music. They might show the rhythm or the shape of the melody. **Could you show the feelings you think the music is expressing?** Play approximately 45 seconds of *Brandenburg Boogie*.

Developing the Lesson

1. Distribute flashlights to several students and invite them to create a light show as they listen to the music. Reassure them that there is no single way to do this. Encourage them to listen carefully and choose some aspect of the music on which to base their show. You may wish to experiment with darkening the room and shining the lights on a screen, the wall, or the ceiling. The closer the lights are to the screen, the more focused they will be. Give several groups of students the opportunity to use the flashlights. Replay a portion of the composition each time the flashlights are distributed to a new group.

2. **Open your books to page 96. Look at the two groups of instruments. Pay careful attention to the sounds of the instruments. Which group is playing?** Play *Brandenburg Boogie* again. Conclude that the group that includes the violin, flute, piano, bass, and percussion is performing.

Create a Light Show

Some of you will "paint" with colored lights.
Experiment with making different lines and shapes.
Will all of the lights be used all of the time?

Others will create music to match the movement of the lights.
Choose a different instrument for each colored light.

97

For Your Information

To provide a medium for a light show, use rubber bands to attach different-colored cellophane paper to the lens of each flashlight.

Brandenburg Boogie is a jazz arrangement of J. S. Bach's *Brandenburg Concerto No. 2*, First Movement. Drums, bass, and keyboard play throughout the composition. The flute and violin play both solo and duet passages.

3. Assign a different color flashlight to represent each of the three most important instruments—the flute, the violin, and the piano. Give the flashlights to a new group of students. **Remember which is your instrument. Shine and dance your light only when you hear it. When it is not heard, switch off your light.** Play the recording again.

Closing the Lesson

Let's turn the activity around. Let's start with the lights and create music to go along with it. Guide the students to make decisions as presented on page 97. Flashlight painters should try making curved lines, sharply pointed lines, or "dots" (produced by turning the flashlight off and on). Composers might decide that non-pitched instruments should match one color, bells a second color, and autoharps a third. (See **Materials.**)

Assign flashlight painters and instrument players. Give them several chances to present their show until painters and players are working closely together. Exchange assignments as time permits.

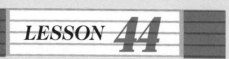 LESSON **44**

Lesson Focus

Time and Place: The way musical elements are combined into a whole reflects the origin of the music. *(D–I)*

Materials

○ **No Piano Accompaniment**
○ **Record Information:**
  • *Brandenburg Boogie*
    (Record 5 Side A Band 2)
  • *Brandenburg Concerto No. 2* in F major, First Movement
    by J. S. Bach **(bahk),** 1685–1750
    Record 5 Side A Band 3
    Marboro Festival Orchestra
    Pablo Casals, Conductor
○ **Other:** flashlights and colored cellophane paper, as prepared for Lesson 43
○ **Teacher's Resource Binder:**
  • Optional—
    Mainstreaming Suggestion 11, page M18
○ **For additional experience with time and place:** Special Times 7, page 229

 LISTENING

Brandenburg Concerto No. 2 in F Major
First Movement
by Johann Sebastian Bach

A conductor must know what each instrumentalist is playing.
This is what the conductor sees for the first nine measures.
A conductor must learn to watch many parts at the same time.

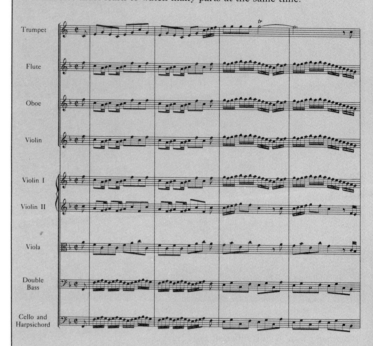

The four solo instruments are at the top of the score.
The accompanying instruments are shown below.

98

Introducing the Lesson

Begin by reviewing *Brandenburg Boogie,* Lesson 43. Choose three students to create the light show as described in that lesson.

Developing the Lesson

1. **Here is a recording I've never played for you, but some sharp ears may find something familiar.** Play *Brandenburg Concerto,* First Movement. This selection may remind some students of *Brandenburg Boogie.* If no one recognizes it, play parts of both compositions. Ask the students if they can identify anything similar about the two.

2. **Which composition do you think was written first? Why?** Students may have a variety of suggestions, such as the choice of instruments and the rhythms. Explain that the second composition (*Brandenburg Concerto*) was composed first. (See **For Your Information.**)

3. Ask the students to turn to page 97 and discuss the differences in instruments used in the two performances. **Now turn to pages 98–99.** Explain that this is a score for Bach's *Brandenburg Concerto.* Each instrumental part is written on a separate staff, just as voice parts may be written on separate staffs for songs the class sings in harmony. Play the recording of the *Brandenburg Concerto* again as the students try to follow the notation.

4. Replay portions of each composition and discuss similarities or differences. The students may notice several aspects:
    • *Brandenburg Boogie* begins with an introduction not found in *Brandenburg Concerto,* which begins with the theme played first by the flute, oboe, and violins.

For Your Information

Bach wrote *Brandenburg Concerto No. 2* in 1721. It is scored for four solo instruments: trumpet, recorder (or flute), violin, and oboe. The solo instruments are supported by strings and harpsichord.

As in *Brandenburg Boogie,* the solo instruments take turns playing the melody and countermelody. The concerto has a bright and brilliant sound because the solo instruments are frequently played in their high registers.

99

• The tempos are similar in both compositions and remain the same throughout. However, the *Brandenburg Boogie* performers add a long *ritard* at the end.
• The solo *Brandenburg Boogie* performers play more *legato,* while the *Brandenburg Concerto* performers attack each sound more cleanly, almost *staccato.*
• The accompanying instruments in *Brandenburg Boogie* play simple patterns, while the *Brandenburg Concerto* accompaniment is constantly moving.
• There is little dynamic contrast in either performance. Changes are primarily a result of the number of instruments playing (softer when solos are heard; louder when accompanying instruments join in).

5. The students may create a light show for the *Brandenburg Concerto* as they did for *Brandenburg Boogie.* Individual instruments are more difficult to follow. Rather than trying to follow a specific instrument, ask the students to focus on either the solo or the accompanying instruments as they hear the recording.

Closing the Lesson

Some fifth graders may be studying piano, violin, or other instruments. Ask if any have ever played compositions by Bach. Invite them to play for the class.

LESSON 45

Lesson Focus

Evaluation: Review concepts and skills studied in the Third Quarter.

Materials

○ **Piano Accompaniment:** page 322
○ **Record Information:**
  • Old Hound Dog Sally
    (Record 5 Side A Band 1)
  • I Believe in Music
  Record 5 Side A Band 4
    Voices: child solos, children's choir
    Accompaniment: trumpet, piano, electric organ, electric bass, percussion
○ **Instruments:** autoharp; bass and alto xylophones; alto and soprano metallophones; soprano glockenspiel
○ **Other:** a pencil for each student
○ **Teacher's Resource Binder:**
  Evaluation • **Review 3,** pages Ev14–Ev15 (Prepare one copy of each page for each student.)
  • **Musical Progress Report 3,** page Ev16

Review 3

Chords not shown on Pupil Page

I Believe in Music

Words and Music by Mac Davis

100

Introducing the Lesson

Tell the students to turn to page 94 and review "Old Hound Dog Sally." Ask them to identify the key signature, locate the tonal center, and name the chords to be used for each phrase. Review the rules for locating tonal centers by studying the key signature.

What information does the meter signature give us? (The top number tells us that the rhythm moves in fours. The lower number indicates that the quarter note moves with the beat.)

Choose several students to add the instrumental accompaniment while the class sings.

Developing the Lesson

1. Distribute Review 3 (*I Believe in Music*) and a pencil to each student. Play "I Believe in Music" through the end of Verse 1 several times as the students answer Question 1.

2. Give the students a few minutes to complete the three parts of Questions 2 and 3.

3. Play the complete recording of "I Believe in Music." Remind the students that they will need to pay particular attention to the final refrain in order to answer Question 4. You may wish to signal when this final refrain begins so the students will attend to the correct portion of the recording.

4. To answer Question 5, play the following chords on the autoharp, strumming slowly from the lowest to the highest strings. Play each chord several times before proceeding to the next:

   F major
   G minor
   C7 major
   C major

For Your Information

Form of "I Believe in Music":

1) Intro 5) Refrain
2) Verse 1 6) Verse 3
3) Refrain 7) Refrain
4) Verse 2

Verse 3 varies slightly from the original score because of the vocal improvisation. Although harmony is not given in the pupil book, the final refrain adds a homophonic part.

Answers for Review 3:
1. 2, 4, 1, 3
2. A. a

   B.

   C. These pitches should be circled: F, G, A, B♭, C, D, E, and F'.
3. A. this song will move in fours.
(or) the meter is in four.
   B. the quarter note will move with the beat.
   C. the eighth note.
4. homophony
5. major, minor, seventh, major
6. I be–lieve in (mu)-sic

(I)(I) be–lieve in (love)

I be–lieve in (mu)-sic

(I)(I) be–lieve in (love)

---

5. Play the complete recording again, this time notifying the students when the second refrain (after Verse 2) is about to begin. Explain that in order to answer Question 6, they will need to circle the word, syllable, or space between words and syllables on which a chord change occurs. Play the recording several times, as needed.

Closing the Lesson

End the class by inviting the students to sing the song with the recorded accompaniment. Adjust the balance on the recording so that only the accompaniment can be heard.

Use the information collected during this activity as well as other observations made during the Third Quarter to complete a copy of *Musical Progress Report 3* for each student. This may be sent to parents as a report and/or filed.

Lesson Focus

Rhythm: A series of beats may be organized into regular or irregular groupings by stressing certain beats. *(P–S)*

Materials

○ **No Piano Accompaniment**

○ **Record Information:**
  • Yankee Doodle Boy
    (Record 4   Side B   Band 5)
  • Norwegian Mountain March
    Record 5   Side A   Band 5
    Ensemble: accordion, violin, double bass, thimble drum

○ **Instruments:** autoharp; resonator bells D, F♯, G, A, B, C, D′, and E′; bell mallets

○ **Teacher's Resource Binder:**
  • Optional—
    Orff Activity 9, page O17

○ **For additional experience with rhythm:** Describe 8, page 180

The Fourth Quarter

Norwegian Mountain March

Traditional

102

Introducing the Lesson

Review "Yankee Doodle Boy" on page 84. **Who remembers why we decided that this song is a march and not a waltz?** (As a rule, marches move in twos; waltzes move in threes.)

There are always exceptions to the rules. Who knows a spelling rule that has an exception to it? ("I" before "E" except after "C") Ask the students if they can figure out the rule and its exception in the music on page 102. Guide the students to conclude that this music is called a march, even though it moves in threes rather than twos. Play the recording. **Can you march to it? Does it seem to move in threes, twos, or fours?** Some students may sense that the "rhythm of the accent" (the first beat of each measure) makes it possible to think of the beats as being grouped in fours (one beat per measure), while others will sense the movement in threes. Play the recording again.

Developing the Lesson

1. Ask the students to look at the meter signature and the notation. **Which note lasts for one beat?** (the quarter note) **Which note represents the shortest sound?** (the same note) **Will the rhythm be easy or difficult to learn?** (It will be easy because most notes are the same length.) Establish the shortest sound. Ask the class to chant the rhythm on the syllable "boo."

2. Explain that many folk dances describe actions that tell a story. In the legend for "Norwegian Mountain March," the march represents a guide walking in front of two mountain climbers. The guide must watch out for them.

    OPTIONAL

3. As the students listen to the recording, they should practice tapping on alternate legs, accenting the first of every three taps: **right**, left, right; **left**, right, left, and so on. With the stu-

Section A:

Step forward, taking small steps:
Right–left–right **Left**–right–left

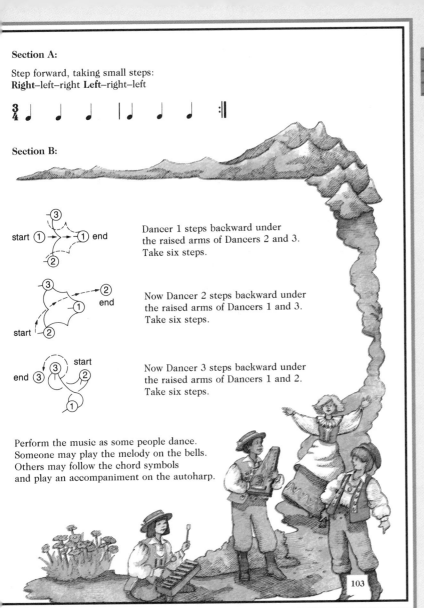

Section B:

Dancer 1 steps backward under
the raised arms of Dancers 2 and 3.
Take six steps.

Now Dancer 2 steps backward under
the raised arms of Dancers 1 and 3.
Take six steps.

Now Dancer 3 steps backward under
the raised arms of Dancers 1 and 2.
Take six steps.

Perform the music as some people dance.
Someone may play the melody on the bells.
Others may follow the chord symbols
and play an accompaniment on the autoharp.

103

For Your Information

Dance formation for "Norwegian Mountain March":

Three people in a triangle formation all hold hands. (See pictures and patterns in the pupil book.) Dancer 1 is the leader; Dancer 2 is on the left, and Dancer 3 is on the right.

Dance steps for "Norwegian Mountain March":

A Section (Measures 1–8):

Starting with the right foot, run forward, one step for each beat: **right**-left-right; **left**-right-left.

B Section (Measures 9–16):

· Measures 9–10: Dancer 1 takes six small steps backward under the raised arms of Dancers 2 and 3 who in turn, take six small steps in place.

Measures 11–12: With right arm raised, Dancer 2 now passes under the arch made by Dancers 1 and 3, completing the movement in six small steps.

Measures 13–14: Dancer 3 passes under arch made by Dancers 1 and 2 in the same manner as Dancer 2 in Measures 11–12.

Measures 15–16: Dancer 1 turns under his or her own raised right arm and all face forward again.

Repeat dance steps for Sections A and B each time the music is repeated.

dents still seated, ask them to transfer the action from hands to feet.

4. Ask the students to listen quietly to the recording. **Raise your hand when you think something in the music suggests we should change motions.** (Measure 9)

5. Demonstrate the dance steps for Section B, using three students as models. (See **For Your Information** and illustrations on the pupil page.) Stress that hands must remain joined. **(No one wants to fall off the mountain!)**

6. Organize the class into groups of three. Help the groups to walk through the entire dance several times without the music. When they can perform the steps in an appropriate tempo, add the music. Play the recording as the students enjoy the dance.

Closing the Lesson

Return to page 102. Help the students learn to play the melody on the bells and the harmony on the autoharp while the class sings on the syllable "loo." When they can perform the two parts together fluently, some students may perform the dance while others sing and play.

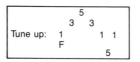

LESSON 47

Lesson Focus

Rhythm: Individual sounds and silences within a rhythmic line may be longer than, shorter than, or the same as other sounds within the line.
Melody: Each pitch within a melody moves in relation to a home tone. *(P–S)*

Materials

- **Piano Accompaniment:** page 326
- **Record Information:**
  - Turn the Glasses Over
    Record 5   Side A   Band 6
    Voices: children's choir
    Accompaniment: woodwind quintet
- **Instruments:** autoharp; resonator bells C and F; bell mallet
- **Other:** Prepare "Plus" and "Minus" cards by drawing a "+" or a "−" on 3 × 5″ index cards. Make approximately 75 "+" and 50 "−" cards.
- **Teacher's Resource Binder:**
  - **Activity Sheet 26,** page A37 (Prepare a copy for each student.)
  - Optional—
    Kodaly Activity 13, page K20
    Orff Activity 1, page O2
- **For additional experience with melody:** Special Times 14, page 244

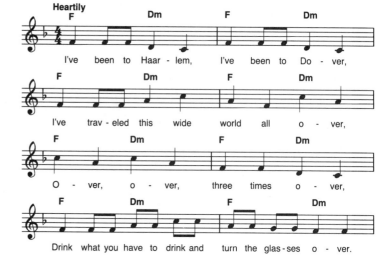

Turn the Glasses Over

American Singing Game

I've been to Haar - lem, I've been to Do - ver,
I've trav - eled this wide world all o - ver,
O - ver, o - ver, three times o - ver,
Drink what you have to drink and turn the glas - ses o - ver.

104

Introducing the Lesson

Have you ever heard of a spelldown or a spelling bee? Explain that students have been playing this game since the days of the one-room schoolhouse. **Who knows how it is played?** (See **For Your Information**.) **Who has ever participated in one?**

Developing the Lesson

1. **Today we are going to play a game that is similar to a spelldown.** Divide the class into four teams. Hand out Activity Sheet 26 (*Spelldown*) to each student. Explain that in Round 1, the students are to look at the rhythm patterns on their sheets. Call out the number of the pattern that they are to chant. (Choose patterns according to the ability of the students. A less able student may be given an easier example than a student with greater

ability. Thus both can succeed.) Give each student one rhythm to chant. Hand out a "Plus" card for each correct response and a "Minus" card for each incorrect response. (See **Materials**.)

2. For Round 2 explain that the rhythms will be chanted from "Turn the Glasses Over" on page 104 in the pupil book. Observe that many of these rhythms were ones that were on the activity sheet used during Round 1. The first student will chant Measure 1, the second will chant Measure 2, and so on. **Be ready to chant your measure without interrupting the flow of the steady beat.** Explain that when one student gets to the end of the song, the next student should begin the song again until all have had an opportunity to chant a pattern. As each performs his or her chant, hand out the appropriate "Plus" or "Minus" cards.

F   Dm   F   Dm

Sail - ing east,   sail - ing west,

F   Dm   F   Dm

Sail - ing o - ver the o - cean,

F   Dm   F   Dm

Bet - ter watch out when the boat be - gins to rock,

F   Dm   F

Or you'll lose your girl in the o - cean.

Learn accompaniment parts for this song.

F   Dm   F   Dm

Strum autoharp: 4/4 ♩ ♩ | ♩ ♩ :||

Play this on bells or piano:

1   5,   1   5,

105

For Your Information

Rules for a spelldown:
Students stand in a line. Each student is given a word to spell. If the word is spelled correctly, the student may continue to stand. If the spelling is incorrect the student must sit down. The last person standing is the winner.

3. For Round 3 return to the patterns on the activity sheet. **Now sing your pattern with scale numbers instead of just chanting the rhythm.** Establish the tonality in F and help the students "tune up." Then engage the students in the game as played in Steps 1 and 2.

4. Ask the students to return to page 104 for Round 4. As before, they should start at the beginning of the song, this time singing scale numbers. **This will be a little harder because you must sing the numbers in the correct rhythm.**

5. **Here is a bonus round!** Each team may pick one person to sing either the first eight or the last eight measures of the song without stopping. The bonus round can be worth up to 8 points, one point per measure. On this round, play the autoharp to accompany the chosen singers.

OPTIONAL

6. Tally up the points. Determine the winning team. **Actually you are all winners! You are learning to read music by yourselves. Many adults cannot do what you are doing.**

Closing the Lesson

Ask the entire class to sing the song. If there is time, add the accompaniments shown at the bottom of page 105.

Lesson Focus

Rhythm: Individual sounds and silences within a rhythmic line may be longer than, shorter than, or the same as other sounds within the line.

Melody: Each pitch within a melody moves in relation to a home tone. *(P–S)*

Materials

○ **Piano Accompaniment:** page 327

○ **Record Information:**
- Garden Song
  Record 5 Side B Band 1
  Voices: children's choir
  Accompaniment: flute, oboe, acoustic guitar, electric piano, electric bass, percussion
- Allegretto from *Symphony No. 7* by Ludwig van Beethoven 1770–1827
  Record 5 Side B Band 2
  New York Philharmonic
  Leonard Bernstein, conductor

○ **Instruments:** autoharp; resonator bells E, F♯, G, G♯, A, and B; bell mallet

○ **Teacher's Resource Binder:**
- Optional—
  Biography 2, page B3

○ **For additional experience with form and expression:** Perform 16, page 164; Describe 3, page 172

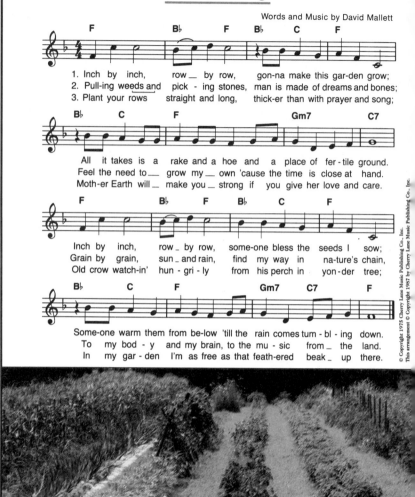

Garden Song

Words and Music by David Mallett

1. Inch by inch, row __ by row, gon-na make this gar-den grow;
2. Pull-ing weeds and pick - ing stones, man is made of dreams and bones;
3. Plant your rows straight and long, thick-er than with prayer and song;

All it takes is a rake and a hoe and a place of fer - tile ground.
Feel the need to __ grow my __ own 'cause the time is close at hand.
Moth-er Earth will __ make you __ strong if you give her love and care.

Inch by inch, row __ by row, some-one bless the seeds I sow;
Grain by grain, sun __ and rain, find my way in na-ture's chain,
Old crow watch-in' hun - gri - ly from his perch in yon-der tree;

Some-one warm them from be-low 'till the rain comes tum - bl - ing down.
To my bod - y and my brain, to the mu - sic from __ the land.
In my gar - den I'm as free as that feath-ered beak __ up there.

© Copyright 1975 Cherry Lane Music Publishing Co. Inc.
This arrangement © Copyright 1987 by Cherry Lane Music Publishing Co. Inc.

Introducing the Lesson OPTIONAL

Read the lyrics to "Garden Song" on page 106. **Is the singer only talking about growing gardens?** Help the students sense that this poem might be considered a metaphor, the words of which suggest a larger idea of growing—the growth of one's self and the growth of others around us.

Developing the Lesson

1. **Can you describe the structure of this song? Let's call the first phrase A. What three choices did the composer have for the next phrase?** (Repeat A, alter it to A', or introduce a new idea, B.) **What did this composer decide?** (B) Follow the same line of questioning to help the students decide that the melody of Phrase 3 is A and that of Phrase 4 is B (except for the slight change made at the end so that the song returns to the tonal center).

Knowing the form should make the song easier to learn. How many lines or phrases do we need to practice? (only two plus the change at the end)

2. Choose a student to set the tempo of the shortest sound and ask the others to read the rhythm of Phrases A and B, chanting on the syllable "too."

3. Scan the melody. We will warm up on measures that go lower than 1. **Which measures are they?** (4 and 7) Ask the students to sing those patterns. Then encourage them to sing the entire melody on the syllable "loo" as you accompany them on the autoharp.

4. Point out that whole songs that use very little material can still be interesting. **The mind likes to hear parts repeated. If there are no repeated parts, it is difficult to remember**

Allegretto

from *Symphony No. 7*

by Ludwig van Beethoven

Slowly

107

LESSON 48

For Your Information

Structure of "Allegretto" (excerpt):

The movement opens with a sustained chord on wind instruments.

Theme is announced by violas, accompanied by cellos.

Theme is repeated, now by second violins. Viola and first cello add countermelody.

Third statement of themes performed by first violins, while the second violins play countermelody.

Fourth statement is played by wind instruments and horns, while countermelody is in first violins.

and make connections to other parts. Explain that Beethoven is a famous composer who liked to expand a little idea by using repetitions. Ask the students to turn to page 107 and look at "Allegretto" from Beethoven's *Symphony No. 7*. **Beethoven used this theme as the basis for a composition that lasts for ten minutes. If you look carefully, you will see that this theme consists of a simple melody. However, Beethoven used it to create a great piece of music.**

Give several students an opportunity to play the theme on resonator bells. (See **Materials**.) Invite the class to hum along so that they may become familiar with the melody before listening to the orchestral piece.

5. Ask the students to listen to the first part of this long composition. They should follow the theme in their books. **The wind instruments begin with a long chord. Then you will hear**

the viola softly introduce the melody. Play the recording through four statements of the theme (marked by a visible band). Then turn down the volume and stop the recording.

6. **Did you hear the theme more than once?** (yes) **Listen again. Count how many times you hear the theme.** (4)

Closing the Lesson

Beethoven made changes each of the four times. What did he do? The students will offer a variety of suggestions. (See **For Your Information**.)

On another day play the rest of the composition to hear what Beethoven did in the middle of the composition and to discover whether he ever returned to this theme.

LESSON 49

Lesson Focus

Form: A musical whole is a combination of smaller segments. *(D–S)*

Materials

- **Piano Accompaniment:** page 328
- **Record Information:**
  - Catch a Falling Star
    Record 5   Side B   Band 3
    Voices: children's choir
    Accompaniment: electric guitar, electric piano, electric bass, percussion
- **Instruments:** two sets of resonator bells and glockenspiels with pitches E, F, G, and A; mallets
- **For additional experience with form:** Special Times 9, page 232; Describe 17, page 196

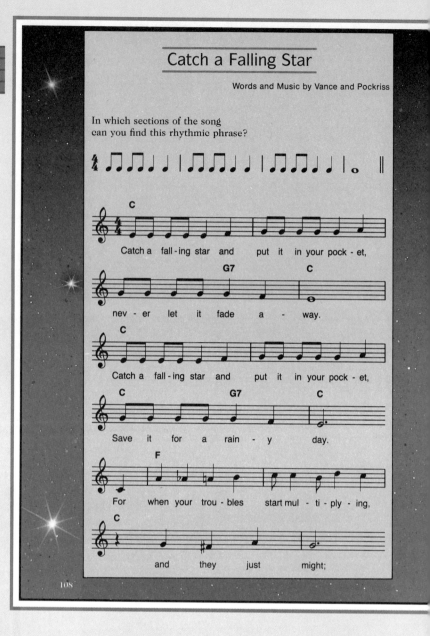

Introducing the Lesson

Ask the students to open their books to page 108 and look at the rhythmic phrase shown at the top of the page. Clap the phrase using "short" for eighth notes, "long" for quarter notes, and "lo-ong" for whole notes.

Developing the Lesson

1. Ask the students to find this rhythmic phrase in the song. **How many times is the phrase repeated?** (4 times) Challenge them to use the location of the phrases as a clue to how many sections there are in this song. They should readily see that the rhythmic phrase shown at the top of the page is found in Section A and that Section B is rhythmically different. The form of the song is **A B A.**

2. Help the students learn to sing the song. The students will discover that the melody in Section A moves up and down in a simple, repeated, stepwise pattern, while the melody in Section B includes some skips. When the students are familiar with the melody, divide them into two groups and sing the last Section A as a round. Group 2 begins when Group 1 reaches the second measure.

Closing the Lesson

Section A may be played either as an introduction, an accompaniment, or a coda on resonator bells or glockenspiels. Give the instruments to at least two students. The students should find this stepwise pattern easy to perform on the bells by reading the song score. **Could this part also be played as a round?** (yes)

LESSON 50

Lesson Focus

Rhythm: A series of beats may be organized into regular or irregular groupings by stressing certain beats. *(D–E)*

Materials

○ **Piano Accompaniment:** page 325
○ **Record Information:**
  • Sim Sa-La-Bim
    Record 5   Side B   Band 4
    Voices: children's choir
    Accompaniment: woodwind quintet
  • Rumanian Dance No. 5 from
    Rumanian Folk Dances
    by Béla Bartók (**bahr**-tawk)
    1881–1945
    Record 5   Side B   Band 5
    Gyorgy Sandor, piano
○ **Instruments:** drum; drumstick or hard mallet
○ **Other:** overhead projector
○ **Teacher's Resource Binder:**
  Activity Sheets • **Activity Sheet 27,** page A38
    (Prepare a transparency of the activity sheet.)
  • Optional—
    Kodaly Activity 10, page K14
    Orff Activity 6, page O10
○ **For additional experience with rhythm:** Describe 13, page 188; Special Times 10, page 233

Sim Sa-La-Bim

Danish Folk Song

1. High in a tree a crow - ow - ow,
2. Then came a wick - ed hunt - er
3. He shot that poor old crow - ow - ow,

Sim sa - la - bim bam boom, sa - la - doo, sa - la - dim!

High in a tree a crow - ow - ow sat.
Then came a wick - ed hunt - er a - long.
He shot that poor old crow - ow - ow dead.

4. Then came a pretty maiden along,
   Sim sa-la-bim bam boom, sa-la-doo, sa-la-dim!
   Then came a pretty maiden along.

5. She took the poor old crow-ow-ow home,
   Sim sa-la-bim bam boom, sa-la-doo, sa-la-dim!
   She took the poor old crow-ow-ow home.

110

Introducing the Lesson

Display a transparency of Activity Sheet 27 (*Sports Chants*). Have the class chant the names of the sports that appear at the top of the activity sheet, noting that the names are grouped according to whether they are comprised of two or three syllables. Discuss the meaning of the terms **symmetrical** and **asymmetrical**. Help the students decide, by examining the pictures, that objects are symmetrical when two halves on either side of an imaginary line are identical but opposite (a mirror image). When the two halves are different, the objects are asymmetrical. Have the students find other objects in the room that are symmetrical or asymmetrical.

Developing the Lesson

1. **Why are the rhythm patterns on the lower left side of the activity sheet described as** **symmetrical and those on the lower right as asymmetrical?** (The notes on the left are grouped the same way for the entire measure either in all sets of two or all sets of three. Those on the right are mixtures of sets of two and sets of three.) Chant the patterns together to help students sense the differences. Guide them to discover that patterns within the same meter may be grouped symmetrically or asymmetrically (such as in the $\frac{4}{4}$ and $\frac{9}{8}$ examples shown on the activity sheet).

2. **Is the rhythm of the song on page 110 symmetrical or asymmetrical? Why?** (It is asymmetrical because there is no way to divide five into symmetrical sets.) Ask the students to chant the words of the song to decide where the natural accents of the text fall. Determine that each measure is organized into a set of three followed by a set of two (3 plus 2).

Forward—Back!

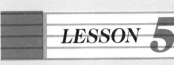

Drummer—Play on drum head: Play on rim of drum:

Movers—Step **forward** when the drummer plays on the drum head.

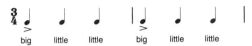

big   little   little   big   little   little

Bend your knee slightly on each accented beat.
Step **backward** when the drummer plays on the rim.

step   step   step   step

LISTENING

Rumanian Dance No. 5

from *Rumanian Folk Dances*

by Béla Bartók

Use your forward-backward movements with this dance.
Listen during the first four measures:

Be ready to move:

Can you describe the changes in meter for the entire dance?

111

---

3. Learn the melody of "Sim Sa-La-Bim" by using scale numbers. Guide the class to identify the tonal center by studying the key signature (F). Tune up using the pitches 1–3–5. Then sing the song, first with scale numbers then with words. Perform the complete song, adding body sounds to reinforce the asymmetrical feeling.

clap   snap   snap   clap   snap

4. Guide the students to follow the instructions on page 111. The drummer should play the ¾ pattern on the head of the drum with a stick or hard mallet. He or she should strike the wooden rim of the drum on the ¾ pattern. The drummer will need to move back and forth between the two meters to create asymmetrical metric groupings while the class steps the pattern as suggested in their books.

Closing the Lesson

Play the recording of "Rumanian Dance No. 5." Discover that it begins with a four-measure introduction, then repeats the asymmetrical pattern shown at the bottom of page 111 four times. Play the recording of this brief composition several times until the students are familiar with the music. Invite them to move to the dance, using the forward-backward step they practiced earlier.

111

Lesson Focus

Rhythm: A series of beats may be organized into regular or irregular groupings by stressing certain beats. *(C–I)*

Materials

○ **Piano Accompaniment:** page 330
○ **Record Information:**
  • Rumanian Dance No. 5
    (Record 5 Side B Band 5)
  • Gerakina
    Record 5 Side B Band 6
    Voices: children's choir
    Accompaniment: clarinet, bouzouki, outi, accordion, acoustic guitar, percussion
○ **Instruments:** finger cymbals; tambourine; assorted non-pitched percussion instruments
○ **Other:** Activity Sheet 27, from Lesson 50; overhead projector
○ **Teacher's Resource Binder:**

  [Activity Sheets] • **Activity Sheet 28**, page A39 (Prepare a copy for each student.)
  • Optional—
    Orff Activity 7, page O12

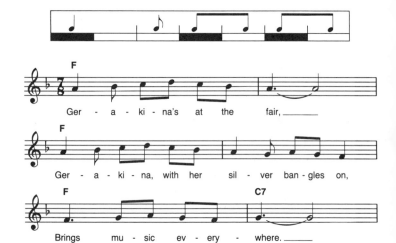

Gerakina

English Words by Margaret Marks

Greek Folk Song

Ger - a - ki - na's at the fair, _____

Ger - a - ki - na, with her sil - ver ban - gles on,

Brings mu - sic ev - ery - where. _____

Introducing the Lesson

Begin the class by reviewing "Rumanian Dance No. 5," page 111. Invite the students to perform the "forward-backward" dance step learned during that lesson.

Developing the Lesson

1. Divide the class into two groups and perform the pattern shown by the rhythm ruler at the top of page 112. Group 1 taps the shortest sound while Group 2 chants the rhythm of the melody on the syllable "doo." **Is this pattern symmetrical or asymmetrical?** (It is asymmetrical because the seven short sounds are grouped unequally: 3 plus 2 plus 2.)

2. Draw attention to the meter signature at the beginning of the song "Gerakina." Agree that

this is the symbol that describes the pattern they just practiced. Play the recording as the students join you in lightly tapping this pattern on the knees:

Right knee: **7**
Left knee: **8**

3. Examine the melodic notation, noticing how frequently the melody is based on these rhythmic patterns:

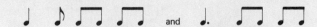

and

Invite the students to softly sing along with the recording. When they can confidently sing the song, some students may add these instrument parts:

Ring, pret - ty sil - ver ban - gles,

Jin - gle jin - gle jan - gle, Sing in the air,

Ger - a - ki - na danc - ing at the fair.

All the vil - lage folk will come to the square,

For the jin - gle jan - gle dance at the fair. _____

113

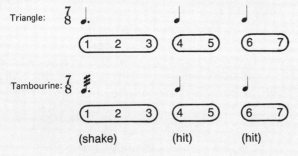

Triangle: $\frac{7}{8}$

① 2 3   ④ 5   ⑥ 7

Tambourine: $\frac{7}{8}$

① 2 3   ④ 5   ⑥ 7

(shake)   (hit)   (hit)

Closing the Lesson

Remind the students of the "sports chants" (Activity Sheet 27) used in the previous lesson. **Today you are to create your own composition based on a category of your choice.** Distribute Activity Sheet 28 (*Asymmetric Composition*). Students may work in small groups.

Give groups approximately ten minutes to plan their compositions, select their instruments (see

Materials), and practice. Call the class together and have each group perform its composition. Decide whether each meets the criteria of the activity sheet and is asymmetrical. Invite those groups whose compositions are particularly interesting and appealing to teach their chants to the rest of the class.

Lesson Focus

Melody: Each pitch within a melody moves in relation to a home tone.
Melody: A series of pitches bounded by the octave "belong together," forming a tonal set. *(D–I)*

Materials

○ **Piano Accompaniment:** page 332
○ **Record Information:**
  • Spider on the Floor
    (Record 4   Side A   Band 7)
  • Magic Penny
    Record 6   Side A   Band 1
    Voices: children's choir
    Accompaniment: two acoustic guitars, double bass, percussion
○ **Other:** Activity Sheets 18 and 19, from Lesson 32
○ **Teacher's Resource Binder:**
  • Optional—
    Curriculum Correlation 10, page C13
    Mainstreaming Suggestion 12, page M19

Magic Penny

Words and Music by Malvina Reynolds

Love is some-thing if you give it a-way,—
Give it a-way,— give it a-way,—
Love is some-thing if you give it a-way,—
You end up hav-ing more.

Introducing the Lesson

Review "Spider on the Floor," page 70. Ask the students to decide which pitch they would like to use as the tonal center. Help them figure out the pitches needed to develop a scale from that pitch. (If necessary, review the information learned when completing Activity Sheets 18 and 19. See **Materials.**) Write the key signature and the scale on the chalkboard.

Developing the Lesson

1. Ask the students to look at the score for "Magic Penny" on page 114. **In what key is this song written?** (E♭) Write the following pattern on the chalkboard:

Explain that there is another way to be sure that the key has been identified correctly. **If the tonal center is E♭, what pitches of the scale will be used most frequently, especially when there are skips?** (1, 3, 5) **In the key of E♭, what will those pitches be?** (E♭, G, B♭)

2. Guide the class to scan the notation and observe that Phrases 1 and 2 begin and end with one or more of these pitches. (Each phrase is four measures long.) In Section B (Phrases 3 and 4) each two-measure pattern also returns to these same pitches.

3. Play the recording while the students determine the design of the complete song. Agree that
  • The song is made up of three sections, each including two phrases.
  • Section A consists of two similar phrases, A and A'.

It's just like a mag - ic pen - ny;

Hold it tight and you won't have an - y.

Lend it; spend_ it, and you'll have so man - y

they'll roll all o - ver the floor, for

D.C. al Fine

115

- Section B has the same form, **B** and **B′**.
- The song comes to a close with a repetition of Section A.

4. Help the students learn the song as you play the accompanying chords on the piano. You may wish to adjust the balance on the recording so that the students may sing independently with the recorded accompaniment.

Closing the Lesson OPTIONAL

When they know the melody, help the students add harmonizing parts. Section A may be accompanied with the following pattern:

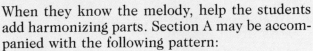

Love is some thing.

During the first six measures of Section B, guide one group to sing the melody a third lower:

End this section by again singing in unison (that is, everyone singing the same pitches).

115

LESSON 53

Lesson Focus

Melody: Each pitch within a melody moves in relation to a home tone.
Melody: A series of pitches bounded by the octave "belong together," forming a tonal set. *(D–I)*

Materials

○ **No Piano Accompaniment**

○ **Record Information:**
  • Magic Penny
    (Record 6   Side A   Band 1)
  • America, America
    Record 6   Side A   Band 2
    Voices: children's choir
  • Whippoorwill Round
    Record 6   Side A   Band 3
    Voices: children's choir
    Accompaniment: recorder

○ **Instruments:** bass xylophone; glockenspiel; mallets

○ **Teacher's Resource Binder:**
  | Evaluation | • Optional—
    Checkpoint 4, page Ev17
    Kodaly Activity 9, page K14

America, America

Traditional

116

Introducing the Lesson

Review "Magic Penny" on page 114, singing the song with the added harmony parts as suggested at the end of the lesson.

Developing the Lesson

1. Ask the students to examine the songs on pages 116 and 117. **In what key are these two songs? How will you decide?** Agree that the students should study the key signatures. Decide that both represent the key of G.

2. **How will you decide if you are right?** Recall the discussion when learning "Magic Penny" that songs frequently center around scale steps 1–3–5. **What pitches will you expect to find at the beginning and end of phrases and in patterns that move by skips?** (G, B, and D)

3. **Does the melody for "Whippoorwill Round" frequently return to these pitches?** (yes) Draw a blank chart (as shown below) on the chalkboard. Ask the students to name all of the pitches found in "Whippoorwill Round." Put them in Row 1 in the order shown:

Whippoorwill Round:	(G)		(A)		(B)	(C)		(D)		(E)		(F#)	(G)
America, America:	(E)		(F#)	(G)			(A)		(B)	(C)		(D)		(E)

Look at the chart on page 117. Do the pitches used in this song form a major scale? (yes)

4. **What about "America, America"?** Guide the class to realize that this melody centers around E, G, and B instead of G, B, and D. **In what key is this song if not in G Major?** Guide the students to follow the same procedure as in Step 3. As they call out the letter names of each different pitch they locate, write them

116

Whippoorwill Round

Traditional

1. Gone to bed is the set - ting sun,

2. Night is com - ing and day is done, Whip-poor -

3. will, whip-poor-will, has just ___ be - gun.

Add an accompaniment:

Glockenspiel

Arrange the pitches used in each song in order,
starting with the last pitch of the song.
Which scale does your pattern match?

Major Scale	X		X		X	X		X		X		X X
Minor Scale	X		X X		X		X X		X		X
Whole Tone	X		X		X		X		X		X		X

117

---

in the appropriate boxes in Row 2 of the chart
on the chalkboard. (Although there is no C in
the melody, add it to the chart.)

5. Ask the students to compare the scale they
built with the chart on page 117. **What kind
of a scale have we created?** (minor)

6. Invite the students to choose one of the songs
to learn to sing. Practice the rhythm. Then
sing the scale on which the song is based
starting on low 5 (5,–6,–7,–1–2–3–4–5).

Closing the Lesson

Help the students perform their chosen song with
the appropriate ostinato accompaniment as
shown below each song on the pupil page.

When the students are secure in their ability to
perform the melody in unison, invite them to
sing the song as a round. Group 2 begins when
Group 1 reaches the numeral 2 in the song.

LESSON 54

Lesson Focus

Timbre: The quality of a sound is determined by the sound source. *(D–I)*

Materials

○ **Piano Accompaniment:** page 334
○ **Record Information:**
  • *Polonaise in A Flat*
    by Frédéric Chopin (**show**-pan), 1810–1849
    Record 6 Side A Band 4
    Vladamir Horowitz, pianist
  • *In Dulci Jubilo*
    by J. S. Bach, 1685–1750
    Record 6 Side A Band 5
    E. Power Biggs, organist
  • *Funkarello* (excerpt)
    by Bill Evans, 1929–1980
    Record 6 Side A Band 6
    The Bill Evans Trio
  • *Joyful*
    by Aaron Briggs
    Record 6 Side A Band 7
    Aaron Briggs, synthesizer
  • Sinfonia from
    Entrance of the Queen of Sheba
    by G. F. Handel, 1685–1759
    Record 6 Side A Band 8
    harpsichord

(continued on next page)

Keyboard Instruments

Can you identify which keyboard instruments you are hearing?

All of these instruments have keyboards. Why don't they sound the same?

In what ways would the music of the pipe-organ selection be different if performed on the harpsichord?

118

Introducing the Lesson

Focus the students' attention on the pictures of keyboard instruments on pages 118–119. Discuss the similarities and differences that can be observed by looking at the pictures. **How do you think each keyboard will sound? Will they have similar or different qualities of sound?**

Developing the Lesson

1. Play the recorded examples of music performed on each of the instruments. Ask the students to identify which keyboard instruments they are hearing. (See **Materials**.) As each is heard, discuss how sound is produced on that instrument. (See **Teacher's Glossary** for information on each.)

2. After the students have associated the sounds of the instruments with the pictures, read the question at the bottom of page 118. Guide the students as they compare the sounds of the instruments.

Closing the Lesson

Play the recording of "The Old Piano Roll Blues." Briefly discuss the sound of this piano and the mechanical roll that was used to create the music. (See **For Your Information.**) **Which of the other instruments we heard sounds most like this?** (a grand piano) Discuss with the students that the piano was a very important object in the home around the turn of the century. People who owned pianos were very popular and often envied. The piano was a popular entertainment center around which family and friends frequently gathered.

Explain that if no one was able to play the piano, the mechanism to turn the piano into a player piano was inserted, making an "expert pianist" out of anyone who had the strength to keep

The Old Piano Roll Blues

Words and Music by Cy Coben

I wanna hear it again, I wanna hear it again,
The Old Piano Roll Blues.
We're sittin' at an upright, my sweetie and me,
Pushin' on the pedals, makin' sweet harmony.
When we hear rinkity tink, and we hear plinkity plink,
We cuddle closer it seems.
And while we kiss, kiss, kiss away all our cares,
The player piano's playin' razz-a-ma-tazz.
I wanna hear it again, I wanna hear it again,
The Old Piano Roll Blues!

119

Materials (*continued*)
- The Old Piano Roll Blues
  Record 6   Side A   Band 9
  Voice: children's choir
  Accompaniment: piano
- **Teacher's Resource Binder:**
  - Optional—
    Biography 3, page B5

For Your Information
A piano roll is a roll of paper that is perforated to allow air to pass through it. The air provides pressure that causes the appropriate piano keys to play. The "performer" pumps pedals to create the air flow. (In modern player pianos, the flow may be created electronically.)

pumping the pedals in a steady rhythm. The family could listen or sing along. **Are player pianos still available?** (While they are not manufactured today as often as in the past, some students may be familiar with their sound.)

Invite the students to follow the words on page 119 and sing along with the recorded player-piano sound.

The Old Piano Roll Blues
Words and Music by Cy Coben

LESSON 55

Lesson Focus

Melody: A series of pitches may move up, down, or remain the same. *(P–I)*

Materials

o **Piano Accompaniment:** page 333
o **Record Information:**
  • The Old Piano Roll Blues
    (Record 6 Side A Band 9)
  • Solomon Levi
    Record 6 Side A Band 10
    Voices: children's choir
    Accompaniment: string ensemble, piano
o **Instruments:** any available keyboard instruments
o **Teacher's Resource Binder:**

  `Activity Sheets` • **Activity Sheet 29,** page A40 (Prepare a copy for each student.)

o **For additional experience with harmony:** Perform 13, page 158

Solomon Levi

Traditional

F
My name is Sol - o - mon Le - vi, and I

B♭
live on Sa - lem Street;

C7
That's where to buy your coats and vests and

F
ev - ery - thing that's neat.

F
Sec - ond - hand - ed ul - ster - ettes and

B♭
o - ver - coats so fine,

C7
For all the boys that trade with me at

C7   **F**
Hun - dred and for - ty - nine.

120

Introducing the Lesson

Ask the students to sing "The Old Piano Roll Blues" (page 119) learned in the previous lesson. Introduce a new song, "Solomon Levi," on page 120. Ask the class to examine the notation and determine how many different pitches there are in the song. (4) **Do the pitches move by steps or by skips?** (by steps) **When do the pitches remain the same?** (Pitches are repeated several times before moving up or down to the next pitch.) Establish the tonality and guide the class to sing the melody.

Developing the Lesson

1. Provide each student with a copy of Activity Sheet 29 (*Play a Keyboard Instrument*). The students should sing the song while using just the index finger on their right hands to tap the rhythm of the melody on the "drum head" shown on the activity sheet.

2. Ask the class to sing the melody of "Solomon Levi" again, this time following the piano score on page 121. Sing in a slow tempo. As the students sing, guide them to play the song by tapping the rhythm and the up-down movement of the melody on the stairsteps found on the activity sheet.

3. **This time tap the pitches on your practice keyboard. The melody begins on C. On what word will you move up to D?** ("live") **to E?** ("where") **Then what happens?** (The melody moves back down.) Discuss the movement of the entire melody in this fashion. Then invite the students to sing the melody as they touch the appropriate keys, tapping the rhythm of the melody.

4. Send several students to the keyboard(s) to play the song while others continue to practice on their activity sheet. Keyboard players

120

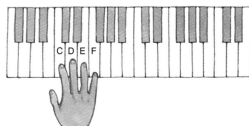

Play a Keyboard Instrument

Play using

- one finger
- several fingers, one after the other

Piano Score:

```
F ————————————————————————————————————————
E ————————————————————————————————————————
D ———————————————————————————— live on Salem Street;
C — My name is Solomon Levi, and I ——————————

F ————————————————————————————————————————
E —— where to buy your coats and vests ——————
D — That's ——————————————————— and ——————
C ———————————————————— everything that's neat.

F ————————————————————————————————————————
E ————————————————————————————————————————
D ———————————————————————————— overcoats so fine,
C — Second-handed ulsterettes and ——————————

F ———————————————————————————————— nine.
E —— all the boys that trade with me ———————— ty
D — For ————————————— at ——————————— for-
C ———————————————————— Hundred and
```

121

---

may use one finger or they may wish to use a different finger for each key (thumb for C, "pointer" for D, and so on). Encourage them to strive for an accurate rhythmic flow of the melody as they play.

Closing the Lesson

Play "Solomon Levi" as a duet. Select one of the performers to play the melody while you play a chordal accompaniment. Perform the song in an **A A′ A** form. For **A** the class sings with the accompaniment. For **A′** the students and teacher play the song with no singing.

LESSON 56

Lesson Focus

Harmony: Chords and melody may move simultaneously in relation to each other. *(P–S)*

Materials

- ○ **Piano Accompaniment:** page 338
- ○ **Record Information:**
  - La Cucaracha
    (Record 2 Side A Band 5)
  - This Land Is Your Land
  - ▭ **Record 6 Side B Band 1**
    Voices: baritone, children's choir
    Accompaniment: banjo, guitar, bass, tambourine
- ○ **Instruments:** autoharp; maracas
- ○ **Teacher's Resource Binder:**
  - **Activity Sheet 30**, page A41 (Prepare a copy for each student.)
  - Optional—
    Biography 4, page B7
    Enrichment Activity 9, page E12
- ○ **For additional experience with harmony:** Perform 9, page 148

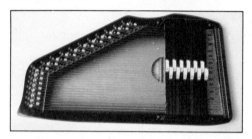

Play the Autoharp

How to play:
Learn the basics.

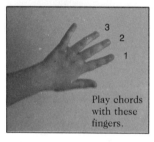

Press chord buttons firmly with fingers of left hand.

Play chords with these fingers.

Strum with right hand crossed over left. Use a pick.

Try different strums.
All strings: up stroke (away from body)
down stroke (toward body)

Some strings: low _____   middle _____   high _____

122

Introducing the Lesson

Introduce several autoharp playing methods to the entire class. Demonstrate the basic playing position and discuss the various procedures. Then assign the students times during music class or at special times through the week to work independently or in pairs. Display Activity Sheet 30 (*Rules for Playing the Autoharp*) in work areas so that it will be readily available for student reference.

Developing the Lesson

1. Ask the students to look at the pictures and instructions on page 122. Guide them to discover that

   - Low strings are the thickest and largest. High strings are the thinnest and shortest.
   - A sound is produced when a string is strummed or picked.

   - To produce a chord, the bar must be pressed down firmly.

2. Ask one or more students to demonstrate the correct playing position. Ask them to locate the G chord. They are to hold the G major button down firmly with the left index finger. Strum from low to high with the right hand crossing over the left. Strum with a steady beat while the class sings "Are You Sleeping?" Ask the performer to strum the G chord once to help the class locate the starting pitch (G) before they begin to sing.

3. Follow the instructions on page 123 and help the students learn to play the chords to accompany "This Land Is Your Land" and "La Cucaracha." (See page 186 for the complete melody to "This Land Is Your Land" and page 26 for the complete melody to "La Cucaracha.") Review the songs if the students are

122

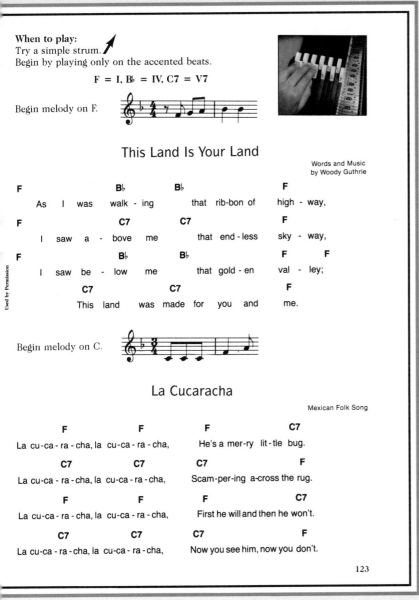

When to play:
Try a simple strum.
Begin by playing only on the accented beats.

F = I, B♭ = IV, C7 = V7

Begin melody on F.

This Land Is Your Land

Words and Music
by Woody Guthrie

Used by Permission

F		B♭		B♭		F	
As	I	was	walk - ing	that rib-bon of	high -	way,	

F		C7		C7		F	
I	saw	a -	bove	me	that end - less	sky - way,	

F		B♭		B♭		F	F
I	saw	be -	low	me	that gold - en	val - ley;	

	C7			C7		F	
This	land	was	made	for	you	and	me.

Begin melody on C.

La Cucaracha

Mexican Folk Song

F	F	F	C7
La cu-ca - ra - cha, la cu-ca - ra - cha,		He's a mer-ry lit-tle bug.	

C7	C7	C7	F
La cu-ca - ra - cha, la cu-ca - ra - cha,		Scam-per-ing a-cross the rug.	

F	F	F	C7
La cu-ca - ra - cha, la cu-ca - ra - cha,		First he will and then he won't.	

C7	C7	C7	F
La cu-ca - ra - cha, la cu-ca - ra - cha,		Now you see him, now you don't.	

123

unsure of the melodies. Stress the importance of singing when playing the autoharp.

Closing the Lesson

When the student accompanists can easily move back and forth between the chords needed to accompany "La Cucaracha," show them how to add a unique sound to their accompaniment. They are to continue to firmly press the chord buttons as before. This time instead of strumming, they may rhythmically tap the strings of the autoharp with a maraca. The sound should combine both the harmony and the timbre of the rattling shaker to suggest the sounds of Latin American accompaniments. Remind the students to sing as they perform the accompaniment.

Lesson Focus

Harmony: Chords and melody may move simultaneously in relation to each other. *(P–S)*

Materials

○ **Piano Accompaniments:** pages 337 and 340

○ **Record Information:**
  • This Land Is Your Land
    (Record 6 Side B Band 1)
  • La Cucaracha
    (Record 2 Side A Band 5)
  • Oh Susannah
    Record 6 Side B Band 2
    Voices: man
    Accompaniment: banjo, bass, percussion
  • Rock Island Line
    Record 6 Side B Band 3
    Voices: man
    Accompaniment: 5-string banjo, guitar, harmonica, fiddle, double bass, percussion

○ **Instruments:** autoharps; kazoos; thumb and finger picks

○ **Teacher's Resource Binder:**
  • Optional—
    Biography 5, page B9
    Kodaly Activity 7, page K11
    Mainstreaming Suggestion 13, page M20

Introducing the Lesson

OPTIONAL

Before proceeding with this lesson, make sure that the students have demonstrated some skill at using a thumb pick or a hand-held pick to play two- and three-chord songs with one or two strokes per measure.

Review "This Land Is Your Land" and "La Cucaracha." Invite the students to experiment with the strums given at the bottom of page 123, using either a thumb pick or a hand-held pick.

Developing the Lesson

1. Ask the students to look at "Oh Susannah." Review the steps needed for adding an autoharp accompaniment:

   • Determine the meter. Set it in a comfortable singing tempo.

   • Locate the starting pitch. Then review the melody.
   • Identify the chords that are to be used in the accompaniment.
   • Place the left hand in the correct fingering position.
   • Strum the first chord to establish tonality.
   • Begin to sing and strum.
   • Always practice using a full stroke first.
   • When sure of chord changes, experiment with other strums.

2. Help the students learn to sing "Rock Island Line" on page 125. After they know the melody, encourage them to experiment with adding a special "train effect." They are to follow the suggestions on the pupil page. The students may find it easier to play this pattern by using a hand-held pick and brushing it back and forth in the rhythm shown.

Rock Island Line

Work Song

With a steady beat

I say the Rock Is - land Line ___ is a
might - y good road. ___ I say the Rock Is - land Line ___
___ is the road to ride; Oh, the Rock Is - land Line ___
___ is a might - y good road. ___ If you want to
ride it, got to ride it like you're fly - in'; Buy your
tick - et at the sta - tion on the Rock Is - land Line.

Create a special train effect.
Form your hand in a loose fist.
Strum only on lowest strings.

Look through your music book.
Choose songs you like.
Plan your own strum.

125

Closing the Lesson

Plan a special performance. Add to the train effect by giving kazoos to some students. They are to play a "train-whistle sound" at the end of each phrase.

LESSON 58

Lesson Focus

Expression: Musical elements are combined into a whole to express a musical or extramusical idea. *(D–I)*

Materials

- **Piano Accompaniment:** page 342
- **Record Information:**
  - *Londonderry Air*
    by Percy Grainger, 1882–1961
    Record 6   Side B   Band 4
    National Symphony Orchestra
    Howard Mitchell, conductor
  - *Galway Piper*
    Record 6   Side B   Band 5
    Voices: children's choir
    Accompaniment: Irish pipes, flute, tin whistle, concertina, Celtic harp, violin, cello, percussion
- **Other:** a blank sheet of paper, a pencil, and colored chalk for each student
- **Teacher's Resource Binder:**
  - Optional—
    Kodaly Activity 3, page K5
- **For additional experience with expression:** Perform 8, page 146

LISTENING

Londonderry Air
by Percy Grainger

Grainger used a very old Irish folk song for this piece. The melody has many names, including "Danny Boy." Londonderry is a county in Ireland where the song originates.

126

Introducing the Lesson

Distribute a blank sheet of paper and a pencil to each student. **You are about to listen to a composition you have not heard before. Write down three things that you notice about the music.** Explain that the purpose is to find out what they focus on when they listen to music. Many people can listen to the same music and notice very different things. All responses are "correct." Play the recording of *Londonderry Air.*

Developing the Lesson

1. Ask each student to share his or her first answer with the class. Write each response on the chalkboard; group the responses by element. (See **For Your Information.**) Reassure the students that there is no single right answer and that it is all right to repeat what someone else has said.

2. Comment that while everyone listened to the same music, everyone focused on different things (the instruments, the mood, the form, and so on). Ask the students to look at their other two items and to add any others that were not shared on the first list.

3. **Listen again. Pick one or two items that you did not have on your list. Try to listen for them this time.** After playing the recording ask the students if they noticed any new things about the music that were not mentioned yet. Add these to the chalkboard list.

4. Distribute colored chalk to each student. Explain that this time, instead of using words to describe what they are hearing, they are to describe it by drawing. Each student may again focus on a different aspect of the composition. They may choose to draw a picture that shows the dynamic changes, the articu-

126

Galway Piper

Irish Folk Song

E
Ev - ery per - son in the na - tion, —

B7
Of a great or hum - ble sta - tion, —

E
Holds in high - est es - ti - ma - tion,

A   B7   E
Pip - ing — Tim — of — Gal - way.

E
Loud - ly — he can play or low;

B7
He can — move you fast or slow;

E
Touch your — hearts or stir your toe,

B7   E
Pip - ing — Tim of Gal - way.

127

For Your Information

Answers that students may give during Step 1:

Instruments—string family (no other instruments are used)

Tempo—slow

Dynamics—sometimes loud, sometimes soft

Articulation—smooth, legato

Melody—wide range from high to low (The melody is an Irish folk song.)

Form—melody repeated

Mood—restful, sweet, peaceful, melancholy

lation, the shape of the melody, or the overall form. Remind the students that the picture is to be abstract, not a picture of a real thing, such as a violin. Play the recording again.

5. Turn the students' attention to page 127. Point out that the theme of this song, "Galway Piper," like that of *Londonderry Air,* is Irish. To learn this new song, challenge the students to use their knowledge of the following musical elements:

- **Form**—Compare two-measure patterns to discover similarities and differences.
- **Rhythm**—Determine the meter, the beat note, and the shortest sound. Then challenge the students to read the rhythm on the syllable "duh."
- **Melody**—Determine the tonality (E) and identify the I chord (E–G♯–B). Guide the class to sing the song with scale numbers.

Closing the Lesson

Draw the following on the chalkboard:

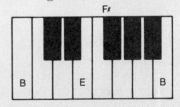

End the class by inviting one student to add a drone-like accompaniment beginning with the interval E-B. Ask the class to help determine when to change to the interval B-F♯.

127

LESSON 59

Lesson Focus

Timbre: The total sound is affected by the number and qualities of sounds occurring at the same time.
Form: A musical whole may be made up of same, varied, or contrasting segments. *(D–S)*

Materials

○ **Record Information:**
  • Norwegian Mountain March
    (Record 5   Side A   Band 5)
  • March from *The Nutcracker Suite*
    by Peter Ilyich Tchaikovsky
    (chie-**kawf**-skee),
    1840–1893
    Record 6   Side B   Bands 6a-6b
    Band 6a: themes only
    Band 6b: complete
    Philadelphia Orchestra
    Eugene Ormandy, conductor
○ **Other:** a pencil for each student; overhead projector
○ **Teacher's Resource Binder:**

Activity Sheets
  • **Activity Sheet 31,** page A42
    (Prepare a copy of the activity sheet for each student and prepare as a transparency.)

(continued on next page)

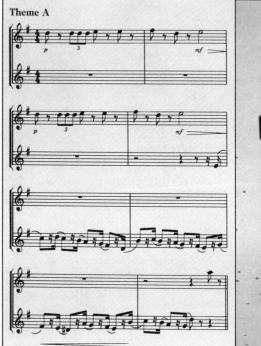

LISTENING

March

from *The Nutcracker Suite*

by Peter Ilyich Tchaikovsky

1. Follow the themes as you listen.
   In what order do you hear them?
   Which one keeps returning?
2. As you listen again, identify the instrument families that play the repeating theme.

Theme A

128

Introducing the Lesson

Review "Norwegian Mountain March," page 102, with the students. Recall that the form of this composition is **A B A. How can you determine the form of a composition?** The students' answers will vary. Help them conclude that they must first decide how many sections are in the music and when each section ends. Then they need to compare each section with preceding ones to decide if they are the same (identified by the same letter), similar (identified by the addition of a prime mark to the letter), or different (identified by a different letter).

Developing the Lesson

1. Ask the students to turn to page 128. **Before we hear the entire composition, listen to each of the themes.** Play Band 6a of "March" from *The Nutcracker Suite* as the students follow the notation for each theme. Play the recording several times until the students feel they will be able to recognize each theme when it is heard in the complete composition.

2. Distribute Activity Sheet 31 (*Musical Form*) and a pencil to each student. Explain to the class that the activity sheet helps them identify the first thing they need to know when describing musical form—the number of sections. **You will hear eleven sections in this composition. As you listen you may follow the notation in your books. Then in the first blank in each box, write the letter that identifies the theme you hear.** Play Band 6b of "March" from *The Nutcracker Suite*. Play it again if the students wish to hear it again. If you wish, call out the number of each box as each new section begins. (Each section is eight measures long.)

Theme B

Theme C

129

Materials (*continued*)
- Optional—
  Curriculum Correlation 12, page C14
- o **For additional experience with form:**
  Describe 15, page 192; Special Times 5, page 226

For Your Information
Answers to Activity Sheet 31:
Boxes I, II, IV, V, VII, VIII, X, and XI:
1. A
2. woodwinds and brass
3. strings

Boxes III and IX:
1. B
2. brass
3. strings

Box VI:
1. C
2. woodwinds
3. strings

In Sections VII, VIII, X, and XI, the strings add a decorative accompaniment.

3. Explain to the students that they are now to identify the most important instrument families that play the main themes during each section. In each section the theme is a dialogue between instruments. One group of instruments will begin. They are then answered by a second group. **In a few cases you may hear two instrument families at the same time, so listen carefully. Then in the second and third blanks in each box on your activity sheet, write down the names of those families.** As before play the recording as many times as needed for the students to complete the activity sheet.

Closing the Lesson

If time allows, display a transparency of the activity sheet. Ask the students to share their answers. Using an overhead pen, fill in the blanks with the correct answers. (See **For Your Information.**) Play Band b once more so that the students can hear the right answers and correct any mistakes that were made.

LESSON 60

Lesson Focus

Evaluation: Review concepts and skills studied in the Fourth Quarter.

Materials

○ **Piano Accompaniment:** page 343

○ **Record Information:**
  • We Shall Overcome
  🔲 **Record 6   Side B   Band 7**
  Voices: children's choir
  Accompaniment: piano, electric organ, electric guitar, acoustic guitar, electric bass, percussion

○ **Instruments:** autoharp; piano; resonator bells with pitches C, D, E, F, G, A, B, and C'; bell mallet

○ **Other:** a pencil for each student

○ **Teacher's Resource Binder:**
  [Evaluation] • **Review 4**, pages Ev19–Ev20 (Prepare one copy of each page for each student.)
  • **Musical Progress Report 4,** page Ev21
  • Optional —
  Curriculum Correlation 12, page C14
  Kodaly Activity 7, page K11

Review 4

Learning a New Song

Review the information you have learned this year that will help you learn a new song from notation.

THE FORM

Can you decide:
  how many **phrases** are in the song?
  whether they are the same, similar, or different?
  whether there are repeated patterns?

The Rhythm

Can you decide:
  how the **beats** are grouped?
  which **note** will move with the beat?
  which note is the shortest sound?

The Melody

Can you decide:
  where the **home tone** is located on the staff?
  whether the song is in major or minor?
  where the scale numbers are for each pitch in the song?

THE HARMONY

Can you decide:
  what pitches belong to the I, IV, and V7 chords?
  which chord to use to accompany the melody?

130

Introducing the Lesson

Ask the students to turn to page 130. Read the discussion together, pausing after each question to discuss the musical aspects the students would need to know in order to be successful.

Ask the students to answer each question in relation to songs that are unfamiliar to them, such as "Let Us Sing Together" (page 146) and "Found a Peanut" (page 152).

Developing the Lesson

1. Comment on how well the students have demonstrated their ability to determine information that is needed to learn a new song. **Let's see how well you can do with these questions.** Distribute Review 4 (*We Shall Overcome*) and a pencil to each student. Give the students time to answer Questions 1 through 4. Then sing the last part of the song "We Shall Over-

come" ("Oh deep in my heart . . ."), or play it on the bells or piano. (See **Materials.**)

Lightly tap the underlying shortest sound, the eighth note, as you perform it. Sing it several times to give the students ample time to complete Questions 5 and 6.

2. Provide time for the students to complete Questions 7 and 8.

3. When all of the students have completed the evaluation, tell them to open their books to page 131. Guide them to compare their answers with the notation and to determine the correct answer for each question.

Closing the Lesson

Follow the suggestions on page 131 and divide the class into small groups of five or six people.

We Shall Overcome

New Words and Musical Arrangement by
Zilphia Horton, Frank Hamilton, Guy Carawan, and Pete Seeger

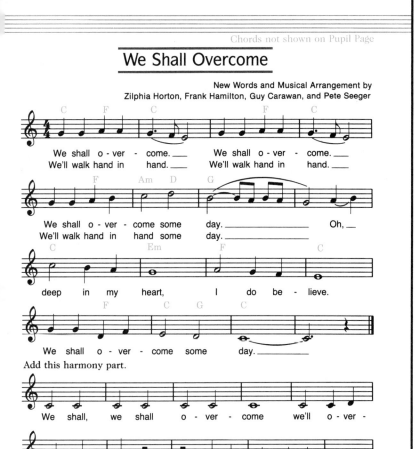

We shall o - ver - come. ___ We shall o - ver - come. ___
We'll walk hand in hand. ___ We'll walk hand in hand. ___

We shall o - ver - come some day. _____ Oh, ___
We'll walk hand in hand some day. _____

deep in my heart, I do be - lieve.

We shall o - ver - come some day. _____

Add this harmony part.

We shall, we shall o - ver - come we'll o - ver -

come some day. Oh, ___ deep in my heart,

I do be - lieve, We'll o - ver - come some day.

131

For Your Information

Answers for Review 4:
1. The letter name is C. The notes of the scale are those of the C major scale.
2.

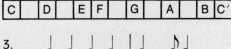

| C | D | E F | G | A | B C' |

3.

4.

We shall o - ver - come. _____

5.  etc.

Oh ____ deep ____ in __ my __

6. The scale numbers are
6 – 7 – 1' – 7 – 6 – 5;
6 – 5 – 4 – 3;
5 – 5 – 2 – 4 – 3 – 2 – 1.
7. I Chord: C – E – G
IV Chord: F – A – C
V7 Chord: G – B – D – F
8. The chords are C, F, C, G7, and C.

Each group is to learn to sing the song, then plan an accompaniment of their choice. They may choose bells or autoharp. Help the students identify the pitches that make up each chord in the accompaniment. Write the pitches on the chalkboard:

C   Dm   F   G7   Am

Give the students approximately ten minutes to prepare their performance. Invite each group to perform for the rest of the class.

Use the information collected during this activity as well as other observations made during the Fourth Quarter to complete *Musical Progress Report 4* for each student. This may be sent to parents as a report and/or retained for your files.

Unit 2

Unit Overview

Unit 2, *More Music to Explore,* provides opportunites for the students to participate in a variety of musical experiences for review, reinforcement, and extension of the core concepts. Each lesson may be used either in conjunction with the core lesson, to which it is cross-referenced, or by itself at any time during the year.

Perform Music contains suggestions for presentations of two-part and round singing, songs sung with instrumental accompaniment, and movement. The students learn to play the ukulele using proper playing technique.

Describe Music helps the students develop a variety of ways to communicate what they hear,

More Music To Explore

using not only words, but movement and notation. The students learn more about form, dynamics, and rhythm patterns.

Create Music offers opportunities for the students to use all that they have learned to create their own music dramas through movement and storytelling. They explore the components of an opera, make creative decisions, and perform the Japanese Noh play "Kantan" as a music drama.

The songs and activities in *Special Times* help the students enjoy the celebration of traditional holidays and understand their meaning. This chapter features excerpts from *Amahl and the Night Visitors* with a narration by the teacher.

Perform Music

Maori Stick Game

Translated by Max Exner   Maori Folk Song

E - pa - pa __ wai - a - ri ta - ku nei __ ma __ hi,
Smile o my __ fa - ther, but nev - er de - ny __ me,

Ta - ku nei __ ma - hi he tu - ku ro - ma - ta
Nev - er de - ny me the pleas - ure of __ dream - ing.

E pa - pa __ wai - a - ri ta - ku nei __ ma __ hi,
Smile o my __ fa - ther, but nev - er de - ny __ me,

134

Lesson Focus

Rhythm: A series of beats may be organized into regular or irregular groupings by stressing certain beats.
Form: A musical whole may be made up of same, varied, or contrasting segments. *(D–I)*

Materials

○ **Piano Accompaniment:** page 344
○ **Record Information:**
   • Maori Stick Game
     Record 7   Side A   Band 1
     Voices: children's choir
     Accompaniment: percussion
○ **Other:** a pair of wooden sticks for each student (Make sticks 15 inches long and 1 inch in diameter from dowels or broom handles.) (Rhythm sticks will work, although they are not quite long enough to be easily grasped or passed.)
○ **Teacher's Resource Binder:**
   • Optional—
     Mainstreaming Suggestion 14, page M20
○ **Extends Lesson 9,** page 22

The Lesson

1. Begin by asking the students to examine the song "Maori Stick Game" on pages 134–135. Guide the students to observe the frequent return of similar phrases and the repetition of patterns within the phrase (such as in Measures 3 and 7, and, one step lower, in Measure 5). The song is made up of two large sections: Section A consists of four phrases, each phrase being four measures long (**a b a b′**). Section B consists of six phrases (**c d e f c d**).

   Play the recording as the students listen for the melodic movement and the pronunciation of the Maori text. While they listen a second time, ask the students to lightly tap the underlying pulse to become familiar with the meter, which moves in threes.

2. Explain that this song is used to accompany a stick dance, a popular game in New Zealand.

Introduce to the students and help them practice the following five basic movements and the musical sequence of the game.

Movements

1. Clap: Player hits own sticks together in a vertical position.
2. Down: Player hits bottom ends of both sticks on floor.
3. Drum: Player hits the tops of sticks on the floor, letting the sticks slide through hands until he or she holds ends that were originally on the bottom.
4. Pass: Player hands one or both sticks to partner.
5. Hold: Sticks are held in place.

Musical Sequence

Measures 1–8: Down, clap, pass right. Down, clap, pass left. (Repeat three times.)
Measures 9–16: Down, clap, pass right, pass right. Down, clap, pass left, pass left. (Re-

134

13 C7 **14** **15** F **16**

Ta - ku nei— ma - hi he ta - ku roi — ma - ta
Nev - er de - ny me the pleas - ure of dream - ing.

17 F **18** **19** B♭ **20** F

E - au - e ka ma - te - au. —
Way a - way, my love is a - way.

21 F **22** C7 **23** F **24**

E - hi - ne ho - ki i - ho ra. —
Girl of mine, come a - gain to me! —

25 F **26** **27** **28** C7

Ma - ku e kau - te o hi - koi tang - a
Cold is the path - way that led her from me,

29 C7 **30** **31** **32** F

Ma - ku e kau - te o hi - koi tang - a.
Warm will the path be that brings her to me.

33 F **34** **35** B♭ **36** F

E - au - e ka ma - te - au. —
Way a - way, my love is a - way.

37 F **38** C7 **39** F **40**

E - hi - ne ho - ki i - ho ra. —
Girl of mine, come a - gain to me! —

135

PERFORM 1

For Your Information

Patterns for ''Maori Stick Game'':
Position—Partners should be seated on the floor, facing each other. Sticks should be held upright, near the center. They are passed vertically. Five basic movements are used throughout the game, as explained in the lesson.
Pronunciation of Maori text:
Ay-pah-pah **wie**-ah-ree
tah-koo nay **mah**-ee.
Tah-koo nay **mah**-ee ay
too-koo roe **mah**-tah.
Ay-oe-ay kah **mah**-tay-oe.
Ay-hee-nay **hoe**-kee **ee**-hoe rah.
Mah-koo ay **kou**-tay oe
hee-koy **tang**-ah.

---

peat twice; note that the sequence now moves in fours, while the music continues to move in threes.)

Measures 17–18: Break, hold for two beats. (Repeat.)

Measures 19–22: Down, clap, double pass outside. (Repeat three times.)

Measures 23–24: Down, hold for five beats.

Measures 25–32: Down, clap, double pass outside. Down, clap, double pass inside. (Repeat three times.)

Measures 33–34: Break, hold for two beats. (Repeat.)

Measures 35–38: Down, clap, double pass outside. Down, clap, double pass inside. (Repeat.)

Measures 39–40: Down, hold for five beats.

When all of the movements have been mastered separately, practice each of the sequences and breaks. Each segment should be practiced with the music in order to establish a feeling for the appropriate tempo and three-beat accent groupings. The students should sense how the music continues to move in threes in Section B while the motions are grouped by fours.

3. Do the entire stick game with the recording. If the students have difficulty keeping up with the recorded tempo, suggest that they chant the words (English or Maori) in a slower tempo. They may continue to practice until they can handle the sticks more quickly and perform the game at the recorded speed.

4. Remind the students of their discovery about the form of the song. **Does each of the sections have its own stick movement?** (yes) Encourage them to sing the song in both Maori and English as they continue to perform the stick game.

Lesson Focus
Rhythm: Music may move in relation to the underlying shortest pulse. *(D–S)*

Materials
○ **Piano Accompaniment:** page 346
○ **Record Information:**
  • I'm Going Crazy
  Record 7   Side A   Band 2
  Voices: child solos, children's choir
  Accompaniment: harpsichord, positive organ, clarinet, synthesizer, sound effects, percussion
○ **Instruments:** tambourine; claves
○ **Other:** a pencil for each student
○ **Teacher's Resource Binder:**
  [Activity Sheets] • **Activity Sheets 32–33,** pages A43–A44 (Prepare a copy for each student.)
○ **Extends Lesson 8,** page 20

For Your Information
Correct answers for Activity Sheet 33:

1. sixteenth note
2. 2
3. 3
4. 4
5. 6
6. 6
7. 10
8. 16

I'm Going Crazy

New Verses by Charles Sharp   Traditional

Can you pat this pattern on the outside of your legs as you sing?

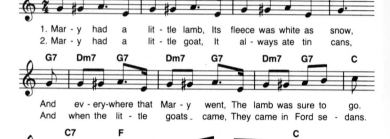

1. Mar-y had a lit-tle lamb, Its fleece was white as snow,
2. Mar-y had a lit-tle goat, It al-ways ate tin cans,

And ev-ery-where that Mar-y went, The lamb was sure to go.
And when the lit-tle goats_ came, They came in Ford se-dans.

I'm go-ing cra-zy, ____ just sing-ing this song. ____

I'm go-ing cra-zy, ____ Don't you wan-ta come a-long? ____

3. Mary had a little cat, It always played with yarn,
   And when the little kittens came, They came with sweaters on.

4. Mary had a little lamb, His fleece was black as soot,
   And everywhere that lamb went, His sooty foot he put.

136

The Lesson

1. Play the recording of "I'm Going Crazy." Enjoy the humorous text with the students. Ask them to examine the pattern at the top of page 136. Determine that the sixteenth note is the shortest sound. Invite the students to tap the shortest sound as they listen to the recording again.

2. Distribute copies of Activity Sheets 32 (*"I'm Going Crazy" Rhythm*) and 33 (*Accompany "I'm Going Crazy"*). **The first two measures to "I'm Going Crazy" are shown on Activity Sheet 32.** The students are to show the remainder of the rhythm for the song on the activity sheet, following the notation in their books. Remind them that the sixteenth note is the shortest sound. Discuss the difference between even and uneven patterns. **Which pair of notes is even?** (two eighths) **Which is uneven?** (dotted eighth followed by a sixteenth) Ask the students to listen to the song, noticing the alternating even and uneven patterns. Invite the students to sing the song.

3. The students should use Activity Sheet 32 to help them complete Activity Sheet 33. (See **For Your Information** for correct answers.) Check their answers and discuss Questions 1–8. Invite the students to share the percussion parts they wrote in response to Question 9. Determine which patterns will fit best with the song. The following patterns might fit well:

Even

or any combination

Uneven

4. Choose combinations of percussion parts to perform with each verse of the song.

136

The Zulu Warrior

Words and Music by Josef Marais

The Chant
Perform this pattern six times:

I - ka-ma zim-ba zim-ba za - yo, I - ka-ma zim-ba zim-ba zee,

End with this pattern:

whispered *f*

chief, chief, chief, chief. Zhe - ka - ma - li - oh zhe, wah!

The Melody
Perform this pattern twice:

See him there, _____ the Zu - lu war - ri - or, _____

See him there, _____ the Zu - lu chief, chief, chief.

End with this pattern:

whispered *f*

chief, chief, chief, chief. Zhe - ka - ma - li - oh zhe, wah!

137

Hampshire House Publishing Corp., New York, N.Y. Used by Permission

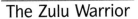

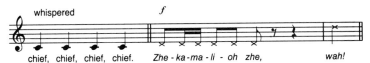

Lesson Focus

Rhythm: Individual sounds and silences within a rhythmic line may be longer than, shorter than, or the same as the underlying shortest pulse. *(P–S)*

Materials

o **Record Information:**
  • Mayo Nafwa
    (Record 3   Side A   Band 3)
  • Zulu Warrior
  Record 7   Side A   Band 3
    Voices: children's choir
    Accompaniment: percussion
o **Instruments:** three drums; beaters (with high, medium, and low pitches); assortment of percussion instruments
o **Other:** a pencil for each student
o **Teacher's Resource Binder:**
  Activity Sheets • **Activity Sheet 34,** page A45 (One copy for each student)
    • Optional—
    Mainstreaming Suggestion 15, page M21
o **Extends Lesson 16,** page 38

For Your Information

Pronunciation for "Zulu Warrior":
Ee-kah-mah **zim**-bah **zim**-bah **zie**-yoe,
Ee-kah-mah **zim**-bah **zim**-bah **zee**.
Tsay-kay-mah-lee-oe-tsay, wah.

The Lesson

1. Review "Mayo Nafwa" (Lesson 16). "Zulu Warrior" on page 137 is also an African song, but it was written about rather than by the Zulu people.

2. Ask the students to discover that this is a two-part song. Begin by learning the repetitive chant. It is to be performed six times, followed by the pattern shown on the second staff. After learning the rhythm, add the pitches.

3. Scan the melody. It is performed twice before proceeding to the last staff for the ending. Warm up by singing 1'-6-5-3-4-2-1. Challenge the class to sight read the melody. When they can perform it, play the recording of "Zulu Warrior" to hear how the harmony (the chant) and melody parts fit together. The chant begins the piece. (The melody enters on the last beat of the second measure.) While some students sing the harmony part, invite a small group of students to sing the melody.

OPTIONAL

4. The students should practice the three drum patterns shown on the upper half of Activity Sheet 34. ("*Zulu Warrior*" *Drum Accompaniment*). Chant the numbers while clapping those that are circled. Divide the class into three groups and have each group clap one pattern. Choose one student to lead each group by playing that part on a drum. Add the drum parts to the song.

5. Provide time for the students to create new percussion parts for instruments of their choice. Use the number grid at the bottom of the activity sheet. Students can "notate" their percussion sounds by circling the numbers on the activity sheet. When the students have practiced their parts, they may add them as an accompaniment to the song.

137

Lesson Focus

Expression: The expressiveness of music is affected by the way dynamics, rhythm, melody, and timbre contribute to the musical whole. *(P–S)*

Materials

○ **Piano Accompaniment:** page 347

○ **Record Information:**
  • Sunshine on My Shoulders
    Record 7   Side A   Band 4
    Voice: man
    Accompaniment: acoustic guitar, electric piano, electric bass, percussion

○ **Instruments:** bass xylophone with pitches G, A, C, D, E, F♯, G′, and A′; alto metallophone, with pitches D, E, F♯, G, A, B, C, and D′; alto and soprano glockenspiels, with pitches D, E, G, A, B, and C′; bell mallets

○ **Teacher's Resource Binder:**
  • Optional—
    Mainstreaming Suggestion 16, page M21

○ **Extends Lesson 22,** page 50

The Lesson

1. Play the recording, "Sunshine on My Shoulders." Invite the students to listen and respond to the shortest sounds (the eighth note) by softly patting the upper part of their legs with their right hands.

   Play the recording again. This time, while remaining seated, the students should add the sound of the underlying beat (the quarter note) by moving their feet.

2. Help the students sense how the rhythmic pattern of the melody relates to the beat and the shortest sounds. Ask them to continue their movements while following the rhythm of the melody in their books as they listen to the recording a third time.

3. Draw attention to the rhythm ruler at the top of page 138. **Where does this pattern appear in the song?** (Phrases 1 and 3) Perform this pattern on the syllable "ch" while continuing to tap the shortest sound and step the beat.

4. Play the recording a fourth time as the students softly perform all three rhythmic ideas with the music.

5. Discuss the melody. **How does the melody help express the words of the song?** (Each phrase moves upward, ending relatively high. This helps reflect the happy, "up" mood of the song.) Ask the students to sing the song.

6. After the students are familiar with the song, ask them to plan their own expressive performance. **How will you use dynamics?** (Choose from *forte, piano, crescendo,* or *decrescendo.*) **tempo?** (Choose from *largo, adagio, andante, allegro,* or *presto.*)

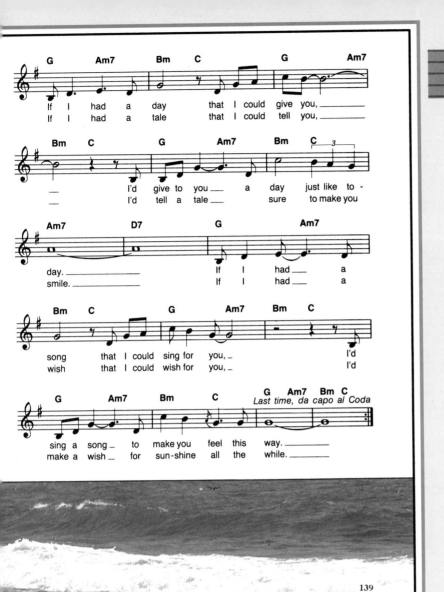

If I had a day that I could give you, ____
If I had a tale that I could tell you, ____

__ I'd give to you __ a day just like to-
__ I'd tell a tale __ sure to make you

day. ____ If I had __ a
smile. ____ If I had __ a

song that I could sing for you, _ I'd
wish that I could wish for you, _ I'd

sing a song _ to make you feel this way. ____
make a wish _ for sun-shine all the while. ____

Last time, da capo al Coda

139

PERFORM 4

7. Perform the song, without accompaniment, using the students' ideas. The class may wish to select a conductor to remind them of how the song will be expressed.

8. Help the students learn the instrumental accompaniment by reading the parts at the bottom of page 140. **Who can read the bass xylophone part? What key are we in?** (G) **What is the first and last pitch in this part?** (G) Invite the students who indicate that they can read this part to go to an instrument and play it. The students may need to be reminded of the pitch names of the staff lines and spaces in order to select the correct bars for the instrument. Select the first student who is able to read the part to play the instrument.

9. Invite two students to read and play the alto metallophone part. One student plays the top pitches: B, C, and D. The other plays the

OPTIONAL

bottom pitches: D, E, F♯, G, and A. Be certain the performers understand the repeat signs.

The soprano and alto glockenspiels reproduce some parts of the vocal melody. (The first pitch has been changed from B to D to accommodate the range of the instrument.) Point out that the large numbers "5" and "4" shown on the glockenspiel staffs indicate that the performers are to rest for five or four full measures. The students may select from these parts to plan an introducton, interlude, or coda. Encourage them to decide how each part should be used to provide contrast and interest to the overall arrangement. Ask the students to perform the song expressively, using the instrumental accompaniment.

139

Coda

Sun-shine_ al-most all the time makes me high,_____

sun-shine_ al-most al - ways. . ._____

Play these parts as an accompaniment
for Phrases 1 through 4:
Bass Xylophone

Play 6 times   Play 8 times

Alto Metallophone

Play 3 times   Play 4 times

Soprano Glockenspiel

Alto Glockenspiel

140

Alleluia

Music by W. A. Mozart

Al - le - lu - ia,

Al - le - lu - ia, al - le - lu - ia,

Al - le - lu - ia, al - le - lu - ia,

al - le - lu - ia.

al - le - lu - ia, al - le - lu - ia.

al - le - lu - ia, al - le - lu - ia.

141

Lesson Focus

Harmony: Two or more musical lines may occur simultaneously. *(P–I)*

Materials

o **No Piano Accompaniment**
o **Record Information:**
  • Alleluia
    by Wolfgang Amadeus Mozart
    (**moet**-sahrt), 1756–1791
    Record 7   Side A   Bands 5a-b
    Voices: children's choir
    Accompaniment: clavichord
o **Teacher's Resource Binder:**
  • Optional—
    Kodaly Activity 18, page K27
    Mainstreaming Suggestion 20, page M26
o **Extends Lesson 36,** page 78

For Your Information

Melodic contour from Sept 5:

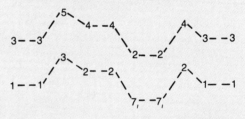

The Lesson

1. Ask the students to follow the notation to "Alleluia" on page 141. Play Band 5a of the recording, which consists of a unison statement followed by a three-part round.

2. Ask the students to learn the round as a unison melody by singing the pitches with scale numbers. Write the numbers on the chalkboard as the class sings.

3. When the students know the melody well, divide the class into three groups and sing it as a round. Guide the students to sing slowly, listening carefully to the interesting sounds created by the combination of sounds.

4. Play the unison statement only to Band 5b of the recording. Ask the students if they recognize anything about the melody. (It uses the same words.) Guide them to realize that this

is the same melody they just learned, now sung backwards. Play this band again. The students should put their fingers on the last note and trace the notation backwards. After playing Band 5b several times, challenge the class to sing the melody. Write the numbers backwards, under the first round.

Forward: 1 2 5 1 5 6 4 5 1

Backward: 1 5 4 6 5 1 5 2 1

5. Write the scale numbers for Phrases 2 and 3 of the original version in contour. (See **For Your Information.**) **What do you notice?** (The two parts follow the same melodic shape, always staying a third apart.) **When this happens we say we are performing parallel harmony.**

141

PERFORM 6

Lesson Focus

Expression: Musical elements are combined into a whole to express a musical or extramusical idea. *(P–I)*

Materials

○ **Piano Accompaniment:** page 350
○ **Record Information:**
  • The Lonely Goatherd
    Record 7   Side A   Band 6
    Voice: woman
    Accompaniment: violin, trumpet, clarinet, accordion, double bass
○ **Instruments:** resonator bells or xylophone with pitches C, D, E, F, C', D', E', and F'; cowbells; woodblocks; mallets
○ **Teacher's Resource Binder:**
  • Optional—
    Curriculum Correlation 13, page C15
○ **Extends Lesson 34,** page 74

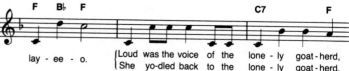

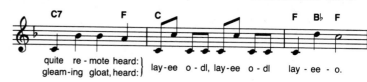

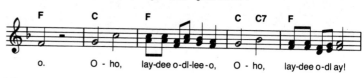

The Lesson

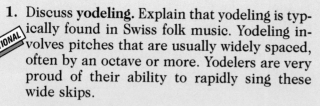

1. Discuss **yodeling.** Explain that yodeling is typically found in Swiss folk music. Yodeling involves pitches that are usually widely spaced, often by an octave or more. Yodelers are very proud of their ability to rapidly sing these wide skips.

2. Invite the students to learn a yodeling song. Play the recording of "The Lonely Goatherd." The students may recognize the music as a song from the movie "The Sound of Music."

3. Look at the music on pages 142–143. **Where do you see yodeling?** (The song alternates words and yodeling every two measures.) **Look at the melodic skips in the yodeling parts. Are these wide skips or small skips?** (wide—an octave plus one step)

4. Invite the students to sing the song. **How accurate can you be when singing the wide melodic skips?**

5. After the class is familiar with the melody, divide it into two groups. The first group sings Part 1, which is the melody. The second group sings Part 2, which consists of the lower notes when the music is written for two parts.

6. The students singing Part 2 will discover that they are singing a third below the melody, except in one place. **Where does Part 2 have an interval other than a third below the melody?** (The interval of a sixth can be found on the last syllable, "ay.")

7. Select several students to learn the instrumental accompaniment on page 144. Use resonator bells or xylophones. The students will

142

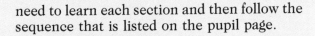

O - ho, lay-dee o - dl lee - o, hod-l - o - dl-lee - o - ay!

Hap-py are they, lay-lee o lay-ee lee-o! O lay-lee o lay-lee lay - ee-o.

Soon the du-et will be - come a tri - o, lay-ee o - dl lay-ee o-dl - o.

Coda Ho-di lay-ee, _____ Ho-di lay-ee, _____ Ho-di lay-ee, Ho-di lay-ee! _

need to learn each section and then follow the sequence that is listed on the pupil page.

8. After the xylophone parts have been learned, invite other students to use small percussion instruments, such as cowbells or woodblocks, to add special effects to the ensemble. These students will need to decide whether they will play all the time, during certain sections, or occasionally.

9. Combine instruments and voices to perform the song.

Add an accompaniment on resonator bells or xylophone.
Play **A** four times. Play **B** once.
Play **A** four times. Play **B** once.
Play **A** four times. Play the coda.

A

B

Use small percussion instruments for special effects:

cowbell   woodblock

Create your own stage production of this song.
Choose: 1. a musical director
         2. composers and instrumental performers
         3. a chorus
         4. choreographers
         5. stagehands
Perform the drama that is told in the song.
Make your performance longer by creating
a dance for the herd of goats.
What kind of music will you play
to accompany the dance?
When will the goats dance?
Could the mother dance?
What kind of music will you create for her dance?

144

Peace of the River

Words by Glendora Gosling

Music by Viola Wood

Follow the dynamic tempo markings as you sing.
Will you perform the song *staccato* or *legato*?

Peace, I ask of thee, O riv - er, Peace, peace, peace.

When I learn to live se - rene - ly, Cares will cease.

From the hills I gath-er cour - age, Vi - sion of the day to be,

Strength to lead and faith to fol - low, All are giv-en un-to me.

Peace, I ask of thee, O riv - er, Peace, peace, peace.

145

PERFORM 7

Lesson Focus
Harmony: Chords and melody may move simultaneously in relation to each other. *(P–S)*

Materials
○ **Piano Accompaniment:** page 352
○ **Record Information:**
  • Peace of the River
▭ **Record 7   Side A   Band 7**
  Voices: children's choir
  Accompaniment: oboe, cello, celesta, harp, percussion
○ **Instruments:** resonator bells with pitches C, D, E, F, G, A, B, C′, D′, and E′; 10 bell mallets
○ **Other:** overhead projector
○ **Teacher's Resource Binder:**
  Activity Sheets • **Activity Sheet 35,** page A46 (Prepare a transparency of the activity sheet.)
○ **Extends Lesson 4,** page 12

The Lesson

1. Play the recording of "Peace of the River." Help the students sense the expressive quality of the song. **Show the length of each phrase by moving your arms in an arc.**

2. **Open your books to page 145.** Challenge the students to learn to sing both parts of Phrase 1 simultaneously. Divide the class into two groups. **How does the song begin?** (repeated tones) **Then what happens?** (Part 1 moves up–down–up–up by steps, while Part 2 moves down–up–down–up by steps.) Help the students perform Phrases 1 and 2 in harmony.

3. Examine Phrases 3 and 4. Discover that Part 2 is always a third lower than the upper part (except on the syllables "Vi-," "all," and "un-"). Guide everyone to sing the upper part in unison. Then help the singers in Group 2

hear and sing Part 2. **Can you sing the last phrase?** (Yes, because it is the same as the first.)

4. Display a transparency of Activity Sheet 35 (*Accompany "Peace of the River"*). Distribute resonator bells and mallets to ten students. Have them play their bells each time their pitch occurs in the boxes above the words. (Chords should be played in the rhythm shown above the chord boxes.)

5. **Are there other ways we could create a different kind of "peaceful" accompaniment?** Encourage the students to experiment with different rhythms and different combinations of the notes shown for each box. Any note will fit with the song so long as it occurs in the box or half-box immediately above a given group of words. Add the patterns the students create as an accompaniment to the song.

OPTIONAL

145

Lesson Focus

Expression: Musical elements are combined into a whole to express a musical or extramusical idea. *(P–S)*

Materials

o **Piano Accompaniment:** page 354

o **Record Information:**
  • Let Us Sing Together
  Record 7 Side B Band 1
  Voices: children's choir
  Accompaniment: violin, clarinet, trumpet, accordion, double bass

o **Other:** overhead projector

o **Teacher's Resource Binder:**
  | Activity Sheets | • **Activity Sheet 36**, page A47 (Prepare a transparency of the activity sheet.) |

  • Optional—
  Orff Activity 12, page O24

o **Extends Lesson 58,** page 126

Let Us Sing Together

Hand Signs Arranged
by Janet Cole

Adapted from a
Czech Folk Song

Learn the melody. Learn the hand signs.
Practice them until you can do them as you sing.

let   us   sing   together

Let us sing to-geth-er, Let us sing to-geth-er

One and all a joy-ous song. Let us sing to-

geth-er, One and all a joy-ous song.

Let us sing a-gain and a-gain, Let us sing a-

146

The Lesson

1. Discuss the use of hand signs as a means of communicating with people who cannot hear.

2. Ask the students to look at pages 146–147. Invite them to describe times when they have seen people using hand signs or learned to use hand signs themselves. Display the transparency of Activity Sheet 36 (*Basic Hand Signs*) and practice the letters shown. All appear in the words of the song.

3. Guide the students to form each word as shown in their books. When the signs have been learned, practice them in the rhythm of the words of the song.

4. When the students can perform the motions in a steady rhythm, suggest that they perform them while listening to the recording.

5. Establish the tonality in G. Ask the students to sing the song using a neutral syllable. Then sing it with the words. Challenge the class to sing and perform the signs at the same time.

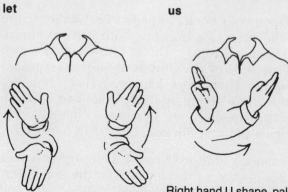

let   us

Both hands open palms.
Bring to upright position.

Right hand U shape, palm in.
Place tips on right side of chest then arc over to left side.

146

G		A7	

gain and a - gain, Let us sing a - gain and a - gain,

D7		G	

One and all a joy - ous song.

one

and

all

a

happy

song

again

147

PERFORM 8

For Your Information

Instructions for hand movements:
Begin with hands down, ready to move upward on Beat 1.

"Let": Hands up.

"us": Move right hand to chest.

"sing": Right hand sweeps out.

"to-": Move fists out in "T" shape.

"gether": Bring fists together.

Repeat the above motions. Then proceed to the next phrase.

"one": Index finger up.

"and": Right hand forms this word.

"all": Both hands form this word.

"a": Bring right fist up.

"joyous": Sweep right hand up and down.

"song": Move right fist over left palm twice.

Repeat these motions as the remainder of the song is performed, altering the rhythm as necessary. End the song.

"again": Right hand moves left, finger tips in left palm.

"and": Right hand moves left to right.

"again": Same motion as above.

sing

Right hand open B, palm up, tips out. Swing fingers of left open B over right palm in rhythmic motion without touching.

and

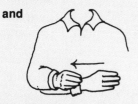

Five shape right palm in, tips left. Move from left to right closing into flat O.

together

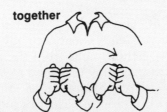

T shape both hands, thumbs out. Bring together.

all

Open B both hands, right palm up, left palm down. Circle right with left ending with back of LH resting on right palm.

happy

Place open B on chest and brush up and out twice.

again

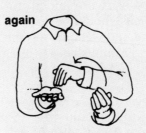

Right hand open B, palm up, tips out. Bent B LH palm up. Arc to right and place tips in right palm.

song

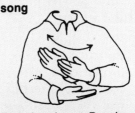

Right hand open B, palm up, tips out. Swing fingers of left open B over right palm in rhythmic motion without touching.

147

Lesson Focus

Harmony: Chords and melody may move simultaneously in relation to each other. *(P–I)*

Materials

○ **Instruments:** soprano ukuleles for each student

○ **Other:** heavy cardboard picks (rectangles cut to 1½ inches × 4 inches) for each student

○ **Teacher's Resource Binder:**
  • Optional—
  Kodaly Activity 15, page K24
  Mainstreaming Suggestion 17, page M25

○ **Extends Lesson 56,** page 122

Play the Soprano Ukulele

1. Learn to hold your ukulele.

2. Find these parts:

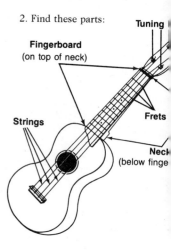

Tuning
Fingerboard (on top of neck)
Strings
Frets
Neck (below finge

3. Learn how to read the chord charts. Fingers are numbered on chord charts.

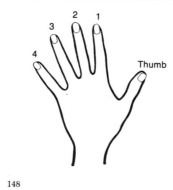

Thumb

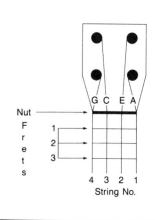

G C E A

Nut

F
r
e
t
s

1
2
3

4 3 2 1
String No.

148

The Lesson

1. Before the students arrive, ukuleles should be tuned, using open tuning. (See **For Your Information.**) Distribute the ukuleles and cardboard picks to the students. (See **Materials.**) Ask the students to follow the steps on page 148. Demonstrate the correct way to hold the instrument. Left-handed students should use the same playing position as right-handed students. The cardboard picks should be gripped between the thumb and index finger of the right hand. (This position establishes a proper strumming technique.)

2. Guide the students to locate the parts on their ukuleles. Be sure they understand that the strings are counted from the "bottom up." When holding the ukulele in the correct position, the string nearest the floor is string number "1."

3. Guide the students to practice keeping a steady beat as they strum downward with their picks from the fourth to the first string. As they continue to strum, begin to sing "Are You Sleeping?" Each chord symbol or slash mark on page 149 indicates where the chords should be strummed. Divide the class into several groups to sing and play the song as either a two- or three-part round.

4. To give the students additional practice with their instruments, ask them to sing and play the other rounds on page 149. Help them adjust their strumming for proper beat and tempo.

5. Challenge the students to combine the rounds and perform them as partner songs. "Three Blind Mice" and "Row, Row, Row Your Boat" are in ⁶⁄₈, while "Are You Sleeping?" is in ⁴⁄₄. Each song should be sung with a feeling of

Learn to Strum on Open Strings

The C Chord

Tune: G C E G

Are You Sleeping?

C   /   /   /
Are you sleeping, are you sleeping,
/   /   /
Brother John, Brother John?
/   /
Morning bells are ringing,
/   /
Morning bells are ringing,
/   /   /
Ding, Ding, Dong, Ding, Ding, Dong.

Row, Row, Row Your Boat

C   / /   /   /   /   /   /
Row, row, row your boat, gently down the stream.
/   /   /   /   /   /   /
Merrily, merrily, merrily, merrily, Life is but a dream.

Three Blind Mice

C   /   /   / /   /   /   /
Three blind mice,   three blind mice,
/ /   / / /   /   /
See how they run,   see how they run.
/   /   /
They all ran after the farmer's wife,
/   /   /
She cut off their tails with a carving knife,
/   /   /   /
Did ever you see such a sight in your life
/   /   /   /
as three blind mice?

149

For Your Information

Soprano ukulele tunings:
Open Tuning (C–G–E–G) allows the students to play with "instant success" and concentrate on holding the ukulele correctly.

Standard Tuning (C–G–E–A) is used most often with younger students. Perform 9–11 use both open and standard tunings.

Another tuning (D–A–F♯–B) is usually used with junior-high students.

two beats per measure. These songs should be combined as shown below.

Row, Row, Row Your Boat

Three Blind Mice

Are You Sleeping?

Lesson Focus

Harmony: Chords and melody may move simultaneously in relation to each other. *(P–I)*

Materials

- **Piano Accompaniments:** page 355, 356, and 358
- **Record Information:**
  - Groundhog
    Record 7 Side B Band 2
    Voice: woman
    Accompaniment: ukulele, guitar, double bass, percussion
  - Found a Peanut
    Record 7 Side B Band 3
    Voices: child solos, children's choir
    Accompaniment: ukulele, synthesizer, percussion
  - The Yellow Rose of Texas
    Record 7 Side B Band 4
    Voices: children's choir
    Accompaniment: piccolos, accordion, ukulele, banjo, double bass, percussion
- **Instruments:** soprano ukuleles
- **Other:** cardboard picks, prepared for Perform 9; overhead projector

(continued on next page)

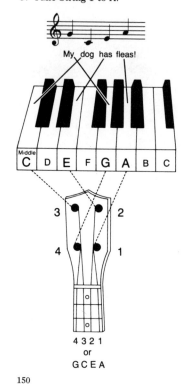

Tune Your Ukulele

1. There is one peg for each string.
   - Find the peg that is attached to String 1.
2. Change the pitch of String 1.
   - Pluck it as you slowly turn its peg until you hear the string change pitch. How did the pitch change?
   - Now turn the peg in the opposite direction until you hear the pitch change again. How did the pitch change this time?
3. Tune String 1 to A.

My dog has fleas!

Middle
C D E F G A B C

3   2
4   1

4 3 2 1
or
G C E A

4. Ukulele strings quickly stretch out of tune. You will often need to re-tune your instrument between songs.

150

The Lesson

1. Review playing the C chord with each ukulele tuned in open tuning. The students may choose from among the three rounds performed in the previous lesson. They may sing them in unison or as partner songs.

2. **Open your books to page 150.** Go around the room showing the students how to retune the first string to change to the standard tuning. (See **For Your Information** in Perform 9.) Display Activity Sheet 37 (*Ukulele Chords*) on the overhead projector. (Cover the C7 and B♭ chords so that only the F chord position can be seen.) Help the students learn to form the F chord as shown at the top of the transparency. Discuss the proper hand position for playing this new chord. The fingers should be curved so that the tips are perpendicular to the finger board. The students must be careful not to allow their fingers to touch any strings other than those marked with circles on the activity sheet. Discuss how to read the diagram, noting the placement of the frets. Help the students realize that the finger tips always press down to the left of the fret.

   When the students can produce a good strumming sound and keep their fingers in position, ask them to play and sing "Are You Sleeping?"now in the key of F.

3. Help the students learn the song "Groundhog" on page 151 while they rest from their practicing. Play the recording or sing the song while the students pretend to strum, following the strum markings above the staff.

4. When the students are familiar with the song, they may return to their ukuleles and add the strum as they sing.

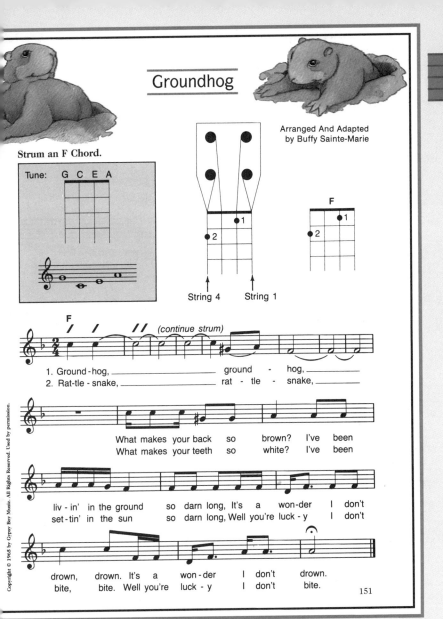

Groundhog

Arranged And Adapted
by Buffy Sainte-Marie

Strum an F Chord.

Tune: G C E A

F

String 4   String 1

F

F   / /   // (continue strum)

1. Ground-hog, _____ ground - hog, _____
2. Rat-tle - snake, _____ rat - tle - snake, _____

What makes your back   so   brown? I've been
What makes your teeth   so   white? I've been

liv - in' in the ground   so   darn long, It's a   won-der   I   don't
set-tin' in the sun   so   darn long, Well you're luck - y   I   don't

drown,   drown. It's   a   won - der   I   don't   drown.
bite,   bite. Well you're luck - y   I   don't   bite.

151

Materials (*continued*)

○ **Teacher's Resource Binder:**
  • **Activity Sheet 37**, page A48
    (Prepare a transparency of the
    activity sheet.)
  • Optional—
    Enrichment Activity 10, page
    E17
    Mainstreaming Suggestion 17,
    page M25

○ **Extends Lesson 56,** page 122

5. Teach the remaining songs on pages 152–153, "Found a Peanut" and "The Yellow Rose of Texas" before proceeding to the next chord. As before suggest that the students pretend to strum in order to get a good feeling for the metric grouping as they listen to the recording and learn the melodies.

6. Help the students practice the chord changes from F to C7 and C7 back to F as shown on the top of page 152 and the activity sheet. (Cover the B♭ chord on the activity sheet so that the students can only see the F and C7 chord positions.) The easiest way to change is to lift the fingers slightly, while tipping the hand down to play the first string (for the C7 chord) with the underside of the index finger (finger "1"). The F chord is easily performed by rocking the hand back to its original position. Finding this "anchor point" should pre-

vent the students from losing their place on the fingerboard.

7. End the class by singing and playing "The Yellow Rose of Texas." As before the students OPTIONAL may take turns singing and playing.

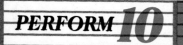
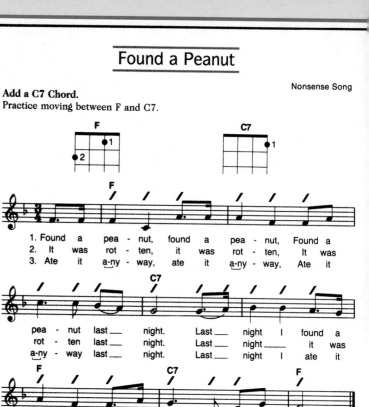

Found a Peanut

Nonsense Song

Add a C7 Chord.
Practice moving between F and C7.

1. Found a pea - nut, found a pea - nut, Found a
2. It was rot - ten, it was rot - ten, It was
3. Ate it a-ny - way, ate it a-ny - way, Ate it

pea - nut last ___ night. Last ___ night I found a
rot - ten last ___ night. Last ___ night _____ it was
a-ny - way last ___ night. Last ___ night I ate it

pea - nut, Found a pea - nut last ___ night.
rot - ten, It was rot - ten last ___ night.
a-ny - way, Ate it a-ny - way last ___ night.

4. Got sick . . .

5. Called the doctor . . .

6. Had an operation . . .

7. I died anyway . . .

8. Went to heaven . . .

9. Woke up . . .

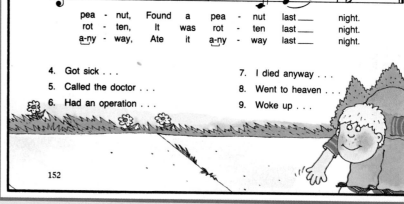

152

Yellow Rose of Texas

American Song

1. There's a yel-low rose in Tex-as, I'm go-ing there to see,

No oth-er fel-low knows her, No-bod-y on-ly me.

She cried so when I left her, it al-most broke her heart,

And if we ev-er meet a-gain, we nev-er more shall part.

Chorus: She's the sweetest rose of color a fellow ever knew,
Her eyes are like the diamonds, they sparkle like the dew.
You may talk about your dearest maids and sing of Rosy Lee,
But the yellow rose of Texas beats the belles of Tennessee.

2. Oh, I'm going back to find her; my heart is full of woe,
We'll sing the songs together we sang so long ago.
I'll pick the banjo gaily and sing the songs of yore,
The yellow rose of Texas, she'll be mine forevermore.

153

PERFORM 10

Lesson Focus

Harmony: Chords and melody may move simultaneously in relation to each other. *(P–I)*

Materials

○ **Piano Accompaniments:** page 360 and 361

○ **Record Information:**
  • The Yellow Rose of Texas
    (Record 7   Side B   Band 4)
  • When the Saints Go Marching In
    Record 7   Side B   Band 5
    The Burly Five Plus One
    Ensemble: trumpet, trombone, clarinet, tuba, banjo, drums
  • Streets of Laredo
    Record 7   Side B   Band 6
    Voice: children's choir
    Accompaniment: ukulele, accordion, acoustic guitar, double bass

○ **Instruments:** soprano ukuleles

○ **Other:** Activity Sheet 37, prepared as a transparency for Perform 10; cardboard picks, prepared for Perform 9; overhead projector

○ **Teacher's Resource Binder:**
  • Optional—
    Mainstreaming Suggestion 17, page M25
    Orff Activity 8, page O15

○ **Extends Lesson 56,** page 122

The Lesson

1. Display Activity Sheet 37 (*Ukulele Chords*) as a transparency. (Cover the B♭ chord position as in the previous lesson.) Review the F and C7 chords by playing "The Yellow Rose of Texas" (page 153).

2. Be sure that the students know the songs on pages 154–155, "When the Saints Go Marching In" and "Streets of Laredo." Challenge the students to sing as much of each as possible by following the notation. Then ask them to listen to the recordings to correct any errors they may have made.

3. Uncover the B♭ chord on the transparency. Help the students practice changing from F to B♭ and back, and from B♭ to C7. The use of an anchor point (the index finger remaining in place for both the B♭ and F chords) will help the students change chords more easily. To play the B♭ chord, the index finger must hold down two strings at the same time. The other fingers must be curved so they do not alter the sound of other strings.

4. When the chord changes have been practiced thoroughly, use the three chords to accompany "When the Saints Go Marching In." The B♭ chord occurs only once in the song. Remind the students to watch and "be prepared" for it.

5. Continue practicing the three chords as the students play "Streets of Laredo."

Streets of Laredo

Cowboy Song

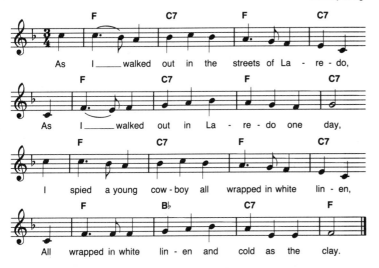

155

PERFORM 11

155

PERFORM 12

Lesson Focus

Harmony: Chords and melody may move simultaneously in relation to each other. *(P–S)*

Materials

○ **Piano Accompaniment:** page 362
○ **Record Information:**
   • Solomon Levi
     (Record 6 Side A Band 10)
   • Spanish Cavalier and Solomon Levi
     Record 7 Side B Band 7
     Voices: man, children's choir
     Accompaniment: pan pipes, ukulele, acoustic guitar, double bass, percussion
○ **Instruments:** autoharp; soprano ukuleles for several students
○ **Other:** cardboard picks, as prepared for Perform 9
○ **Extends Lesson 5,** page 14

Spanish Cavalier and Solomon Levi

Words and Music by William Hendrickson

Perform two melodies at the same time.
Add a ukulele accompaniment.

156

The Lesson

1. Review Lesson 55, pages 120–121, where students learned to play the melody of "Solomon Levi" on a keyboard instrument. Invite one student to play this melody while the class sings.

2. Ask the students to open their books to page 156 and examine the score for "Spanish Cavalier and Solomon Levi." **What in the score indicates that both songs can be sung at the same time?** (The same chord sequence is used for both songs.) Remind the students of their discoveries when they combined "Oh, Dear, What Can the Matter Be?" "Skip to My Lou," and "Ode to a Washerwoman" in Lesson 5, page 14.

3. Help the students learn the new song, "Spanish Cavalier." Draw attention to the skips,

which use pitches of the I, IV, and V7 chords. Play the autoharp as the students sing the melody on the syllable "loo" and then with words.

4. When the students are familiar with the melody, divide them into two groups. Help them learn to sing "Solomon Levi" and "Spanish Cavalier" at the same time. Draw attention to the fact that one song moves in fours, while the other moves in twos. The ⁶₈ meter is felt with two "large" beats per measure. Therefore Group 2 will sing two measures to each one measure sung by Group 1.

5. Draw attention to the verse of "Spanish Cavalier" on the bottom of page 157. Sing it to the melody in Part 1. **Can we sing "Solomon Levi" along with this verse?** (Yes, because both melodies are still the same. Only the words have changed.) End the class by singing the song in this form:

156

F

Bright sun - ny days will

Sec - ond - hand - ed ul - ster - ettes, and

B♭

soon fade a - way, Re -

o - ver - coats so fine, For

C7

mem - ber what I say and be

all the boys that trade with me at

C7   **F**

true dear.

Hun - dred and for - ty nine.

Add this verse to "Spanish Cavalier":

> A Spanish cavalier stood in his retreat,
> And on his guitar played a tune dear;
> The music so sweet would oft times repeat,
> The blessing of my country and you, dear.

157

- two-part refrain
- unison verse
- two-part refrain

6. Draw attention to the fact that this song is accompanied by the same three chords the students have learned to play on the ukulele. Some may accompany the class on the ukulele while others continue to sing the two parts.

OPTIONAL

Lesson Focus

Harmony: Chords and melody may move simultaneously in relation to each other. *(P–I)*

Materials

o **Piano Accompaniment:** page 331
o **Record Information:**
  • Spanish Cavalier and Solomon Levi **(Record 7 Side B Band 7)**
  • The Bee and the Pup **Record 8 Side A Band 1**
    Voices: children's choir
    Accompaniment: recorder, bassoon, harpsichord, percussion
o **Instruments:** keyboard instruments
o **Other:** Activity Sheet 29, prepared for Lesson 55
o **Teacher's Resource Binder:**
  • Optional—
    Enrichment Activity 11, page E20
    Mainstreaming Suggestion 18, page M25
o **Extends Lesson 55**, page 120

Learn to Play a C Chord

Play on the low part of the keyboard. Press the **root** of the chord with your left index finger. Play the other two tones of the chord with the thumb and middle finger of your right hand.

Use this chord to accompany a familiar song. The beginning pitch for the song is E.

Three Blind Mice

    /   /   /   /
Three blind mice, three blind mice,

    /   /   /   /
See how they run, see how they run.

        /   /
They all ran after the farmer's wife,

        /   /
She cut off their tails with a carving knife,

        /   /
Did ever you see such a sight in your life

        /   /
as three blind mice?

158

The Lesson

1. Review the keyboard lessons on pages 118–121 and the songs "Solomon Levi" and "Spanish Cavalier" on page 156. Discuss the fact that since the students could play the piano accompaniment when they sang "Solomon Levi," they should also be able to play the melody while they sing that song and "Spanish Cavalier" as partner songs. Provide an opportunity for the students to play the melody on their practice keyboards as well as on a sounding keyboard instrument.

2. Ask the class to sing the familiar song "Three Blind Mice." Begin the melody on E. Play a one-chord piano accompaniment. **I was playing a chordal accompaniment while you sang the song. How many times did I change the chord?** If necessary, repeat the song so the students can determine that there was only one chord used throughout the song.

3. Invite the students to learn how to play the C chord on the piano. Follow the instructions on page 158. Tell the students to play all three pitches of the chord at the same time, using both hands as shown in the illustration at the top of the page. Have the students take turns at the piano or some other keyboard instruments as they practice this chord.

4. Ask the class to sing "Three Blind Mice" while playing the C chord accompaniment. The students should play the C chord each time a slash mark appears over a word in the song.

5. Help the students learn "The Bee and the Pup" on page 159. Explain that they can play a two-chord accompaniment for this song. First they must learn how to play a G7 chord. They are to follow the instructions on the top of the page. When the students are relatively skillful at moving back and forth between the

158

The Bee and the Pup

Traditional

Learn to play a G7 Chord.
Change the finger positions from the C chord to the G7 chord.
Move the index finger of your left hand from C to B.
Leave the middle finger of your right hand on G.
Put your index finger on F.
Remove your thumb from E.
Practice moving back and forth between the chords several times.
Practice the C and G7 chords in this sequence:

There was a	C C	C C	G7 G7	G7 G7	G7 G7	G7 G7	C C	C C

Play and sing this song:

1. There was ____ a bee - i - ee - i - ee,
2. There was ____ a pup - i - up - i - up,

Sat on ____ a wall - i - all - i - all,
Sat on ____ the bee - i - ee - i - ee,

And he ____ went buzz - i - uzz - i - uzz,
Some - one ____ went Ki - yi - yi - yi - yi,

And that ____ was all - i - all - i - all.
And that ____ was he - i - ee - i - ee.

159

C and G7 chords, guide them to play the sequence to a steady beat.

6. Conclude the class with the students singing and playing the song at the same time.

7. Explain to the students that if interested, other keyboard materials are available for their individual use. (See **Materials.**)

OPTIONAL

PERFORM 14

Lesson Focus
Harmony: Chords and melody may move simultaneously in relation to each other. *(P–S)*

Materials
- **Piano Accompaniment:** page 364
- **Record Information:**
  - Deep in the Heart of Texas
  Record 8   Side A   Band 2
  Voices: children's choir
  Accompaniment: electric guitar, pedal steel guitar, bass, piano
- **Instruments:** autoharps; soprano ukuleles
- **Other:** cardboard picks, prepared for Perform 9
- **Extends Lesson 2,** page 8

The Lesson

1. Ask the students to stand beside their chairs. **How good are your ears?** Play an F chord on the autoharp in a steady rhythm, on the first and third beats of each four-beat measure. **Step in place as long as you hear this sound.** Ask the students to squat down whenever they hear a different sound (a C7 chord). Continue to play in the same rhythm, changing between the two chords, F and C7, in the order shown in "Deep in the Heart of Texas" on page 160.

2. Tell the students to open their books to page 160. **Do you think you moved at the right time? What clue on the page tells you when to move?** (the chord symbols above the staff) Ask the students to follow the notation and indicate the chord changes with their hands as they listen to the recording. Their hands

should remain in their laps when the F chord is heard. One hand should be raised when the C7 chord is heard.

3. **Can you sing what you hear?** Help the students learn to sing the verse and refrain by listening to the recording or by singing the melody with scale numbers.

4. When the melody is familiar, follow the suggestions at the top of page 160. Recall that the class has added harmony by singing in thirds, sixths, or other intervals. **Here is a new way to add a harmonizing part. If I said that the two pitches you will sing, F and C, are the chord roots, can you decide what a chord root is?** (the lowest pitch in the chord, the one for which the chord is named)

Choose some singers to add the chord root as a harmonizing part while the rest of the class

160

heart of Tex-as! _____ The prai-rie sky is

wide and high, Deep in the heart of Tex-as! _____ The

sage in bloom is like per-fume, Deep in the heart of

Tex-as! _____ Re-minds me of the one I

love, Deep in the heart of Tex-as! _____

161

continues to sing the refrain melody. **On what pitch will the harmonizing part begin?** (F) **On what word will you change to C?** ("Texas") To help the students hear the chord changes, invite one student to play the auto-harp accompaniment, strumming twice per measure.

5. The students may also enjoy accompanying this song on the ukulele.

OPTIONAL

6. Challenge the students to add a "root bass" vocal accompaniment to other two-chord songs they know, such as "Found a Peanut" (page 152).

Lesson Focus

Melody: A series of pitches bounded by the octave "belong together," forming a tonal set. *(P–S)*

Materials

o **No Piano Accompaniment**
o **Record Information:**
  • Soldier's Song
    from *The Lark*
    by Leonard Bernstein, 1918–
  ▭ **Record 8   Side A   Band 3**
    Voices: children's choir
    Accompaniment: flute, oboe, clarinet,
    French horn, bassoon, percussion
o **Instruments:** piano; autoharp; hand drum
o **Teacher's Resource Binder:**
  • Optional—
    Biography 6, page B11
o **Extends Lesson 32,** page 70

Soldier's Song

Words by Jean Anouilh

Music by Leonard Bernstein

Vi - ve la Jean-ne, la __ jo -lie, jo -lie Jean-ne,
jo - lie, jo-lou, jo - la la la, Jean - ni, Jean-non, Jean - na na na,
Ô -la jo - lie, jo - lie, Jean - ne. vi - ve la Jean - ne,
la __ jo - lie, jo - lie, Jean - ne, jo - lie, jou lou; jo - la la la,
Jean - ni, Jean-nou, Jean - na na na, O la jo - lie, jo - lie Jean - ne.

162

The Lesson

1. Ask the students to listen to the recording of "Soldier's Song." **What kind of song do you think this probably is?** (a marching song) Invite the students to tap the drum pattern on page 163 on their legs as they listen again.

2. Play the recording again. **Can you hear any changes in the music?** (The song gradually becomes louder. A change occurs at the beginning of the middle section.) To help the students understand the cause for the change, ask them to hum the tonal center for the first section (C). One student may play it on the piano. **Can you keep that sound "in your head" and hum it again when the music reaches the end of the first section?** Play the recording. Stop the music where the changes occur. Agree that the tonal center is still C.

3. Play the recording through the middle section. The students should sense that the melody no longer centers around C but has now shifted to F. **When this happens we say the music modulates. Look at the notation on page 162. What do you think happens in the third section?** (It returns to C.) Guide the students to learn to sing the song, listening carefully to the pronunciation of the French text. (See **For Your Information.**)

4. **Look at the bottom of page 163. To accompany this song you will need three different chords: I, IV, and V7.** Explain that since the melody modulates in the middle of the song, the students will need to play two different sets of chords on the autoharp. **Which chords will you need when the song is in the key of C?** Help the students recall the letter names of the C scale. Determine that the chords will

Whistle:

Add this pattern throughout on a hand drum:

Can you hear the melody change
from one tonal center to another?
When that happens we say there is a **modulation.**
Add an autoharp accompaniment.
You will play the I, IV, and V7 chords in the key of C,
then in the key of F.
Can you figure out the letter names
for each set of chords?

163

For Your Information

Pronunciation for French text of "Soldier's Song":
Vee-veh la Jon-nuh, la jo-lee.
jo-lee Jon-nuh,
Jo-lee, Jo-lou, jo-la-la-la, Jon-nee, jon-nohn, jon-na-na-na,
O-la, jo-lee, jo-lee Jon-nuh.

English translation:
"Long live Joan (of Arc), the pretty Joan." Many of the words are simply a play on the name Joan.

Structure of "Soldier's Song":
The song begins in the key of C, modulates to F, and then modulates back to C. All of the modulations are abrupt.

be C (I), F (IV), and G7 (V7). For the key of F, the chords will be F (I), B♭ (IV), and C7 (V7).

5. Distribute autoharps and give the students time to practice playing the two sets of chords. Give as many students as possible an opportunity to play while others sing. Choose other students to add the drum part.

Lesson Focus

Expression: The expressiveness of music is affected by the way melody and form contribute to the musical whole. *(P–I)*

Materials

o **Piano Accompaniment:** page 366

o **Record Information:**
  • Sing
    Record 8   Side A   Band 4
    Voices: children's choir
    Accompaniment: acoustic guitar, electric piano, electric organ, electric bass, drums

o **Other:** paper and pencil for each student

o **Teacher's Resource Binder:**
  • Optional—
    Mainstreaming Suggestion 19, page M26

o **Extends Lesson 48,** page 106

Sing

Words and Music
by Joe Raposo

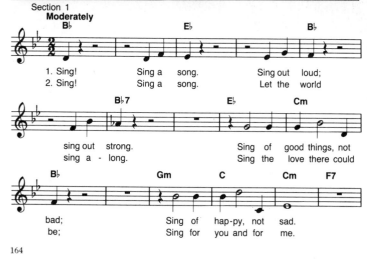

164

The Lesson

1. Play the recording of "Sing." Discuss the expressiveness of the words. Distribute a piece of paper and pencil to each student. Explain that the students are to draw a line each time the singers begin to sing. **Draw only as long as the sound of the singers' voices are heard. Then move your pencil down a space and start a new line.** Play the first section (the first sixteen measures) several times until the students are satisfied that they have drawn their lines appropriately.

   Repeat the activity for the second section (the next 16 measures). Ask the students to draw lines for this section beside the first. Their final pictures should look something like this:

   Section 1   Section 2

2. Ask the students to compare the two pictures. They begin the same way, but the third and fourth musical ideas are extended in the second section. **What if this section had been the same as the first? Would the song have been as interesting?** Ask the students to turn to the song on page 164 and experiment by singing the first section twice. Discuss the effect of stretching out the patterns in the second section. It gives a feeling of something about to happen, of something important being said. It helps build to the climax, the important point of the song.

3. Explore the melodic structure. **Draw a shape for each melodic fragment.** The students' designs should look something like this:

   Section 1

   Section 2

164

4. Comment to the students about how each fragment of melody moves a little higher until it reaches its highest point in the second section. **Does the gradually rising movement help give a special feeling? What would happen if the composer chose to repeat the melodic shape at the same pitch level?** Ask the students to try singing the first eight measures, using only the pitches used in the first two measures.

5. **What other things do you hear in the music that help move the music to a climax near the end of the second section?** Draw the students' attention to the accompaniment as they listen again to the recording. Notice the ways that the instruments help "move the music forward" by "filling in" rests with interesting rhythms and by adding dynamic intensity.

Lesson Focus

Harmony: Two or more musical lines may occur simultaneously. *(P–S)*

Materials

○ **Piano Accompaniment:** page 370
○ **Record Information:**
  • The Inchworm
  Record 8   Side A   Band 5
  Voices: children's choir
  Accompaniment violins, trumpet, trombone, French horn, guitar, electric bass, harp, drums
○ **Instruments:** piano or low-pitched instrument, such as a chromatic bass xylophone, with pitches C, D♭, D, E♭, F, G, A, B♭, and C'; alto metallophone or glockenspiel with pitches B♭, C, and D; mallets
○ **Extends Lesson 35,** page 76

The Inchworm

Words and Music by Frank Loesser

Slowly

Two and two are four, four and four are eight;

That's all you have on your busi-ness-like mind.

Two and two are four, four and four are eight;

How can you be so blind? _____

Refrain

Two and two are four, Four and four are eight,

Inch-worm, inch-worm, mea-sur-ing the mar-i-golds,

Eight and eight are six-teen, Six-teen and six-teen are thir-ty two.

You and your a-rith-me-tic, you'll prob-a-bly go far. _____

166

The Lesson

1. Put the words of the first line of the song "The Inchworm" on the chalkboard. Ask the class to tap a steady beat while chanting the words over and over until a rhythm emerges. Choose one student to mark the accented words while the class continues to chant. A possible solution appears below:

Student chant |Two| and |two| are |four|, |Four| and |four| are |eight|.

Play the recording. Ask the students to continue to tap a steady beat while a second student marks the words accented in the song:

Song   Two and two |are| four, |Four| and four |are| eight.

Discuss possible reasons why the composer chose to set the chant in threes. (It causes accents to occur in unexpected places, making the chant more interesting rhythmically.)

2. **Listen again. Does the melody line move unexpectedly in relation to the words?** Help the students realize that the melodic skip to the unimportant word "and" makes the melody unexpected and interesting. Another unimportant word, "are," occurs at the highest point of the melodic line.

3. Ask the students to scan the melody of the first section on page 166. Draw attention to the recurring skip from D to A. Help the students determine that this skip is a fifth by calling D "1" and counting scale steps up to A. Comment that another name for the distance between pitches is **interval**. Establish the tonality by playing F major and D minor chords. Challenge the class to sing the first section.

4. Ask the students to examine the refrain. **Can you locate an interval that recurs in the low**

166

Two and two are four, Four and four are eight,

Inch-worm, inch-worm, mea-sur-ing the mar-i-golds,

Eight and eight are six-teen, Six-teen and six-teen are thir-ty two.

Seems to me you'd stop and see how beau-ti-ful they are.

Use a low-pitched instrument. Play this bass pattern as an accompaniment for the refrain.

C Bb A G F Eb D Db C C C F

Improvise a melodic interlude that "sounds good" with the bass pattern. Use only these three pitches:

For Your Information

"The Inchworm" is from the movie "Hans Christian Andersen." Andersen lived during the early nineteenth century. He wrote numerous fairy tales that are known and loved all over the world. In the movie Andersen tells children his stories as he wanders through the streets of Copenhagen.

part? (a sixth, at the beginning of Measures 1 through 5) Practice singing the melody of this section.

5. **Is there any interval that occurs frequently in the upper voice of the refrain?** (a third) Compare this melody with that of the first section. Notice that it has a similar up-down contour, but that its range is narrower. Choose some students to learn this melody.

6. Choose one student to add the bass pattern shown on page 167 on the piano or bass xylophone as an accompaniment while the other students sing. (Mark the keys for students who do not play the piano.)

7. Invite the students to improvise a 16-measure interlude while others continue to play the bass accompaniment. Another performer may improvise a melody on an alto metallophone
OPTIONAL

or glockenspiel, using the pitches shown at the bottom of page 167. The interlude may be added between performances of the song.

Lesson Focus

Melody: Individual pitches, when compared to each other, may be higher, lower, or the same. *(D–I)*

Materials

○ **Piano Accompaniment:** page 374

○ **Record Information:**
  • Put On a Happy Face
  📼 **Record 8   Side A   Band 6**
  Voices: children's choir
  Accompaniment: small show orchestra

○ **Teacher's Resource Binder:**
  • Optional—
  Kodaly Activity 1, page K2

○ **Extends Lesson 21,** page 48

Describe Music

Put On a Happy Face

Words by Lee Adams   Music by Charles Strouse

168

The Lesson

1. Ask the students to look at pages 168 and 169. **These pages do not look like most of the pages in our book because there is no musical notation. Yet they can give us many clues about the song to make it easy to learn. Who can find a clue to the melody?** (the line contour) **the rhythm?** (the rhythm bars) **the mood?** (the masks on page 168 and the lyrics on page 169) **the form?** (the order of the masks placed beneath the rhythm bars)

2. Direct the students to follow the row of faces across page 169 while they listen to the recording. Ask the students to be ready to describe the form (a a' b b' a a' c d).

3. **Listen again. This time follow the melodic contour at the top of page 169. Which phrases fit this contour?** (Phrases 2 and 6 fit exactly. Phrases 1 and 5 fit, except for the last pitch. Phrases 3 and 4 start in a similar fashion but end differently. Phrases 7 and 8 are different.)

4. **Now follow the rhythm bars while you listen. Which phrases match these patterns?** (Phrases 1, 2, 5, and 6 fit exactly. Phrases 3 and 4 start the same. Phrases 7 and 8 are different.)

5. **Can you now sing the song?** When the students have demonstrated that they know the melody, suggest that they plan gestures and facial expressions that show the organization of the music. Enjoy singing the song.

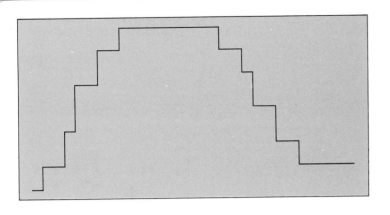

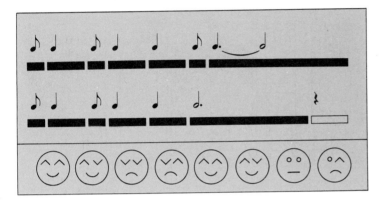

Gray skies are gonna clear up, Put on a happy face!
Brush off the clouds and cheer up, Put on a happy face!
Take off the gloomy mask of tragedy, It's not your style;
You'll look so good that you'll be glad you decided to smile!
Pick out a pleasant outlook, stick out that noble chin;
Wipe off that "full of doubt" look, slap on a happy grin!
And spread sunshine all over the place,
Just put on a happy face!

169

Put On a Happy Face

Words by Lee Adams
Music by Charles Strouse

Johnny's My Boy

Ghana Folk Song

John-ny's my boy, I sent him to school, to

learn how to spell John Pool, John-ny, John-ny, John-ny.

Lesson Focus

Melody: A series of pitches bounded by the octave "belong together," forming a tonal set. *(D–S)*

Materials

○ **Piano Accompaniment:** page 336

○ **Record Information:**
  • Johnny's My Boy
    Record 8   Side A   Band 7
    Voices: children's choir
    Accompaniment: percussion

○ **Instruments:** six sets of resonator bells or xylophones; sets 1 and 2 with pitches C, E, F, A, and C′; sets 2 and 3 with pitches A, B♭, C′, D′, E′, and F′; sets 5 and 6 with pitches C, F, G, A, B♭, and C′; mallets

○ **Other:** paper and a pencil for each team leader

○ **Teacher's Resource Binder:**
  • Optional—
    Kodaly Activity 1, page K2

○ **Extends Lesson 36,** page 78

170

The Lesson

1. Challenge the students to figure out the song "Johnny's My Boy" on page 170 by reading the notation. Guide the class to determine the meter, the scale, the starting pitch, and the shortest sound. Ask the students to sing the two-phrase song.

2. Divide the class into six teams. Each team is to learn a countermelody. Since there are three countermelodies, two teams will learn each. Write these items on the chalkboard:
   • Countermelody number:
   • Starting pitch? meter?
   • Shortest sound for entire song?
   • Shortest sound for assigned part?
   • Scale numbers of assigned part?
   Give blank paper and a pencil to each team leader. Explain that each team is to answer the questions for the part they are assigned.

3. Assign parts. Allow ten minutes for the teams to answer the questions written on the chalkboard and to prepare to sing and play their parts. **Appoint someone in your group to set the shortest sound and give the starting pitch each time you practice your part.** Provide a set of resonator bells for each team. (See **Materials.**) Circulate as the students work, helping those teams who request it.

4. Assemble the class. Ask the teams with the first countermelody to perform their parts while others follow the notation. **Were their performances the same? Were both groups correct?** If needed, point out places that must be corrected. Continue with the second and third countermelodies.

5. Choose a team to sing the melody while the other teams sing the parts they learned.

OPTIONAL

170

Countermelodies to "Johnny's My Boy":

Arranged by Max Exner

Lesson Focus

Form: A musical whole may be made up of same, varied, or contrasting segments. *(D–S)*

Materials

- ○ **No Piano Accompaniment**
- ○ **Record Information:**
  - Allegretto, from *Symphony No. 7*
    (Record 5   Side B   Band 2)
- ○ **Instruments:** resonator bells E, F♯, G, G♯, A, and B; bell mallets
- ○ **Teacher's Resource Binder:**
  - Optional—
    Biography 2, page B3
- ○ **Extends Lesson 48,** page 106

LISTENING

Allegretto

from *Symphony No. 7*

by Ludwig van Beethoven

Compare these themes by Beethoven to the one on page 107. How are they different?

Theme 1

Theme 2

Can you hear the cello and bass instruments play?

172

The Lesson

1. Review the first theme of "Allegretto," from Beethoven's *Symphony No. 7*, page 107. Ask a volunteer to play the theme on resonator bells. Play the recording of the first section of the movement, which features the first theme. (The first section lasts for approximately four minutes.)

2. Explain that Beethoven used two themes in the second section of this music. **These two themes are shown on page 172. Compare them with the theme on page 107.** (They are very different from the theme of the first section. That theme has many repeated pitches, while the themes in the second section move up and down with a distinctive contour.) Play this section of the recording and help the students hear the themes.

3. Call attention to the rhythm pattern played by the cellos and basses as notated on the bottom of page 172. Play the middle section again as the students focus their attention on this accompaniment pattern.

4. Point out that the second section ends with a descending passage. It starts with the high woodwinds, passes to the violins and violas, and finally reaches the cellos and basses. **Listen carefully. What does Beethoven do in the final section?** (He returns to the first theme.)

5. Play the entire movement as the students listen quietly.

Old Dan Tucker

Circle Dance

F

1. Old Dan Tuck - er went to town,
2. First to the right and then to the left, And

F   C7   F

Swing - ing the la - dies all a - round.
then to the one that you love best.

F

Prom - e - nade, Old Dan Tuck - er,

[1.]
C7   F

Prom - e - nade, Old Dan Tuck - er,

[2.]
C7   F

Came too late to get your sup - per.

Measure 5–6
("First to the right and
then to the left . . .")

173

Lesson Focus
Time and Place: The way musical elements are combined into a whole reflects the origin of the music. *(D–S)*

Materials
o **Piano Accompaniment:** page 373
o **Record Information:**
  • Old Dan Tucker
    Record 8   Side A   Band 8
    Voices: children's choir
    Accompaniment: fiddle, guitar, banjo, bass,
o **Teacher's Resource Binder:**
  • Optional—
    Mainstreaming Suggestion 21, page M26
o **Extends Lesson 42,** page 94

For Your Information
Formation for the dance:
Partners stand in a circle, with boys on the inside and girls on the outside. All face counterclockwise. One boy is "Old Dan." He stands in the center and tries to steal a partner during the song.

The Lesson

1. Warm up by singing an F pentatonic scale (F–G–A–C–D). Practice the following patterns:

   1–2–3–5–6–5–3–2–1 and 1–6–5–6–1

   These are the patterns you will find often in the song on page 173. Can you sing the melody? Establish the pulse of the eighth note. Challenge the students to sing the song on the syllable "doo." Play the recording so that the students may check their performance and enjoy the humorous words. Here are the words to Verse 2:
   Old Dan Tucker's a very fine man;
   He washed his face in a frying pan,
   Combed his hair with a wagon wheel,
   And died with a toothache in his heel.

2. Discuss the early days in America. Because there were no VCRs, TVs, radios, or tele-phones, people held parties and dances for entertainment. Play-party games allowed for boys and girls to get to know one another.

3. Help the students learn the dance. (See **For Your Information.**)

   • Measures 1–4: Stand still and clap hands.
   • Measure 5: The boy takes partner's right hand in his right hand and walks around her.
   • Measure 6: The boy repeats the action with the girl on his left.
   • Measures 5–6: The person in the middle ("Old Dan") tries to get a partner by taking the place of one of the boys in the circle.
   • Measures 7–8: "Swing your partners."
   • Measures 9–16: Partners "promenade." (They circle counterclockwise.)

4. Walk through the dance without the music. Then perform it with the recording.

173

Lesson Focus

Form: A musical whole may be made up of same, varied, or contrasting segments. *(D–S)*

Materials

- ○ **Piano Accompaniment:** page 376
- ○ **Record Information:**
  - • Happiness
    Record 8   Side B   Band 1
    Voices: children's choir
    Accompaniment: trumpet, trombone, flute, tenor saxophone, guitar, bass, percussion
- ○ **Teacher's Resource Binder:**
  - • Optional—
    Curriculum Correlation 14, page C15
- ○ **Extends Lesson 28,** page 62

Happiness

Words and Music by Clark Gesner

1. Hap - pi - ness   is   two kinds of   ice   cream,
2. Hap - pi - ness   is   five dif-fer-ent cray - ons,

Find - ing your skate key,   tell - ing   the   time.
Know-ing   a   se - cret,   climb-ing   a   tree.

1. Hap - pi - ness   is   learn - ing   to   whis - tle,
2. Hap - pi - ness   is   find - ing   a   nick - el,
3. Hap - pi - ness   is   hav - ing   a   sis - ter,

Ty - ing your shoes for the   ver - y   first   time.
Catch-ing   a   fire - fly, ___   set-ting him   free.
Shar - ing   a   sand - wich, ___   get-ting a - long.

Hap-pi-ness   is   play - ing the drum in your   own   school   band.
Hap-pi-ness   is   be - ing a-lone ev-ery   now   and   then.
Hap-pi-ness   is   sing-ing to-geth - er when   day   is   through.

And   Hap-pi-ness   is   walk-ing hand   in   hand. ___
And   Hap-pi-ness   is   com - ing home a -
And   Hap-pi-ness   is   those who sing with

174

The Lesson

1. When you are in a shopping center, a park, or a museum, you may see a map that says "You are here." If you know how to follow the map, you can figure out where to go next. Explain that one may also need a map to learn a new song. Music signs can help a person figure out where to go next in a music score. "Happiness," on pages 174–175, is a song that uses a map. Draw musical signs on the chalkboard. (See **For Your Information.**) Ask the students to locate these signs in the song. **Listen to the recording and follow the map. Can you figure out what each sign means?**

2. Solicit answers from the class. Play the recording to verify their answers. **Why do you think these signs are used?** (They make it unnecessary to write out all the music.)

3. **The composer has made the rhythm an interesting feature of this song. As you listen again, decide what ideas he used to create such an interesting rhythm.** (He used many different lengths of sound. He started measures with rests. He put complete measures of rests in the middle of the verses. He stressed normally unaccented words or syllables by using longer sounds on those words. He used very long sounds at the end.)

4. Play the recording again. Invite the students to sing the song with the accompaniment. Turn the balance knob so that only the accompaniment is heard. After the students are comfortable singing the song as a group, ask for volunteers to sing solos.

5. Invite the students to create new verses to complete the idea, "Happiness is . . ." **Can you**

gain. _____ / you. _____ Hap-pi-ness is morn-ing and eve - ning,

Day - time and night - time too.

For Hap-pi-ness is an-y-one, and an-y-thing at all,

repeat from 𝄋 to Fine.

That's loved by you. _____

Fine

For Your Information

Definitions of musical signs:

𝄆 𝄇 means to repeat whatever music is between the signs.

1. _____ means "the first ending." Sing this section the first time through. At the end of the repeat, skip this section and proceed to the second ending.

2. _____ means "the second ending." Do not sing this section the first time through. On the repeat, skip the first ending and sing this one instead.

𝄋 means "from the sign." Return to this sign rather than to the beginning.
Fine means "the end."

think of things that could not have been enjoyed by people long ago? (Answers will vary. They may include "Happiness is watching a video," "flying in an airplane," "learning to breakdance," and so on.)

6. **Can you make up a verse about things people enjoyed long ago that we don't do today?** (Answers may include "riding in a chariot," "waiting for the iceman," or "drinking from a river.") Sing the new verses.

OPTIONAL

DESCRIBE 6

Lesson Focus

Harmony: Chords and melody may move simultaneously in relation to each other.
Harmony: Two or more pitches may be sounded simultaneously. *(P–S)*

Materials

- ○ **Piano Accompaniment:** page 380
- ○ **Record Information:**
  - One Bottle of Pop
    Record 8   Side B   Band 2
    Voices: children's choir
    Accompaniment: synthesizer, acoustic guitar, electric bass, percussion
- ○ **Other:** five soda bottles, tuned to pitches E♭, G, A♭, B♭ and D; sterilizer and wiping cloth
- ○ **Teacher's Resource Binder:**
  - Optional—
    Curriculum Correlation 15, page C18
- ○ **Extends Lesson 2,** page 8

One Bottle of Pop

Traditional
Arranged by Marie Winn

Tune up:

Each measure uses the **root** of a chord.
Can you name each chord?

One bot-tle of pop,   Two bot-tles of pop,   Three bot-tles of pop,

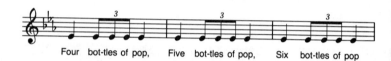

Four bot-tles of pop,   Five bot-tles of pop,   Six bot-tles of pop

Sev - en bot - tles of pop,   Pop!

Which measures of the next melody are based on tones of the
I chord? the **V7** chord?

Do they match those of the first melody?

Don't throw your junk in   my back - yard,   my back - yard,

176

The Lesson

1. **Today we are going to form a pop-bottle band.** Ask the students to listen while you blow into one of the five bottles. (See **Materials.**) **Do you know something about science that will help you predict the sounds produced by the other bottles? Which bottles will sound higher?** (those with more water and less air) **Which will sound lower?** (those will less water and more air) .

2. Choose five students to blow into the bottles. Explain that they must not blow too hard or forget to breathe. If they begin to feel dizzy or lightheaded, they should take a couple of deep breaths before continuing.

3. Be sure the students know which pitches they will be playing. Guide them to play the following musical pattern:

This will be the accompaniment for the songs on pages 176 and 177. First we will need to learn the melodies.

4. Guide the students to answer the questions at the top of page 176 and learn the first melody. Establish the tonality. (Measures 1, 2, 4, 5, 6, and 8 use the I chord. Its root is E♭. Measures 3 and 7 use the V7 chord. Its root is B♭.) Guide the students to sing the tune-ups and encourage them to sing the first melody.

5. Examine the second melody so that the students can answer the questions given in the middle of the page. Guide the students to realize that the answers are the same as they were for the first melody. Write the following chord pattern on the chalkboard:

176

my back - yard. Don't throw your junk in my back - yard,

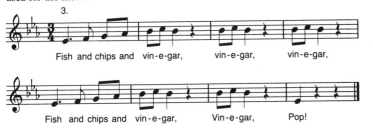

My back - yard's full.

The third melody moves by scale steps.

Can you accompany it with the same chord sequence used for the first two melodies?

3.

Fish and chips and vin-e-gar, vin-e-gar, vin-e-gar,

Fish and chips and vin-e-gar, Vin-e-gar, Pop!

For Your Information

Instructions for tuning bottle pitches: Assemble five empty soda bottles. Pour varying amounts of water into them until the appropriate pitches can be sounded. (See **Materials**.) Mark the water levels with tape. In order to play the bottles, the lips must blow across them like a flute. Experiment until the right amount of lip tension and the correct bottle angle are found to produce a good tone.

A sterilizer can be purchased at any music store that sells band instruments. Remind the students to wipe each bottle before and after playing it.

177

E♭–E♭–B♭–E♭–E♭–E♭–B♭–E♭

Play the chord pattern on the piano while the students learn the second melody. Play the same pattern as they review the first melody. **Does the pattern sound right for both melodies?** (yes)

6. Ask the students to examine the third melody. Challenge them to sing it while you play the accompaniment. **Does the accompaniment still fit?** (yes) **All three songs have the same chordal pattern. Therefore they could be combined.** Review the three songs. If the students can confidently sing the three melodies, divide them into three groups to sing them at the same time.

7. Add the pop-bottle accompaniment to the songs.

OPTIONAL

Lesson Focus

Expression: The expressiveness of music is affected by the way meter contributes to the musical whole. **(D–E)**

Materials

○ **Piano Accompaniment:** page 382
○ **Record Information:**
  • Put On a Happy Face
    (Record 8 Side A Band 6)
  • Edelweiss
  ⊡ **Record 8 Side B Band 3**
    Voices: children's choir
    Accompaniment: small show orchestra
○ **Extends Lesson 43,** page 96

Edelweiss

Words by Oscar Hammerstein II   Music by Richard Rodgers

E - del - weiss, E - del - weiss,
Ev - ery morn - ing you greet me.
Small and white, Clean and bright,
You look hap - py to meet me.

178

The Lesson

1. Explain that in the musical *The Sound of Music*, "Edelweiss" is sung by the Von Trapp family just before they escape from the Nazis. They are sad to leave their Austrian homeland with its beautiful mountains and flowers. **How do you think they would sing this song?** (slowly and sadly, yet with hope for the future and happiness in recalling the beauty of their country) **Is the mood different from "Put On a Happy Face"?** (yes) Play the recording. Discuss the students' reactions.

2. **Because "Edelweiss" is an emotional song, it would be inappropriate to sing or play it like a football march. What has the composer done to achieve both peacefulness and melancholy?** Play the recording again before calling on the students for answers. Some things that might be noticed are the rise and fall of the melodic countour moving by leaps; the rhythm of the melody, which usually moves with tones that are longer than the beat; the $\frac{3}{4}$ meter, which gives a sense of a waltz; a moderate tempo; and *legato* singing.

3. Play the recording once again so that all may listen for the ideas offered. **What movements could you show with your arms that might describe the musical feeling?** Play the recording again while the students experiment.

4. Suggest to the students that, using both arms, they describe the music by making large circles in the air. One circle should be made per measure. The students' hands should touch gently on the first beat of each measure.

5. Show the students the gesture for conducting a $\frac{3}{4}$ meter. Play the recording as the students *OPTIONAL* practice.

Blos - som of snow, may you bloom and grow,

Bloom and grow for - ev - er.

E - del - weiss, E - del - weiss,

Bless my home - land for - ev - er.

For Your Information

Edelweiss is an herb with small, white leaves and flowers. It grows abundantly in the Alps.

179

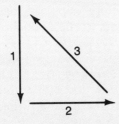

6. End the class by singing the song on pages 178–179 with the recorded accompaniment.

Lesson Focus

Rhythm: Individual sounds and silences within a rhythmic line may be longer than, shorter than, or the same as other sounds within the line. *(D—E)*

Materials

o **No Piano Accompaniment**
o **Record Information:**
  • *St. Louis Polka*
  by J. Biskart and F. Yankovic
  Record 8   Side B   Band 4
  Frankie Yankovic and his Yanks
o **Extends Lesson 46,** page 102

For Your Information

Form of the polka:
  Part A (16 measures): Take 16 polka steps.
  Part B (16 measures): Promenade in a circle.
  Part C (16 measures): Girls take 16 polka steps while boys stand in place. The rhythmic values of "short–short–long," "left–right–left," and "hop–step–hop" are eighth note–eighth note–quarter note.
  Part D (16 measures): Promenade in a circle.

St. Louis Polka

Music by J. Biskart and F. Yankovic

Follow these dance steps:
A. Face your partner. Dance the polka step.

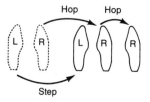

hop - step - hop   hop - step - hop
right - left - right   left - right - left

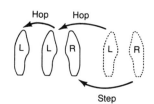

B.

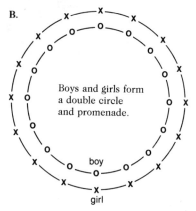

X = girl
O = boy

Each boy should have his hand on the shoulder of the person in front of him.

Boys and girls form a double circle and promenade.

boy

girl

C. Boys should stand still and clap while the girls perform the polka step.

180

The Lesson

1. **People everywhere enjoy the polka.** Play the recording of "St. Louis Polka." As the music begins, clap in a short–short–long pattern. (See **For Your Information.**) Ask the class to join you.

   Let's clap a new way this time. Demonstrate by clapping your own hands on the short sounds. On the long sound, turn your hands outward to the side to suggest clapping the hand of the neighbor on either side of you.

2. While still standing, ask the students to practice tapping with their feet: right–left–right, left–right–left, and so on.

3. Ask the class to form a circle, with all facing the center. Teach the students the basic polka step: right foot–hop; left foot–step; both feet together; right foot–hop. Suggest that the stu-

dents chant "hop–step–hop" as they practice. Practice moving in the opposite direction, beginning with the left foot.

4. Play the recording as the students practice. Those who know the step should stand next to others who are having difficulty. Once individuals master the step, they may practice as couples. One partner starts on the right foot while the other starts on the left.

5. Teach the dance to "St. Louis Polka." **Turn to page 180.** The instructions and pictures will help the students learn the dance. Challenge them to dance by playing the recording.

6. Skilled dancers may embellish their performance by dancing the first polka step face to face, the second back to back, and so on. To do this they must pivot in the opposite direction on the last step of each measure.

OPTIONAL

Black-Eyed Susie

Traditional

What do you notice about the rhythm of the melody?

Here is the rhythm of "Black-Eyed Susie" shown
in relation to the shortest sound.

1. All I want in   this cre-a-tion: pret-ty wife and   big plan-ta-tion.

Hey there pret-ty   black-eyed Su-sie,   Hey there pret-ty   black-eyed Su-sie,

Hey there pret-ty   black-eyed Su-sie,   Hey there pret-ty   black-eyed Sue.

2. All I want in this old world: little kid with hair that's curled.
Hey pretty black-eyed Susie, Hey pretty black-eyed Sue.
Hey pretty black-eyed Susie, Hey there black-eyed Sue.

3. All I want on earth: happiness and mirth.
Hey! Black-eyed Susie! Hey! Sue!
Hey! Black-eyed Susie! Hey! Sue!

181

Lesson Focus
Rhythm: Music may move in relation to the
underlying shortest pulse. **(D–S)**

Materials
○ **Piano Accompaniment:** page 379
○ **Record Information:**
  • Black-Eyed Susie
  Record 8   Side B   Band 5
  Voice: man
  Accompaniment: fiddle, five-string
  banjo, acoustic guitar, double bass,
  harmonica
○ **Other:** a pencil for each student
○ **Teacher's Resource Binder:**
  Activity Sheets • **Activity Sheet 38,** page A49
  • Optional—
  Kodaly Activity 14, page K20
○ **Extends Lesson 9,** page 22

For Your Information
Rhythm ruler answers to Steps 3 and 5:
Phrase 1 of second verse:

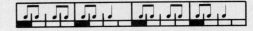

Phrase 1 of third verse:

The Lesson

1. **Look at the song "Black-Eyed Susie" on page
181. What do you notice about the rhythm
of the melody?** (Every note is the same
length.) Ask the class to chant this rhythm
while tapping the short sounds.

2. Hand out Activity Sheet 38 (*Black-Eyed Susie*). **Here is the second verse. As you chant,
can you find the rhythm changes?** ("world,"
"curled," "Hey," "there," and "Sue") **What is
the relationship between these words and the
shortest sound?** (They are twice as long.)

3. Ask the students to write notes in the rhythm
ruler to show the rhythm of the melody of
Verse 2. **What note will you use to begin?** (an
eighth note, same as Verse 1) Show the students how to draw and place the notes so that
each eighth note occupies one segment of the
ruler. (See **For Your Information.**)

4. **What new note will you need? How will you
draw it in the ruler?** (a quarter note, which
will last for two segments on the words
"curled," "Hey," "there" and "Sue")

5. Continue the same process with Verse 3.
Agree that some of the words ("earth,"
"mirth," "hey," and "Sue") need to be four
times as long as the shortest sound.

6. **Listen to the entire song while lightly tapping
the shortest sound.** Challenge the students to
OPTIONAL write the scale numbers for the first verse on
the reverse side of the activity sheet. Sing
with numbers as shown below, and then with
words.

5–5–5–3–4–4–4–2
3–3–3–1–2–7,–6,–5,
1–1–3–3–2–1–6,–5, (three times)
1–1–5,–5,–1–1–1

Lesson Focus

Time and Place: The way musical elements are combined into a whole reflects the origin of the music. *(D–S)*

Materials

- o **Piano Accompaniment:** page 384
- o **Record Information:**
  - Tina Singu

  Record 8   Side B   Band 6

  Voices: folksingers

  Accompaniment: kara
- o **Instruments:** resonator bells with pitches D, G, A, B, C, and D'; tub drum; drums of various sizes; mallets
- o **Extends Lesson 38,** page 84

Tina Singu

African Folk Song

Ti - na sing - u le - lu - vu - tae - o.

Wat-sha, Wat-sha, Wat-sha, Ti - na! Ti - na sing - u

le - lu - vu - tae - o. Wat - sha, Wat - sha,

Wat - sha, Wat - sha. La - la - la - la - la

182

The Lesson

1. Play the recording of "Tina Singu." Share information with the students regarding the song's origin and meaning. (See **For Your Information.**)

2. Review syncopation (the occurrence of melodic rhythm accents before or after the accents of the beat). **What other songs do we know that include syncopated rhythms?** ("Fifty Nifty United States," "You're a Grand Old Flag," and "Life in the Army") **Can you find a syncopated pattern in "Tina Singu" by looking at the notation?** Ask the students to follow the notation of the song on page 182 as they tap the steady beat and listen to the recording. **Which words or syllables have syncopated patterns?** ("Wat-sha" and "vu-tae") The accent falls on the second syllable, which comes after the beat.

3. As one student taps a steady beat on a tub drum, invite the class to chant the rhythm, stressing the "lo-ong" part of each "short-lo-ong" pattern.

4. Draw the following patterns on the chalkboard:

How will you find the tonal center so that you can sing these patterns? (Look at the key signature. G is the tonal center.) Establish the sound of the tonal center on the resonator bells. Ask a volunteer to play each pattern on the bells. The students should then echo each pattern.

5. Direct the students' attention back to their books. **How much of the song have you**

For Your Information

This music is from the southern part of Africa. Typical musical characteristics include a call-response form, repeated melodic patterns, and complex rhythms.

Phonetic pronunciation of "Tina Singu":
tee-nah **seeng** goo
leh-loo-voo-**tah**-eh-oh
waht-shah **waht**-shah **waht**-shah.
Translation of "Tina Singu":
We are the burning fire.
We burn, we burn, we burn.

learned by singing these patterns? (the first section and the upper voice of the second section)

6. Focus the students' attention on the harmonizing part (the lower voice). **Why will this part be easy to learn?** Discover that each pattern begins with a skip up a fourth. All patterns but the first then move downward by steps.

7. **Can you sing both parts together? Which voice will start?** (Voice 1) Divide the class into two groups. Establish the tonality in G and then challenge the class to sing both parts simultaneously.

8. Choose a soloist to be the leader in the first section. When the students know the song, invite them to develop rhythmic accompaniments on drums of different sizes. They may choose rhythmic patterns taken from the melody to use as a basis for their improvisations.

OPTIONAL

DESCRIBE 11

Lesson Focus

Expression: The expressiveness of music is affected by the way dynamics contribute to the musical whole. *(D–S)*

Materials

- **No Piano Accompaniment**
- **Record Information:**
  - *Elfin Dance*
    by Edvard Grieg (**greeg**),
    1843–1907
    Record 8   Side B   Band 7
    Janet Pummill, piano
- **Teacher's Resource Binder:**
  - **Activity Sheet 39,** page A50
- **Extends Lesson 13,** page 30

Elfin Dance

by Edvard Grieg

184

The Lesson

1. Ask the students to imagine that they have just finished composing a piano piece called *Elfin Dance* and have written out the melody and rhythm on music manuscript paper. **Now you have to decide when you want it played loud or soft and where to add markings so that the piano player will know how it should be performed.** Hand out Activity Sheet 39 (*Elfin Dance*). The students are to follow the score as they listen for dynamic changes. Comment that the title *Elfin Dance* might imply some surprises, so they should watch and listen carefully.

2. Review the following musical symbols that are used to describe dynamic levels. Draw them on the chalkboard.

pp	(pianissimo)	very soft
p	(piano)	soft
f	(forte)	loud
ff	(fortissimo)	very loud
sfz	(sforzando)	suddenly very loud
⟨	(crescendo)	gradually louder
⟩	(decrescendo)	gradually softer

3. As the students listen again to the recording, they are to choose the appropriate markings and write them on the score to show what they hear.

4. **Open your books to page 184. Did you make the same decisions as Grieg?** Compare answers. Play the recording again until a consensus is reached.

5. Ask the students to identify other symbols on the page, such as *staccato* and *marcato*. Listen a final time and have them decide whether or not the pianist observes these signs.

OPTIONAL

185

Lesson Focus

Harmony: Two or more pitches may be sounded simultaneously. *(D–S)*

Materials

- **Piano Accompaniment:** page 338
- **Record Information:**
  - This Land Is Your Land
    (Record 6   Side B   Band 1)
- **Teacher's Resource Binder:**
  - Optional—
    Biography 4, page B7
    Curriculum Correlation 16, page C18
    Kodaly Activity 9, page K14
- **Extends Lesson 1**, page 6

The Lesson

1. Many students may already know "This Land Is Your Land." Invite those who do to sing softly along with the recording. Ask the others to listen while they follow the notation on pages 186 and 187.

2. Explain that there are many versions of this song. Some students may have learned a different one. **One version is not necessarily right and another version is not necessarily wrong. That just happens to be the nature of folk songs.** Explain that many people learn folk songs by hearing them sung. They then change a note or two either deliberately or because they forgot how the tune went after they first heard it. Play the recording again. Have the students raise their hands whenever they hear parts of the song they have learned differently. Explain that everyone will need to learn this version so that it will sound pleasing when they sing it together.

3. **Listen to the refrain. Does it sound like the verse or is it different?** (The lower part sings the same melody as in the verse. The upper part adds a new melody, a descant.) Ask the students to sing the lower part without the descant to verify that the tune is the same as in the verse.

4. Ask the class to compare the melody of the descant with the main melody. Call attention to the fact that sometimes the descant moves in the opposite direction of the melody (first and third staffs on page 187), and sometimes it moves in the same direction (second and fourth staffs on page 187). Help a few students learn to sing the descant while the others continue to sing the melody.

186

Refrain

A♭ ... E♭

This land is your land, this land is my land,

B♭7 ... E♭

From Cal - i - for - nia to the New York is - land,

A♭ ... E♭

From the red-wood for - est to the Gulf Stream wa - ters;

B♭7 ... E♭

This land was made for you and me. _____

187

5. Discuss the importance of singing expressively. Ask the class to sing in a style that expresses the pride and wonder they might feel when gazing at a mighty skyscraper or a giant redwood tree. Help the students sing with assurance and in a brisk rhythm, carrying each phrase through without a break.

6. Draw the following patterns on the chalkboard:

Section:

Phrase:

Motive:

If I tell you that each of the three lines I've drawn describes something about the form,

who can figure out what each is describing? To help the students decide, ask some of them to go to the chalkboard. Explain that when the music begins, they are to draw a line with two arcs. They should finish the first arc at the conclusion of the verse and the second arc when the song ends. Agree that this line shows the two sections of the song.

7. Follow the same procedure to help the students realize that each section consists of two phrases (as shown by the second line on the chalkboard) and that each section has seven motives (as reflected in the third line).

DESCRIBE 13

Lesson Focus

Rhythm: A series of beats may be organized into regular or irregular groupings by stressing certain beats. *(D–S)*

Materials

○ **No Piano Accompaniment**

○ **Record Information:**
  • *Blue Rondo à la Turk*
  by Dave Brubeck
  Record 9   Side A   Band 1
  The Dave Brubeck Quartet
  • A Blue Song
  Record 9   Side A   Band 2
  Voices: children's choir
  Accompaniment: synthesizer

○ **Instruments:** assortment of soft percussion instruments, such as triangles, finger cymbals, gongs, guiros, sand blocks, or hand drums

○ **Extends Lesson 50,** page 110

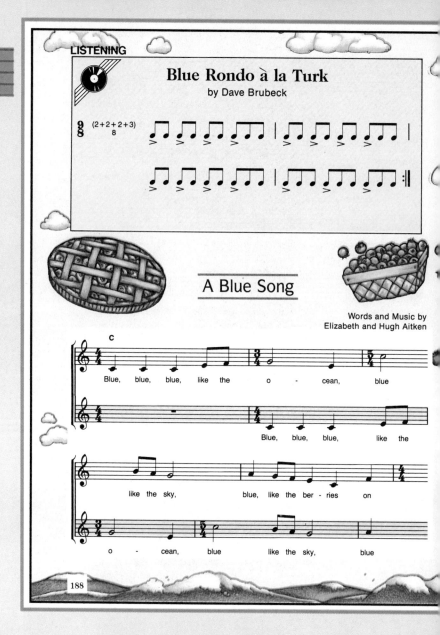

The Lesson

1. Review symmetrical and asymmetrical metric groupings by having the students examine the rhythm patterns shown at the top of page 188. **Which measure is symmetrical?** (Measure 4) **Which measures are asymmetrical?** (Measures 1, 2, and 3) Add the names of sports (such as those used in Lesson 50) to the rhythms. Practice chanting the four-measure pattern.

2. Ask the students to lightly tap the rhythmic sequence on the palms of their hands. Play the recorded excerpt of *Blue Rondo à la Turk* while the students continue to softly tap the pattern.

3. Ask the students to look at the music for "A Blue Song," focusing their attention on the top part of each pair of staffs. Help the students

sense the shift between symmetrical and asymmetrical groupings. The song begins in an asymmetrical feeling, as one measure of ¼ is immediately followed by a measure of ¾. The next two measures of ⅝ continue the asymmetrical feeling. The following four measures of ¼ provide a symmetrical "interlude." Help the students chant the words of the song in rhythm while lightly tapping a steady beat, being careful to place the accents on the correct beats as indicated by the bar lines.

4. Play the recording through the unison statement of the melody as the students evaluate their performance of the rhythm.

5. **As you listen again, focus on the melodic contour. Does it usually move by steps or skips?** Play the recording. Agree that it moves more frequently in steps or small skips. **Do**

188

blue - ber-ry pie, yum,   yum, yum, yum,

like the ber - ries on   blue - ber-ry pie, yum,   yum, yum, yum,

C

blue, blue, blue like the   o - cean,   blue

blue, blue, blue like the

like the sky,   blue like the ber - ries on

o - cean, blue   like tho sky,

F   G7

blue like the ber - ries on

blue like the ber - ries on   blue like the ber - ries on

C
(Both)   Shout

blue-ber - ry pie, yum, yum, yum, yum, yum, yum, yum, yum,   Yum!

189

For Your Information

The rhythm pattern in *Blue Rondo à la Turk,* as shown on page 188, alternates between the saxophone and the piano.

Form of "A Blue Song":
   Introduction
   Song (unison)
   Song (sung in canon)
   Song (unison)

you think you can sing the melody yet? Help the students perform the top part in unison.

6. Allow a few students to choose percussion instruments that seem most appropriate to the "blue feeling." Experiment with the "soft" qualities of various instruments. (See **Materials.**) These students should play the underlying beat, accenting in appropriate sets of two or three beats while the class sings the melody in unison.

OPTIONAL

7. Compare the music on the lower part of each pair of staffs with the upper part the students have just learned. Help them realize that this is a **canon.** That is, the two parts sing the same melody but at different times. Listen to the complete recording to hear how the two parts fit together. Help the students realize that this is an example of polyphonic harmony because each part has an independent melody. When the canon is mastered, sing the entire song with the recording, adjusting the balance so that only the accompaniment is heard.

Lesson Focus

Harmony: Chords and melody may move simultaneously in relation to each other. *(P–S)*

Materials

○ **Piano Accompaniment:** page 386
○ **Record Information:**
  • The Lost Lady Found
  Record 9 Side A Band 3
  Voice: tenor
  Accompaniment: oboe, harp, cello
○ **Instruments:** autoharp; resonator bells with pitches C, D, E, F, G, and A; bell mallets
○ **Extends Lesson 38,** page 84

The Lost Lady Found

English Folk Song

1.'Twas down in a val-ley a fair maid did dwell,
She lived with her un-cle, as all knew full well,
'Twas down in the val-ley where vi-o-lets were gay,
Three gyp-sies be-trayed her and stole her a - way!

2. Long time she'd been missing and could not be found,
Her uncle, he searched the country around,
Till he came to her trustee, between hope and fear,
The trustee made answer, "She has not been here."

3. The trustee spake up with a courage so bold,
"I fear she's been lost for the sake of her gold;
So we'll have life for life, sir," the trustee did say,
"We shall send you to prison, and there you shall stay."

4. There was a young squire that loved her so,
Oft times to the school house together they did go;
"I'm afraid she is murdered; so great is my fear,
If I'd wings like a dove I would fly to my dear!"

190

The Lesson

1. Introduce the students to "The Lost Lady Found" on page 190 by telling them that it is a ballad. **Listen to this recording. Can you decide what a ballad is by describing this song?** Play the recording. Guide the students to conclude that a ballad is a song that tells a story. The same melody is repeated many times as each verse is added to tell the complete tale.

2. Guide the students to study the notation in preparation for learning the song. **Will the rhythm move with a feeling of twos or threes? How will you know?** (It moves in threes, because the meter signature indicates three beats per measure.)

3. Ask the students to stand and step on the first, accented, beat of each measure while clapping the rhythm of the melody.

OPTIONAL

4. Play the recording again. **Is this song based on a major or minor scale?** (minor) **Can you find any repeated sections that will help you learn the melody more quickly?** (Phrases 1 and 4 are identical. Phrase 2 begins the same as Phrase 1. Phrase 3 is different.) Play an autoharp accompaniment as the students softly sing the melody. Play the first verse of the recording as the students listen for sections where they had problems. When the melody is familiar, ask the students to sing all nine verses of the ballad.

5. Invite the students to add an accompaniment. **Look at the chord symbols above the staff. How many different chords will you use to accompany this song?** (three: D minor, A minor, and C major) Distribute resonator bells for each chord, one bell and mallet to each of six students. (See **Materials.**)

5. He travelled through England, through France
    and through Spain,
   Till he ventured his life on the watery main;
   And he came to a house where he lodged for a night,
   And in that same house was his own heart's delight.

6. When she saw him, she knew him, and flew to his arms,
   She told him her grief while he gazed on her charms.
   "How came you to Dublin, my dearest, I pray?"
   "Three gypsies betrayed me, and stole me away."

7. "Your uncle's in England; in prison doth lie,
   And for your sweet sake is condemned for to die,"
   "Carry me to old England, my dearest," she cried;
   "One thousand I'll give you and will be your bride."

8. When she came to old England, her uncle to see,
   The cart it was under the high gallows tree.
   "Oh, pardon! Oh, pardon! Oh, pardon! I crave!
   Don't you see I'm alive, your dear life to save?"

9. Then straight from the gallows they led him away,
   The bells they did ring, and the music did play;
   Every house in the valley with mirth did resound,
   As soon as they heard the lost lady was found.

191

6. Write the three chords on the chalkboard. Ask each bell player to identify the chords that he or she will play. The A and C bell players should realize that they must each play on two chords.

Dm   C   Am

7. Guide the students to follow the chord symbols in their books to determine the sequence in which the chords are to be played. Play the chords two different ways: a) as a full chord on the first beat of each measure:

b) in a rhythmic pattern:

Suggest that the students may wish to alternate these or other ideas they develop while accompanying the many verses of the song.

191

DESCRIBE 15

Lesson Focus
Form: A musical whole may be made up of same, varied, or contrasting segments. *(D—I)*

Materials
○ **No Piano Accompaniment**
○ **Record Information:**
  • The Lost Lady Found
    (Record 9   Side A   Band 3)
  • The Lost Lady Found
    from *Lincolnshire Posy*
    by Percy Grainger, 1882–1961
    Record 9   Side A   Band 4
    The Cleveland Winds
    Frederick Fennell, conductor
○ **Extends Lesson 59,** page 128

LISTENING

The Lost Lady Found
from *Lincolnshire Posy*
by Percy Grainger

Follow the chart as you listen to the composer's use of an ancient melody.
Then add movements to describe the form.

The Music (Theme and Variations)	Movement
1. The theme is stated simply, in unison, by two clarinets.	Listen to and feel the underlying accent.
2. A chordal accompaniment is added by brass instruments.	Group 1: Move in this way: heel - toe - stamp, stamp, stamp
3. The lower brasses play a rhythmic accompaniment of broken chords.	Group 1: Repeat your ideas while a soloist adds an improvised movement.
4. The piccolo plays the melody, now very *legato*.	Group 2: Two members begin the movement — out, in, turn around. . . .
5. Other instruments join in playing the *legato* version of the melody.	Group 2: All members join the movement.

192

The Lesson

1. Review the song "The Lost Lady Found" on pages 190 to 191. **How many verses are in this song?** (nine) Ask the students to turn to page 192. **Here is an orchestral setting of this song.** Explain that the composer set each verse as a variation so the music is never boring, even though the melody is stated nine times. Guide the students to follow the boxes on the left side of each page as they listen to the music. Play the complete recording.

2. Tell the students to work in pairs, with one partner's book open to pages 190–191 while the other's is open to pages 192–193. **As you listen, look back and forth from the words and music to the description of each variation.** Play the recording again, pausing after each section to discuss what the students have heard and how they feel the variation

might help express the ideas of the ballad. (Answers will vary.)

3. Draw attention to the instructions in the boxes on the right side of both pupil pages. Explain that these boxes give instructions for moving to the theme and variations. Divide the class into three groups. Play the recording again, asking each group to read the suggested movements for each variation as they listen. Because the movement suggestions are general, each group will need to plan more detailed floor patterns and gestures to express their parts of the music. They may decide to move with partners, in a line, in a circle, or be spaced randomly about the room.

4. Play the first theme, asking all to move on the accented beat of each measure. Continue to play the first variation as Group 1 practices the heel-toe-stamp motion suggested on page

192

6. The French horn plays a countermelody.	**Group 2:** Continue while a soloist improvises.
7. The accompaniment is again very rhythmic. The theme is in the low brasses. Then. . .	**Group 3:** Move this way: 3/4 pat knees — clap — clap — pat — clap — clap step sideways — together — step sideways
8. a trumpet is heard above the other brasses. Suddenly a fanfare announces. . .	**Group 3:** Continue.
9. the big, majestic statement of the theme played by the full band and timpani.	**All Groups:** Repeat movements, this time reflecting the full, heavy sounds of the accompaniment.

193

192. They will also need to select a soloist to improvise movements while the other group members continue the stepping pattern.

5. Repeat each variation several times, giving the appropriate group time to work out their movement before going on to the next variation. Proceed in this manner until all nine sections have been planned. Note that all groups will perform their movements simultaneously during the final statement of the theme.

6. After planning and rehearsing movements for each section, perform the entire piece.

OPTIONAL

DESCRIBE 16

Lesson Focus
Expression: Musical elements are combined into a whole to express a musical or extramusical idea. **(D–I)**

Materials
○ **No Piano Accompaniment**
○ **Record Information:**
   • Hoe-Down from *Rodeo*
   by Aaron Copland, 1900—
   Record 9   Side A   Band 5
   Morton Gould Orchestra
   Morton Gould, conductor
○ **Extends Lesson 25,** page 56

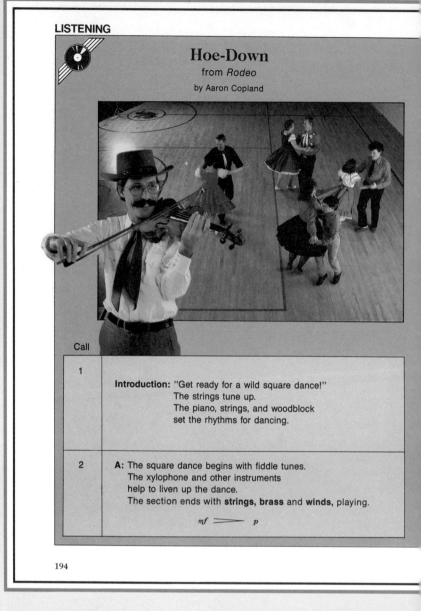

LISTENING

Hoe-Down
from *Rodeo*
by Aaron Copland

Call	
1	**Introduction:** "Get ready for a wild square dance!" The strings tune up. The piano, strings, and woodblock set the rhythms for dancing.
2	**A:** The square dance begins with fiddle tunes. The xylophone and other instruments help to liven up the dance. The section ends with **strings, brass** and **winds,** playing. $mf \Longrightarrow p$

194

The Lesson

1. Ask the class to look at the call chart on pages 194 and 195. Discuss the words "Hoe-Down" and "Rodeo" used in the title. Some students will probably know that a rodeo is a contest of various cowhand skills, such as riding and roping cattle. **What do you think a hoe-down is?** Suggest that the students look at the illustrations and the description of the first sections of the music. Agree that a hoe-down is a type of dance. After a rodeo is over, the participants and friends often hold a dance to celebrate.

2. Ask the students to scan the call chart. **What will you expect to hear at the end of Call Section 2?** (The music will become gradually softer.) **What will you expect to hear in the middle of Call Section 4, the interlude?** (A melody will move gradually downward.)

3. Explain that the numbers shown in the left-hand column will be spoken by a voice on the recording. This will tell them when to move to the next section of the chart.

4. Play the complete recording. **Were you able to hear the musical ideas described in each box?** Replay each section. Pause after each to give the students an opportunity to describe what they heard. Their descriptions should be in relation to the ideas listed in the chart as well as other musical aspects they may have noticed. Replay the complete composition, guiding the students to follow the complete chart. **Which section is repeated?** (Section A is repeated in Call Section 5.)

5. **Do you think you know what a Western hoe-down might be like after hearing this music? What do you think happens?** (The fiddles tune up. The orchestra plays several different

OPTIONAL

194

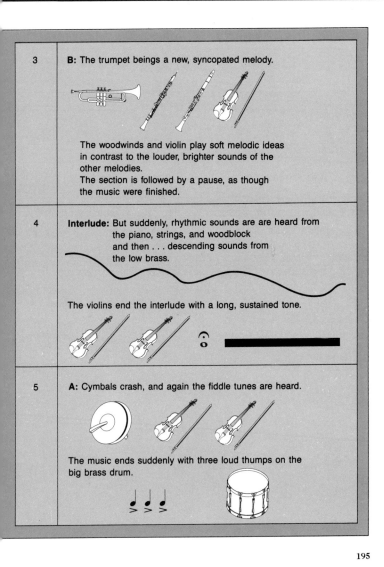

3   **B:** The trumpet beings a new, syncopated melody.

The woodwinds and violin play soft melodic ideas in contrast to the louder, brighter sounds of the other melodies.
The section is followed by a pause, as though the music were finished.

4   **Interlude:** But suddenly, rhythmic sounds are are heard from the piano, strings, and woodblock and then . . . descending sounds from the low brass.

The violins end the interlude with a long, sustained tone.

5   **A:** Cymbals crash, and again the fiddle tunes are heard.

The music ends suddenly with three loud thumps on the big brass drum.

195

dance tunes. The hoe-down must be a fast, boisterous dance, for the tempo is fast and the melodies are "jumpy.")

6. Invite the students to develop their own hoe-down to match the design of the music. Form "squares" of four couples. Count the number of beats in each section. Plan dance patterns for each section, drawing on the following traditional square-dance figures.

- Promenade—Walk or skip around the square, holding your partner's hand.
- "Honor your partner, honor your corner" — Bow to your partner and to the person on the other side of you.
- The head couple may skip around the outside of the ring.
- Partners swing, then turn and swing their corner.

Lesson Focus

Form: A musical whole is a combination of smaller segments. *(D–S)*

Materials

○ **Piano Accompaniment:** page 388

○ **Record Information:**
  • Ode to a Washerwoman
    (Record 1   Side A   Band 6)
  • One Bottle of Pop
    (Record 8   Side B   Band 2)
  • Oh, It's Great to Be Livin' This Morning
    Record 9   Side B   Band 1
    Voices: man, children's choir
    Accompaniment: piccolo, flute, oboe, clarinet, bassoon, French horn, electric piano, clarinet, double bass, percussion

○ **Extends Lesson 49,** page 108

Chords not shown on Pupil Page

Oh, It's Great to Be Livin' This Morning

Words and Music by Doug Nichol

The Lesson

1. Begin by reviewing "Ode to a Washerwoman" (page 14) and "One Bottle of Pop" (page 176). Help the students enjoy the pleasing sound that harmony produces.

2. **How did we achieve harmony?** (Two or three different melodies are combined at the same time.) **Sometimes a melody can be combined with itself. The song "Oh, It's Great to Be Livin' This Morning" is that kind of song. When we know it well we can sing the refrain at the same time as the verse.**

3. Ask the students to scan the notation on pages 196 and 197. **Which note represents the shortest sound?** (sixteenth note) Draw a rhythm ruler on the chalkboard.

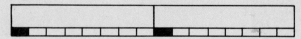

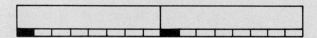

Ask a student to fill in the ruler to show the rhythm of the first phrase of the refrain.

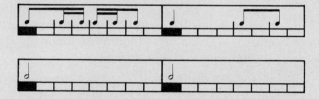

4. Challenge the students to find phrases with the same rhythm as Phrase 1 (Phrase 3) and phrases that are similar but not exactly the same (Phrases 2 and 4). Remind them that they are looking for rhythmic, not melodic, similarity.

5. Draw another rhythm ruler on the chalk-

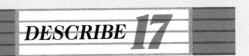

Verse

1. It makes no dif-fer-ence if it's sun-ny or not,
2. I've found that I can make the sun shine in - side,

The rain just can't de - press me.
When Moth - er Na - ture's gloom - y.

I'm real - ly thank-ful for this new day I've got.
There's no ex - cuse I've found to make my sun hide,

1. Just be - in' here a - live on earth can im - press
2. When there's so ma - ny things that keep com-in' to

D.C. al Fine

me. _____
me. _____

197

board. Ask a volunteer to draw the first phrase of the verse.

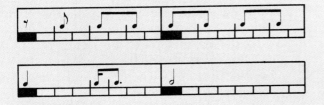

6. Repeat Step 4, this time looking at the phrases in the verse. Here, Phrases 3 and 4 are the same as Phrase 1. (Phrase 4 is extended to the end of the song.) Phrase 2 is similar. Give the students an opportunity to chant the rhythm of the entire song using the nonsense syllable "doo." *OPTIONAL*

7. When the students realize that the entire song is built out of only two contrasting rhythmic ideas, focus their attention on the melody. **Is the same true for the melody?** (yes) Ask the students to sing the first phrase with numbers after determining that the song begins on the tonal center (1). When the refrain melody has been learned, proceed with the verse in the same manner. (The verse begins on 5.)

8. Play the recording for the students. Encourage them to check the accuracy of their singing. Call attention to the expressiveness of the singing.

9. When the students know the song well, divide the class into two groups. Both groups should sing the refrain. Then one group continues with the verse while the other group sings the refrain again.

197

Lesson Focus

Harmony: Two or more pitches may be sounded simultaneously. *(C–I)*

Materials

○ **No Piano Accompaniment**

○ **Record Information:**
  • Pachycephalosaurus
    Record 9   Side B   Band 2
    Voices: children's choir
    Accompaniment: saxophone quartet
  • "Fossils" from *Carnival of the Animals*
    by Camille Saint-Saëns, 1835–1921
    Record 9   Side B   Band 3
    New York Philharmonic
    Leonard Bernstein, conductor

○ **Teacher's Resource Binder:**
  • Optional—
    Curriculum Correlation 17, page C19

○ **Extends Lesson 19**, page 44

Create Music

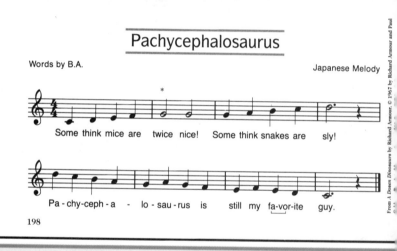

Pachycephalosaurus

Words by B.A.   Japanese Melody

Some think mice are   twice nice!   Some think snakes are   sly!

Pa - chy-ceph - a - lo - sau - rus   is   still my fa-vor-ite   guy.

198

The Lesson

1. Challenge the students to learn to sing the melody to "Pachycephalosaurus" on page 198 by reading the notation, using the syllable "loo." **Will you be able to do this easily?** (Yes, because the melody moves up or down by steps, and the rhythm usually moves with the shortest sound.) Establish the tonality. Ask the students to warm up by singing the scale from 1 up to 2' and then back down to 1.

2. When the students can sing the melody on the syllable "loo," help them learn to pronounce pachycephalosaurus (**pak-i-sef-a-lo-saw-rus**). **What do you think a pachycephalosaurus was?** (The students may know that it was a type of dinosaur.) Read the poem to discover that it was, indeed, a dinosaur. (See **For Your Information.**) Ask the students to describe what they think this dinosaur looked like and how it might have moved.

3. **The composer Saint-Saëns used music to describe fossils that might have been dinosaur bones.** (Fossils are bones or other remnants of life embedded in stone.) Explain that Saint-Saëns wrote this music in a very playful way, by borrowing melodies from other compositions for his themes. Theme 1 is from *Danse Macabre* (page 44). Themes 2 and 3 might be recognized by the class as "Twinkle, Twinkle Little Star" and "In the Moonlight." Draw attention to the three themes shown on page 199. **Listen to the music. Raise your hand when you hear one or more of these melodic ideas.** Ask the students to follow the notation in their books while they listen.

4. **Here is a fourth theme, which is also borrowed.** Explain that Theme 4 is a melody used in *The Barber of Seville,* an opera by Rossini. Play this theme on the piano or resonator bells for the class. Then play the recording

198

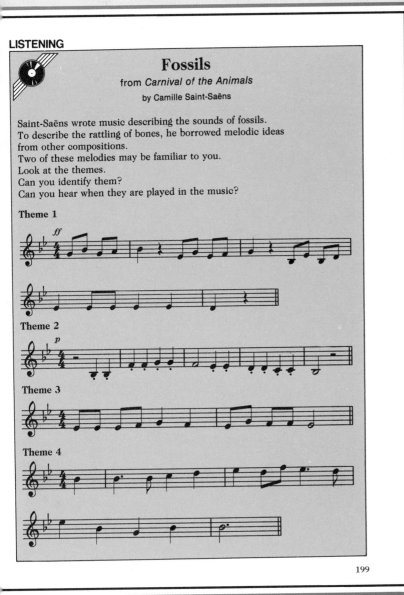

Fossils

from *Carnival of the Animals*

by Camille Saint-Saëns

Saint-Saëns wrote music describing the sounds of fossils.
To describe the rattling of bones, he borrowed melodic ideas
from other compositions.
Two of these melodies may be familiar to you.
Look at the themes.
Can you identify them?
Can you hear when they are played in the music?

Theme 1

Theme 2

Theme 3

Theme 4

199

CREATE 1

For Your Information

Pachycephalosaurus
by Richard Armour

Among the later dinosaurs
  Though not the largest, strongest,
Pachycephalosaurus had
  The name that was the longest.

Yet he had more than syllables,
  As you may well suppose.
He had great knobs upon his cheeks
  And spikes upon his nose.

Ten inches thick, atop his head,
  A bump of bone projected.
By this his brain, though hardly worth
  Protecting, was protected.

No claw or tooth, no tree that fell
  Upon his head kerwhacky,
Could crack or crease or jar or scar
  That stony part of Paky.

And so he nibbled plants in peace
  And lived untroubled days.
Sometimes, in fact, as Paky proved,
  To be a bonehead pays.

again as the students follow the themes in their books, this time listening especially for Theme 4.

5. **Why was the xylophone a good instrument to feature in this music?** (It suggests the idea of brittle bones or fossils.)

6. Return to the song on page 198. Organize the class into small groups. (The students may also work individually, if they so choose.) They are to replace the words "twice nice" and "sly" with words that suggest a new idea about mice and snakes. They must also make up a new imaginary animal that uses the same number of syllables as "Pachycephalosaurus." Invite the students to sing their new verses. Select several verses for the entire group to sing.

7. Create harmony by singing the song as a two-part canon, using either the original or the new verses. Divide the class into two groups. The second group begins when Group 1 reaches the asterisk.

OPTIONAL

199

CREATE 2

Lesson Focus

Form: A musical whole is a combination of smaller segments. *(C–I)*

Materials

○ **No Piano Accompaniment**

○ **Record Information:**
   • Every Morning When I Wake Up
   Record 9 Side B Bands 4a–b
   Voices: children's choir
   Accompaniment: percussion

○ **Instruments:** bass, alto, and soprano xylophones; alto metallophone; alto and soprano glockenspiels, all with pitches D, E, F♯, A, B, and D'; various non-pitched percussion instruments; mallets

○ **Extends Lesson 5**, page 14

For Your Information

Further recording information for "Every Morning When I Wake Up":
Band a—The song is performed first as a single melody and then as a three-part round.
Band b—The song is used as Section A of a rondo.

Every Morning When I Wake Up

Words and Music by Avon Gillespie

Ev - e-ry morn - ing when I wake _ up

I have a new song to sing, my chil - dren.

Ev - e-ry morn - ing when I wake _ up

I have a new song to sing. ____

Create an accompaniment for this round.
Create special parts to perform as a rondo.

200

The Lesson

1. Sing or play the recording of "Every Morning When I Wake Up" for the students. **Listen to the song. Decide if this melody begins high and moves down or begins low and moves up.** (It begins high and moves down.) **This time show with your hand how the melody moves. If I sing the first phrase, can you answer with Phrase 2?** (Yes, because it's the same, except for the ending.) After they sing the phrases as an echo, ask the students to sing the complete song.

2. Invite the students to plan an instrumental accompaniment. Guide them to make decisions about how each part may be played. All parts must be in ⁴⁄₄ meter. (See **Materials.**)

   • Bass xylophone: Choose pitches. Reinforce the steady beat.
   • Alto metallophone: Choose pitches. Play only on the first and third beat.
   • Alto or soprano xylophone: Choose pitches. Play eighth-note patterns.
   • Glockenspiels or small non-pitched percussion instruments: Create melodic or rhythmic ideas for sections of the rondo.

3. Organize the composition as a rondo (**A B A C A D A**), using the song as the A section. Glockenspiel players are to improvise melodies for the B, C, and D sections of the rondo. Rhythmic accompaniments may be added using the students' choice of non-pitched percussion instruments for each improvised section. These rhythmic accompaniments may be continued throughout the entire piece, if desired.

4. The song may also be performed as a three-part round. See the score for the voice entrances.

OPTIONAL

Glee Reigns in Galilee

Traditional Israeli Song

Refrain   Em

Glee reigns in Gal - i - lee, the Gal - il re - joic - es,

Fine

The day and night a - round;— lift up your voic - es.

Verse   G

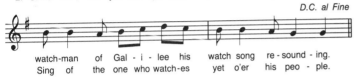

1. Through night __ witch-ing dark-ness, bells soft - ly sound-ing, the
2. Strike out the lyre and cym-bals, call all the peo - ple;—

D.C. al Fine

watch-man of Gal - i - lee his watch song re - sound - ing.
Sing of the one who watch-es yet o'er his peo - ple.

Bass xylophone (refrain)   (verse)

Alto metallophone (refrain)   (verse)

Create other instrumental parts.

201

CREATE 3

Lesson Focus

Harmony: Chords and melody may move simultaneously in relation to each other. *(C–S)*

Materials

○ **Piano Accompaniment:** page 390
○ **Record Information:**
  • Glee Reigns in Galilee
    Record 9   Side B   Band 5
    Voices: children's choir
    Accompaniment: clarinet, trumpet, trombone, tuba, cimbalom, violin, accordion, mandolin, percussion
○ **Instruments:** bass xylophone; alto metallophone with pitches E, G, B, and D; autoharp; tambourines; timpani; cymbals; finger cymbals; drums; chromatic resonator bells with pitches E to E'; mallets
○ **Teacher's Resource Binder:**
  • Optional—
    Orff Activity 12, page O25
○ **Extends Lesson 27,** page 60

The Lesson

1. Warm up by singing an E major and then an E minor scale on the syllable "loo." Ask the students to turn to page 201 and follow the notation for "Glee Reigns in Galilee" as they listen carefully to the recording. **Can you decide on which scale this song is based? Does it seem to be in major, like the first scale you sang, or in minor, like the second one?** Play the recording. Guide the students to realize that this song uses both major and minor modalities. **Listen again. Decide which section is in major and which is in minor.** (The verse is in major. The refrain is in minor.)

2. Observe the rhythm. Note that each measure begins with the same pattern (short–long–short). Tap the shortest sound and ask the students to read the words, stressing the long sound. Establish the tonality on the autoharp and help the students learn the melody.

3. Guide the students to learn the accompaniment parts that reinforce the major-minor qualities as shown on the bottom of the page. The students should notice that each part consists of a one-measure ostinato. Combine these to create an accompaniment for Verse 1.

4. **Look at Verse 2. Decide which instruments would best help express the ideas of this text.** The autoharp might suggest a lyre. Use either regular or finger cymbals. Ask the autoharp player to strum E minor and G major chords. The cymbals performers might play a short–long pattern at the beginning of each measure.

5. Other students may add other accompaniments, using appropriate small nonpitched percussion instruments.

OPTIONAL

201

Lesson Focus

Form: A musical whole may be made up of same, varied, or contrasting segments. *(C–I)*

Materials

○ **Record Information:**
- The Dove from *Noye's Fludde* by Benjamin Britten, 1913–1976
  Record 9   Side B   Band 6
  Ensemble conducted by Buryl Red
- By the Brook from *Symphony No. 6* (excerpt) by Ludwig van Beethoven, 1770–1827
  Record 9   Side B   Band 7
  The Cleveland Orchestra
  George Szell, conductor

○ **Instruments:** whistles; glockenspiels; mallets

○ **Teacher's Resource Binder:**
- Optional—
  Biography 2, page B3
  Curriculum Correlation 18, page C19

○ **Extends Lesson 6,** page 16

Sky Singers

Bird songs are a part of nature's music.
What do you think birds are saying to each other?
Do they ever just sing for fun?

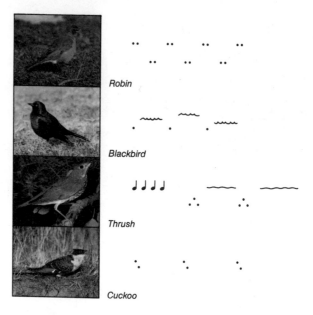

Robin

Blackbird

Thrush

Cuckoo

A musical strategy:
1. Use vocal sounds, whistles, or instruments to perform your interpretation of these bird songs.
2. Work in groups.
   Combine bird songs to make a musical form.
   Create a suite entitled "Sky Singers."
   What musical forms will each movement in the suite use?
   A B A? A A B A? canon? rondo?

202

The Lesson

1. Write the words "Sky Singers" on the chalkboard. **What do you think "Sky Singers" could be?** If the students do not readily think of birds, add the word "Nature's" in front of the words. Invite the students to suggest times when they have enjoyed the songs of "sky singers." Ask them to open their books to page 202. Discuss the beautiful sounds of birds and invite the students to offer answers to the questions at the top of the pupil page.

Explain that researchers study the sounds of birds. The students are to take on the role of researchers. Ask them to explore ways birds communicate with each other. Birds use their sounds to tell other birds "get out of my tree," "this is my bug," or "hello." Birds also seem to make sounds just for their own pleasure.

2. Draw the students' attention to the illustrations of bird songs on the pupil page. **This is the way the researchers have written down bird songs. Can you interpret their "notation"?** Suggest that the students use vocal sounds (including whistling), whistles, or other high-pitched instruments such as glockenspiels to interpret the bird sounds shown in their books. Provide individual practice time and then give each student an opportunity to perform the bird song of his or her choice.

3. Divide the class into several groups. Each group is to create a bird song for a suite entitled "Sky Singers." Explain that a **suite** is a long composition divided into small sections called **movements.** Each movement has a form of its own. Each group may choose a form for its movement, such as **A B A, A B,** rondo (**A B A C A**), or theme and variations. Each group should decide which bird songs it

LISTENING

The Dove
from *Noye's Fludde*
by Benjamin Britten

Listen to how other composers have expressed their ideas of
bird songs in music.
Britten created the sound of the dove by having
a recorder "fluttertongue." That is, the tongue is whirred
against the back of the player's teeth while he or she blows.

Noye speaks, and the dove appears at the cabin window.
Can you hear when the dove sings?

LISTENING

Symphony No. 6 ("Pastoral")
by Ludwig van Beethoven

One of the most famous examples of birdsong in music is in
Beethoven's *Pastoral Symphony,* where three instruments
imitate the sound of a cuckoo, a quail, and a nightingale.

Follow this score.
Can you hear when the different birds enter with their songs?

203

CREATE 4

will interpret and how it will organize the
songs to create the form it has chosen.

4. Give the groups a few minutes to plan and
practice their compositions. Then perform
the entire suite.

5. Focus the students' attention on page 203.
Explain that composers have used bird songs
in their music. Benjamin Britten wrote a composition called "The Dove." Explain that this
selection is from an opera that tells the story
of Noah's Ark. During the opera, Noye (Noah)
sends a raven to search for dry land. Noye
sings, "Ah Lorde, wherever this raven be?
Somewhere is drye, well I see." A dove appears at the window. "But yet a dove, by my
lewtye (faith) after I will send." He sends the
dove to follow the raven. The dove begins to
circle away and disappears.

OPTIONAL

Noye again sings about the dove: "Thou wilt
turne again to me, for of all fowles that may
flye, Thou art most make and hend." (kind)
The dove returns with an olive branch in its
beak, indicating that dry land has been found.

Play the recording. Ask the students to listen
for the sound of the dove cooing and then
flying away to find land.

6. **Listen to another famous piece of music that
uses instruments to imitate birds.** Explain
that this music is a small part of a movement
from a symphony by Beethoven. This symphony is known as the *Pastoral Symphony*
because Beethoven's music suggests scenes of
the countryside. Help the students follow the
score while they listen to the segment that
contains the bird songs.

203

CREATE 5

Lesson Focus
Form: A musical whole is a combination of smaller segments. *(C–I)*

Materials
○ **Record Information:**
  - Autre Choral
  from *En Habit de Cheval*
  by Erik Satie (sah-**tee**), 1886–1925
  Record 9   Side B   Band 8
  French National Radio and Television Orchestra
  Manual Rosenthal, conductor
○ **Instruments:** piano; resonator bells or chromatic xylophone with pitches C♯, D♯, F, G, A, B, C♯', and D♯'; mallets
○ **Extends Lesson 24,** page 54

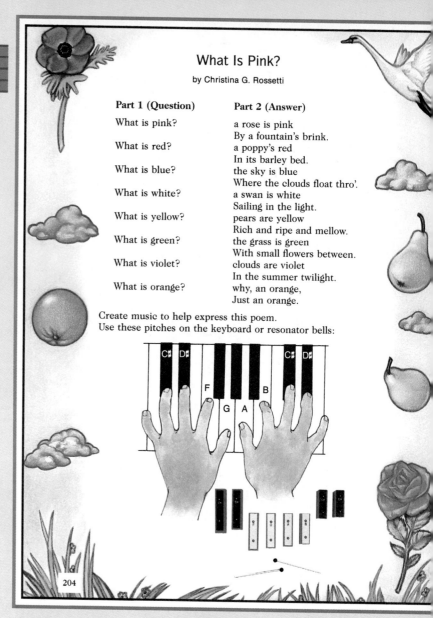

What Is Pink?
by Christina G. Rossetti

Part 1 (Question)	Part 2 (Answer)
What is pink?	a rose is pink
	By a fountain's brink.
What is red?	a poppy's red
	In its barley bed.
What is blue?	the sky is blue
	Where the clouds float thro'.
What is white?	a swan is white
	Sailing in the light.
What is yellow?	pears are yellow
	Rich and ripe and mellow.
What is green?	the grass is green
	With small flowers between.
What is violet?	clouds are violet
	In the summer twilight.
What is orange?	why, an orange,
	Just an orange.

Create music to help express this poem.
Use these pitches on the keyboard or resonator bells:

204

The Lesson

1. Ask the students to read the poem on page 204 to themselves. Then divide the class into two groups and assign parts. Perform the poem as a choral reading several times until a rhythmic pattern emerges and members of each group can rhythmically read in unison.

2. Put out the resonator bells or chromatic xylophone with pitches of the whole-tone scale or mark these pitches on the piano. (See **Materials**.) As the class chants the poem, invite one student to improvise a melodic descant, using any of the indicated pitches. The student should play in the rhythm of the words. Give several students the opportunity to improvise.

   Explore the different qualities of instrumental sounds (the bells versus the piano) and pitch levels (the high octaves versus the low octaves

of the piano). Suggest to the students that they think about ideas suggested by the words of the poem. Suggest that they express those ideas by choosing an instrument and improvising a melodic shape at an appropriate pitch level.

3. Give several students the opportunity to improvise while the class reads the poem. Focus on the sounds of the instruments. Tell the class to "take the words inside." That is, think the words but not to speak them aloud. This time choose two students to perform the "poem without words" as an instrumental question-and-answer piece. Performer 1 plays the question, "What is pink?", Performer 2 plays the answer, "a rose is pink. . . ."

4. Ask the students to create another instrumental composition by following the score titled "Largo" on page 205. The score indicates the

204

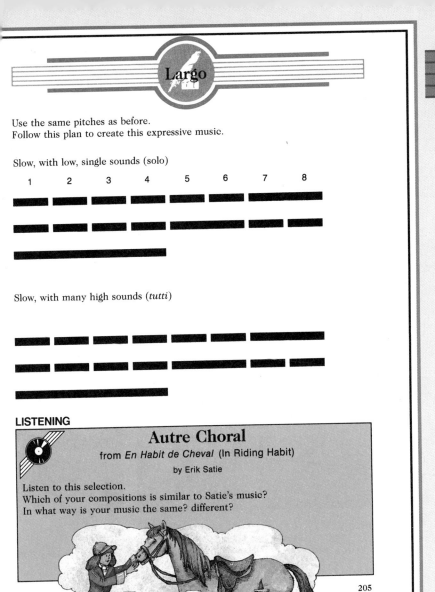

Largo

Use the same pitches as before.
Follow this plan to create this expressive music.

Slow, with low, single sounds (solo)

1   2   3   4   5   6   7   8

Slow, with many high sounds (*tutti*)

LISTENING

Autre Choral
from *En Habit de Cheval* (In Riding Habit)

by Erik Satie

Listen to this selection.
Which of your compositions is similar to Satie's music?
In what way is your music the same? different?

205

duration of the piece. It is defined by the length of the lines and numbers written across the top of the score. Each number equals one short sound. The tempo is identified at the top of the score. The performer must choose the pitches to be played, selecting from the whole-tone scale used in the previous improvisation activity. He or she will also have to make decisions about dynamics.

Draw attention to the word "solo" at the end of the instructions at the top of the page. **How many performers will play this part?** (only one) **How many will play the second part?** The students may be unsure. Explain that **tutti** is a musical term that means "all." This part may be played by several students, depending on the number of instruments available. Give several soloists and groups the opportunity to improvise a question-and-answer composition.

OPTIONAL

5. Read the discussion at the bottom of the page regarding the composition "Autre Choral" by Erik Satie. Play the recording. The students should discover that Satie's music is rhythmically the same as "Largo." It follows the same plan for solo-tutti sections but uses different instruments and pitch ideas.

Lesson Focus

Expression: The expressiveness of music is affected by the way melody, dynamics, rhythm, and timbre contribute to the musical whole. *(C–E)*

Materials

○ **Extends Lesson 17,** page 40

Speech to Song

Speaking and singing have many things in common.
Words may be spoken or sung.
Words express our feelings.
They can express excitement, happiness, sadness, or fright.
We use voice inflection when we speak.

Ba — na - nas for sale

We use exaggerated voice inflections when we sing.

Yes! We have no ba - na - nas,

Gestures help punctuate and emphasize our words.
Look at this storyboard.
What could these people be saying to each other?

Work with a partner.
Decide who the characters will be.
Play the roles of these two people.
Speak their conversation.
Perform the roles again by singing the conversation.

206

The Lesson

1. Read the discussion on page 206 with the students. Help them understand that vocal inflection can be used to express different ideas. Ask the class to read "Bananas for sale," following the contour shown on the page. Compare it with the melody for "Yes! We have no bananas." Agree that both have high and low sounds. The melodic contour of the song, however, is more exaggerated, and it stretches over a wider range from low to high.

2. Read the sentence about gestures. Ask the students to look at the storyboard in the middle of the page. Ask them to describe what they think is happening, based on the gestures of the characters. **What could these people be saying to each other? Who could they be? What are they feeling? Where might they be?** Assign each student to work with a partner.

They are to

- decide who the characters are; they might be parents, two strangers, or a vendor trying to sell something to a passerby.
- create the conversation ("Excuse me, but are you the chef?" "Yes I am, madam." "This food is very good. Did you prepare it?" "Yes, madam. I'm glad you like it.")

3. Give the students a brief time to plan their conversation. Then invite them to speak it for the class. After several groups have presented their dialogues, ask them to change from speaking to singing. They may use any pitches they choose. Encourage them to think about the melody they are using and how to use loud and soft voices, long and short sounds with some words accented, and different qualities of voice to express the emotions of the characters.

The Makings of an Opera

Opera is a story told with voices and an orchestra.
An opera has different kinds of songs.

1. An **aria** is a song usually written for just one singer.
   It expresses the inside thoughts of the character,
   such as joy, sorrow, or fright.
   Make up an aria for one of these feelings.

joyful   terrified   angry   mournful

2. A **recitative** is "song-talking."
   It is like a conversation, and it is sung between
   the main songs of the opera.
   It can help move the plot of the story.
   Find a partner and sing a recitative.

Have you ever sung a recitative before?

207

4. Continue on to page 207. Discuss the different kinds of music used as part of an opera. **Arias** are sung to express the character's feelings. They often have wide ranges, and they may include a variety of dynamics, tempos, accents, and vocal qualities in order to help the audience sense how the character feels. The students may take turns improvising an aria to express the feeling of a character chosen from the first row of boxes.

5. **Look at the lower row of boxes.** A recitative helps carry along the plot of the opera. A recitative often has a more limited melodic range than an aria. The words are frequently sung in a rhythm that closely follows the natural rhythm of the spoken words. Encourage the students to consider the same points as they did when planning the aria. Ask them to perform their recitatives. Help the students realize that they have already sung a recitative when they followed the storyboard on the previous page.

CREATE 7

Lesson Focus

Time and Place: The way musical elements are combined into a whole reflects the origin of the music. *(P–S)*

Materials

○ **Piano Accompaniment:** page 391
○ **Record Information:**
  • A Little Love Goes a Long Way
  ▪ **Record 10 Side A Band 1**
    Voices: child solo; children's choir
    Accompaniment: electric organ, electric guitar, electric bass, tin whistle, steel drum, percussion
○ **Instruments:** Latin rhythm instruments, such as conga and bongo drums, maracas, and claves
○ **Extends Lesson 16,** page 38

A Little Love Goes a Long Way

Words and Music by Alfred Balkin

Learn to sing this song.
Use Latin rhythm instruments to create an accompaniment.

The Lesson

1. Introduce the song "A Little Love Goes a Long Way." Challenge the students to learn Part 1 of the refrain melody by singing the pitch numbers. Make a pitch ladder on the chalkboard. Place the following numbers vertically: 7,, 1, 2, 3, 4, and 5. Ask the students to establish the sound of the pitches. Begin and end on 1. Then ask them to sing as you point rhythmically to the pitch numbers on the ladder. Use the following example to aid you when directing the students.

   ```
   1 1 1  1    1 1 1  7, 7,
   A lit– tle love goes a lo– ng way.
   2 2 2  2    1 7, 7, 1  1
   A lit– tle love goes a lo– ng way.
   1 1 1  1    2 3 3  4  4
   A lit– tle love goes a lo– ng way.
   3 2 1  5    3 4 2  1
   A lit– tle love, A lit– tle love.
   ```

2. Learn Part 2 of the refrain using the same procedure.

   ```
   3    1  2
   Love, love, love.
   4    2  3
   Love, love, love.
   5    3    4 4 4 4  4
   Love, love, love, A lit– tle love,
   3 2 1  5  7, 2  4  3
   A lit– tle love, A lit– tle love.
   ```

3. Ask the students to open their books to page 208. Ask them to look at Part 1 of the refrain. They are to follow each note as you sing the melody using numbers. Discuss how the melody remained the same, moving up and down almost entirely by steps. Repeat this procedure with Part 2 of the refrain.

4. Invite the students to sing each part of the

208

Verse Eb / Bb7

1. Lends   a   warm   and   friend-ly   hand,___
2. Puts   you   on   your   spe-cial   cloud,___
3. Helps   keep spring-time   in the   air,___
4. Gets   you   sing-ing   loud and   strong,___

Bb7 / Eb

When   it's   hard to   un-der-stand.___
When   you're   lone-ly   in a   crowd.___
Though the   trees are   cold and bare.___
E-   ven when life's go-ing wrong.___

Eb7 / Ab

Lends   a   warm   and   friend-ly   hand,___
Puts   you   on   your   spe-cial   cloud,___   A lit-tle
Helps   keep spring-time   in the   air,___
Gets   you   sing-ing   loud and   strong,_

Bb7 / Eb   D.C. al Fine

love,_____ a lit-tle love.

refrain by reading from the book. Divide the class into two groups and sing the refrain in harmony.

5. Play the recording. Ask the students to sing the refrain with the recorded voices. Ask them to listen and follow the words of each verse.

6. When the students are familiar with the verses, ask them to sing the entire song.

7. Distribute Latin rhythm instruments. (See **Materials**.) Ask the students to improvise rhythm patterns while you play the recording. Develop a signal for all to play or for an instrumental soloist to be heard.

OPTIONAL

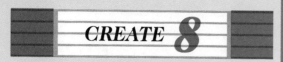

CREATE 8

Lesson Focus

Expression: Musical elements are combined into a whole to express a musical or extramusical idea. *(C–I)*

Materials

- **Instruments:** various small percussion instruments, such as woodblocks or temple blocks, tuned water glasses, finger cymbals, windchimes, gong, timpani, metallophones, or resonator bells; mallets
- **Teacher's Resource Binder:**
  - Optional—
    Curriculum Correlation 19, page C20
- **Extends Lesson 26,** page 58

Kantan

Japanese Noh Play

Use this play as a basis for an opera.
This story begins by establishing the setting
and the characters.

Rosei: I have traveled so fast that I have already come to the village of Kantan. Though the sun is still high, I will lodge here tonight. (*knocking*) May I come in?

Hostess: Who is it?

Rosei: I am a traveler; pray give me lodging for the night.

Hostess: Yes, I can give you lodging. Pray come this way. (He seems to be traveling all alone.) Tell me, where have you come from, and where are you going?

The story then presents the problem.

Rosei: I come from the land of Shoku. They tell me that on the Hill of the Flying Sheep, there lives a sage; and I am visiting him so that he may tell me by what rule I should conduct my life.

Hostess: It is a long way to the Hill of the Flying Sheep. Listen! A wizard once lodged here and gave us a marvelous pillow called the Pillow of Kantan. He who sleeps on it sees all his future in a moment's dream.

Rosei: Where is this pillow?

Hostess: It is on the bed.

Rosei: I will go and sleep upon it.

Hostess: And I, meanwhile, will heat you some millet at the fire.

Rosei: (*going to the bed*) Upon the borrowed Pillow of Kantan, I will lay my head and sleep . . . .

There needs to be a resolution to the problem.
Complete this drama.
What will happen in Rosei's dream?
How will his problem be solved?

210

The Lesson

1. Help the students create their own opera. Discuss that a good story needs a beginning, a setting, and characters. There is usually a problem that needs solving. The students may use the Noh play that appears on pages 210 and 211 as the basis for their opera.

   This story is set in early Japan in the village of Kantan. It is an excerpt from a Noh play created many years ago. The hero is seeking dreams about his future. The hostess of the lodge provides him with a mystical pillow. The students will need to provide a story line to decide what the hero's future will be and who will help him solve his problems. A moral might evolve related to the idea that it may not always be good to know one's future.

2. After the students have developed the story, they may write it down or decide to improvise a dialogue as they dramatize it. When they have dramatized the story, ask them to perform it again, this time as an opera. The characters will now get to sing their parts. They may use any pitches they choose. Remind them that they may wish to plan to include arias, recitatives, and ensembles.

3. Assign some students to be the opera orchestra. They are to use non-pitched instruments when accompanying the arias or recitatives, but they may use pitched instruments at other times in the opera when there is no singing. Provide a variety of instruments from which the orchestral players may choose to improvise ideas that will enhance the singers' words and actions. Some ideas might be

   - Dream music—metallophones or tuned water glasses
   - Hostess' footsteps—temple blocks or woodblocks

- Rosei's footsteps—timpani
- Pillow theme—finger cymbals or wind-chimes
- Fire theme—gong

4. Simple kimono-like costumes may be created from sheets, crepe paper, or robes. Props, such as folded paper fans and parasols made from paper fans attached to sticks, will serve to further create the feeling of an ancient Japanese scene.

OPTIONAL

CREATE 9

Lesson Focus

Harmony: Chords and melody may move simultaneously in relation to each other. *(C–I)*

Materials

○ **Piano Accompaniment:** page 394
○ **Record Information:**
  • Tzena, Tzena
    Record 10   Side A   Band 2
    Voices: children's choir
    Accompaniment: clarinet, trumpet, trombone, tuba, cimbalom, violin, accordion, mandolin, double bass, percussion
○ **Teacher's Resource Binder:**
  • Optional—
    Enrichment Activity 12, page E25
○ **Extends Lesson 3,** page 10

The Lesson

1. Challenge the students to use their knowledge of rhythm and melody to sightread the three melodies that make up the folk tune "Tzena, Tzena" on pages 212–213. Examine each melody. Note that Part 1 uses both skips (usually drawn from tones of the I chord) and stepwise patterns. Parts 2 and 3 move mostly by scale steps. When the students are familiar with each melody, divide the class into three groups. Ask each group to sing the three melodies at the same time to create harmony.

2. Challenge the class to create a dance for each melody. Discuss the character of each as described on page 213. Organize the class into three groups again. Assign one melody to each group. **What formation will your group use?** (line dance, circle, partners, and so on) **What motions will the foot patterns include?** (heel-toe, stamp, hop, step-slide, and so on)

3. Give the groups time to plan and practice their dances. When the groups are ready, ask each to perform the dance while the rest of the class sings the appropriate melody. Then sing all three melodies and perform the three dances simultaneously.

Part 3

C   F

Tze - na,   Tze - na,   stop   your hes - i - ta - ting.

G   C   G

There's   a   par - ty,   come and join   us,   We   are   wait - ing.

C   F

Tze - na,   Tze - na,   We're   an - tic - i - pat - ing

G   C

your   ar - riv - al,   Tze - na, Tze - na, Tze - na.

Choreograph this music.
Divide into three groups.
Create dances for each melody.
Each melody has its own character.

As you plan movements for each
melody, consider that

- Melody 1 is a simple, pleasant statement.

- Melody 2 is more uplifting and has a soaring feeling.

- Melody 3 has **syncopation** that adds drive and strong feelings.

Each dance must last for eight measures.

213

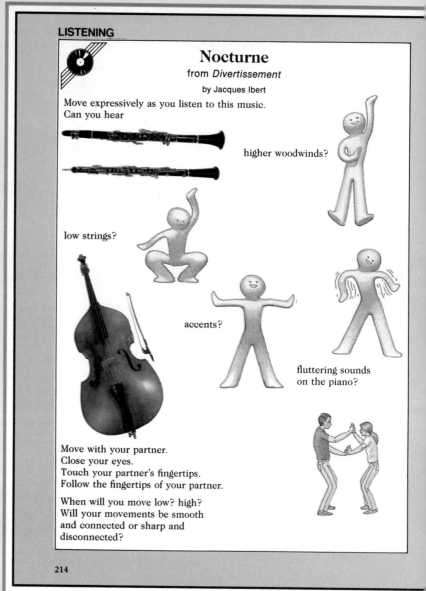

CREATE 10

Lesson Focus

Expression: Musical elements are combined into a whole to express a musical or extramusical idea. *(C–I)*

Materials

- ○ **No Piano Accompaniment**
- ○ **Record Information:**
  - Nocturne from *Divertissement* by Jacques Ibert (ee-**behr**), 1890–1962
    Record 10   Side A   Band 3
    Philadelphia Orchestra
    Eugene Ormandy, conductor
- ○ **Instrument:** finger cymbals
- ○ **Teacher's Resource Binder:**
  - Optional—
    Biography 7, page B13
- ○ **Extends Lesson 43**, page 96

The pupil page (214) reads:

LISTENING

Nocturne

from *Divertissement*

by Jacques Ibert

Move expressively as you listen to this music. Can you hear

higher woodwinds?

low strings?

accents?

fluttering sounds on the piano?

Move with your partner.
Close your eyes.
Touch your partner's fingertips.
Follow the fingertips of your partner.

When will you move low? high?
Will your movements be smooth
and connected or sharp and
disconnected?

214

The Lesson

1. Play the recording of "Nocturne" as the students follow the pictures on page 214. **Can you hear when the music is low? high? accented? When do different instruments join the strings?**

2. Invite the students to use movement to show what is happening in the music. Play the recording again.

3. Ask the students to mirror your movements. Slowly move one hand. Then add a full arm movement.

4. Do the same with the other hand and arm. Then let the arm lead the entire body. Again the students should mirror your movements.

5. Invite each student to find a partner. One person in each couple should be designated

the "lead" partner. They are to close their eyes, barely touch their partner's fingertips, and then listen and move to the music as signaled by the lead partner. Periodically tap once on the finger cymbals to signal when the leadership should change.

6. After the students have moved to the music, discuss why they moved in the way they did. Guide them to answer the questions on the pupil page. The students should conclude that the music expressed a sense of smooth, connected, and flowing movements as suggested by the low, *legato* string sounds. **How did your movements change when you heard *crescendos* or the distinctive sounds of specific instruments?**

7. Ask the students to repeat the experience, listening for new ideas they may have missed on previous listenings.

OPTIONAL

Farewell My Own True Love

American Folk Song
Collected by William S. Haynie

1. Fare - well, my own true love,
2. Ten thou - sand mile, my love,
3. Oh, don't you see that dove

Fare - well a lit - tle while;
Through Eng - land, France, and Spain;
That flies from vine to vine,

I'm goin' a - way but I'll come a - gain,
My rov - ing mind shall nev - er rest,
A - mourn - ing for his own true love,

If I go ten thou - sand mile.
Till I see your face a - gain.
Just as I will mourn for mine.

Create a shadow dance to express the words
of this song.
Move between the light and the screen.
When does your image become larger? smaller?

215

Lesson Focus

Expression: Musical elements are combined into a whole to express a musical or extramusical idea. *(C–I)*

Materials

o **Piano Accompaniment:** page 396
o **Record Information:**
  • Farewell My Own True Love
    Record 10   Side A   Band 4
    Voice: soprano
    Accompaniment: woodwind quintet
o **Other:** a large white sheet attached to a pole at each end; overhead projector
o **Teacher's Resource Binder:**
  • Optional—
    Curriculum Correlation 11, page C20
o **Extends Lesson 25,** page 56

The Lesson

1. Challenge the students to learn "Farewell My Own True Love" by reading the notation on page 215. Listen to the recording to check for errors.

2. Invite the students to use movement to express the ideas in each verse. The following are some possible ways:

   Verse 1: Wave, then walk away and return, as though having journeyed many miles.
   Verse 2: Use gestures to suggest journeying many miles from country to country, and then returning.
   Verse 3: Move like a flying dove, ending in a mournful position.

3. Set up a large sheet as a shadow screen. (See **Materials.**) Assign two students to hold the posts and keep the screen taut. Place an over-head projector on the floor or on a low table about 12 to 15 feet behind the screen. Darken the room. Invite dancers, either as individuals or in small groups, to take turns moving between the light and the screen to cast shadows. **How will the shadows express going and coming?** Move forward or backward between the light and the screen.

4. Students who are not dancing should form a chorus and sit in front where they can see the screen. They should sing while the dancers interpret the words.

5. Provide opportunities for the students to take turns shadow dancing. Repeat the song as often as needed. Encourage the students to create other ways in which to express the ideas in the song.

OPTIONAL

Lesson Focus

Expression: Musical elements are combined into a whole to express a musical or extramusical idea. *(C–I)*

Materials

○ **No Piano Accompaniment**

○ **Record Information:**
  • The Slitheree Dee
    Record 10   Side A   Band 5
    Voices: children's choir
    Accompaniment: synthesizer, sound effects

○ **Teacher's Resource Binder:**
  • Optional—
    Curriculum Correlation 21, page C22

○ **Extends Lesson 26**, page 58

The Slitheree Dee

Words and Music by Shel Silverstein

Oh, the Slith-e-ree dee has crawled out of the sea;

He may catch all the oth-ers, But he won't catch me.

No you won't catch me, old Slith-er-ee dee;

you may catch all the oth-ers, but you won't

216

The Lesson

1. Before singing "The Slitheree Dee" for the students, explain that the words are a joke and the music is an important part of this joke. **Listen. What is the joke?** (The Slitheree Dee catches the person who thought he or she was so smart.) **How does the music help you know this?** (The music stops in the middle of the last measure. Instead of going to the I chord as expected, the music leaves the listener feeling as though it should continue.)

2. Invite the students to open their books to page 216 and sing the song. Practice several times to make sure that everyone stops before the sentence ends.

3. Ask the students to move while singing, to express the ideas of the song. They are to be the "Slitheree Dees" for the first five measures of the song. Then they are to switch characters and complete the song by being the smart person who could not be caught.

4. Turn the dance into a game. Whisper in several students' ears but appoint only one of them to be the Slitheree Dee. This time each student is to touch someone else's hand as everyone "slithers" through the room. The Slitheree Dee is the only one who can squeeze a hand as he or she passes. **If your hand is squeezed it means that the Slitheree Dee has cast a spell upon you. At the end of the song all others should freeze, but since you have been caught you are to collapse to the floor in a most dramatic way.**

The song continues with the Slitheree Dee back in action and all dancers stepping over or around the students who were just caught. The Slitheree Dee will have some time to

216

Use movement to help express the ideas in this song. Can you move like a mysterious Slitheree Dee?

Can you change and become the smart person who could not be caught?

Can you really make us believe the Slitheree Dee got you?

217

catch several students each time the song is sung. The students may stop the game when they can identify the Slitheree Dee.

Yes Indeed

Words and Music by Sy Oliver

Refrain
Yes in - deed, _____ Yes in - deed, _____
I've got that feel-in' _____ in me, Yes in - deed. _____

Verse
You will shout when it hits you, Yes in - deed. _____
out if it's in you, Yes in - deed. _____

CREATE 13

Lesson Focus

Harmony: Chords and melody may move simultaneously in relation to each other. *(C–E)*

Materials

○ **Piano Accompaniment:** page 396
○ **Record Information:**
  • Yes Indeed
    Record 10 Side A Band 6
    Voices: children's choir
    Accompaniment: piano, electric organ, electric guitar, electric bass, percussion
○ **Extends Lesson 7**, page 18

The Lesson

1. Ask the students to listen to the recording of "Yes Indeed." Help them become familiar with the song by asking them to softly tap their toes and lightly clap the beat.

2. Tell the students to open their books to page 218 and examine the notation. Draw their attention to the long, sustained sounds that occur whenever the syllables "-deed" and "-jah" are sung. Play the recording again as the students follow the notation. Ask them to softly sing "Yes indeed" each time these words appear in the song. Continue to listen to the rest of the song. Remind the students to "spin out" the long sound for the full amount of time. **How long will that be?** (usually three beats, or six short sounds) Play the recording as the students sing the repeated word pattern. Ask them to sing the complete song.

3. Divide the class into two groups. Group 1 is to sing the song as learned. Group 2 is to create an echo each time the syllable "-deed" is sustained. This group may either rhythmically chant or sing their echo. If the group chooses to sing, they may either use the pitch being sustained or choose any of the pitches that they hear within the chordal accompaniment. **How many echos will you sing?** (six)

4. Perform the entire song in this way. Provide opportunities for the groups to sing each other's parts.

Yes, you'll shout when it hits you, Yes in - deed. _____
Makes you shout, "Jack it sends you" Yes in - deed. _____

When the spir - it moves you, you'll shout,
When that jive starts jump - in', you'll shout,

B♭

"Hal - le - lu - jah." _____ When it hits you _
"Let me in there." _____ When it hits you _

C   **F** |1. |2.   *D.S. al Fine*

You'll hol-ler _ "Yes in - deed." _____ It comes
You'll hol-ler _ "Yes in - deed." ___   ___ Yes in -

219

Lesson Focus

Harmony: Chords and melody may move simultaneously in relation to each other. *(P–S)*

Materials

○ **Piano Accompaniment:** page 398
○ **Record Information:**
  • Ever Onward!
  📼 **Record 10   Side A   Band 7**
    Voices: children's choir
    Accompaniment: trumpet, French horn, trombone, tuba, percussion
○ **Instruments:** autoharp or piano; bass xylophone; mallet
○ **Other:** overhead projector
○ **Teacher's Resource Binder:**
  [Activity Sheets] • **Activity Sheet 40,** page A51 (Prepare as a transparency.)
○ **Extends Lesson 35,** page 76

Special Times

Ever Onward!

Words by Norman Bell   Music by David A. Pollock

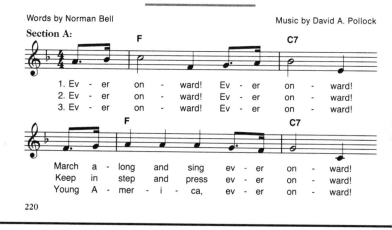

220

The Lesson

1. Music is an effective means to help students express their feelings about their pride and patriotism. Begin by reading the following poem by Ralph Waldo Emerson to the students.

                A Nation's Strength
    Not gold, but only man can make
    A people great and strong;
    Men who, for truth and honor's sake,
    Stand fast and suffer long.
    Brave men who work while others sleep,
    Who dare while others fly;
    They build a nation's pillars deep
    And lift them to the sky.

   Discuss the meaning of the poem from the standpoint that a nation's wealth is in its human resources, the value of each individual.

2. Ask the students to look at the transparency of Activity Sheet 39 (*A Nation's Strength*), which shows this poem as a scale song. Establish the tonality. Ask the students to sing the song independently, stepping up to each new pitch as indicated on the activity sheet.

3. When the students are familiar with the song, use the bass xylophone or piano to play the following descending bass accompaniment:

   Observe that this pattern steps downward each time the voice part steps upward.

4. Continue the feeling of national pride by asking the students to learn to sing a song that

March with heads high, Sing with hearts high,
Stand to - geth - er, For to - geth - er,
Ev - er on - ward, Ev - er on - ward,

F   C7   F   *(To Section B after Verse 2)*

And go on - ward to vic - to - ry.
We'll go on - ward to vic - to - ry.
Ev - er on - ward on vic - to - ry.

Section B:

F   C7

Like the o - cean's might - y roar, As it beats a - gainst the shore,

F   C7

Comes the sound of voic - es ring - ing loud and clear.

F   C7

From the North and from the South, From the East and from the West,

F   C7   F   *(To Verse 3)*

It's the sound of Young A - mer - i - ca we hear.

221

expresses the need for unity. Ask the students to examine Section A of the song "Ever Onward!" on page 220. Help them note that it moves by scale steps or skips within either the I or V7 chord. Practice singing 1–5–1, 5, –2–5,, 7,–4–7,, and 1–5–1 as you play the appropriate chords on the piano or autoharp (I, V7, V7, I). Then ask the students to read the melody as you add the piano accompaniment.

5. Scan the entire song. **How many times will you sing this same section?** (three times) **How many more sections will you need to learn?** (one) The students should identify the complete song form as **A A B A**.

6. Follow a similar procedure to learn Section B. Sing the chordal skips. Then sing the melody with the accompaniment.

OPTIONAL

7. **Although the melodies in both sections are different, there is something the same. What is it?** (The chordal sequence is the same.) The students should recall from previous lessons that when the chordal accompaniment is the same, two different melodies may be sung at the same time. **Sing both sections at the same time. Do they fit?** (yes)

8. Ask the students to listen to the recording to hear the arrangement of this song. First Section A is sung twice. Then Section B is heard. Finally Sections A and B are sung at the same time. Divide the class into two groups and sing this arrangement of the song.

Lesson Focus

Form: A musical whole may be made up of same, varied, or contrasting segments. *(P–S)*

Materials

○ **Piano Accompaniment:** page 400
○ **Record Information:**
 • Little Lamb
 📷 **Record 10 Side A Band 8**
  Voices: children's choir
  Accompaniment: flute, harp, electric piano, percussion
○ **Instruments:** two sets of resonator bells: one with pitches C, C♯, D, D♯, E, F, F♯, G, G♯, A, A♯, and B (Pitch Set 1); one with F, G, A, B♭, C, D, E, and F′ (Pitch Set 2); mallets
○ **Extends Lesson 6,** page 16

Little Lamb

Words by Stephen Sondheim

Music by Jule Styne

1. Lit-tle lamb, lit-tle lamb, My birth-day is here at last.
   bear, lit-tle bear, You sit on my right, right there.

Lit-tle lamb, lit-tle lamb, A birth-day goes by so fast. 2. Lit-tle
Lit-tle hen, lit-tle hen, What game should we play, and

when? Lit-tle cat, lit-tle cat, Ah, why do you look so blue?

Did some-bod-y paint you like that, Or is it your birth-day too? ____

Lit-tle fish, lit-tle fish, Do you think I'll get my wish?

The Lesson

1. Find musical ways to make each student's birthday very special. Invite twelve students to perform a special birthday greeting to honor the birthday boy or girl. They are to stand in a row. All are to chant and clap the rhythm of the traditional "Happy Birthday" song. Repeat the chant, moving from left to right down the row of students. Each student is responsible for clapping only one note of the rhythm when it is his or her turn in the sequence.

When all in the row have clapped, they will find that the chant is not completed. They are then to reverse the clap (without breaking the rhythm) and clap from right to left to complete the row. The pattern will eventually end with the second student in the row. The students are then to take the chant "inside," and clap the word rhythm without speaking.

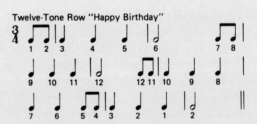

Twelve-Tone Row "Happy Birthday"

2. Distribute the twelve resonator bells and mallets from Pitch Set 1 to twelve students. (See **Materials.**) Repeat the activity as described in Step 1, this time playing each individual bell rather than clapping. Help the students become aware that they have played a twelve-tone row in its original form and then its retrograde (backwards) version to create a variation of this familiar birthday greeting. Explain that grouping pitches in this manner is one of the techniques used by contemporary composers when planning their music.

Lit-tle lamb, lit-tle lamb, I won-der how old I am.

I won - der how old I am. _____

The form of this song is

Intro A A B A Coda
Can you hear when Section A is played? Section B?
Play this bell accompaniment with Section A.
Move downward on the first beat of each measure.

F E D C

B♭ A G F

3. **Open your books to pages 222–223.** Ask the students to listen to the recording of this gentle birthday song while following the words and musical score on the pupil pages. After the students have listened a second time, guide them to review the score for information about the form of the piece. Then ask them to sing the complete melody. Identify Section A and distribute the eight bells from Pitch Set 2. (See **Materials.**) Ask the students to play the descending accompaniment part as they sing the melody.

SPECIAL TIMES 3

Lesson Focus

Expression: The expressiveness of music is affected by the way rhythm, melody, form, and texture contribute to the musical whole. *(C–I)*

Materials

○ **Instruments:** timpani or hand drums; bass xylophone, with pitches D′ and A; slide whistles; any pitched instruments, such as resonator bells, xylophones, or keyboards, with pitches D, E, F, G, and A; any non-pitched percussion instruments; mallets

○ **Extends Lesson 14,** page 34

On October

by Sharon Falk

On October thirty-first,
That's when witches do their worst;
You'll turn into a frog if you are curs'd,
On October thirty-first.

(Improvisation 1)

On October thirty-one,
That's when vampires have their fun;
If you see them flying you'd better run,
On October thirty-one.

(Improvisation 2)

On October's final night,
Pumpkins glow with an eerie light;
Little children scream with fright,
On October's final night.

(Improvisation 3)

Timpani and Bass Xylophone Accompaniment:

Improvisation 1	Improvisation 2	Improvisation 3
Slide Whistle	D minor melodies	Tone Block

224

The Lesson

1. Provide opportunities for the students to create an instrumental setting for "On October," a Halloween poem on page 224. Begin by asking everyone to read the poem rhythmically. Ask two students to improvise an accompaniment on timpani and bass xylophone while the class reads the poem again. The players may improvise the accompaniment using pitches D′ and A, playing with the underlying beat.

2. Assign other students to improvise during the interludes between each verse. The steady beat accompaniment should continue throughout the piece. Use the following instruments for each improvisation:

   • Improvisation 1—one or more slide whistles
   • Improvisation 2—all available pitched instruments (see **Materials**)

   • Improvisation 3—miscellaneous non-pitched percussion instruments

   Encourage the students to work together, listening carefully to each other's improvisations to develop interesting interludes. **Should everyone play all of the time? part of the time? Should everyone echo ideas?**

3. When all ideas have been developed and practiced, invite the students to make decisions about an introduction and coda. **Should you use the same ideas used during the interludes? Should new ideas be developed?** Perform the complete poem in its musical setting.

224

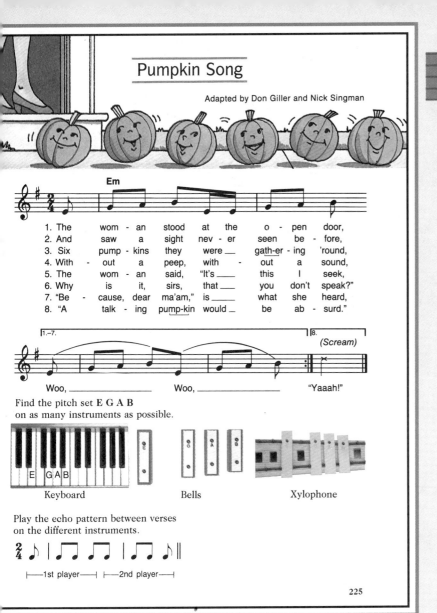

Pumpkin Song

Adapted by Don Giller and Nick Singman

Em

1. The wom - an stood at the o - pen door,
2. And saw a sight nev - er seen be - fore,
3. Six pump - kins they were gath-er - ing 'round,
4. With - out a peep, with - out a sound,
5. The wom - an said, "It's this I seek,
6. Why is it, sirs, that you don't speak?"
7. "Be - cause, dear ma'am," is what she heard,
8. "A talk - ing pump-kin would be ab - surd."

1.–7.

8.

(Scream)

Woo, _____ Woo, _____ "Yaaah!"

Find the pitch set **E G A B**
on as many instruments as possible.

E G A B

Keyboard   Bells   Xylophone

Play the echo pattern between verses
on the different instruments.

├──1st player──┤ ├──2nd player──┤

225

SPECIAL TIMES 4

Lesson Focus

Form: A musical whole is a combination of smaller segments *(P–I)*

Materials

- **Piano Accompaniment:** page 399
- **Record Information:**
  - Pumpkin Song
    Record 10   Side B   Band 1
    Voices: child solos, children's choir
    Accompaniment: pipe organ, prepared piano, rubbed glasses, percussion
- **Instruments:** assorted pitched instruments, with pitches E, G, A, and B; assorted non-pitched instruments; mallets
- **Teacher's Resource Binder:**
  - Optional—
    Orff Activity 4, page O9
- **Extends Lesson 17,** page 40

The Lesson

1. Play the four pitches E, G, A, and B on any pitched instrument for the students. Explain that the song they are about to learn uses only these four pitches, repeated many times. Ask the students to sing the pitches upward and downward. Then invite them to open their books to page 225 and locate the repeated pitch pattern in "Pumpkin Song." **How many times will we sing this pattern for each verse?** (twice) The students will quickly realize that the entire song is made up of this short pattern and that it is heard four times for each verse and interlude.

2. **What do you notice about the rhythm? Is it repetitive as well?** (Yes, as it usually moves with the shortest sound.) Ask the students to sing the first verse. Perform with the recorded or piano accompaniment.

3. Invite up to nineteen students to find the pitch set shown on the pupil page on available pitched instruments. Invite them to practice playing the pattern, moving from one instrument to another without interrupting the rhythm pattern. The effect should be that of multiple echoes with each echo having its own distinctive timbre.

4. Perform the song, adding two instrumental echoes after each verse is sung, as shown on the pupil page.

5. *OPTIONAL* Invite other students to experiment with special "spooky" sound effects created on non-pitched percussion instruments to complete an arrangement of this strange Halloween song.

225

Lesson Focus

Form: A musical whole may be made up of same, varied, or contrasting segments. *(P–S)*

Materials

○ **Piano Accompaniment:** page 401
○ **Record Information:**
  • Hayride
  📼 **Record 10   Side B   Band 2**
  Voices: children's choir
  Accompaniment: piccolo, clarinet, trumpet, violin, accordion, mandolin, double bass, percussion
○ **Instruments:** several sets of resonator bells or xylophones, with pitches B,, C, D, E, F, G, A, B, and C'
○ **Extends Lesson 59**, page 128

Hayride

Words and Music by Richard C. Berg

Come on a - long, we're go - ing for a hay - ride,

Fill up the wag - on with a load of hay;

Come on a - long, we're go - ing for a hay - ride,

Frost's on the pump - kin, au - tumn's on its way.

Gid - dy up, Dob - bin, oh, here we go a - jog - ging;

226

The Lesson

1. **Open your books to page 226.** Sing the first two phrases for the students, using the syllable "loo." Ask the students to follow the score and echo you as you sing this part again. When they are familiar with this melody, ask them to search the score and discover how many times they find this same idea. (It is heard three times.) **When is this melody not heard?** (on the third phrase, "Giddy up, Dobbin, . . .") Guide the students to label these phrases, using the letter A for the first idea and B for the second idea. The students will discover that the form of the piece is **A A B A.**

2. Invite the students to listen to Part 1 of the recording. (See **For Your Information.**) Then ask them to sing the melody. Repeat this activity several times until the students have achieved rhythmic and melodic accuracy.

Clap the rhythm of the words if necessary to refine the performance.

3. Direct the students' attention to the descant on page 227. Ask them to study the score and be ready to independently learn to sing this special part. They should be able to easily determine that the descant is made up of descending and ascending C major scales.

4. After the students have studied this special part, invite several of them to take turns demonstrating how they think it will sound. Help them begin by sounding the beginning pitch for them. After the demonstration and discussion of their interpretations, ask the entire class to sing the descant.

5. Divide the class into two groups and sing the melody and descant of the song.

226

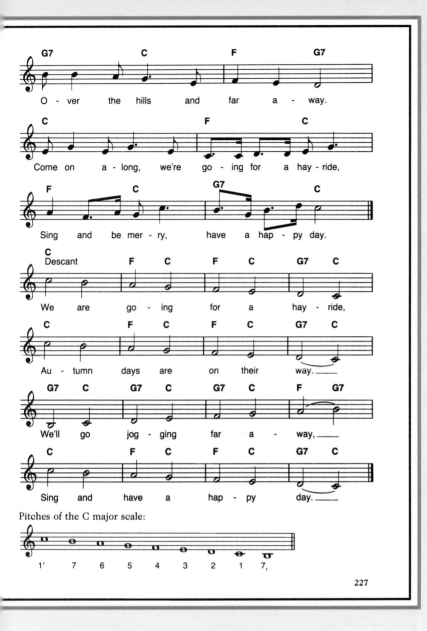

Over the hills and far away.

Come on along, we're going for a hay-ride,

Sing and be mer-ry, have a hap-py day.

Descant
We are go-ing for a hay-ride,

Au-tumn days are on their way.____

We'll go jog-ging far a-way,____

Sing and have a hap-py day.____

Pitches of the C major scale:

1' 7 6 5 4 3 2 1 7,

227

For Your Information
Recording information of "Hayride":
Part 1—melody
Part 2—descant
Part 3—melody and descant together

6. Distribute several sets of bells. (See **Materials.**) Challenge several students to play the descant as a special instrumental accompaniment as others sing the song.

OPTIONAL

SPECIAL TIMES 6

Lesson Focus
Harmony: A series of simultaneous sounds may alternate between activity and rest. *(P–E)*

Materials
○ **No Piano Accompaniment**
○ **Record Information:**
   • Harvest Time
   Record 10   Side B   Band 3
   Voices: children's choir
   Accompaniment: violin, balalaika, mandolin, cimbalum, accordion, acoustic guitar, double bass
○ **Instruments:** alto xylophone, with pitches D, G, A, B, C, and D′; bass xylophone, with pitches D and G; alto metallophones, with pitches D, F♯, G, A, B, C, and D′; tambourine; mallets
○ **Extends Lesson 31,** page 68

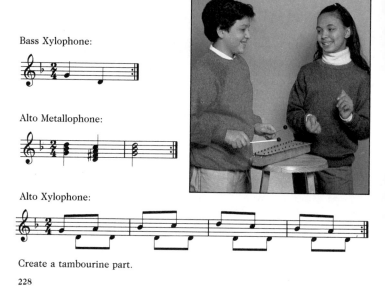

Bass Xylophone:

Alto Metallophone:

Alto Xylophone:

Create a tambourine part.

228

The Lesson

1. Help the students learn "Harvest Time" on page 228. Begin by asking them to look at the notation of the first phrase and describe the rhythm, the repetition of phrases, and the melodic direction. Establish the G minor tonality and ask the students to sing the first phrase.

2. Help the students learn the second phrase in the same way. Note the sharp preceding the seventh step in Measures 3 and 7. **How will this note be sung?** (a little higher than usual) Explain that the raised seventh step often occurs in minor songs to help give a sense of finality to the final pitch, which in this song is G.

3. When the students can sing the entire tune, ask them to practice the rhythm of each instrumental part shown on the bottom of the

page. Practice using hand clapping or *patschening* (slapping thighs), using gestures that move the same way as mallets will move when playing the instrumental parts. Assign several students to play these accompaniment parts on the appropriate instrument as others sing the melody. (See **Materials.**)

4. *OPTIONAL* The students should be very familiar with the melody by this time. They should now be able to sing it as a round. Begin by dividing the class into two groups and singing the melody as a two-part round. On another day, perform the round in three or four parts.

228

Now Thank We All Our God

Words by Martin Rinckart
Translation by Catherine Winkworth

Melody by Johann Crüger

1. Now thank we all our God With heart and hands and voic - es,
2. O may this boun-teous God Through all our life be near us,

Who won-drous things hath done, In whom his world re - joic - es,
With ev - er joy - ful hearts And bless-ed peace to cheer us,

Who, from our moth-ers' arms, Hath blessed_us on our way
And keep us in his grace, And guide_us when per - plexed,

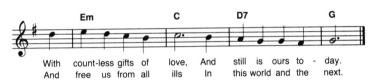

With count-less gifts of love, And still is ours to - day.
And free us from all ills In this world and the next.

Listen to the recording of this well-known chorale.
First you will hear it sung with an organ accompaniment
written by Felix Mendelssohn.
Then you will hear Johann Sebastian Bach's arrangement,
which has been recorded with choir, two trumpets,
and organ.
The trumpets play interludes between the sung phrases.

229

Lesson Focus

Time and Place: A particular use of mel-ody, harmony, rhythm, and form reflects the origin of the musical whole. *(D–I)*

Materials

○ **Piano Accompaniment:** page 404
○ **Record Information:**
  • Now Thank We All Our God
    Record 10 Side B Band 4a
    Voices: children's choir
    Accompaniment: pipe organ
    Record 10 Side B Band 4b
    Voices: mixed choir
    Accompaniment: two trumpets, organ
○ **Extends Lesson 44,** page 98

The Lesson

1. Read together the words of this joyful song of thanksgiving. **What kind of song do you think this might be?** (a thanksgiving hymn) Play Band 4a of the recording. Ask the students to focus on how the words are set to music and to suggest why this setting is described as "hymn style":

   • The words are set in a steady rhythm, re-flecting the way the words would be spoken.
   • The melody moves usually by steps, with a different chord occurring on almost every beat.
   • The phrases are all of equal length.

2. Review the function of the fermata. If the stu-dents cannot recall its purpose, play the re-cording again. **What do the singers do at this point?** (They sustain the tone longer than it is usually held.)

OPTIONAL

3. When the students have listened carefully to the music, invite them to sing with the re-cording.

4. Play another arrangement of this well-known hymn. Band 4a is by Mendelssohn and was composed during the nineteenth century, over a hundred years ago. Band 4b is by Bach, who was born 300 years ago. Ask the students which arrangement they prefer, and why. (There is no correct answer.)

229

Lesson Focus

Harmony: Two or more pitches may be sounded simultaneously. *(P–S)*

Materials

- o **Piano Accompaniment:** page 405
- o **Record Information:**
  - • Pat-A-Pan
  - **Record 10 Side B Band 5**
    Voices: children's choir
    Accompaniment: two piccolos, percussion
- o **Other:** paper and a pencil for each student
- o **Extends Lesson 34,** page 74

Pat-A-Pan

Words Adapted by Kurt Miller

French Carol
Arranged by Kurt Miller

230

The Lesson

1. Ask the students to listen to the recording of "Pat-A-Pan." Call attention to the characteristics of French folk music that are found in this song:
   - • the melody based on the minor scale
   - • the dance-like rhythms
   - • the repetition of the opening melodic idea
   - • the use of piccolo and percussion.

2. Begin to learn the song on pages 230–231 by dividing the class into high and low voice parts. Ask each group to examine its melodic part and compare it to the other group's part. **When do the voice parts move in the same direction, even though one group is higher than the other?** (during Section 1, except for the last two measures) Label this as "parallel motion." **When do the two voice parts move in opposite directions?** (during the last two

   measures in Section 1 and the first half of Section 2) Label this as "contrary motion." **What happens next?** (The voice parts return to parallel motion.)

3. Play the recording again. Distribute paper and a pencil to each student. Ask everyone to draw pictures of their own melodic and rhythmic part. (See **For Your Information** for possible examples.)

4. Encourage the students to practice the two parts simultaneously. Isolate problem spots as they occur.

5. This appealing carol should be sung in a steady, moderately fast tempo with crisp enunciation of the words. Suggest that the students imitate the crispness of the drum with their voices.

OPTIONAL

For Your Information

Possible melodic and rhythmic pictures made by the students, as discussed in Step 3:

- Beginning of Section 1:

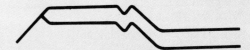

- Beginning of Section 2:

Lesson Focus
Form: A series of sounds may form a distinct musical idea within the musical whole. *(P–S)*

Materials
○ **No Piano Accompaniment**
○ **Record Information:**
   • Christmas Is Coming
   📼 **Record 10   Side B   Band 6**
   Voices: children's choir
   Accompaniment: racket, shawm, crumhorn, sackbut, lute, viola da gamba, percussion
○ **Instruments:** bass xylophone; alto metallophone, with pitches C, E, F, G, and A; glockenspiels; mallets
○ **Extends Lesson 49,** page 108

Christmas Is Coming

English Melody

The Lesson

1. Ask the students to look at the notation of "Christmas Is Coming" on page 232 as you sing Phrase 2 on the syllable "loo." **Which phrase am I singing?** They are to look for clues in the notation to answer the question. **What clues helped you know?** (large skips and the up-down direction of the melody) Repeat the activity singing Phrase 3 and then Phrase 1.

2. Invite the students to sing the melody, following the notation. When they are familiar with the song, add an instrumental accompaniment. (See **Materials.**) Invite all of the students to practice each part by first tapping their legs or pretending to hold mallets, moving in the direction they will need to move when playing the patterns. For example, the bass xylophone part on the bottom of the page begins left-right-left, cross-over, and so on.

When the students can "play" each rhythmic pattern correctly, assign several students to play the parts on the designated instruments while the class sings.

3. Help the students perform the song as a three-part canon. Ask the students to form three groups, each forming a circle. All groups are to perform the same motions, but they are to begin singing and moving one phrase behind the other to create a canon in movement as well as in song.

• Phrase 1: Circle to the right.
• Phrase 2: Step to the middle.
• Phrase 3: Step backward from the middle.

Repeat the same motions for the second verse or invite the students to make up their own motions.

232

Here We Come A-Wassailing

Old English Carol

Verse Eb

1. Here we come a-was-sail-ing A-mong the leaves so green;
2. We are not dai-ly beg-gars That beg from door to door;
3. Good mas-ter and mis-tress, As you sit by the fire,
4. God bless the mas-ter of this house, Like-wise the mis-tress, too,

Ab   Eb   Bb7

Here we come a-wan-d'ring, So fair to be seen.
But we are neigh-bors' chil-dren Whom you have seen be-fore.
Pray think of us poor chil-dren Who wan-der in the mire.
And all the lit-tle chil-dren That round the ta-ble go.

Refrain   Eb

Love and joy come to you, And to you glad Christ-mas

Eb   Ab   Bb7   Eb

too; And God bless you and send you a hap-py New

Ab   Eb   Ab   Bb7   Eb

Year, And God send you a hap-py New Year.

233

Lesson Focus

Rhythm: Individual sounds and silences within a rhythmic line may be longer than, shorter than, or the same as the underlying steady beat. *(D–S)*

Materials

○ **Piano Accompaniment:** page 408

○ **Record Information:**
  • Here We Come A-Wassailing
    Record 10   Side B   Band 7
    Voices: children's choir
    Accompaniment: lute

○ **Teacher's Resource Binder:**
  • Optional—
    Orff Activity 12, page O27

○ **Extends Lesson 50,** page 110

The Lesson

1. Play the recording of "Here We Come A-Wassailing" with the books closed. **How does the rhythm move? Does it move the same way all of the time?** Guide the students to conclude that the underlying beat moves in groups of twos throughout. However, the melodic rhythm changes. It moves unevenly during the verse and evenly during the refrain.

2. **Open your books to page 233 and locate the two meter signatures.** Discuss the fact that in this song, the ⁶⁄₈ meter sounds in two. The beat note is actually the dotted quarter note. In the ²⁄₂ section the beat note is the half note. Draw these patterns on the chalkboard:

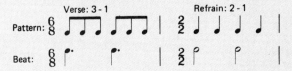

Discuss the differences in the way the melodic pattern moves in relation to the underlying beat. In the ²⁄₂ section it moves with two sounds to the beat. In the ⁶⁄₈ section it moves with three sounds to the beat.

3. Guide the students to practice tapping the two patterns against a steady beat until they can easily switch from threes to twos. Note that the dotted quarter note in ⁶⁄₈ meter lasts for the same length of time as the half note in ²⁄₂ meter.

   OPTIONAL

4. Play the recording again. Draw attention to the accompaniment played on the lute. **Why is this appropriate?** (This is a very old carol from England, where the lute was a popular stringed instrument.) Invite the students to sing the song.

Lesson Focus

Expression: Musical elements are combined into a whole to express a musical or extramusical idea. *(D–I)*

Materials

○ **No Piano Accompaniment**

○ **Record Information:**
  • Amahl and the Night Visitors by Gian Carlo Menotti (meh-**naht**-tee), 1911–
  Record 11   Side A   Bands 1a–h
  Grossman Orchestra and Chorus
  Herbert Grossman, conductor

○ **Other:** paper and a pencil for each student

○ **Teacher's Resource Binder:**
  • Optional—
  Biography 8, page B15

○ **Extends Lesson 19,** page 44

LISTENING

Amahl and the Night Visitors
by Gian Carlo Menotti

234

The Lesson

1. Discuss the difference between a play and an opera with the students. **An opera is much like a play, except that the conversations are usually sung.** Help the class determine the number of singers who would be needed for a solo, duet, trio, quartet, and quintet by examining the first part of each word and relating it to other quantity words that use the same prefix. Describe the characters that will be heard in *Amahl and the Night Visitors* for the class. (See **For Your Information.**)

2. Ask the students to follow the themes and pictures on pages 234 to 239 while you read the story and play each band of the recording as indicated in the text. Ask the students to focus their attention on each of the characters, what they are like, and what they appear to be feeling in the opera.

3. After playing the complete recording, distribute blank paper and a pencil to each student. Play each band of the recording again, pausing after each so that the students may list any moods and feelings that were described by the story and music. Have them also describe any musical devices the composer used to create the moods and feelings. (See **For Your Information** for possible answers.) Discuss each section and encourage the students to share their findings.

4. Read the story again, playing each of the bands of the recording at the appropriate time, while the students follow the pictures and themes in their books. Encourage them to focus their attention on the findings they recorded on their lists.

Amahl:

Moth-er, Moth-er, Moth-er, come with me;

I want to be sure that you see what I see.

235

For Your Information

This lesson requires repeated listenings. It should be used over a span of several class periods. The following characters appear in *Amahl and the Night Visitors*:

Amahl—a poor shepherd boy
Mother—his mother
Kings Kaspar, Melchior, and Balthazar—three kings in search of the Child
The Page—attendant to the kings

Possible answers for Step 3:

Band a: peaceful (slow tempo, soft, *legato*, use of sustained strings); lively dance tune (imitation of shepherd's pipe, lively dance-like rhythms); agitated (less *legato*, faster tempo)

Band b: soothing (slow tempo, soft, lilting feeling created by accented groups of three — $\frac{9}{8}$ and $\frac{6}{8}$ meters; *legato*)

Band c: agitated, excited (faster, louder, pizzicato strings); calm (when kings enter) (long note values, male trio—very *legato*, slower)

Band d: excited, curious (faster, louder, pizzicato strings)

Band e: excited, playful (faster, louder, pizzicato strings, use of some slower and repeated sections for emphasis)

Band f: lively, dance-like, expressive, exciting (detached, *staccato*, in sets of three— $\frac{12}{8}$ meter; faster tempo, use of dynamic contrasts, soprano descant)

(*continued on next page*)

THE STORY

Somewhere in the world there is a poor, crippled shepherd boy named Amahl. He and his mother live in a shepherd's hut and have very little to eat. As the opera begins, Amahl is sitting outside the hut on a rock, playing his shepherd's pipe. It is nighttime. The sky is filled with stars. One of the stars is very bright.

(*Play Band a of the recording.*)

Amahl has enjoyed looking at the stars. He even imgaines that the clouds and wind are the setting for a king's ball. The brightest star looks like it has a fiery tail and is a chariot on fire.

Amahl begs his mother to come outside and see the wonderful things he is dreaming about. Thinking he is telling another of his usual tall tales, she makes him promise never to tell another lie. His mother is very sad because they

have so little to eat. To make her feel better, he sings this song.

(*Play Band b.*)

Amahl and his mother go to sleep for the night, but soon Amahl is awakened by the sound of someone approaching the hut. He hobbles over to the window to see who it is. Outside, he sees a kingly procession approaching led by the kings' page. When they knock on the door, Amahl opens the door a crack. Excitedly, he calls to his mother to come.

(*Play Band c.*)

After the kings enter the hut, Amahl begins to ask them all kinds of questions. King Kaspar, who is slightly deaf, has a parrot that especially interests Amahl.

(*Play Band d.*)

235

236

Kaspar shows Amahl a jeweled box and begins opening its three drawers, one at a time, to show Amahl their contents.

(Play Band e.)

After Amahl has eaten some licorice the kings have brought, his mother asks him to go find the other shepherds so they may bring gifts to the three kings. Amahl's mother looks at all the gold and gifts that the three kings have with them for the Child. She begins to think about all she could do for Amahl if she had some of the gold.

She tells the kings about Amahl and what a special child he is. The kings reply that the Child they are looking for is also poor but they must find him by following the bright Eastern star.

The shepherds, led by Amahl, begin to enter the house with their gifts.

(Play band f.)

After offering their gifts to the kings, the shepherds dance. When the dancing ends, the shepherds say goodnight and the kings prepare to go to sleep.

Amahl's mother again looks at the gold and thinks of all she could do for Amahl if she had some of it. She slowly moves near the gold. As she takes it, the page awakens and begins to shout.

(Play Band g.)

The kings awaken. Sensing that Amahl and his mother really need the gold, they tell her she may keep it because the Child they are seeking doesn't need the gold. The mother asks the kings to take the gold back and adds that she, too, would like to send their child a gift, but she has none to offer.

Amahl wants to give a gift to the Child and offers to send the crutch that he has made. As

The Shepherds:

Em - i - ly, Em - i - ly, Mi-chael, Bar-thol - o-mew,

How are your chil-dren and how are your sheep?

Dor - o-thy, Dor - o-thy, Pe - ter, E - van - ge-line,

Give me your hand, come a - long ___ with me.

All the chil-dren have mumps. All the

flocks are a - sleep. We are go-ing with A -

mahl, bring - ing gifts to the Kings.

237

he hands the crutch to the kings, he realizes that he no longer needs it. He is so overjoyed that he tells them he would like to go with them so he can give the crutch to the Child himself.

As the opera ends, the kings and Amahl are leaving to follow the star that will guide them to the Child.

(Play Band h.)

Amahl:

Look, Moth-er, I can dance, I can jump, I can run!

The Kings:

Tru - ly, he can dance, he can jump, he — can — run!

Tru - ly, he can dance, he can jump, he — can — run!

Tru - ly, — he can dance, — he can run! —

239

SPECIAL TIMES **12**

Lesson Focus

Harmony: Chords and melody may move simultaneously in relation to each other. *(P–S)*

Materials

○ **Piano Accompaniment:** page 410

○ **Record Information:**
  • Silver Bells

📼 **Record 11   Side B   Band 1**
  Voices: children's choir
  Accompaniment: electric piano, celesta, acoustic guitar, electric bass, glockenspiel, carillon, handbells, percussion

○ **Instruments:** all available high-pitched instruments, such as glockenspiels, with pitches D, F, G, and B♭; mallets

○ **Extends Lesson 7,** page 18

Silver Bells

Words and Music by
Jay Livingston and Ray Evans

Verse

1. Cit-y side-walks, bus-y side-walks
2. Strings of street lights, e-ven stop lights

dressed in hol-i-day style;
blink a bright red and green;

In the air there's a feel-ing of Christ-mas. ___
As the shop-pers rush home with their trea-sures. ___

Chil-dren laugh-ing, peo-ple pass-ing,
Hear the snow crunch, see the kids bunch,

meet-ing smile af-ter smile,
this is San-ta's big scene,

And on ev-ery street cor-ner you hear: ___
And a-bove all this bus-tle you hear: ___

240

The Lesson

1. Toll the following bell pattern for the students as it might be played on church bells or a carillon:

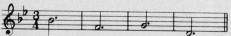

Distribute as many glockenspiels or other high-pitched instruments as are available to the students. Invite these students to use pitches D, F, G, and B♭ and to copy what you play. Imitate the tolling bells of a city where the sounds of the bells "pile" up. The students may begin after your pattern begins, and randomly play the pattern at any point they choose.

2. Ask the students to select their favorite bell-tolling ideas and to use them as an introduction for a new song, "Silver Bells," after it has been learned.

3. Ask the students to turn to page 240 and learn the melody of the verse while listening to the recording.

4. After the students can sing the verse, ask them to examine the refrain. **What do you notice?** (It is to be performed in two-part harmony.) **Which part sings the melody?** (Part 2) **What does Part 1 do?** (It adds a vocal echo, which suggests the tolling of bells.) **What happens when Part 1 is not echoing Part 2?** Help the students realize that during Phrases 2 and 4 the two parts usually move in parallel motion, with Part 1 usually a third higher than Part 2. Divide the class into two groups and learn to sing the refrain.

5. Invite the students to select additional places within the song where the bells might be played.

OPTIONAL

240

241

Encourage Group 1 to sing their echo with a
light head tone to accommodate the high
pitch in the second pattern and to suggest the
light quality of high-pitched bells.

SPECIAL TIMES 13

Lesson Focus

Rhythm: Individual sounds and silences within a rhythmic line may be longer than, shorter than, or the same as the underlying shortest pulse. *(P–S)*

Materials

o **Piano Accompaniment:** page 414
o **Record Information:**
  • I Had a Dream, Dear
    Record 11   Side B   Band 2
    Voices: children's choir
    Accompaniment: piano, banjo, percussion
o **Extends Lesson 37,** page 82

The Lesson

1. Enjoy the valentine season by having the students create and chant their own rhymes. Begin with "Roses are red, violets are blue . . ." The students should make up the last line of the rhyme, such as "I've got a gal, how about you?" or "My best guy fell in the glue."

2. Establish the underlying shortest sound. Ask the students to tap this steady short sound as they speak their rhymes.

    Perform the students' rhymes in a "rhythm chain" by moving down the row of students, with each speaking his or her rhyme without interrupting the steady flow of the rhythm.

3. **Look at a musical "valentine," "I Had a Dream, Dear" on pages 242–243.** Challenge the students to learn the rhythm of the verse by tapping the shortest sound on their legs while chanting the rhythm of the melody. They should first determine that the shortest sound is represented by a quarter note. You may wish to ignore the fermatas at first.

    After the students have chanted the rhythm correctly, discuss how the duration of the notes marked with the fermatas should be extended. (It should be approximately twice the original length of the note.) Chant the words again, this time observing the fermatas.

4. Play the recording and enjoy the shift between the smoothly flowing, "romantic," quality of the first section and the bouncy, lighthearted feeling of the second section. **How many times will you need to listen before you can sing the song without help?** Keep track of the listenings as the students practice listening and singing until they can perform the entire song accurately.

242

G

B - E - S - T,   B - E - S - T best of all the

A

R - E - S - T,   R - E - S - T rest, 'cause I

D   **G**

love you, I love you, I love you all the T - I - M - E time.

Slower **C**   **G**   **E**   **C**   **D7**   **G**

You   tell   me   your   dream,   I'll   tell   you   mine.

243

Lesson Focus

Melody: A series of pitches may move up or down by steps or skips. *(P–S)*

Materials

- **Piano Accompaniment:** page 413
- **Record Information:**
  - Somebody Waiting
    Record 11   Side B   Band 3
    Voices: child solos, children's choir
    Accompaniment: string ensemble
- **Instruments:** four sets of resonator bells and xylophones, with pitches D, E, F♯, G, A, and B; mallets
- **Extends Lesson 47,** page 104

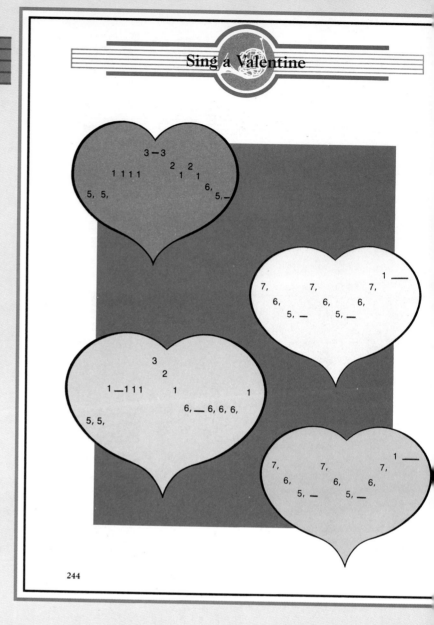

Sing a Valentine

244

The Lesson

1. Invite the students to send musical valentines to each other. Select four students to play mallet instruments. (See **Materials.**) Identify the pitches by number: 5, is D; 6, is E; 7, is F♯; 1 is G; 2 is A; and 3 is B. Ask the students to open their books to page 244 and direct their attention to the four valentines. The first student is to "send" the first valentine by playing the indicated pitches. Note that the long line indicates a longer sound. The second student sends the next valentine by playing the numbers in the second valentine and so on until all four valentines have been sent. Provide opportunities for several groups to send valentines.

2. Explain that the valentines are made up of phrases of the song "Somebody Waiting" on page 245. Ask all of the students to sing the song, first using the numbers as given in the four valentines. Then ask the students to sing the scale numbers while following the notation. Take time to make the transfer to the notation by identifying the scale number of each note in the musical score.

3. Ask the students to sing the words to the song. When they can sing it, invite them to perform it with the recorded accompaniment.

4. When the students are familiar with the song, play a game. All form a circle with one person in the center. On Verse 1, all join hands, with the circle moving to the left while the player in the center moves to the right. On Verse 2, all change directions. During Verse 3, the person in the center chooses two people standing next to each other. The three of them join hands and skip together in the center of the circle. The first person then skips with one of the other two people during Verse 4. They

OPTIONAL

Somebody Waiting

Play Party Song

1. As I look in-to your eyes, I be-hold a sweet sur-prise,

There is some-bod-y wait-ing for me. _____

2. There is some - bod - y wait - ing,
3. Choose _____ two and leave the oth - er,
4. Choose _____ one and leave the oth - er,

There is some - bod - y wait - ing,
Choose _____ two and leave the oth - er,
Choose _____ one and leave the oth - er,

There is some - bod - y wait-ing for me. _____
Choose _ two and leave the oth - er for me. _____
Choose _ one and leave the oth - er for me. _____

245

both join the circle at the end of the verse. The remaining player becomes the new center person and the game continues. More students can be involved in the game by initially placing more than one student in the center.

Lesson Focus

Expression: Musical elements are combined into a whole to express a musical or extramusical idea. *(D–I)*

Materials

○ **Piano Accompaniment:** page 416
○ **Record Information:**
  • You're a Grand Old Flag
    Record 11   Side B   Band 4
    Voices: mixed choir
    Accompaniment: piccolo, trumpet, French horn, trombone, percussion
○ **Teacher's Resource Binder:**
  • Optional—
    Kodaly Activity 7, page K11
○ **Extends Lesson 22,** page 50

You're a Grand Old Flag

Words and Music by George M. Cohan

246

The Lesson

1. Begin the lesson by asking the students to sing their favorite patriotic songs. These might include such songs as "America," "America, the Beautiful," and "This Land Is Your Land." **What do all of these songs have in common?** (All express ideas of love for our nation.)

2. Introduce the students to another patriotic song. **Look at pages 246–247.** Read the words of "You're a Grand Old Flag," and ask the students to describe the feelings suggested by the words. They might suggest senses of pride, brightness, joy, and confidence. **Listen to the music. How does it help to communicate these feelings?** The students might suggest some of the following ways:

   • the march-like beat over which the syncopated rhythms of the melody move
   • the moderately fast tempo
   • the instrumental accompaniment

   • the melody that outlines either the I or V7 chord or the steps of the scale.

   Draw attention to the hint of the traditional tune "Auld Lang Syne" that occurs in the final phrase. Mention to the students that "You're a Grand Old Flag" was written by George M. Cohan, a popular songwriter and performer of the early twentieth century. **"Auld Lang Syne" is a Scottish melody, very popular during Cohan's time and still often sung on New Year's Eve.**

3. Review what the students have learned about musical form. **Listen and count the phrases. How do you know when one has ended?** (There is a long tone, a feeling of momentary rest.) **Can you describe the form with letters? (A B A' C)**

4. Invite the students to listen again. Then ask them to sing the song without assistance.

F

Ev - ery heart beats true un - der red, white, and blue,

D   G   C

Where there's nev - er a boast or brag; ___

F   C

But should auld ac - quaint - ance be for - got,

B♭   C   F

Keep your eye on the grand old flag. ___

247

SPECIAL TIMES 16

Lesson Focus

Melody: Each pitch within a melody moves in relation to a home tone.
Melody: A series of pitches bounded by the octave "belong together," forming a tonal set. *(D–S)*

Materials

○ **Piano Accompaniment:** page 420
○ **Record Information:**
• Tallis's Canon
  Record 11 Side B Band 5
  Voices: children's choir
  Accompaniment: brass quintet
• Haleluyoh
  Record 11 Side B Band 6
  Voices: woman, man
  Accompaniment: clarinet, accordion, guitar, double bass, percussion
○ **Instruments:** resonator bells, with pitches G, A, B♭, C, and D; mallets
○ **Extends Lesson 32,** page 70

Tallis's Canon

Words by Thomas Ken · Music by Thomas Tallis

All praise to Thee, my God, this night,
For all the bless-ings of the light,
Keep me, oh keep me, King of kings
Be-neath Thine own Al-might-y wings.

Haleluyoh

Jewish Folk Song

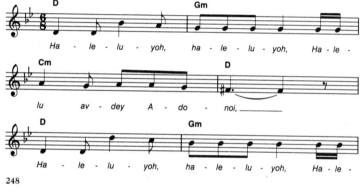

Ha-le-lu-yoh, ha-le-lu-yoh, Ha-le-lu av-dey A-do-noi, Ha-le-lu-yoh, ha-le-lu-yoh, Ha-le-

248

The Lesson

1. Ask the students to scan the notation for "Tallis's Canon" on page 248 and determine the scale on which the song is based. **To do this, let's identify each different pitch that's used in the melody.** Ask the students to name each pitch by its letter name. As they are named, write them on a staff on the chalkboard. When the letter named F is identified, draw attention to the sharp in the key signature and agree that its name must be F♯, to indicate that this pitch will sound one half-step higher than F "natural."

2. Sing the pattern that has resulted and agree that it is the sound of a scale. **Look again at the song. Around which pitch does the mel-**ody seem to center and return to at the end? (G) Agree that the song is based on the G major scale.

3. Ask the students to sing the melody on the syllable "loo." **Will you have difficulty singing the rhythm?** (No, because all notes are the same length, moving with the beat.) Practice the melody, singing first with scale numbers and then with words.

4. Follow the same procedure used in Step 1 to determine the scale on which "Haleluyoh" on pages 248–249 is based. **Be sure to look at the key signature as you name the pitches to see if any should have a sharp or flat added to its name.** The resulting pattern should look like this:

248

Cm   D

lu   es   shem   A - do - noi.

Gm   D   Gm   D

Ha - le - lu - yoh, _____ ha - le - lu - yoh,

D   Gm   D

Ha - le - lu - yoh,   ha - le - lu - yoh, _____

Gm   D   Gm   D

Ha - le - lu - yoh, _____ ha - le - lu - yoh,

D   Gm

Ha - le - lu - yoh,   ha - le - lu - yoh.

After you have learned to sing "Haleluyoh," add this **descant.**
Begin the descant with the ninth measure of the song.

6/8

Ha - le,   ha - le - lu - yoh,   Ha - le,   ha - le - lu - yoh,

Ha - le,   ha - le - lu - yoh,   Ha - le,   ha - le - lu - yoh.

249

SPECIAL TIMES 16

For Your Information

"Haleluyoh" is sung at Passover, the celebration of the exodus of the Jews from Egypt. The Angel of Death killed the first-born child of every Egyptian home but "passed over" Israelite homes. Passover is sometimes called the "Feast of Unleavened Bread" because in their haste to flee from Egypt, the Jews were forced to pack the bread they were baking before it could rise. The story of Passover can be found in the Old Testament 12: 3-40.

Phonetic pronunciation of "Haleluyoh": hah-leh-**loo**-yoh, hah-leh-**loo**, ahv-**day** ah-doy-**noy**, ehs **shehm** ah-doh-**noy**.

---

5. Draw attention to the fact that this song also ends on G. Sing the pattern up and down with numbers, ending on 1 (G). Identify this scale for the class as a harmonic minor scale. Compare the two scales. **Which steps are different?** (Steps 3 and 6) **What gives the harmonic minor scale its special sound?** (the wide space between Steps 6 and 7)

6. Remind the students that "Tallis's Canon" moved in fours, with the quarter note serving as both the shortest sound and the note that moved with the beat. **How does "Haleluyoh" move?** Help the students recall previous discussions of the 6/8 meter signature. Songs with this meter usually move with a feeling of twos. The dotted quarter note moves with the beat. The eighth note is the shortest sound. Establish a tempo by lightly tapping the shortest sound in sixes. Ask the students to chant the rhythm of the melody, using the syllable "lu."

7. Play the recording as the students follow the notation, noticing that Phrases 3 and 4 are almost identical. Then challenge the students to sing the song.

8. Some students who can confidently sing the song well may be selected to learn the descant on the bottom of page 249. Give them a set of resonator bells (see **Materials**) and send them to a quiet corner of the room to learn it independently. While they are practicing, the rest of the class may return to "Tallis's Canon" and learn to perform it as a round.

9. Invite the descant singers to return and perform their part while the remaining members of the class sing the melody of "Haleluyoh."

OPTIONAL

SPECIAL TIMES 17

Lesson Focus

Expression: Musical elements are combined into a whole to express a musical or extramusical idea. *(P–I)*

Materials

○ **Piano Accompaniment:** page 418

○ **Record Information:**
  • Let There Be Peace on Earth
  🔲 **Record 11   Side B   Band 7**
  Voices: children's choir
  Accompaniment: piano, electric organ, electric guitar, electric bass, percussion

○ **Extends Lesson 23,** page 52

The Lesson

1. Write the poem "Tear Down the Walls" on the chalkboard. (See **For Your Information.**) Ask the students to read the words quietly. Then discuss the meaning of the poem. **Do we really want brick walls torn down?** (This is a metaphor. The poet means to tear down the walls of distrust, discrimination, and fear that separate us.)

2. Read the poem aloud together. Ask the students to consider how to expressively speak the words by using voice inflection, volume, and tempo. Assign solo parts and perform again.

3. Read the words of "Let There Be Peace on Earth" on pages 250–251 as a choral reading. Discuss the meaning and ways that speaking might enhance this meaning. **What about a**

musical setting? How should it sound? After the students have given their suggestions, establish the meter in threes and the tonality in C major. Encourage the students to try sight-reading the song. Listen to the recording.

4. Discuss the effectiveness of the musical setting. **Would it have been more effective as a march tune moving in twos?** (Probably not, because the meter in threes allows us to "lean" on certain words to emphasize their importance. The heavy beat in each measure stresses important words such as "let," "there," "peace," and "Earth.") Agree that meter is important in communicating the message of the words. **How does the melody help convey the message?** (It gradually moves upward, with each of the first three phrases beginning slightly higher. Important words appear frequently on the highest pitch of the phrase, such as "care" and "perfect.")

250

Am7   D   G

Let me walk with my broth-er, _____ In

Am   D7   G7

per - fect har - mo - ny. _____

[2.]
C   Am

take each mo - ment and live each mo - ment in

F   D   Fm

peace e - ter - nal - ly; _____

C   E   F   C

Let there be peace on Earth, And

F   G7   C

let it be - gin with me. _____

251

For Your Information

Tear Down the Walls
by Fred Nell

All: Tear down the walls,
Solo 1: Listen to freedom singing out,
All: Tear down the walls,
Solo 2: Can't you hear the church bells ringing out?
Solo 3: Give every man the chance to take his brother's hand.
All: Tear down the walls,
         Tear down the walls.

5. Encourage the students to think about ways of singing this song as expressively as possible. They will need to prepare by having good singing posture so that they can support a pleasing, full tone. They must plan when to take breaths before singing so they can support the long phrases. They should be prepared to use contrast in volume as indicated in the score.

Glossary

Adagio moderately slow, *47*

Allegretto moderately fast, *107*

Allegro fast, *47*

Andante medium speed (a walking tempo), *47*

Aria a song in an opera that expresses the inside thoughts of the character, *207*

Beat the steady pulse of the music, *130*

Brass Family wind instruments made of brass or other metal including the trumpet, French horn, trombone, and tuba, *194*

Canon the form of imitation in which each part plays or sings the same melody at different times, *29*

Chord three or more pitches occurring at the same time, *154*

Coda a short concluding section of a piece, *89*

Descant a harmony part that is played or sung above the melody, *249*

Dynamics the loud and soft changes in music, *48*

Form the design of a piece of music made up of same, similar, or different parts, *37*

Forte (*f*) loud, *48*

Fortissimo (*ff*) very loud, *51*

Glissando movement from one pitch to another by sliding, *55*

Harmony two or more melodies performed at the same time or one melody accompanied by chords, *130*

Home Tone scale step 1, also called the tonal center, *130*

Homophony music in which other voices move with the main melody, *75*

Improvisation creating or composing music as one performs it, without reading musical notation, *54*

Interlude a section between two parts of the music, *195*

Introduction a section that comes before the main part of the music, *194*

Largo very slowly, *47*

Legato performed in a smooth, connected way, *59*

Maestoso a direction indicating a stately, dignified manner of performance at a slower pace than *andante, 50*

Melody a series of tones arranged rhythmically to make a musical idea, *130*

Meter Signature the two numbers at the beginning of a piece of music that tell how the beats are grouped and show the kind of note that moves with the beat, *21*

Mezzo Forte (*mf*) medium loud, *32*

Mezzo Piano (*mp*) medium soft, *48*

Moderato at a moderate speed, *50*

Modulation the change of a melody from one tonal c[...] to another, *163*

Note a sign that shows the pitch and the length of a [...] *130*

Opera a story set to music, using voices and an orch[...] *207*

Ostinato an accompaniment pattern repeated ove[...] over, *77*

Percussion Family instruments played by shaking [...] striking, including the trap set, celesta, chime[...] chestra bells, and timpani, *81*

Phrase a complete musical idea, *130*

Pianissimo (*pp*) very soft, *32*

Piano (*p*) soft, *32*

Pitch the highness or lowness of a musical sound, [...]

Polyphony two or more different melodies heard a[...] same time, *76*

Presto very fast, *47*

Recitative a vocal style used in opera that imitate[...] natural rhythms of speech, *207*

Rhythm the pattern of long and short sounds and [...] *130*

Root the bass note upon which a chord is built, *15*[...]

Sostenuto sustained, *32*

Staccato a series of tones that are separated by [...] silences, *59*

String Family instruments played by plucking or b[...] strings, including the violin, viola, cello, and d[...] bass, *194*

Syncopation a type of rhythm that is created whe[...] accents in a melody occur at a different time fro[...] accented beat, *213*

Tempo the speed of the beat, *48*

Tie a musical addition sign used to join two or [...] notes, *21*

Tonal Center the pitch to which all tones in a song [...] to return—the home tone, *66*

Variation a musical idea that is repeated with [...] change, *29*

Woodwind Family wind instruments usually ma[...] wood or metal, including the piccolo, flute, oboe, [...] inet, and bassoon, *194*

Piano Accompaniments

6. On the Road Again

Words and Music by Willie Nelson

On the road a - gain,_____ Just can't

wait to get on the road a - gain._____

_____ The life I love is mak - ing mu - sic with my friends, and

I can't wait to get on the road_ a - gain._____ On the

road a - gain,_____ Like a band of gyp - sies we go down the

high - way._____ We're the best of friends,_____ In - sist - ing that the

D. C. al Fine

world keep turn - ing our way,_____ and our way_____ is

8. Hey Dum Diddeley Dum

Words and Music by Marc Stone

Hey   dum   did - de - ley - dum,____

Hey   dum   did - de - ley - dum,____   Hey   dum   did - de - ley,

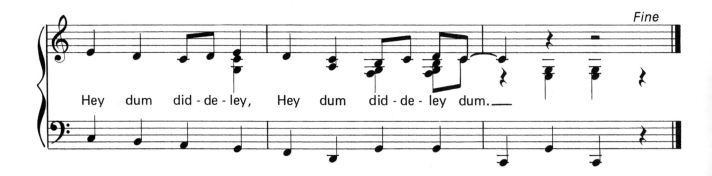

Hey   dum   did - de - ley,   Hey   dum   did - de - ley dum.____

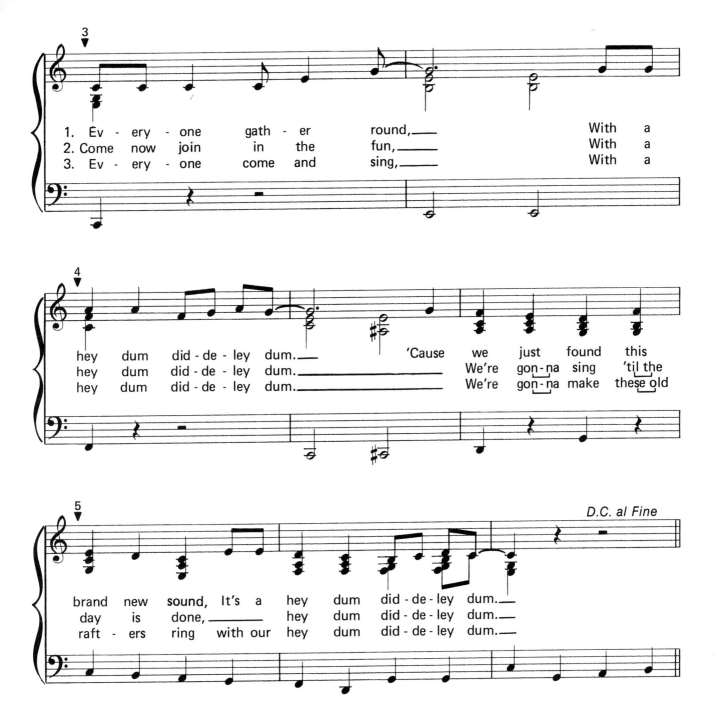

1. Ev - ery - one gath - er round,___ With a
2. Come now join in the fun,___ With a
3. Ev - ery - one come and sing,___ With a

hey dum did - de - ley dum.__ 'Cause we just found this
hey dum did - de - ley dum._____ We're gon - na sing 'til the
hey dum did - de - ley dum._____ We're gon - na make these old

D.C. al Fine

brand new **sound**, It's a hey dum did - de - ley dum.__
day is done,___ a hey dum did - de - ley dum.__
raft - ers ring with our hey dum did - de - ley dum.__

10. Mockin' Bird Hill

Words and Music by Vaughn Horton

1. When the sun in the morn-in' peeps o-ver the hill, And
2. Got a three-cor-nered plow and an a-cre to till, And a
3. When it's late in the eve-ning, I climb up the hill, And sur-

kiss-es the ro-ses 'round my win-dow-sill; Then my
mule that I bought for a ten-dol-lar bill; There's a
vey all my king-dom while ev-ery-thing's still; On-ly

heart fills with glad-ness when I hear the trill, Of the
tum-ble-down shack and a rust-y ole mill, But it's
me and the sky and an ol' whip-poor-will, Sing-in'

birds   in   the   tree - tops   on   Mock - in'   Bird   Hill.
my   Home   Sweet   Home   up   on   Mock - in'   Bird   Hill.
songs   in   the   twi - light   on   Mock - in'   Bird   Hill.

Tra - la

la   Twit - tle - dee   Dee,   Dee,   it   gives   me   a   thrill,   To   wake   up   in   the

morn - in'   to   the   mock - in'   bird's   trill;   Tra   la   la   Twit - tle - dee   Dee,   Dee,   there's

peace   and   good   will;   You're   wel - come   as   the   flow - ers   on   Mock - in'   Bird   Hill.

12. Skip to My Lou

Traditional Folk Song

Choose your part-ner, skip to my Lou, Choose your part-ner, skip to my Lou,

Choose your part-ner, skip to my Lou, Skip to my Lou, my dar-ling.

13. Oh, Dear, What Can the Matter Be?

Traditional Folk Song

Oh, dear, what can the mat-ter be? Oh, dear, what can the mat-ter be?

Oh, dear, what can the mat-ter be? My maid has gone to the fair._____

14. Ode to a Washerwoman

Traditional Folk Song

Here's a wo-man, a wo-man, a good wash-er-wo-man, A

wo-man, a wo-man, a good wash-er-wo-man, A wo-man, a wo-man, a

good wash-er-wo-man. She dan-ces and sings as she wash-es the clothes.

17. Wade in the Water

Afro-American Melody

Wade_____ in the wa - ter,_____ Wade_____ in the

wa - ter, child - ren; Wade_____ in the wa - ter,_____

God's goin' to trou - ble the wa - ter._____ *Fine*

1. See that band all dressed in white,____ } God's goin' to trou - ble the
2. See that band all dressed in red,____ }

262

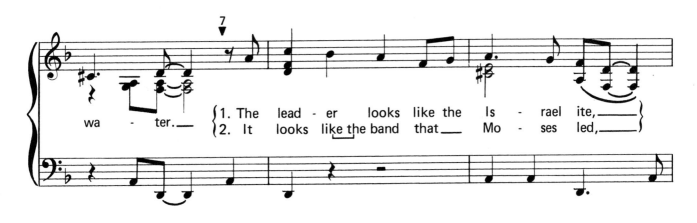

1. The lead - er looks like the Is - rael ite,___
2. It looks like the band that___ Mo - ses led,___

D. C. al Fine

God's goin' to trou - ble the wa - ter.___

26. La Cucaracha

Mexican Folk Song

Allegro

La Cu - ca - ra - cha, La Cu - ca - ra - cha, He's a mer - ry lit - tle

bug. La Cu - ca - ra - cha, La Cu - ca - ra - cha, Scam - per - ing a - cross the rug.

18. My Aunt Came Back

Traditional

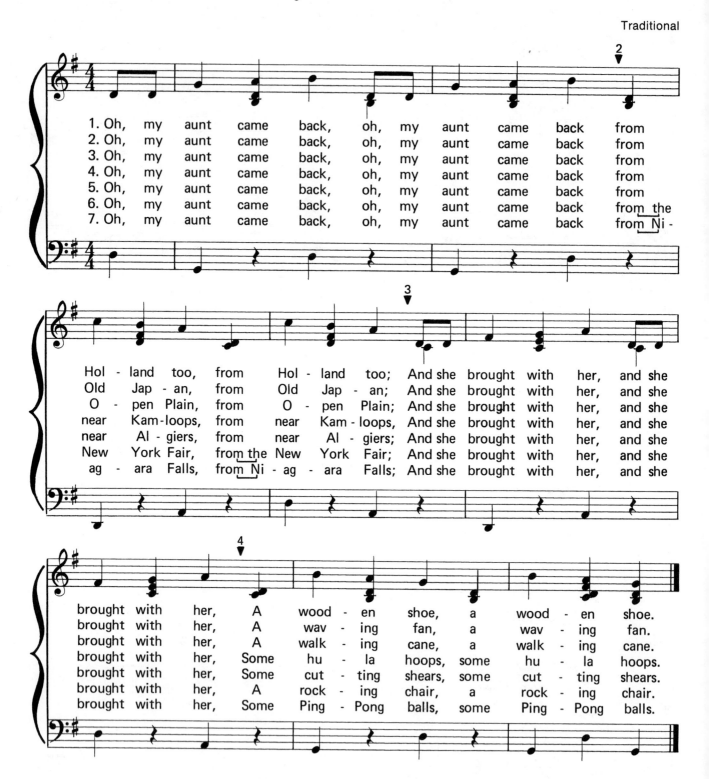

22. Morning Comes Early

Slovak Folk Song

1. Morn-ing comes ear-ly, the dew so bright.
2. Lis-ten, my com-rade: When work seems long,

Come with me, lad-die, in day's first light. Dawn o-ver-takes me,
Light-en each mo-ment with mer-ry song. Wel-come to-mor-row,

morn-ing a-wakes me, To the green mead-ows the herd I lead.
wait not for sor-row, Mu-sic and laugh-ter are all we need!

20. Bicycle Built for Two

Words and Music by by Harry Dacre

Dai - sy, Dai - sy, Give me your

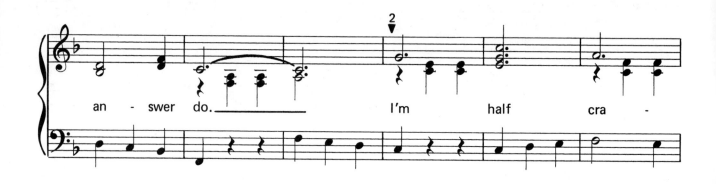

an - swer do._____ I'm half cra -

zy, All for the love of you._____ It

won't be a styl - ish mar - riage;_____ I can't af - ford a

car - riage,_____ But you'll look sweet on a

seat of a bi - cy - cle built for two._____

22. The Turtle's Song—"I Can Win!"

Words and Music by
Therese McGrath

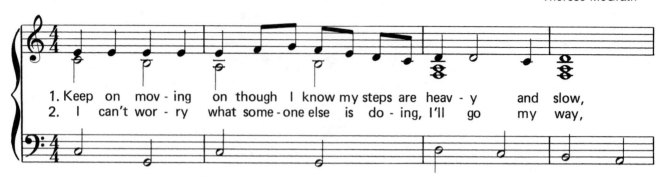

1. Keep on mov - ing   on though I know my steps are heav - y   and slow,
2. I   can't wor - ry   what some - one else is do - ing, I'll go   my way,

One foot out and then one foot af - ter is the way that I go!
I   know where I'm go - ing and I will sure - ly get there some day;

Tho' they laugh to see me plod a - long and ask, "Why be - gin?"
Tho' they tease me and they taunt me I re - ply with a grin.

Just for me to start and keep go-ing, in a way is __ to win.

Let them laugh and let them de-ride__ me, Let them point their fin - gers and chide__ me,

I know deep in - side me__ I can win!

24. Sarah the Whale

Words by Tom Glazer

Music by Daniel D. Emmett

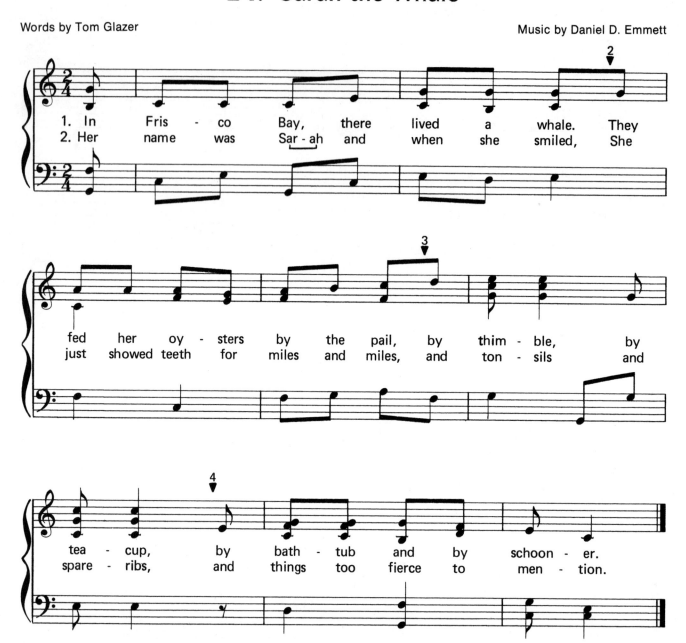

1. In Fris - co Bay, there lived a whale. They
2. Her name was Sar - ah and when she smiled, She

fed her oy - sters by the pail, by thim - ble, by
just showed teeth for miles and miles, and ton - sils by

tea - cup, by bath - tub and by schoon - er.
spare - ribs, and things too fierce to men - tion.

25. On Top of Old Smoky

Kentucky Folk Song

1. On top of Old Smok - y All cov - ered with snow, I lost my true lov - er By court - ing too slow.
2. O court - ing's a plea - sure, But part - ing's a grief, And a false - heart - ed lov - er Is worse than a thief.
3. A thief will but rob you Of all that you save, But a false - heart - ed lov - er Sends you to your grave.
4. The grave will de - cay you And turn you to dust, But a false - heart - ed lov - er You nev - er can trust.

27. Oleana

English Words by Beth Landis

Norwegian Folk Song
Arranged by Kurt Miller

Refrain

O - le, O - le,   O - le, O - le,

(Melody)

O - le, O - le - an - a,   O - le, O - le - an - a,

(R. H. plays melody, or accompaniment may
be omitted altogether throughout Refrain.)

O - le, O - le, O - le, O - le - an - a.

O - le, O - le, O - le, O - le, O - le, O - le - an - a.

1. O that is where I'd like to be, There where the land is free;
2. The hens lay eggs as big as rocks, Roost-ers crow like eight-day clocks,
3. The sal - mon leap so high up there, Hold your ket - tle in the air;
4. O come and bring your fid - dle, Dance to the mid - dle,

D. C. al Fine

Wheat and corn they grow so high, The tas - sels dust-ing off the sky!
Roast - ed pigs run all a - bout With knives and forks stuck in their snouts!
They'll jump in, pull on the lid, And cook them-selves to look like squid!
O - le with his vi - o - lin Will help us make a mer - ry din!

28. Simple Gifts

Shaker Song

'Tis the gift to be sim - ple, 'tis the gift to be free, 'Tis the gift to

come down where you ought to be. And when we find our - selves in the

place just right, 'Twill be in the val - ley of love and de - light.

274

When true sim-pli-ci-ty is gained, To bow and to bend we shan't be a-shamed. To turn, turn will be our de-light, Till by turn-ing, turn-ing we come 'round right.

34. Battle Hymn of the Republic

Words by Julia Ward Howe

Music Attributed to William Steffe

Mine eyes have seen the glo - ry of the com - ing of the Lord; He is

tram - pling out the vin - tage where the grapes of wrath are stored; He hath

loosed the fate - ful light - ning of his ter - ri - ble swift sword; His

truth is march-ing on.   Glo - ry, glo - ry, hal - le - lu - jah!

Glo - ry, glo - ry, hal - le - lu - jah!   Glo - ry, glo - ry, hal - le -

lu - jah! His   truth is   march - ing   on.

36. There's Work To Be Done and No Need to Hurry

Words and Music by Richard C. Berg

Hur - ry, hur - ry, hur - ry, hur - ry, come on the run;

All right, I come now; all right, I come;

Hur - ry, hur - ry, hur - ry, hur - ry, day is be - gun;

No need to hur - ry, no need to run.

3

Come a - long and hur - ry now, there's work to be done;

It is too ear - ly where is the sun?

4

When you have fin - ished there'll be time for fun.

I am so tired that I can - not run.

42. The Music Goes 'Round and Around

Words by "Red" Hodgson

Music by Edward Farley and Michael Riley

I blow through here;_____ The mu-sic goes 'round and a-round. Whoa-ho-

ho - ho - ho - ho and it comes up here._____ I

push the first valve down The mu-sic goes down and a - round. Whoa

ho - ho - ho - ho and it comes up here_____ I

push the mid-dle valve down.__ The mu-sic goes down a - round_ be -low,_ be-low,_

__ be-low,__ Dee-dle-dee ho - ho - ho. List-en to the ja-azz come out. I

push the oth-er valve down. The mu-sic goes 'round and a - round. Whoa-ho -

ho - ho - ho-ho and it comes out here.

46. There's a Hole in the Middle of the Sea

Anonymous

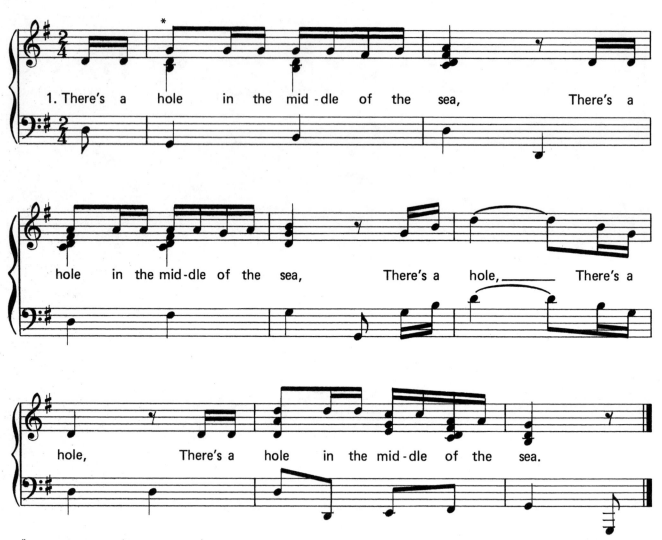

1. There's a hole in the mid-dle of the sea, There's a hole in the mid-dle of the sea, There's a hole,_____ There's a hole, There's a hole in the mid-dle of the sea.

verses accumulate:

2. There's a log. . .
3. There's a bump on the log. . .
4. There's a frog on the bump on the log. . .
5. There's a fly on the frog on the bump on the log. . .
6. There's a wing on the fly on the frog on the bump on the log. . .
7. There's a flea on the wing on the fly on the frog on the bump on the log. . .

282

48. Anyone Can Move a Mountain

Words and Music by Johnny Marks

An-y-one can move a moun-tain if one real-ly tries;

An-y-one can move a moun-tain you must re-al-ize.

It will take a lit-tle time, a lot of faith, make up your mind and

you'll ar - rive at where you strive to go.＿＿＿＿ So,

nev - er be a - fraid to dream for that's what you must do;

If you nev - er dream at all then your dreams can't come true.

An - y - one can move a moun - tain, ev - ery - one should know,

1. **8** *mp*

Just be-lieve it and you'll find it so.____

2. **9** *mf*   *mp*   *mf*   *mp*

Just be-lieve it, (just be-lieve it) just be-lieve it, (just be-lieve it)

10 *rit.*

And you'll find it so.____

50. Lift Every Voice and Sing

Words by James Weldon Johnson

Music by J. Rosamond Johnson

Moderato e maestoso

Lift ev-ery voice and sing Till earth and heav-en ring, Ring with the har - mo -

nies of lib - er - ty. Let our re - joic - ing rise High as the

list - 'ning___ skies, Let it re - sound loud as the roll - ing sea.

Sing a song full of the faith that the dark past has taught us, Sing a song full of the

hope that the pres-ent has brought us. Fac-ing the ris - ing sun Of our new

day be - gun, Let us march on till vic-to-ry is won.

52. I Believe

Words and Music by Ervin Drake,
Irvin Graham, Jimmy Shirl, and
Al Stillman

way. _____ I be - lieve, _____

I be - lieve. way, _____ Then I know

why I be - lieve! _____

60. Lord, Lord, Lord

Melody arranged by
Walter F. Anderson

Lord, Lord, Lord, you've sure been good to me. I'm sing-ing

Lord, Lord, Lord, you've sure been good to me. Well it's Lord, Lord, Lord, you've

sure been good to me. For you've done what the world could not do. Oh you

feed me when I'm hun-gry, you've sure been good to me. O Lord you

Fine

feed me when I'm hun - gry, you've sure been good to me. Well you

feed me when I'm hun - gry, you've sure been good to me. For you've

D. C. al Fine

done what the world could not do. I'm sing - ing

62. I'd Like to Teach the World to Sing
(In Perfect Harmony)

Words and Music by B. Backer,
B. Davis, R. Cook,
and R. Greenaway

I'd like to build_ the world_ a home_ and fur-nish it with love,_ Grow

ap-ple trees_ and hon-ey bees_ and snow-white tur-tle doves._ I'd

like to teach_ the world_ to sing_ in per-fect har-mo-ny,_ I'd

like to hold it in my arms__ and keep it com - pa - ny.__

I'd like to see the world__ for once__ all

stand - ing hand in hand,__ And hear them ech - o through__ the hills__ for

peace through - out the land.__ That's the song I hear,__

Let the world sing to-day,_____

A

song of peace that ech-oes on__ and nev-er goes a-way.__

Put your hand in my hand; Let's be-gin to-day.

Put your hand in my hand; Help me find the way. I'd

D. S. al Fine

294

64. Seven Limericks

Words by Edward Lear

Music by Emma Lou Diemer

1. There was a young
2. There was an Old

La - dy of Nor - way, _____ Who ca - su - al - ly sat in a
Man who said, "Well! _____ Will no - bo - dy an - swer this

door - way; _____ When the door squeezed her flat, she ex - claimed "What of
bell? _____ I have pulled day and night, till my hair has grown

that?" This cou - ra - geous young la - dy of Nor - way. _____
white, _ But no - bo - dy an - swers this bell!" _____

3. There is a young
4. There was an Old

la - dy whose nose _____ con - tin - u - al - ly pros-pers and
Man of Dum - bree _____ who taught lit - tle owls to drink

grows; _____ When it grew out of sight, she ex - claimed in a
tea; _____ For he said, "To eat mice is not prop - er or

fright, "Oh! Fare - well to the end of my nose!" _____
nice," __ That am - i - ca - ble Man of Dum - bree. _____

5. There was an old
6. There was a Young
7. There was an Old

per - son of Ware _____ Who rode on the back of a
La - dy of Bute, _____ Who played on a sil - ver - gilt
Man who, when lit - tle, _____ Fell ca - su - al - ly in - to a

bear. _____ When they asked, "Does it trot?" He said, "Cer - tain - ly
flute; _____ She played sev - er - al jigs to her un - cle's white
ket - tle; _____ But grow - ing too stout he could nev - er get

5. & 6.

not! He's a Mop - pi - si - kon Flopp - si - kin bear!" _____
pigs; That's a - mus - ing Young La - dy of Bute. _____

297

out, So he passed all his life in that ket-tle! _____

70. Spider on the Floor

Words and Music by Bill Russell

1. There's a spi-der on the floor, on the floor. There's a

spi-der on the floor, on the floor. Who could ask for an-y more than a

spi-der on the floor. There's a spi-der on the floor, on the floor.   2. Now the

spi-der's on my leg, on my leg.   Oh the spi-der's on my leg, on my

leg.   Oh he's real-ly, real-ly big, This old spi-der on my leg. There's a

spi-der on my leg, on my leg.   3. Now the

spi-der's on my stom-ach, on my stom-ach.____   Oh, the

spi - der's on my stom - ach, on my stom - ach.___ Oh, he's

just a dumb old lum - mock, this old spi - der on my stom - ach. There's a

spi - der on my stom - ach, on my stom - ach.___ 4. Now the

spi - der's on my neck, on my neck. Oh, the spi - der's on my neck, on my

neck. Oh, I'm gon-na be a wreck, I've got a spi-der on my neck. There's a

spi-der on my neck, on my neck. 5. Now the spi-der's on my face, on my

face, Oh, the spi-der's on my face, on my face. Oh,

what a big dis-grace, I've got a spi-der on my face. There's a

spi - der on my face, on my face. 6. Now the

spi - der's on my head, on my head. Oh, the spi - der's on my head, on my

head. Oh, I wish that I were dead, I've got a

spi - der on my head. There's a spi - der on my head, on my head.

72. Sweet Potatoes

Adapted and Arranged by Jean La Coste

Creole Folk Song

76. Dobbin, Dobbin

Dutch Tune

Dob-bin, Dob-bin on your way, We've been to-geth-er for man-y a day, So let your
Dob-bin, Dob-bin don't you stop, Just let your feet__ go clip-pe-ty clop, And let your

tail go swish as the wheels go 'round, Gid-dy-ap! We're home-ward bound.
tail go swish as the wheels go 'round, Gid-dy-ap! We're home-ward bound.

Refrain

I like to take a horse and bug-gy When I go trav-'ling to the

town. I like to hear old Dob-bin's clip-clop. I like to feel the wheels go 'round.__

78. A Smile Is a Frown Upside Down

Words and Music by Fred Willman

A smile is a frown up-side down, A smile is a frown up-side down, So when you are smil - ing, you can't frown, You'll have a great new day. If you have a frown,

turn it a-round. If you have a____ frown, turn it a-round. You'll

see the__ world in a dif-ferent way. You'll have a great new day.

mp
Days are bright - er, work seems light - er,

Love will come your way to - day.

Let your friends all know you care. Make them hap-py, do you dare? When you smile they'll try it too. So let it start with you. So smile, smile, turn it a-round, So smile and you won't frown, You'll see the world in a dif-ferent way. You'll have a great new day.

307

84. Yankee Doodle Boy

Words and Music by
George M. Cohan

I'm a Yan-kee Doo-dle Dan - dy, A Yan - kee

Doo-dle, do or die;_____ A real live neph-ew of my Un - cle

Sam, Born on the Fourth of Ju - ly._____ I've

got a Yan-kee Doo-dle sweet - heart, She's my Yan-kee Doo-dle joy._____ Yan-kee Doo-dle came to Lon-don, just to ride the po - nies, I am that Yan-kee Doo-dle boy._____

83. Life in the Army

Traditional

Vigorously

1. The bis-cuits in the ar-my they say are might-y fine, But
2. The cof-fee in the ar-my they say is might-y fine, It
3. The chick-en in the ar-my they say is might-y fine, But

one rolled off the ta-ble and killed a friend of mine, Oh,
looks like mud and wa-ter and tastes like i-o-dine,
once two drum-sticks got up and start-ed beat-ing time,

I have had e-nough of ar-my life, Gee Ma, I wan-na go,

Hey Ma, I got to go, Gee Ma, I wan-na go home.

86. Fifty Nifty United States

Words and Music by Ray Charles

Fif - ty nif - ty U - nit - ed States from thir - teen o - rig - i - nal col - o - nies,

Fif - ty nif - ty stars in the flag that bil - lows so beau - ti - f'ly in__ the breeze.

Each in - di - vid - u - al state con - trib - utes a qual - i - ty that is great.

Each in - di - vid - u - al state de - serves a bow,

Let's sa - lute them now! Fif - ty nif - ty

2nd time to Coda ⊕

U - nit - ed States from thir - teen o - rig - i - nal col - o - nies,

Shout 'em, scout 'em, Tell all a - bout 'em, One by one, 'til we've

giv - en a day to ev - ery state that's in the U. S.

A., in the U. S. A., in the U. S.

A. _____ Al - a -

ba - ma, A - las - ka, Ar - i - zo - na, Ar - kan - sas, Cal - i - for - nia, Col - o -

ra - do, Con - nect - i - cut, Del - a - ware, Flo - ri - da,

Geor - gia, Ha - wai - i, I - da - ho, Il - li - nois, In - di - an - a.

I - o - wa, Kan - sas, Ken - tuck-y, Lou - i - si - an - a, Maine,

Mar - y - land, Mas - sa - chu - setts, Mich - i - gan. Min - ne -

so - ta, Mis - sis - sip - pi, Mis - sou - ri, Mon - tan - a, Ne -

bras - ka. Ne - vad - a.

Chant

New Hamp - shire, New Jer - sey, New Mex - i - co, New York,

North Car - o - li - na, North Da - ko - ta, O - hi -

o! Ok - la - ho - ma, Or - e - gon, Penn - syl - va - nia, Rhode Is - land,

South Ca - ro - li - na, South Da - ko - ta, Ten - nes - see, Tex - as.

U - tah, Ver - mont, Vir - gin - ia, Wash - ing - ton,

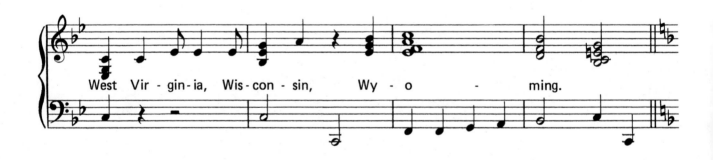

West Vir - gin - ia, Wis - con - sin, Wy - o - ming.

* Insert the name of any state.

92. The Lion Sleeps Tonight

New lyrics and revised music by
Hugo Peretti, Luigi Creatore,
George Weiss, and Albert Stanton

Introduction

Wee_____ ooh wim - o - weh.___

Refrain

Wim - o - weh, o - wim - o - weh, o - wim - o - weh, o - wim - o - weh, o -

wim - o - weh, o - wim - o - weh, o - wim - o - weh, o - wim - o - weh.

Verse

1. In the jun - gle, the might - y jun - gle, The li - on sleeps to - night.
2. Near the vil - lage, the peace - ful vil - lage, The li - on sleeps to - night.
3. Hush, my dar - ling, don't fear my dar - ling, The li - on sleeps to - night.

In the jun-gle, the qui-et jun-gle, The li-on sleeps to-night.
Near the vil-lage, the qui-et vil-lage, The li-on sleeps to-night.
Hush, my dar-ling, don't fear my dar-ling, The li-on sleeps to-night.

Wee_____ ooh wim-o-weh.____

Coda

Wee_____ ooh wim-o-weh.____

D. S.

90. Look Down that Lonesome Road

Traditional

Look down, look down__ that lone - some road,__ Hang
down your head and sigh. The best of friends__ must
part some day,__ And why not you and I?

94. Old Hound Dog Sally

Southern Folk Song
Adapted by Sharon Falk

1. Way down yon-der in the green, green val - ley, Hey did-dle-i-
2. Fox he run__ till he come to the "hol - ler." Hey did-dle-i-
3. We searched all day__ and we searched all night.__ Hey did-dle-i-

ay. I took my old hound dog named Sal - ly.
ay. Me and Sal - ly up and "fol - ler."
ay. But the fox he was no - where in sight.____

Hey did - dle - i - ay. I turned old hound dog
Hey did - dle - i - ay. Old hound dog Sal - ly
Hey did - dle - i - ay. The fox was hid - ing

Sal - ly loose. Hey did - dle - i - ay. To
smelled the ground. Hey did - dle - i - ay. But the
in his den. Hey did - dle - i - ay. So

catch the fox that stole our gray goose. Hey did - dle - i - ay.
fox was no - where to be found.____ Hey did - dle - i - ay.
me and Sal - ly went home a - gain.____ Hey did - dle - i - ay.

100. I Believe in Music

Words and Music by Mac Davis

1. Well, I could just sit a-round mak-ing __ mu - sic
2. Mu - sic is love, _____ love is __ mu - sic if you
3. Mu - sic is the u - ni - ver - sal lan - guage__ and

all day long. _____
know what I mean. _____
love is the key. _____

Long as I'm mak-ing mu-
Peo - ple who be - lieve in mu-
To broth-er-hood and peace and un -

- sic, I know I can't do no-bod-y wrong. __ And
- sic are the hap-pi-est peo-ple I ev-er seen. __ So
- der - stand - ing to liv-ing in har-mo-ny. _____ So

who knows,   may-be some-day I'll __ come up with a song. _____
clap your hands,   stomp your feet, ____ shake __ your tam - bour-ine. _
take your bro - ther __ by the hand ___ and sing a - long __ with me. _

__ That makes peo-ple want to stop their fuss - ing and fight-ing just
__ Lift __ your __ voic - es to ____ the sky. _____ God
__ And find __ out __ what it real - ly means __ to be

long e-nough to sing a - long. ____
loves ____ you when __ you sing. ____
young __ and rich ___ and free. ____

1.

110. Sim Sa-La-Bim

Danish Folk Song

1. High in a tree a crow-ow-ow,
2. Then came a wick-ed hunt - er
3. He shot that poor old crow-ow-ow,
4. Then came a pret - ty mai - den
5. She took the poor old crow-ow-ow,

Sim sa-la-bim bam boom, sa-la-doo, sa-la-dim!

High in a tree a crow-ow-ow sat.
Then came a wick-ed hunt-er a - long.
He shot that poor old crow-ow-ow dead.
Then came a pret-ty mai-den a - long.
She took the poor old crow-ow-ow home.

104. Turn the Glasses Over

American Singing Game

106. Garden Song

Words and Music by David Mallett

1. Inch by inch, row by row, gon-na make this gar-den grow;
2. Pull-ing weeds and pick-ing stones, man is made of dreams and bones;
3. Plant your rows straight and long, thick-er than with prayer and song;

All it takes is a rake and a hoe and a place of fer-tile ground.
Feel the need to __ grow my __ own 'cause the time is close at hand.
Moth-er Earth will __ make you strong if you give her love and care.

Inch by inch, row by row, some-one bless the seeds I sow;
Grain by grain, sun __ and rain, find my way in na-ture's chain,
Old crow watch-in' hun-gri-ly from his perch in yon-der tree;

Some-one warm them from be-low 'till the rain comes tum-bl-ing down.
To my bod-y and my brain, to the mu-sic from __ the land.
In my gar-den I'm as free as that feath-ered beak __ up there.

108. Catch a Falling Star

Words and Music by Vance and Pockriss

Catch a fall - ing star and put it in your pock - et,

nev - er let it fade a - way. Catch a fall - ing star and

put it in your pock - et, Save it for a rain - y day. For

when your trou - bles start mul - ti - ply - ing, and they just might; It's

easy to forget them without trying, with just a pocket full of starlight. Catch a falling star and put it in your pocket, never let it fade away. Catch a falling star and put it in your pocket, Save it for a rainy day.

112. Gerakina

English Words by Margaret Marks

Greek Folk Song

Ger - a - ki-na's at the fair, _____ Ger - a - ki - na, with her

sil - ver ban-gles on, Brings mu-sic ev-ery - where. _____

Ring, pret - ty sil - ver ban - gles, Jin - gle jin - gle

jan - gle, Sing in the air, Ger-a - ki - na danc - ing at the

fair. All the vil - lage folk will come to the

square, For the jin - gle jan - gle dance at the fair.

159. The Bee and the Pup

Traditional

1. There was __ a bee - i - ee - i - ee, Sat on __ a wall - i - all - i -
2. There was __ a pup - i - up - i - up, Sat on __ the bee - i - ee - i -

all, And he __ went buzz - i - uzz - i - uzz, And that __ was all - i - all - i - all.
ee, Some - one __ went Ki - yi - yi - yi - yi, And that __ was he - i - ee - i - ee.

114. Magic Penny

Words and Music by Malvina Reynolds

Love is some-thing if you give it a-way,— give it a-way,— give it a-way,—

Love is some-thing if you give it a-way— You end up hav-ing— more.

It's just like a mag-ic pen-ny,— Hold it tight and you won't have an-y;—

Lend it; spend— it and you'll have so man-y— they'll roll all o - ver the floor, for

120. Solomon Levi

Traditional

My name is Sol-o-mon Le-vi, and I live on Sa-lem Street; That's where to buy your coats and vests and ev-ery-thing that's neat. Sec-ond-hand-ed ul-ster-ettes and o-ver-coats so fine, For all the boys that trade with me at Hun-dred and for-ty nine.

119. The Old Piano Roll Blues

Words and Music by Cy Coben

I wan-na hear it a-gain, _ I wan-na hear it a-gain, _

The Old Pi-a-no Roll Blues, ___ We're

sit-tin' at an up-right, My sweet-ie and me, ___

Push-in' on the ped-als, mak-in' sweet har-mo-ny. When we hear

rink - i - ty tink, __ And we hear plink - i - ty plink, __

We cud-dle clos-er, it seems. __ And while we kiss, kiss, kiss a -

way all our cares, __ The play - er pia - no's play - in'

razz - a - ma - tazz, __ I wan - na hear it a - gain, __ I wan - na

hear it a - gain, _ The Old Pi - a - no Roll Blues. _____

170. Johnny's My Boy

Ghana Folk Song

John - ny's my boy, I sent him to school, to

learn how to spell John Pool, John - ny, John - ny, John - ny.

124. Oh Susannah

Words and Music by Stephen Foster

1. I __ came from Al - a - bam-a, With my ban-jo on my knee; I'm __
2. It __ rained all night the day I left, The weath-er it was dry, The __

going to Loui - si - an - a, There my true love for to see.
sun so hot I froze to death, Su - san-nah, don't you cry.

Refrain

Oh! Su - san-nah, Oh, don't you cry for me, I've __

come from Al - a - bam - a With my ban - jo on my knee.

123. This Land Is Your Land

Words and Music by Woody Guthrie

1. As I was walk-ing that rib-bon of high-way, I saw a-
2. I've roamed and ram-bled and I fol-lowed my foot-steps To the spar-kling
3. When the sun comes shin-ing, and I ___ was stroll-ing And the wheat fields

bove me that end-less sky-way, I saw be-low me that gold-en
sands of her dia-mond des-erts, And all a-round me a voice came
wav-ing and the dust clouds roll-ing, As the fog was lift-ing a voice was

val - ley,
sound - ing,   This land was made for you and me. ___
chant - ing,

125. Rock Island Line

Work Song

With a steady beat

I say the Rock Is - land Line ____ is a

might - y good road, ____ I say the Rock Is - land Line ____ is the

road to ride; Oh, the Rock Is - land Line ____ is a

might - y good road._____ If you want to

ride it, got to ride it like you're fly - in'; Buy your

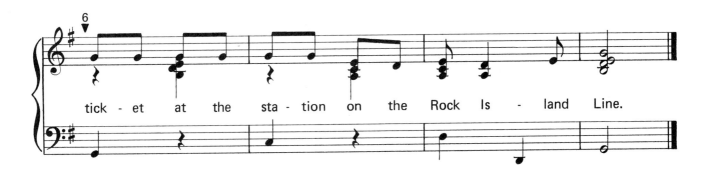

tick - et at the sta - tion on the Rock Is - land Line.

127. Galway Piper

Irish Folk Song

342

131. We Shall Overcome

New Words and Musical Arrangement
by Zilphia Horton, Frank Hamilton,
Guy Carawan, and Pete Seeger

343

134. Maori Stick Game

Translated by Max Exner

Maori Folk Song

E - pa - pa ___ wai - a - ri ta - ku nei ___ ma ___ hi,
Smile o my ___ fa - ther, but nev - er de - ny ___ me,

2
Ta - ku nei ___ ma - hi he tu - ku ro - ma - ta.
Nev - er de - ny me the pleas - ure of ___ dream - ing.

3
E - pa - pa ___ wai - a - ri ta - ku nei ___ ma ___ hi,
Smile o my ___ fa - ther, but nev - er de - ny ___ me,

4
Ta - ku nei ___ ma - hi he ta - ku roi - ma ta. E - au
Nev - er de - ny me the pleas - ure of dream - ing. Way a -

5

e ka ma-te-au. _____ E - hi - ne ho - ki i - ho -
way, my love is a-way. Girl of mine, come a-gain to

ra. _____ Ma-ku e kau-te o hi-koi tang-a
me! _____ Cold is the path-way that led her from me,

Ma-ku e kau-te o hi-koi tang-a. E - au -
Warm will the path be that brings her to me. Way a-

e ka ma-te-au. _____ E - hi-ne ho-ki i-ho ra. _____
way, my love is a-way, Girl of mine, come a-gain to me! _____

136. I'm Going Crazy

New Verses by Charles Sharp

Traditional

1. Mar - y had a lit - tle lamb, Its fleece was white as snow, And
2. Mar - y had a lit - tle goat, It al - ways ate tin cans, And
3. Mar - y had a lit - tle cat, It al - ways played with yarn, And
4. Mar - y had a lit - tle lamb, His fleece was black as soot, And

ev - ery - where that Mar - y went, The lamb was sure to
when the lit - tle goats____ came, They came in Ford se -
when the lit - tle kit - tens came, They came with sweat - ers
ev - ery - where that lamb____ went, His soot - y foot he

go.
dans.
on.
put.

I'm go-ing cra - zy, ____ just sing-ing this song. ____ I'm go - ing

cra - zy, ____ Don't you wan-ta come a - long? ____

138. Sunshine on My Shoulders

Words by John Denver

Music by John Denver,
Mike Taylor, and Dick Kniss

al - ways___ makes me high._____

If I___ had a day that I could give you,_____ I'd
If I___ had a tale that I could tell you,_____ I'd

give to you___ a day just like to - day._____
tell a tale_____ sure to make you smile._____

If I___ had___ a song that I could sing for__ you,__ I'd
If I___ had___ a wish that I could wish for__ you,__ I'd

Last time Da Capo al Coda

sing a song___ to make you feel this way._____
make a wish___ for sun-shine all the while._____

Coda

Sun-shine___ al-most all the time makes me high,_____

___ sun-shine___ al-most al-ways..._____

349

142. The Lonely Goatherd

Words by Oscar Hammerstein II

Music by Richard Rodgers

1. High on a hill was a lone-ly goat-herd, } lay-ee-o-dl lay-ee-o-dl lay-ee-o.
2. One lit-tle girl in a pale pink coat heard: }

Loud was the voice of the lone-ly goat-herd, } lay-ee-o-dl, lay-ee-o-dl - o.
She yo-dled back to the lone-ly goat-herd, }

Folks in a town that was quite re-mote heard: } lay-ee-o-dl, lay-ee-o-dl lay-ee-o.
Soon her ma-ma with a gleam-ing gloat, heard: }

Lus-ty and clear from the goat-herd's throat heard: } lay-ee-o-dl lay-ee-o-dl-o.
What a du-et for a girl and goat-herd! }

O - ho, lay-dee-o-dl-lee - o, O - ho, lay-dee-o-dl - ay!

O - ho, lay-dee-o-dl-lee - o, ho-dl-o-dl lee - o ay!

Hap-py are they, lay-lee-o lay-ee lee-o! O lay-lee-o lay-lee lay-ee-o.

Soon the du-et will be-come a tri-o, lay-ee-o-dl lay-ee-o-dl-o.

Coda

Ho-di lay-ee,_____ Ho-di lay-ee,_____ Ho-di lay-ee,_ Ho-di lay-ee!_

145. Peace of the River

Words by Glendora Gosling

Music by Viola Wood

Peace, I ask of thee, O riv - er, Peace, peace, peace.

When I learn to live se - rene - ly, Cares will cease.

From the hills I gath-er cour - age, Vi - sion of the day to be,

Strength to lead and faith to fol - low, All are giv-en un-to me.

Peace, I ask of thee, O riv - er, Peace, peace, peace.

146. Let Us Sing Together

Adapted from a
Czech Folk Song

Let us sing to-geth - er, Let us sing to-geth - er one and all a joy - ous song.

Let us sing to - geth - er One and all a joy - ous song.

Let us sing a - gain and a - gain, Let us sing a - gain and a - gain,

Let us sing a - gain and a - gain, One and all a joy - ous song.

153. Yellow Rose of Texas

American Song

1. There's a yel - low rose in Tex - as, I'm go-ing there to see, No
Chorus: She's the sweet-est rose of col - or a fel-low ev - er knew, Her
2. Oh, I'm go - ing back to find her; my heart is full of woe, We'll

oth - er fel - low knows her, No - bod - y on - ly me. She
eyes are like the dia - monds, they spar - kle in the dew. You may
sing the songs to - geth - er we sang so long a - go. I'll

cried so when I left her, it al-most broke her heart, And
talk a - bout your dear-est maids and sing of Ro - sy Lee, But the
pick the ban - jo gai - ly and sing the songs of yore, The

if we ev - er meet a - gain, we nev - er more shall part.
yel - low rose of Tex - as beats the belles of Ten - nes - see.
yel - low rose of Tex - as, she'll be mine for-ev - er - more.

151. Groundhog

Arranged and Adapted
by Buffy Sainte-Marie

1. Ground - hog,
2. Rat-tle - snake,

ground - hog,
rat - tle - snake,

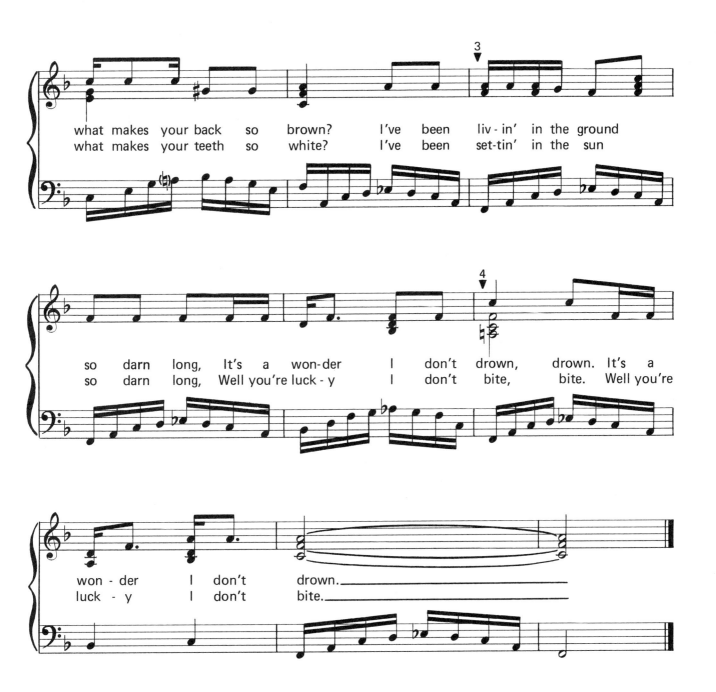

what makes your back so brown? I've been liv-in' in the ground
what makes your teeth so white? I've been set-tin' in the sun

so darn long, It's a won-der I don't drown, drown. It's a
so darn long, Well you're luck-y I don't bite, bite. Well you're

won - der I don't drown._____
luck - y I don't bite._____

152. Found a Peanut

Nonsense Song

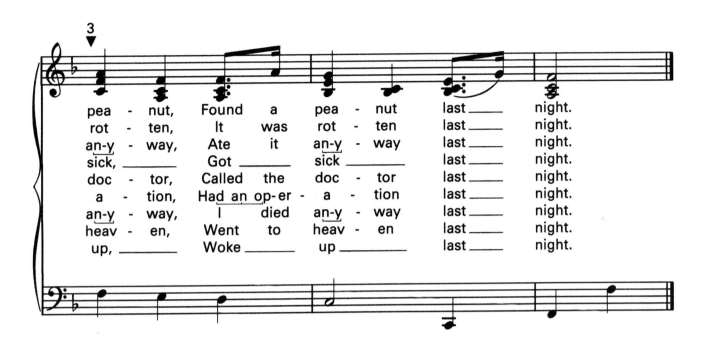

pea - nut, Found a pea - nut last ____ night.
rot - ten, It was rot - ten last ____ night.
an-y - way, Ate it an-y - way last ____ night.
sick, ____ Got ____ sick ____ last ____ night.
doc - tor, Called the doc - tor last ____ night.
a - tion, Had an op-er - a - tion last ____ night.
an-y - way, I died an-y - way last ____ night.
heav - en, Went to heav - en last ____ night.
up, ____ Woke ____ up ____ last ____ night.

154. When the Saints Go Marching In

Traditional

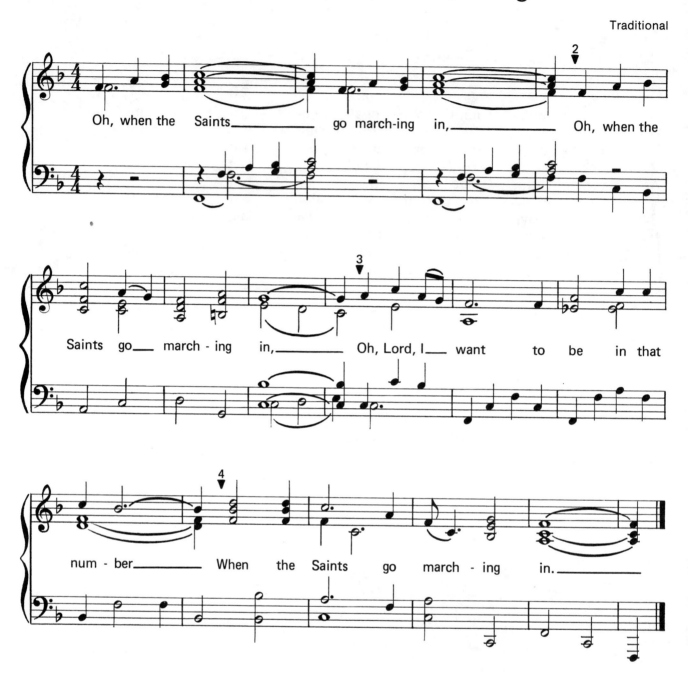

Oh, when the Saints_____ go march-ing in,_____ Oh, when the Saints go_____ march-ing in,_____ Oh, Lord, I___ want to be in that num-ber_____ When the Saints go march-ing in._____

155. Streets of Laredo

Cowboy Song

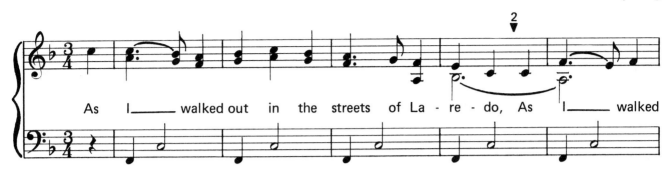

As I_____ walked out in the streets of La - re - do, As I_____ walked

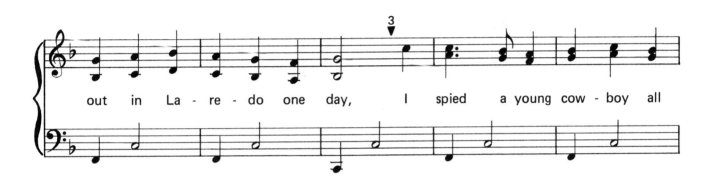

out in La - re - do one day, I spied a young cow - boy all

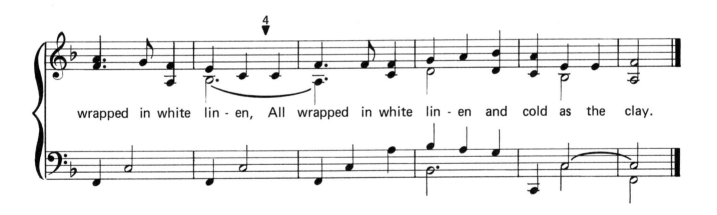

wrapped in white lin - en, All wrapped in white lin - en and cold as the clay.

156. Spanish Cavalier and Solomon Levi

Words and Music by William Hendrickson

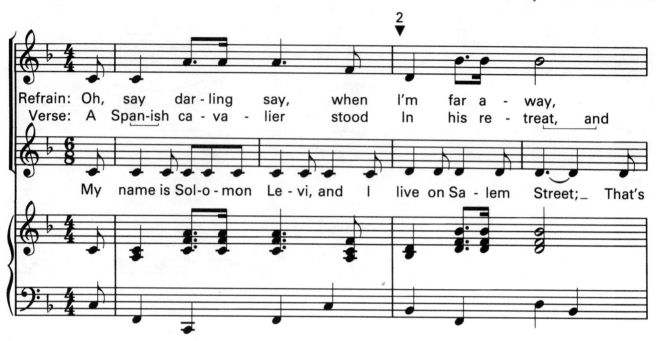

Refrain: Oh, say dar-ling say, when I'm far a - way,

Verse: A Span-ish ca-va - lier stood In his re - treat, and

My name is Sol-o - mon Le - vi, and I live on Sa - lem Street;_ That's

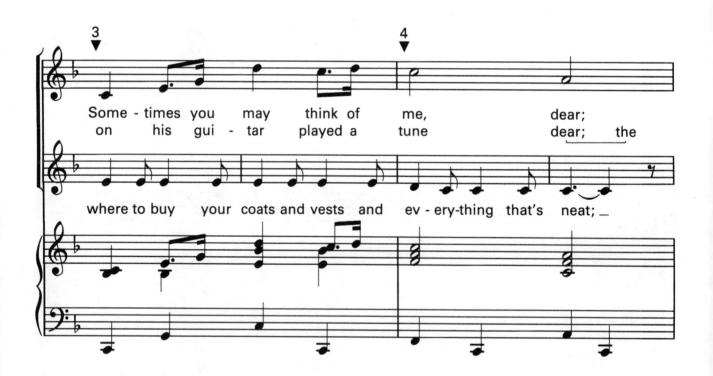

Some - times you may think of me, dear;

on his gui - tar played a tune dear; the

where to buy your coats and vests and ev - ery-thing that's neat; _

Bright sun-ny days will soon fade a - way, Re -
mu - sic so sweet would oft times re - peat, the

Sec-ond-hand - ed ul - ster-ettes, and o - ver-coats so fine. ___ For

mem-ber what I say __ and be true dear.
bless-ing of my coun - try and you, dear.

all the boys that trade with me at Hun-dred and for - ty - nine. __

160. Deep in the Heart of Texas

Words by June Hershey

Music by Don Swander

There is a land, a west-ern land, Might-y won-der-

ful to see._____ It is the land I

un-der-stand, And it's there I long to be._____

Refrain

The stars at night are big and bright, *(clap)* Deep in the heart of

Tex - as! The prai - rie sky is wide and high,

Deep in the heart of Tex - as! The sage in bloom is

like per - fume, Deep in the heart of Tex - as! Re - minds me

of the one I love, Deep in the heart of Tex - as!

164. Sing

Words and Music by Joe Raposo

*Cue notes represent harmony part.

bad;
be;
(sing,) Sing of hap - py, not
(sing,) Sing for you and not for

sad.
me.
Sing!
Sing a

song,
Make it sim - ple to last your whole life

Don't wor-ry that it's not good e-nough for

long._____ Don't wor - - ry,

an - y-one else to hear.

let's hear. Sing! Sing a

song!_____ La la do la da, La

da la do la da, La da da la do la la.____

La do la da, La

da la la da, Lo da da la do lo da.____

1.   2.

repeat and fade

La la do la da, La da la do la da, La da da la do la da.____

166. The Inchworm

Words and Music by Frank Loesser

Two and two are four, four and four are eight; That's all you
have on your busi - ness - like mind. Two and two are four,
four and four are eight; How can you be so blind?_____

Two and two are four, Four and four are eight,

Inch - worm, inch - worm, mea - sur - ing the mar - i - golds,

Eight and eight are six - teen, Six - teen and six - teen are thir - ty two.

Seems to me you'd stop and see how beau - ti - ful they are.

173. Old Dan Tucker

Circle Dance

Old Dan Tuck-er went to town, Swing-ing the la-dies all a-round.

First to the right and then to the left, And then to the one that you love best.

Prom - e-nade, Old Dan Tuck-er, Prom - e-nade, Old Dan Tuck-er,

Prom - e-nade, Old Dan Tuck-er, Came too late to get your sup-per.

168. Put On a Happy Face

Words by Lee Adams

Music by Charles Strouse

Gray skies are gon-na clear up, ___ Put on a hap-py face!

Brush off the clouds and cheer up, ___ Put on a hap-py face!

Take off the gloom-y mask of trag-e-dy, It's not your style;

You'll look so good that you'll be glad_ you de - cid-ed to smile!_

Pick out a pleas-ant out-look, ___ Stick out that no-ble chin;

Wipe off that "full of doubt" look, ___ Slap on a hap-py grin! And spread

sun-shine all o-ver the place, Just put on a hap-py face!

174. Happiness

Words and Music by Clark Gesner

1. Hap - pi - ness   is   two kinds of ice   cream,
2. Hap - pi - ness   is   five dif - fer-ent cray - ons,

Find - ing your skate key, tell - ing the time.
Know-ing a se - cret, climb-ing a tree.

1. Hap - pi - ness   is   learn - ing   to   whis - tle,
2. Hap - pi - ness   is   find - ing   a   nick - el,
3. Hap - pi - ness   is   hav - ing   a   sis - ter,

Ty - ing your shoes for the   ver - y first time.
Catch-ing a   fire - fly, ___ set-ting him free.
Shar-ing a sand - wich, ___ get-ting a - long.

Hap - pi - ness   is   play-ing the drum in your own   school band.   And
Hap - pi - ness   is   be - ing a - lone ev - ery   now   and   then.   And
Hap - pi - ness   is   sing-ing to-geth-er when day   is   through.   And

Hap-pi-ness   is   walk - ing hand   in   hand. _____
Hap-pi-ness   is   com - ing home   a -
Hap-pi-ness   is   those who sing   with

gain.
you.

Hap-pi-ness is morn-ing and eve-ning,

Day-time and night-time too. For Hap-pi-ness is an-y-one, and

an-y-thing at all, That's loved

D.S. 𝄋 to Fine   Fine

by you.

181. Black-Eyed Susie

Traditional

Moderately

1. All I want in this cre - a - tion: pret - ty wife and big plan - ta - tion.
2. All I want in this old world:___ lit - tle kid with hair that's curled.___
3. All I want on earth: _____ hap - pi - ness and mirth._____

Hey there pret - ty black - eyed Su - sie, Hey there pret - ty black - eyed Su - sie,
Hey___ pret - ty black - eyed Su - sie, Hey___ pret - ty black - eyed Su - sie,
Hey!_____ black - eyed Su - sie, Hey!_____ Sue!_____

Hey there pret - ty black - eyed Su - sie, Hey there pret - ty black - eyed Sue.
Hey___ pret - ty black - eyed Su - sie, Hey___ there___ Sue._____
Hey!_____ black - eyed Su - sie, Hey!_____ Sue!_____

379

176. One Bottle of Pop

Traditional

One bot-tle of pop, Two bot-tles of pop, Three bot-tles of pop, Four bot-tles of pop,

Five bot-tles of pop, Six bot-tles of pop, Sev-en bot-tles of pop, Pop!

Don't throw your junk in my back - yard, my back - yard, my back - yard,

Don't throw your junk in my back-yard, My back-yard's full.

Allegro

Fish and chips and vin-e-gar, vin-e-gar, vin-e-gar,

Fish and chips and vin-e-gar, vin-e-gar, Pop!

178. Edelweiss

Words by Oscar Hammerstein II

Music by Richard Rodgers

E - del - weiss, E - del - weiss, Ev - ery

morn-ing you greet me. Small and white,

Clean and bright, You look hap-py to meet me.

Blos - som of snow, may you bloom and grow,

Bloom and grow for - ev - er. E - del - weiss,

E - del - weiss, Bless my home-land for - ev - er.

182. Tina Singu

African Folk Song

190. The Lost Lady Found

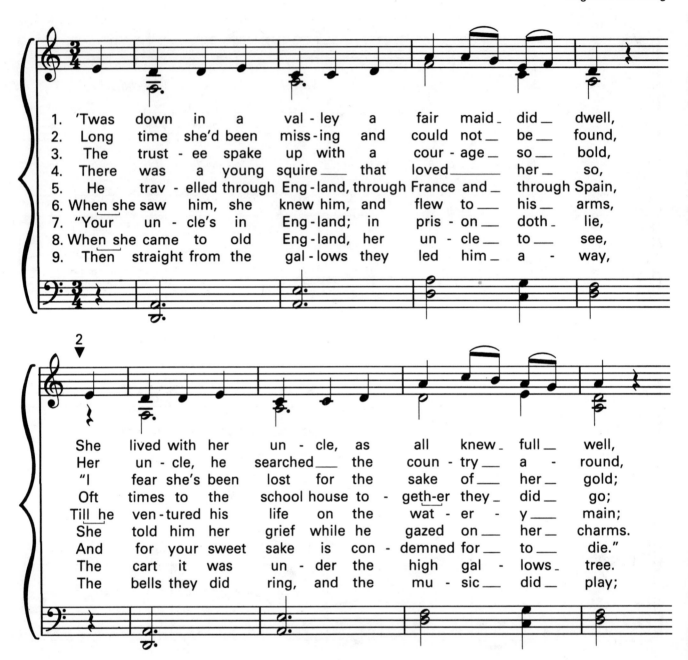

1. 'Twas down in a val - ley a fair maid＿ did＿ dwell,
2. Long time she'd been miss - ing and could not＿ be＿ found,
3. The trust - ee spake up with a cour - age＿ so＿ bold,
4. There was a young squire＿ that loved＿ her＿ so,
5. He trav - elled through Eng - land, through France and＿ through Spain,
6. When she saw him, she knew him, and flew to＿ his＿ arms,
7. "Your un - cle's in Eng - land; in pris - on＿ doth＿ lie,
8. When she came to old Eng - land, her un - cle＿ to＿ see,
9. Then straight from the gal - lows they led him＿ a - way,

She lived with her un - cle, as all knew＿ full＿ well,
Her un - cle, he searched＿ the coun - try＿ a - round,
"I fear she's been lost for the sake of＿ her＿ gold;
Oft times to the school house to - geth-er they＿ did＿ go;
Till he ven - tured his life on the wat - er - y＿ main;
She told him her grief while he gazed on＿ her＿ charms.
And for your sweet sake is con - demned for＿ to＿ die."
The cart it was un - der the high gal - lows＿ tree.
The bells they did ring, and the mu - sic＿ did＿ play;

386

3

'Twas down in the val-ley where vi-o-lets were gay,
Till he came to her trust-ee, be-tween hope and fear,
So we'll have life for life, sir," the trust-ee did say,
"I'm a-fraid she is mur-dered; so great is my fear,
And he came to a house where he lodged for a night,
"How came you to Dub-lin, my dear-est, I pray?"
"Car-ry me to old Eng-land, my dear-est," she cried;
"Oh, par-don! Oh, par-don! Oh, par-don! I crave!
Ev-ery house in the val-ley with mirth did re-sound,

4

Three gyp-sies be-trayed her and stole her a-way!
The trust-ee made an-swer, "She has not been here."
"We shall send you to pris-on, and there you shall stay."
If I'd wings like a dove I would fly to my dear!"
And in that same house was his own heart's de-light.
"Three gyp-sies be-trayed me, and stole me a-way."
"One thou-sand I'll give you and will be your bride."
Don't you see I'm a-live, your dear life to save?"
As soon as they heard the lost la-dy was found.

196. Oh, It's Great To Be Livin' This Morning

Words and Music by Doug Nichol

Refrain

Oh, it's great_ to be liv - in' this morn - ing.

2

Oh, it's great_ to be here on this earth._____

3

And I feel_ that my life is just dawn - ing.

4

Fine

Moth-er Na-ture has just giv-en me new birth._____

5 *Verse*

1. It makes no dif-fer-ence if it's sun - ny or not,
2. I've found that I can make the sun shine in - side,

6   **7**

The rain just can't de - press me. I'm real-ly
When Moth-er Na - ture's gloom - y. There's no ex -

8

thank-ful for this new day I've got. Just be - in' here a - live on
cuse I've found to make my sun hide, When there's so ma-ny things that

9   *D.C. al Fine*

earth can im - press me. _____
keep com-in' to me. _____

201. Glee Reigns in Galilee

Traditional Israeli Song

208. A Little Love Goes a Long Way

Words and Music by Alfred Balkin

love _____ a lit - tle love.   love.

love _____ a lit - tle love.   love.

love _____ a lit - tle love.   love.

Verse 3   4

1. Lends a warm and friend-ly hand, _ When it's hard to
2. Puts you on your spe-cial cloud, _ When you're lone-ly
3. Helps keep spring-time in the air, ____ Though the trees are
4. Gets you sing-ing loud and strong,_ E - ven when life's

5

un - der - stand. __
in a crowd. __
cold and bare. __
go - ing wrong. _

Lends a warm and
Puts you on your
Helps keep spring - time
Gets you sing - ing

6

D.C. al Fine

friend-ly hand, __
spe - cial cloud, __
in the air, __
loud and strong, __

A lit - tle love, _____ a lit - tle love.

212. Tzena, Tzena

Israeli Folk Song

1. Tze - na, Tze - na, Tze - na, Tze - na, can't you hear the mu - sic play - ing
2. Tze - na, Tze - na, Tze - na, Tze - na, there's no use in your de - lay - ing

on _____ this love-ly night.
for _____ the time is right.

Tze - na, Tze - na, join the ce - le - bra - tion,

Join the hap-pi-ness and ju - bi - la - tion, Danc - ing, sing - ing,

what a grand oc-ca-sion   on _____ this love-ly   night.

Part 3

Tze - na,   Tze - na,   stop your hes - i - ta - ting, There's a   par - ty,

come and join   us,   We are wait - ing.   Tze - na,   Tze - na,

We're an - tic - i - pat-ing   your ar - riv - al,   Tze -na, Tze -na, Tze -na.

215. Farewell, My Own True Love

American Folk Song
Collected by William S. Hayne

1. Fare - well, my own true love, Fare - well a lit - tle while; I'm
2. Ten thou - sand mile, my love, Through Eng - land, France, and Spain; My
3. Oh, don't you see that dove That flies from vine to vine, A -

goin' a - way but I'll come a - gain, If I go ten thou - sand mile.
rov - ing mind shall nev - er rest Till I see your face a - gain.
mourn - ing for his own true love, Just as I will mourn for mine.

218. Yes Indeed

Words and Music by Sy Oliver

Refrain

Yes in - deed, Yes in - deed, I've got that

Fine

feel - in' in me. Yes in - deed.

220. Ever Onward!

Words by Norman Bell

Music by David A. Pollock

Section A

1. Ev-er on-ward! Ev-er on-ward! March a-long and sing ev-er on-ward! March with
2. Ev-er on-ward! Ev-er on-ward! Keep in step and press ev-er on-ward! Stand to-
3. Ev-er on-ward! Ev-er on-ward! Young A-mer-i-ca, ev-er on-ward! Ev-er

(To Section B after Verse 2) Fine

heads high, Sing with hearts high, And go on-ward to vic-to-ry.
geth-er, For to-geth-er, We'll go on-ward to vic-to-ry.
on-ward! Ev-er on-ward, Ev-er on-ward to vic-to-ry.

Section B

Like the o-cean's might-y roar, As it beats a-gainst the shore, Comes the

sound of voic-es ring-ing loud and clear. From the North and from the South, From the

East and from the West, It's the sound of Young A-mer - i - ca we hear.

225. Pumpkin Song

Adapted by Don Giller and Nick Singman

1. The wom - an stood at the o - pen door,
2. And saw a sight nev - er seen be - fore,
3. Six pump - kins they were ___ gath-er - ing 'round,
4. With - out a peep, with - out a sound,
5. The wom - an said, "It's ___ you I seek,
6. Why is it, sirs, that ___ you don't speak?"
7. "Be - cause, dear ma'am," is ___ what she heard,
8. "A talk - ing pump-kin would ___ be ab - surd."

woo, ___

(Tremolo)

8. Scream

"Yaaah!"

woo, ___

222. Little Lamb

Words by Stephen Sondheim

Music by Jule Styne

1. Lit-tle lamb, lit-tle lamb, My birth-day is here at last. Lit-tle
bear, lit-tle bear, You sit on my right, right there. Lit-tle

lamb, lit-tle lamb, A birth - day goes by so fast. 2. Lit-tle
hen, lit-tle hen, What game should we play, and when? Lit-tle

cat, lit-tle cat, Ah, why do you look so blue? Did some-bod-y paint you

like that, Or is it your birth-day too? _____ Lit-tle fish, lit-tle

fish, do you think I'll get my wish? Lit-tle lamb, lit-tle lamb, I

won-der how old I am. I won-der how old I am. _____

226. Hayride

Words and Music by Richard C. Berg

Descant

We are go - ing for a

Melody

Come on a-long, we're go-ing for a hay-ride, Fill up the wag-on

hay - ride, Au - tumn days are
with a load of hay; Come on a-long, we're go-ing for a hay-ride,

on their way. _____ We'll go
Frost's on the pump-kin, au-tumn's on its way. Gid-dy up, Dob-bin, oh,

jog - ging   far   a - way, _____

here we go a-jog-ging   O - ver   the   hills   and   far   a - way.

Sing   and   have   a   hap - py   day. _____

Come on a-long, we're go-ing for a hay-ride; Sing and be mer-ry,   have a hap-py day.

229. Now Thank We All Our God

Words by Martin Rinckart
Translation by Catherine Winkworth

Melody by Johann Crüger

1. Now thank we all our God With heart and hands and voic - es, Who
2. O may this boun-teous God Through all our life be near us, With

won-drous things hath done, In whom his world re - joic - es, Who,
ev - er joy - ful hearts And bless - ed peace to cheer us, And

from our moth-ers' arms, Hath blessed us on our way, With
keep us in his grace, And guide us when per - plexed, With

count - less gifts of love, And still is ours to - day.
free us from all ills In this world and the next.

230. Pat-A-Pan

Words Adapted by Kurt Miller

French Carol

Pat-a-pat-a - pan, _____ Tu-re-lu - re-

ley, _____ Fife and drum to - geth - er

play on this joy - ous hol - i - day.

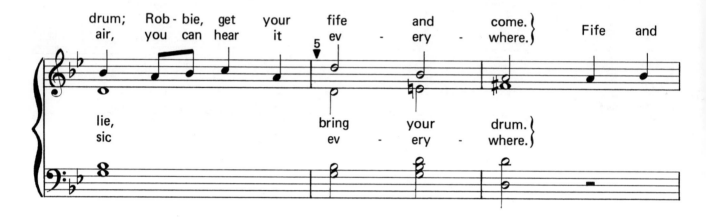

play; Fife and drum to - geth - er play on this joy - ous

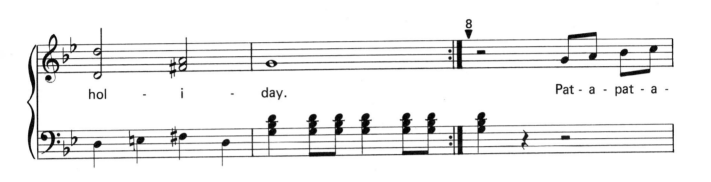

hol - i - day. Pat - a - pat - a -

pan.

233. Here We Come A-Wassailing

Old English Carol

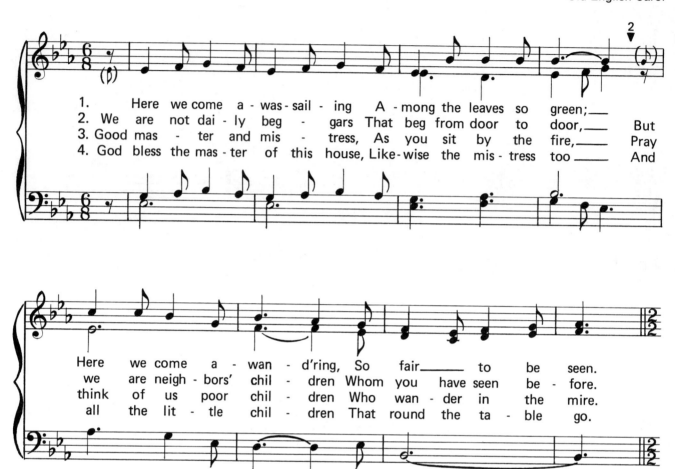

1. Here we come a - was - sail - ing A - mong the leaves so green;___ Here we come a - wan - d'ring, So fair___ to be seen.
2. We are not dai - ly beg - gars That beg from door to door,___ But we are neigh - bors' chil - dren Whom you have seen be - fore.
3. Good mas - ter and mis - tress, As you sit by the fire,___ Pray think of us poor chil - dren Who wan - der in the mire.
4. God bless the mas - ter of this house, Like - wise the mis - tress too ___ And all the lit - tle chil - dren That round the ta - ble go.

Love and joy come to you And to you glad Christ - mas

too, And God bless you and send__ you a hap - py New

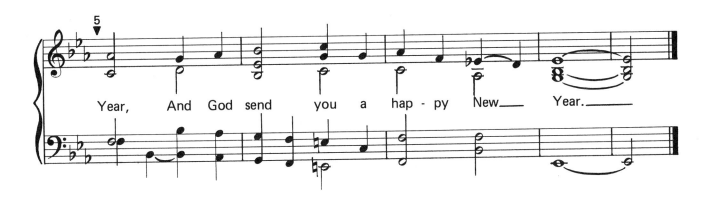

Year, And God send you a hap - py New__ Year.__

240. Silver Bells

Words and Music by
Jay Livingston and Ray Evans

1. Cit - y   side - walks, bus - y   side - walks dressed in   hol - i - day
2. Strings of   street lights, e - ven   stop lights blink a   bright red and

style;   In the   air there's a   feel - ing   of   Christ - mas. _____
green;   As the   shop - pers rush   home with   their   trea - sures _____

—   Child - ren   laugh - ing,   peo - ple   pass - ing, meet - ing
—   Hear the   snow crunch, see the   kids   bunch, this is

smile af - ter   smile,   And on   ev - ery street   cor - ner you   hear: _____
San - ta's big   scene,   And a - bove all this   bus - tle you   hear: _____

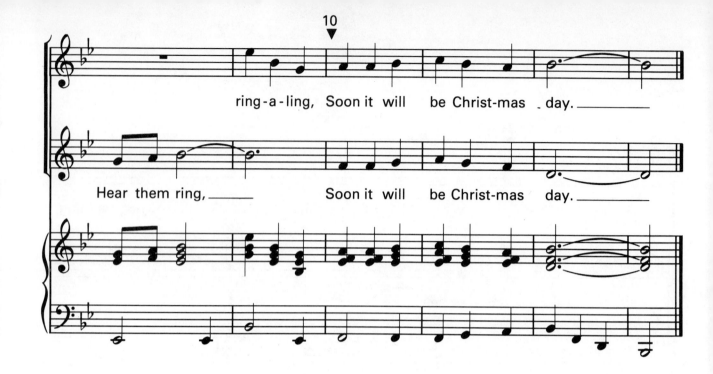

ring-a-ling, Soon it will be Christ-mas day.

Hear them ring,_____ Soon it will be Christ-mas day._____

245. Somebody Waiting

Play Party Song

1. As I look in-to your eyes, I be - hold a sweet sur - prise, There is

some-bod-y wait - ing for me._____

2. There is some - bod - y
3. Choose_ two and leave the
4. Choose_ one and leave the

wait - ing, There is some - bod - y wait - ing, There is
oth - er, Choose_ two and leave the oth - er, Choose_
oth - er, Choose_ one and leave the oth - er, Choose_

some - bod - y wait - ing for me._____
two and leave the oth - er for me._____
one and leave the oth - er for me._____

242. I Had a Dream, Dear

I had a dream, dear, you had one too, Mine was the best, for it was of you. Come, sweet-heart, tar - ry, now is the time. You tell me your dream, I'll tell you mine. M - I - N - E, M - I - N - E mine, I'll be T - H - I - N - E, T-

H - I-N - E thine, and I love you, I love you all the T - I - M - E

time. ___ You are the B - E - S - T, B - E-S - T best of all the R - E - S - T,

R - E-S - T rest, 'cause I love you I love you, I love you all the T - I - M - E

time. You tell me your dream, I'll tell you mine.

246. You're a Grand Old Flag

Words and Music by George M. Cohan

(Introduction not accounted for in pupil book)

You're a grand old flag, You're a high-fly - ing flag, And for-ev - er in peace may you wave;_____ You're the em - blem of the land I love, The home of the free and the

brave._____ Ev - ery heart beats true un - der
red, white, and blue, Where there's nev - er a boast or
brag;_____ But should auld ac - quain - tance be for -
got, Keep your eye on the grand old flag._____

250. Let There Be Peace on Earth

Words and Music by
Sy Miller and Jill Jackson

1. Let there be peace on Earth, and let it be-
2. Let peace be - gin with me. Let this be the

gin with me; _____ Let there be peace on
mo - ment now; _____ With ev - ery step I

Earth. The peace that was meant to be. _____ With
take, Let this be my sol - emn vow: _____ To

God as our Fa - ther, _____ Broth-ers all are we. _____

Let me walk with my broth-er, _____ In per-fect har - mo - ny. _____

take each mo-ment and live each mo-ment in peace e - ter - nal - ly; _____

Let there be peace on Earth, And let it be - gin with me. _____

248. Haleluyoh

Jewish Folk Song

Ha - le - lu - yoh,   ha - le - lu - yoh, Ha - le - lu   av - dey A - do - noi, _____

Ha - le - lu - yoh,   ha - le - lu - yoh, Ha - le - lu   es shem A - do - noi. _____

Ha - le - lu - yoh, _   ha - le - lu - yoh,   Ha - le - lu - yoh,   ha - le - lu - yoh, _____

Ha - le - lu - yoh, _   ha - le - lu - yoh,   Ha - le - lu - yoh,   ha - le - lu - yoh.

Teacher's Glossary

Accidental A notational sign indicating that single tones within a measure should be raised or lowered a half step.

Aerophone An instrument whose sound is made by blowing into an opening to vibrate a column of air.

Articulation The manner in which a tone is produced, smoothly (*legato*) or detached (*staccato*).

Beat The basic unit of time in music, usually organized within a certain meter into groups of two or three. The underlying pulse of the music.

Brass family Instruments made of brass or other metal on which sound is produced by blowing into a mouthpiece. Pitch changes result from altering the length of tubing through which the air moves. This family includes the trumpet, French horn, and tuba.

Call-response A musical form in which a musical idea is stated (usually by one voice) and echoed (usually by a group).

Canon A composition in which one line of music is strictly imitated in another line of music at any pitch or time interval.

Cheng A Chinese zither dating from the Ch'in Dynasty. It usually has between thirteen and sixteen strings. Each string has its own tuning peg and moveable bridge.

Chord The simultaneous sounding of three or more tones.

Chordophone An instrument whose sound is produced by the vibration of stretched strings.

Chromatic scale In Western music the octave is divided into twelve half steps. When these half steps are played one after the other, they form a chromatic scale.

Coda A section added to the end of a composition as a conclusion.

Concerto A piece of music for one or more soloists and orchestra, usually in symphonic form with three contrasting movements.

Consonance A combination of tones within a given musical system that creates an agreeable effect or a feeling of repose.

Countermelody A melody added to another to provide rhythmic or harmonic contrast, or harmonic tone color.

Crescendo A gradual increase in volume.

Da Capo (D.C.) From the beginning. Indicates that the composition should be repeated from the beginning to the end or until the word *Fine* appears.

Dal Segno (D.S.) From the sign. Indicates that the composition should be repeated from the sign until the word *Fine* appears.

Decrescendo A gradual decrease in volume.

Descant A countermelody usually played or sung above the main melody of a song.

Dissonance A combination of tones within a given musical system that creates a disagreeable effect or a feeling of tension.

Dynamics The expressive markings used to indicate the degree of intensity of sound or volume. The most common are pianissimo (*pp*): very soft; piano (*p*): soft; mezzo piano (*mp*): moderately soft; mezzo forte (*mf*): moderately loud; forte (*f*): loud; fortissimo (*ff*): very loud; *crescendo*: increase in loudness; *decrescendo* or *diminuendo*: decrease in loudness.

Electric piano A keyboard instrument whose sounds are activated by keys and produced electronically.

Fermata Hold or pause.

Fine End or close.

Glissando A rapid slide over the scale on a keyboard instrument or harp.

Grand piano A keyboard instrument whose strings are struck by hammers activated by keys.

Harmony The sound that occurs when two or more tones are produced simultaneously.

Harpsichord A keyboard instrument resembling the grand piano in shape and producing tones by the plucking of wire strings with quills or leathery points.

Home tone The tonal center, or first tone of a scale.

Idiophone An instrument whose sound is produced by the vibration of a solid material; the sound is initiated by striking, scraping, or rattling.

Imitation The repetition by one voice or instrument of a melody previously sung or played by another voice or instrument, as in a round, canon, or fugue.

Improvisation Performing or creating music spontaneously without the use of printed music, notes, or memory.

Interlude A section of music inserted between the parts of a long composition. In this text, it often refers to brief instrumental sections between verses of songs on the recordings.

Interval The distance in pitch between two tones.

Introduction An opening section of a composition.

Key The key of a composition indicates the scale on which the work is based.

Key signature A number of sharps or flats present on a staff at the beginning of a piece or section that indicates its key or tonality.

Legato An indication that tones should be performed in a smooth, connected manner.

Major scale A scale consisting of seven different pitches and an eighth pitch that is a higher repetition of the first. Each pitch is separated by the following sequence of steps: whole, whole, half, whole, whole, whole, half.

Marcato The performance of a tone in a marked or stressed manner.

Measure A group of beats, the first of which is usually accented. The number of beats in the group is determined by the meter signature. Measures are separated from each other by bar lines.

Melodic contour The shape of a succession of musical tones.

Melody A succession of tones having both motion and rhythm.

Membranophone An instrument whose sound is produced by vibrating a stretched skin or membrane.

Meter The organization of a specific number of beats into a group. The groupings are determined by the frequency of the underlying accents.

Meter signature A numerical indication found at the beginning of a piece of music or section that tells the number and types of beat found in each measure.

Minor scale A scale consisting of seven different pitches and an eighth pitch that is a higher repetition of the first. Each pitch is separated by the following sequence of steps: whole, half, whole, whole, half, whole, whole.

Mode A scalewise arrangement of tones that may form the basic tonal material of a composition.

Modulation The process of changing from one key to another during the course of a composition.

Motive The shortest recognizable unit of notes of a musical theme or subject.

Movement An independent section of a larger instrumental composition such as a symphony or concerto.

Octave The interval between two tones having the same name and located eight notes apart.

Organ A keyboard instrument that consists of a series of pipes standing on a wind chest and is operated by the player's hands and feet.

Ostinato A short pattern repeated over and over.

Patschen A physical movement in which one slaps his or her thighs rhythmically.

Pentatonic scale A five-tone scale with no half steps between any two tones. The scale can be produced on the piano by playing only the black keys.

Percussion family A group of instruments played by shaking or striking. This family includes the celesta, orchestra bells, timpani, maracas, woodblock, castanets, cymbals, drums, xylophone, glockenspiel, tambourine, and claves.

Phrase A natural division of the melodic line, comparable to a sentence in speech.

Pitch The highness or lowness of a musical sound, determined by the frequency of the sound waves producing it.

Pizzicato In string music, the sound produced by plucking the strings rather than bowing them.

Prime mark A marking that indicates the upper octave of notes; e.g., 1′ is higher than 1. Also used to describe sections of music that are similar; e.g., A′ is similar to A.

Pulse See *Beat*.

Rauschfeiff A medieval and renaissance double-reed instrument.

Ritard A gradual slowing of tempo.

Rondo A musical form resulting from the alternation of a main theme with contrasting themes (**A B A C A** etc.).

Root The note on which a chord is built. A chord is said to be in root position if the root is the lowest sounding note.

Round A melody sung or played by two or more musicians. Each musician or group starts at a different time and repeats the melody several times.

Sanza An African melody instrument known by many names such as *mbira, hand piano,* and *kalimba.* It consists of a series of metal or split-cane strips of graduated lengths arranged on a sounding board or resonator box.

Scale A series of tones arranged in ascending or descending order according to a plan.

Score Printed music.

Sequence Immediate repetition of a tonal pattern at a higher or lower pitch level.

Slur A curved line placed above or below two or more notes of different pitch to indicate that they are to be sung or played without separation.

Sonata A composition for piano or some other instrument (violin, flute, cello, etc.), usually with piano accompaniment, which consists of three or four separate sections called movements.

Staccato An indication that tones should be performed in a short, detached manner.

Staff A group of five horizontal lines on and around which notes are positioned.

String family A group of instruments on which sound is produced by rubbing a bow against strings. Includes the violin, viola, cello, and double bass (bass viol).

Suite A musical form consisting of a set of pieces or movements.

Symphony A sonata for orchestra.

Syncopation The temporary displacement of a regular rhythmic pulse.

Synthesizer An electronic instrument used to produce and organize a wide variety of sounds.

Tempo Rate of speed.

Texture The density of sound in a piece of music. This thickness or thinness of sound is created by the number of instruments or voices heard simultaneously.

Theme A complete musical idea that serves as the focus or subject of a musical composition.

Tie A curved line between two or more successive tones of the same pitch. The tones so connected are sounded as one tone that is equal in length to the combined duration of the individual tones.

Timbre The quality or ''color'' of a tone unique to the instrument or voice that produces it.

Tonal center The first degree of the scale on which a melody is constructed. Also called the *tonic.*

Tonality Feeling for a key or tonal center.

Unison All voices or instruments singing or playing the same pitch. The playing of the same notes by various instruments, voices, or a whole orchestra, either at the same pitch or in different octaves.

Variation The modification of a musical theme to create a new musical idea. This modification may be the result of melodic, rhythmic, or harmonic alteration.

Water drum A percussion instrument found in Africa, Central America, and South America. It consists of a half calabash or gourd that floats open side down in a container of water and is struck with small sticks.

Whole-tone scale A six-tone scale with one whole step between any two tones.

Woodwind family A group of instruments on which sound is produced by vibrating one or two reeds. Includes the clarinet, oboe, and saxophone.

Acknowledgments and Credits

ACKNOWLEDGMENTS

Grateful acknowledgment is made to the following copyright owners and agents for their permission to reprint the following copyrighted material. Every effort has been made to locate all copyright owners; any errors or omissions in copyright notice are inadvertent and will be corrected as they are discovered.

"Amahl and the Night Visitors," text Copyright © 1986 by William Morrow and Company, Inc. Adapted from AMAHL AND THE NIGHT VISITORS by Gian Carlo Menotti. Copyright © 1951, 1952, 1980 by G. Schirmer, Inc. Illustrations Copyright © 1986 by Michele Lemieux. Recording licensed through the Harry Fox Agency.

"Anyone Can Move a Mountain," by Johnny Marks, copyright 1966 St. Nicholas Music Inc. All Rights Reserved. Reprinted by Permission. This arrangement copyright 1986 St. Nicholas Music Inc. Recording licensed through the Harry Fox Agency.

"A Blue Song," words and music by Elizabeth Aitken and Hugh Aitken. © Copyright 1967 Hugh Aitken. Reprinted and recorded by permission of Hugh Aitken.

"Catch A Falling Star," by Paul J. Vance and Lee Pockriss. Copyright by Marvin Music Company. Reprinted and recorded by permission of Emily Music Corporation and Paul J. Vance Publishing.

"Deep in the Heart of Texas," words by June Hershey, music by Don Swander. Copyright © 1941 (Renewed) by Melody Lane Publications, Inc. Reprinted by permission of Columbia Pictures Publications. Recording licensed through the Harry Fox Agency.

"Edelweiss," music by Richard Rodgers, lyrics by Oscar Hammerstein II. Copyright © 1959 by Richard Rodgers and Oscar Hammerstein II. Williamson Music Co., owner of publication and allied rights throughout the Western Hemisphere and Japan. All Rights Administered by Chappell & Co., Inc. International Copyright Secured. All Rights Reserved. Reprinted in the United States and Canada by Permission of Hal Leonard Publishing Corporation. Recording licensed through the Harry Fox Agency.

"Ever Onward," words by Norman Bell and music by David A. Pollock. Copyright 1958 by Norman Bell and David A. Pollock. Reprinted and recorded by permission of David A. Pollock.

"Every Morning When I Wake Up," by Avon Gillespie, from *Zing, Zing, Zing: A Collection of Games and Songs Designed for Vocal Improvisation and Body Movement*, by Avon Gillespie. Copyright by Belwin Mills. Reprinted by permission of Columbia Pictures Publications. Recording licensed through the Harry Fox Agency.

"Farewell My Own True Love," American folk song collected by William S. Haynie. Copyright 1966 by Gulf Music Company. Reprinted and recorded by permission.

"Fifth Nifty United States," words and music by Ray Charles. Copyright © 1961 by Roncom Music Company. Reprinted and recorded by permission.

"Garden Song," words and music by David Mallett. © Copyright 1975 Cherry Lane Music Publishing Co., Inc. This arrangement © Copyright 1987 Cherry Lane Music Publishing Co., Inc. International Copyright Secured. All Rights Reserved. Used by permission. Recording licensed through the Harry Fox Agency.

"Gerakina," Greek folk song, English translation by Margaret Marks, from *Making Music Your Own*, Grade 6, © 1968 by Silver Burdett Company. Reprinted and recorded by permission of the publisher.

"Ground Hog," adapted and arranged by Buffy Sainte-Marie. Copyright © 1965 Gypsy Boy Music. All Rights Reserved. Reprinted by permission. Recording licensed through the Harry Fox Agency.

"Happiness," by Clark Gesner. Copyright © 1965, 1967 by Jeremy Music Inc. All Rights Reserved. Reprinted in the United States and Canada by Permission. HAPPINESS originated in the play YOU'RE A GOOD MAN, CHARLIE BROWN, a musical entertainment based on the comic strip "PEANUTS" by Charles M. Schulz.

"Harvest Time," Finnish folk melody. Words by Tossi Aaron, from *In Canon: Explorations of Familiar Canons for Voices, Recorders and Orff Instruments* by Erling Bisgaard in collaboration with Tossi Aaron, Copyright © 1978 by Magnamusic/Edition Wilhelm Hansen. Words reprinted and recorded by permission of MMB Music, Inc.

"Hayride," words and music by Richard C. Berg, from *Studying Music: Music for Young Americans* by Richard C. Berg, Lee Kjelson, Eugene W. Troth, Daniel S. Hooley and Josephine Wolverton. Copyright © 1966 by American Book Company. Reprinted and recorded by permission of D. C. Heath and Company.

"Hey Dum Diddeley Dum," words and music by Marc Stone. © 1979 Pachyderm Music. Reprinted and recorded by permission of Elephant Records.

"I Believe," words and music by Ervin Drake, Irvin Graham, Jimmy Shirl and Al Stillman. TRO — © Copyright 1952 (renewed 1980) and 1953 (renewed 1981) Hampshire House Publishing Corp., New York, NY. Reprinted by Permission of The Richmond Organization. Recording licensed through the Harry Fox Agency.

"I Believe in Music," words and music by Mac Davis, © Copyright 1970, 1972 by SCREEN GEMS-EMI MUSIC INC. and SONGPAINTER MUSIC. All administrative rights for the entire World controlled by SCREEN GEMS-EMI MUSIC INC., Hollywood, CA 90028. All Rights Reserved. Reprinted by permission of Warner Bros. Music. Recording licensed through the Harry Fox Agency.

"I'd Like To Teach the World To Sing (In Perfect Harmony)," words and music by B. Baker, B. Davis. R. Cook and R. Greenaway. Copyright © 1971 by The Coca-Cola Company. Copyright assigned to Shada Music Inc., ASCAP, 2527 Miami Ave., Nashville, TN 37214. Reprinted and recorded by permission.

"If You Should Meet," poem from ALLIGATOR PIE by Dennis Lee, © Copyright, 1974, by Dennis Lee. Reprinted by permission of Macmillan of Canada, A Division of Canada Publishing Corporation.

"I Had a Dream, Dear," arranged by Sigmund Spaeth. Copyright © 1942 by Mills Music, Inc. International Copyright Secured. All Rights Reserved. Reprinted by permission of Columbia Pictures Publications. Recording licensed through the Harry Fox Agency.

"I'm Going Crazy," source of melody unknown. Additional verses by Charles E. Sharp, from *Songs for Fellowship and Recreation: Singing Is Fun!*, Volume II, compiled and arranged by Mark Blankenship. Copyright © 1981 Broadman Press. Reprinted by permission. Recording licensed through SESAC, Inc.

"The Inch Worm," from *Hans Christian Andersen*, by Frank Loesser. © 1951, 1952 FRANK MUSIC CORP. © Renewed 1979, 1980 FRANK MUSIC CORP. International Copyright Secured. All Rights Reserved. Reprinted by permission. Recording licensed through the Harry Fox Agency.

"La Cucaracha," Mexican folk song, from *1001 Folk Tunes*, copyright © 1976 by Shattinger International Music Co. Reprinted and recorded by permission of Charles Hansen Music and Books.

"Let There Be Peace On Earth," by Sy Miller and Jill Jackson. Copyright © 1955 (Renewed 1983) by Jan—Lee Music (ASCAP). Reprinted by permission of the publisher. Recording licensed through the Harry Fox Agency.

"Lift Ev'ry Voice and Sing," words by James Weldon Johnson, music by J. Rosamond Jackson. Copyright © 1921 (Renewed)

ment © Copyright 1987 Cherry Lane Music Publishing Co., Inc. International Copyright Secured. All Rights Reserved. Reprinted by permission. Recording licensed through the Harry Fox Agency.

"Sweet Potatoes," Creole folk song adapted and arranged by Jean La Coste. Words by William S. Haynie, © 1966 Gulf Music Co. Reprinted and recorded by permission of the publisher.

"Tear Down the Walls," words and music by Fred Neil. TRO—© Copyright 1964 and 1965 Folkways Music Publishers, Inc., New York, NY. Reprinted by Permission of The Richmond Organization. Recording licensed through the Harry Fox Agency.

"There's Work To Be Done—No Need To Hurry," words and music by Richard C. Berg, from *Experiencing Music* of the NEW DIMENSIONS IN MUSIC series, by Robert A. Choate, Lee Kjelson, Richard C. Berg and Eugene W. Troth, copyright © 1970 by American Book Company. Reprinted and recorded by permission of D. C. Heath and Company.

"This Land is Your Land," words and music by Woody Guthrie. TRO—© Copyright 1956 (renewed 1984), 1958 (renewed 1986) and 1970 Ludlow Music, Inc., New York, NY. Reprinted by permission of The Richmond Organization. Recording licensed through the Harry Fox Agency.

"Titi-Toria," Maori folk song translated by Max Exner, from *Tent and Trail Songs*, copyright by World Around Songs. Reprinted and recorded by permission.

"The Turtle Song—'I Can Win!'" words and music by Therese McGrath, copyright © 1985 by Therese McGrath Meyer. Reprinted and recorded by permission of the author.

"Tzena Tzena," Israeli folk song. Copyright © 1950 by Edwards Music Co., Inc. Reprinted by permission of Columbia Pictures Publications. Recording licensed through the Harry Fox Agency.

"Voiles," by Claude Debussy. © 1910 Durand S.A. Used By Permission Of The Publisher. Theodore Presser Company, Sole Representative USA & Canada. Recording licensed through the Harry Fox Agency.

"We Shall Overcome," by Zilphia Horton, Frank Hamilton, Guy Carawan and Pete Seeger. TRO—© Copyright 1960 and 1963 Ludlow Music, Inc., New York, NY. Reprinted by permission of The Richmond Organization. Recording licensed through the Harry Fox Agency. Royalties from this composition are being contributed to The Freedom Movement under the trusteeship of the writers.

"West African Rhythm Complex," transcribed by Nicholas M. England from various Ghanaian songs, © Copyright 1966, Juilliard School of Music. Material Reprinted Courtesy The Juilliard School.

"Yankee Doodle Boy," words and music by George M. Cohan. Copyright © 1986 by Hal Leonard Publishing Corporation. International Copyright Secured. ALL RIGHTS RESERVED. Reprinted by Permission of Hal Leonard Publishing Corporation. Recording licensed through the Harry Fox Agency.

"Yes, Indeed," by Sy Oliver. Copyright © 1940, 1941 (Renewed) by Embassy Music Corporation (BMI). International Copyright Secured. All Rights Reserved. Reprinted by Permission of Music Sales Corporation. Recording licensed through the Harry Fox Agency.

"You're A Grand Old Flag," words and music by George M. Cohan. Copyright © 1906 and renewed by George M. Cohan Music Publishing Co. International Copyright Secured. ALL RIGHTS RESERVED. Reprinted in the United States and Canada by permission of Hal Leonard Publishing Corporation; outside the United States and Canada by George M. Cohan Music Publishing Co. Recording licensed in the United States through the Harry Fox Agency, and in Canada through CMRRA.

"The Zulu Warrior," words and music by Josef Marais. TRO—© Copyright 1946 (renewed 1974), 1952 (renewed 1980) and 1974 Hampshire House Publishing Corp., New York, NY. Reprinted by permission of The Richmond Organization. Recording licensed through the Harry Fox Agency.

Classified Index of Music, Art, and Poetry

*Topics of special interest to teachers who use the Kodaly and Orff methods are indicated with a **K** and an **O**.*

ART REPRODUCTIONS

Castle on the Rhine (*G.C. Bingham*), 30
Concert in a Garden (*F. Falciatore*), 99
Shore at Cas-Butin, Honfleur, (*G. Seurat*), 58

COMPOSED SONGS

Alleluia (*W.A. Mozart*), 141
Anyone Can Move a Mountain (*F.J. Marks*), 48–49
Battle Hymn of the Republic (*W. Steffe*), 34–35
Bicycle Built for Two (*H. Dacre*), 20
Blue Song, A (*E. and H. Aitken*), 188–189
Catch a Falling Star (*Vance and Pakriss*), 108–109
Deep in the Heart of Texas (*D. Swander*), 160–161
Edelweiss (*R. Rodgers*), 178–179
Ever Onward! (*D.A. Pollock*), 220–221
Every Morning When I Wake Up (*A. Gillespie*), 200
Fifty Nifty United States (*R. Charles*), 86–89
Garden Song (*D. Mallett*), 106
Groundhog (*B. Sainte-Marie*), 151
Happiness (*C. Gesner*), 174–175
Hayride (*R.C. Berg*), 226–227
Hey Dum Diddeley Dum (*M. Stone*), 8
I Believe (*E. Drake, I. Graham, J. Shirl, A. Stillman*), 52–53
I Believe in Music (*M. Davis*), 100–101
I'd Like to Teach the World to Sing (In Perfect Harmony) (*B. Backer, B. Davis, R. Cook, R. Greenaway*), 62–63
Inchworm, The (*F. Loesser*), 166–167
Let There Be Peace on Earth (*S. Miller and J. Jackson*), 250–251
Lift Every Voice and Sing (*J.R. Johnson*), 50–51
Lion Sleeps Tonight, The (*H. Peretti, L. Creatore, G. Heiss, A. Stanton, S. Linda, and P. Campbell*), 92–93
Little Lamb (*J. Styne*), 222–223
Little Love Goes a Long Way, A (*A. Balkin*), 208–209
Lonely Goatherd, The (*R. Rodgers*), 142–143
Magic Penny (*M. Reynolds*), 114–115
Mockin' Bird Hill (*V. Horton*), 10–11

Music Goes 'Round and Around, The (*E. Farley and M. Riley*), 42–43
No Need to Hurry (*R.C. Berg*), 37
Now Thank We All Our God (*J. Crüger*), 229
Oh, It's Great to Be Livin' This Morning (*D. Nichol*), 196–197
Oh Susannah (*S. Foster*), 124
Old Piano Roll Blues, The (*C. Cohen*), 119
On the Road Again (*W. Neslon*), 6–7
Peace of the River (*V. Hood*), 145
Put on a Happy Face (*C. Strouse*), 168–169
Sarah the Whale (*D.D. Emmett*), 24
Seven Limericks (*E.L. Diemer*), 64–65
Silver Bells (*J. Livington and R. Evans*), 240–241
Sing (*J. Raposo*), 164–165
Slitheree Dee, The (*S. Silverstein*), 216
Soldier's Song (*L. Bernstein*), 162–163
Spanish Cavalier (*H. Hendrickson*), 156–157
Spider on the Floor (*B. Russell*), 70–71
Sunshine on My Shoulders (*J. Denver, M. Taylor, and D. Knoss*), 138–140
Tallis's Canon (*T. Tallis*), 248
There's Work to Be Done (*R.C. Berg*), 36
This Land Is Your Land (*W. Guthrie*), 123, 186–187
Turtle's song, The — "I Can Win!" (*T. McGrath*), 22–23
Yankee Doodle Boy (*G.M. Cohan*), 84–85
Yes Indeed (*S. Oliver*), 218–219
You're a Grand Old Flag (*G.M. Cohan*), 246–247
Zulu Warrior, The (*J. Marais*), 137

CONTEMPORARY

Amahl and the Night Visitors (*G.C. Menotti*), 234–239
Blue Rondo à la Turk (*D. Burbeck*), 188
Brandenburg Boogie (*arr. L. Holloway*), 96
Dove, The, from Noye's Fludde (*B. Britten*), 203
Hoe-Down from Rodeo (*A. Copland*), 194–195
Variations on a Shaker Tune (*A. Copland*), 29
Wade in the Water, 16–17

COWBOY SONG

Streets of Laredo, 155

CUMULATIVE SONGS

My Aunt Came Back, 19
There's a Hole in the Middle of the Sea, 46

DESCANTS

Haleluyoh, 248–249
Hayride, 226–227
Little Lamb, 222–223
Old Hound Dog Sally, 94–95
Sweet Potatoes, 72–73

FOLK SONGS—K, O

African

Johnny's My Boy, 170
Mayo Nafwa, 38–39
Tina Singu, 182–183

American

Farewell My Own True Love, 215
Lord, Lord, Lord, 60
Old Dan Tucker, 173
Old Hound Dog Sally, 94
On Top of Old Smoky, 25
Sweet Potatoes, 72
Wade in the Water, 17
Yellow Rose of Texas, 153

Czech

Let Us Sing Together, 146–147

Danish

Sim Sa-La-Bim, 110

Dutch

Dobbin, Dobbin, 76–77

English

Christmas Is Coming, 232
Here We Come A-Wassailing, 233
Lost Lady Found, The, 190

Finnish

Harvest Time, 228

French

Pat-A-Pan, 230–231

Greek

Gerakina, 112–113

Irish

Galway Piper, 127

Israeli

El Yivne Ha Galil, 74–75
Glee Reigns in Galilee, 201
Haleluyoh, 248–249
Toembaï, 69
Tzena, Tzena, 212–213

Maori

Maori Stick Game, 134–135

Mexican

La Cucaracha, 26, 123

Norwegian
Oleana, 27

Slovak
Morning Comes Early, 22

FOREIGN-LANGUAGE SONGS

African languages
Mayo Nafwa, 38–39
Tina Singu, 182–183
Zulu Warrior, The, 137

French
Soldier's Song, 162

Hebrew
El Yivne Ha Galil, 74–75
Haleluyoh, 248–249
Toembaï, 69

Maori
Maori Stick Game, 134–135

FUN AND NONSENSE
Bee and the Pup, The, 159
Found a Peanut, 152
Hey Dum Diddeley Dum, 8
I'm Going Crazy, 136
Life in the Army, 83
Lonely Goatherd, The, 142–143
My Aunt Came Back, 19
Oleana, 27
One Bottle of Pop, 176–177
Seven Limericks, 64–65
Slitheree Dee, The, 216
Spider on the Floor, 70–71
There's a Hole in the Middle of
  the Sea, 46

HOLIDAYS, SPECIAL DAYS, PATRIOTIC

Birthday
Little Lamb, 222–223

Christmas
Amahl and the Night Visitors,
  234–239
Christmas Is Coming, 232
Here We Come A-Wassailing, 233
Pat-A-Pan, 230–231
Silver Bells, 240–241

Halloween
On October, 224
Pumpkin Song, 225

Martin Luther King Day
We Shall Overcome, 131

Patriotic
America, America, 116
Battle Hymn of the Republic, 34–
  35
Ever Onward!, 220–21
Fifty Nifty United States, 86–89
Lift Every Voice and Sing, 50–51
Nation's Strength, A, 220
This Land Is Your Land, 123, 186–
  187

Yankee Doodle Boy, 84–85
You're a Grand Old Flag, 246–
  247

Passover
Haleluyoh, 248–249

Thanksgiving and Harvest Time
Harvest Time, 228
Hayride, 226–227
Now Thank We All Our God, 229
Tallis's Canon, 248

Valentine's Day
I Had a Dream, Dear, 242
Somebody Waiting, 245

LISTENING LESSONS
Allegretto from Symphony No. 7
  (*L. van Beethoven*), 107, 172
Amahl and the Night Visitors (*G.C.
  Menotti*), 234–239
Autre Choral (*E. Satie*), 205
Battle Hymn of the Republic, 34–
  35
Bicycle Built for Two (*H. Dacre,
  arr. M. Matthews*), 20–21
Blue Rondo à la Turk (*D. Brubeck*),
  188
Brandenburg Boogie (*arr. L. Hol-
  loway*), 96
Brandenburg Concerto (*J.S.
  Bach*), 98–99
Danse Macabre (*C. Saint-Saëns*),
  44–45
Dove, The, from Noye's Fludde (*B.
  Britten*), 203
Elfin Dance (*E. Grieg*), 184–185
Fossils from Carnival of the Ani-
  mals (*C. Saint-Saëns*), 199
Hoe-Down from Rodeo (*A. Cop-
  land*), 194–195
Londonderry Air (*P. Grainger*),
  126
Lost Lady Found, The (*P. Grain-
  ger*), 192–193
March from The Nutcracker Suite,
  (*P.I. Tchaikovsky*), 128–129
Moonlight Sonata, (*L. van Bee-
  thoven*), 32–33
Nocturne from Divertissement (*J.
  Ibert*), 214
Piano Quintet (''The Trout''), (*F.
  Schubert*), 15
Rumanian Dance No. 5 (*B. Bar-
  tók*),), 111
St. Louis Polka (*J. Biskart and F.
  Yankovic*), 180
Shepherd's Hey (*P. Grainger*), 66–
  67
Sound Categories, 40–41
Souvenir d'Amerique (*H. Vieux-
  temps*), 16
Symphony No. 6 (excerpt) (*L. van
  Beethoven*), 203
Variations on a Shaker Tune (*A.
  Copland*), 29
Voiles (*C. Debussy*), 56–57

Wade in the Water, 16–17

MINOR, MODAL, AND PENTA-TONIC SONGS—K, O

Dorian
Lost Lady Found, The, 190

Minor
America, America, 116
Glee Reigns in Galilee, 201
Haleluyoh, 248–249
Harvest Time, 228
Pat-A-Pan, 230–231
Pumpkin Song, 225
Toembaï, 69
Wade in the Water, 17

Pentatonic
Farewell My Own True Love, 215
Mayo Nafwa, 38
Old Dan Tucker, 173

NATURE, SEASONS, AND WEATHER
Edelweiss, 178–179
Garden Song, 106
Mockin' Bird Hill, 10–11
Morning Comes Early, 22
Oh Susannah, 124
Sunshine on My Shoulders, 138–
  140
Whippoorwill Round, 117

ONE-CHORD SONGS—O
Every Morning When I Wake Up,
  200
Groundhog, 151
Mayo Nafwa, 38–39
Pumpkin Song, 225

PARTNER SONGS
Dobbin, Dobbin, 76–77
No Need to Hurry, 37
Solomon Levi, 156–157
Spanish Cavalier, 156–157
There's Work to Be Done, 36

PART SINGING

Five-part
Smile Is a Frown Upside Down, A,
  78–80

Four-part
Johnny's My Boy, 170–171

Three-part
Alleluia, 141
Hey Dum Diddeley Dum, 8–9

Two-part
Blue Song, A 188–189
El Yivne Ha Galil, 74–75
Inchworm, The, 166–167
Lion Sleeps Tonight, The, 92–93
Little Love Goes a Long Way, A,
  208–209
Lonely Goatherd, The, 142–143
On the Road Again, 6–7
Pat-A-Pan, 230–231

427

Peace of the River, 145
Silver Bells, 240–241
Sweet Potatoes, 72
This Land Is Your Land, 186–187

PATRIOTIC SONGS (SEE *HOLIDAYS, SPECIAL DAYS, PATRIOTIC*)

PENTATONIC (SEE *MINOR, MODAL, AND PENTATONIC SONGS*)

POETRY AND CHANTS—O
Fifty Nifty United States, 88
On October, 224
Pachycephalosaurus, 199
Sports Chants, 110
Tear Down the Walls, 250
What Is Pink?, 204
Zulu Warrior, The, 137

ROUNDS AND CANONS
Alleluia, 141
America, America, 116
Blue Song, A, 188
Catch a Falling Star, 108
Christmas Is Coming, 232
Every Morning When I Wake Up, 200
Pachycephalosaurus, 199
Tallis's Canon, 248
Toembaï, 69
Whippoorwill Round, 117

SINGING GAMES, PLAY-PARTY SONGS, AND DANCES—K, O
Maori Stick Game, 134–135
Mockin' Bird Hill, 94–95
Norwegian Mountain March, 102–103
Old Dan Tucker, 173
St. Louis Polka, 180
Somebody Waiting, 245
Turn the Glasses Over, 104–105
Tzena, Tzena, 212–213

SONGS IN $\frac{5}{4}, \frac{4}{2}, \frac{3}{4}, \frac{7}{8}, \frac{6}{8}$, AND CHANGING METERS—O

Five-four
Sim Sa-La-Bim, 110

Four-two
Tallis's Canon, 248

Three-four
Bicycle Built for Two, 20
Edelweiss, 178–179
Found a Peanut, 152
Inchworm, The, 166–167
La Cucaracha, 26, 123
Let There Be Peace on Earth, 250–251
Lost Lady Found, The, 190

Maori Stick Game, 134–135
Mockin' Bird Hill, 10–11
Norwegian Mountain March, 102
On Top of Old Smoky, 25
One Bottle of Pop, 176–177
Seven Limericks, 64–65
Silver Bells, 240–241
Streets of Laredo, 155

Seven-eight
Gerakina, 112–113

Six-eight
Bee and the Pup, The, 159
Haleluyoh, 248–249
Here We Come A-Wassailing, 233
Lift Every Voice and Sing, 50–51
Ode to a Washerwoman, 14
Oh, Dear, What Can the Matter Be?, 13
Solomon Levi, 120
Whippoorwill Round, 117

Changing Meters
Blue Song, A, 188–189
Mayo Nafwa, 38–39

THREE-CHORD SONGS
Battle Hymn of the Republic, 34–35
Catch a Falling Star, 108–109
Christmas Is Coming, 232
Galway Piper, 127
Haleluyoh, 248–249
Hayride, 226–227
Here We Come A-Wassailing, 233
Johnny's My Boy, 170–171
Let Us Sing Together, 146–147
Life in the Army, 83
Lion Sleeps Tonight, The, 92–93
Little Love Goes a Long Way, A, 208–209
Lost Lady Found, The, 190
Magic Penny, 114–115
No Need to Hurry, 37
Norwegian Mountain March, 102
Ode to a Washerwoman, 14
Oh, Dear, What Can the Matter Be?, 13
Oh, Susannah, 124
Old Hound Dog Sally, 94
Oleana, 27
On Top of Old Smoky, 25
Pat-A-Pan, 230–231
Sarah the Whale, 24
Slitheree Dee, 216
Solomon Levi, 120, 156–157
Spanish Cavalier, 156–157
Spider on the Floor, 70
Streets of Laredo, 155
There's Work to Be Done, 36
This Land Is Your Land, 123, 186–187
Turtle's Song, The—"I Can Win!", 22–23

Tzena, Tzena, 212–213
When the Saints Go Marching In, 154

TRADITIONAL
America, America, 116
Bee and the Pup, The, 159
Black-Eyed Susie, 181
I Had a Dream, Dear, 242–243
I'm Going Crazy, 136
Life in the Army, 83
Look Down That Lonesome Road, 90
My Aunt Came Back, 19
Norwegian Mountain March, 102
Ode to a Washerwoman, 14
Oh, Dear, What Can the Matter Be?, 13
One Bottle of Pop, 176–177
Simple Gifts, 28
Solomon Levi, 120
There's a Hole in the Middle of the Sea, 46
When the Saints Go Marching In, 154
Whippoorwill Round, 117

TRAVEL AND TRANSPORTATION
Bicycle Built for Two, 20
Dobbin, Dobbin, 76–77
Hayride, 226–227
Oh Susannah, 124
On the Road Again, 6–7
Rock Island Line, 125
This Land Is Your Land, 123, 186–187
Turn the Glasses Over, 104–105

TWO-CHORD SONGS
America, America, 116
Bee and the Pup, The, 159
Deep in the Heart of Texas, 160–161
Dobbin, Dobbin, 76–77
Ever Onward!, 220–221
Found a Peanut, 152
Gerakina, 112–113
Glee Reigns in Galilee, 201
Harvest Time, 228
La Cucaracha, 26, 123
Maori Stick Game, 134–135
My Aunt Came Back, 19
Old Dan Tucker, 173
One Bottle of Pop, 176–177
Sim Sa-La-Bim, 110
Simple Gifts, 28
Sweet Potatoes, 72
There's a Hole in the Middle of the Sea, 46
Turn the Glasses Over, 104
Whippoorwill Round, 117
Yellow Rose of Texas, 153

WORK SONG
Rock Island Line, 125

Classified Index of Activities and Skills

*Topics of special interest to teachers who use the Kodaly and Orff methods are indicated with a **K** and an **O**.*

ACTIVITY PAGES IN THE PU-PIL BOOK

Adagio for Percussion, 31
Chords and Melody Go Hand in Hand, 12
Create a Light Show, 97
Forward-Back!, 111
Improvisation on Whole Tones, 54–55
Keyboard Instruments, 118
Largo, 205
Learn to Play a C Chord, 158
Learn to Strum on Open Strings, 149
Learning a New Song, 130
Make Musical Decisions, 34
Makings of an Opera, 207
Moonlight, 30
More About Rhythmic Relationships, 21
Patriotic Polyrhythms, 85
Play a Keyboard Instrument, 121
Play the Autoharp, 122
Play the Soprano Ukulele, 148
Rhythm Challenge, A, 82
Sea, The, 58–59
Sing a Valentine, 244
Sky Singers, 202
Speech to Song, 206
Theme and Variations, 16
Tune Your Ukulele, 150

ART ACTIVITIES, 30, 56–58, 96–98

CREATIVE ACTIVITIES—O

adding new verses, 18–19, 83, 199
arranging, 34, 225, 240–241
creative dramatics, 56–57, 142–144, 206–207, 210–211
drawing pictures, 126–127
games, 26, 68–70, 76, 82, 86, 90–91, 104–105, 134–135, 216–217, 244–245
improvising and composing, 54–55, 58–59, 63, 97, 113, 167, 202, 204–205, 224
improvising accompaniments, 130–131, 200, 210–211, 225
improvising melodies, 204
improvising movements and dances, 23, 56–57, 84, 111–112, 192–193, 212–217
improvising rhythm patterns, 30, 136–137, 145, 183, 209
light shows, 96–98
performing, 99, 113, 130–131, 193, 202–203, 212, 225
student as conductor, 58–59, 139, 178–179
whistling, 202
writing poems, 56–57, 242

CURRICULUM CORRELATION

Language Arts—O

foreign languages
African languages, 38–39, 137, 182–183
French, 162–163
Hebrew, 74–75, 248–249
Maori, 134–135

limericks, 64–65

metaphors, 106, 250

Music Drama
Amahl and the Night Visitors, 234–239
Kantan, 210–211

Poetry
Nation's Strength, A (R.W. Emerson), 220
On October (S. Falk), 224
Pachycephalosaurus (R. Armour), 199
Tear Down the Walls (F. Nell), 250
What Is Pink? (C. Rossetti), 204–205

Mathematics
rhythm equations, 20

Science
birdsong, 202
fossils, 198
sounds produced by bottles, 176

Social Studies
hand signs, 146–147
old-time entertainment, 173
presidents of the USA, 87–88
states of the USA, 87–89
West Africa, 38

ELECTRONIC MUSIC, 21

EVALUATIONS, 36–37, 66–67, 100–101, 130–131

EXPRESSION—O

articulation, 31
overall expressive quality, 30–32, 34, 50, 52, 56–59, 96–97, 138–139, 145, 164, 178, 192–195, 204, 234–239, 246, 250
tempo, 30, 46–47, 49
text setting, 166, 216, 229
volume, 31, 48, 65, 184, 205

FOLK DANCE
circle dance, 9, 94–95, 173
Hora, 75
polka, 180
square dance, 194–195

FORM—K, O
A B A, 13, 16, 37, 108, 114–115, 128, 222–223
aria, 207
call-response, 18–19, 39
interludes, 224
phrases, 10, 50, 84, 106, 134, 196–197, 221, 226
recitative, 207
rondo, 15–16, 200
same-different, 127, 190–191
sections, 78, 128–129
theme and variations, 16–17, 29, 107, 192–193
two- and three-part form, 137, 187

HARMONY
chords, 6, 12–14, 28, 90–92, 94, 122, 150–151, 158–163, 176
chord sequence, 14–15, 24, 26–27, 36–37, 77–78, 92, 176–177, 221
ostinato, 76, 117, 201
parallel and contrary motion, 74, 78, 115, 141, 145, 230, 240–241
selecting chords for accompaniment, 11, 24–26, 127, 130–131

INSTRUMENTAL ACTIVITIES—O
autoharp, 24–28, 36–37, 58–59, 68, 76–77, 82–83, 90–93, 96–97, 100–107, 122–125, 130–131, 160–163, 201, 220–221
castanets, 64–65
claves, 36–37, 60–62, 78–81, 136, 208–209
coconut shells, 76–77
cowbells, 38, 60–61, 142–144
cymbals, 30–31, 64–65, 84–85, 201
drums of all kinds, 6, 20–21, 36–39, 64–65, 78–81, 110, 137, 162–163, 182–183, 188–189, 201, 207–208, 224
environmental soundmakers, 40–41
finger cymbals, 74, 96–97, 112–113, 188–189, 210–211, 214
glockenspiel, 108, 116–117, 202–203, 232, 240–241
   alto, 138–139, 166–167
   soprano, 94–95, 100–101, 138–139, 200
gongs, 38–39, 188–189, 210–211
guiro, 36–37, 84–85, 188–189
kazoo, 124–125
maracas, 36–39, 60–61, 64–65, 78–81, 96–97, 122–123, 208–209
metallophone, 210–211
   alto, 94–95, 100–101, 138–

139, 166–167, 200–201, 228, 232
  soprano, 94–95, 100–101
piano, 162–163, 166–167, 204–205, 220–221
rattles, 38–39
resonator bells, 10–12, 14, 36–37, 52–59, 64–65, 70–74, 96–97, 102–108, 130–131, 142–145, 170, 172, 182–183, 190–191, 201, 204–205, 210–211, 222–227, 224–225, 248–249
sandblocks, 188–189
slide whistles, 224
soda bottles, 176–177
tambourine, 46, 60–61, 64–65, 74, 96–97, 112–113, 134, 201, 228
temple blocks, 210–211
timpani, 201, 210–211, 224
triangle, 30–31, 64–65, 96–97, 188–189
tuned water glasses, 210–211
ukulele
  soprano, 148–157, 160–161
unspecified keyboard instruments, 120–121, 156, 158–159, 224, 240–241
unspecified mallet instruments, 54–59
unspecified percussion instruments, 30–31, 38–39, 84–85, 96–97, 112–113, 137, 188–189, 200–201, 208–211, 224–225
whistles, 202–203
windchimes, 210–211
woodblocks, 30–31, 64–65, 76–77, 84–85, 96–97, 142–144, 210–211
xylophone, 142–144, 170, 204–205, 224, 226–227, 244–245
  alto, 94–95, 100–101, 200, 228
  bass, 76–77, 94–95, 100–101, 116–117, 138–139, 166–167, 200–201, 220–221, 224, 228, 232
  soprano, 200

INSTRUMENTS FEATURED IN LISTENING LESSONS

Bagpipes, 40–41

Banjo, 40–41

Carillon, 40–41

Cheng, 40–41

Clarinet, 40–41

Electric piano
Funkarello (*B. Evans*), 118–119

Ground Rattles, 40–41

Guitar, 40–41

Harmonica, 40–41

Harpsichord
Sinfonia from Entrance of the Queen of Sheba (*G.F. Handel*), 118–119

Jazz Ensemble
Battle Hymn of the Republic, 34–35
Brandenburg Boogie (*J.S. Bach, arr. L. Holloway*), 96–97
Wade in the Water, 16–17

Orchestra
Allegretto from Symphony No. 7 (*L. van Beethoven*), 106–107, 172
Amahl and the Night Visitors (*G.C. Menotti*), 234–239
Autre Choral from En Habit de Cheval (*E. Satie*), 204–205
Battle Hymn of the Republic, 34–35
Brandenburg Concerto No. 2 in F Major, First Movement (*J.S. Bach*), 98–99
Danse Macabre (*C. Saint-Säens*), 44–45
Dove, The, from Noye's Fludde (*B. Britten*), 202–203
''Fossils'' from Carnival of the Animals (*C. Saint-Säens*), 198–199
Hoe-Down from Rodeo (*A. Copland*), 194–195
Londonderry Air (*P. Grainger*), 126–127
March from The Nutcracker Suite (*P.I. Tchaikovsky*), 128–129
Moonlight Sonata (*L. van Beethoven*), 30–33
Nocturne from Divertissement (*J. Ibert*), 214
Symphony No. 6, excerpt (*L. van Beethoven*), 202–203
Variations on a Shaker Tune from Appalachian Spring (*A. Copland*), 28–29, 42

Organ
In Dulci Jubilo (*J.S. Bach*), 118–119

Piano
Elfin Dance (*E. Grieg*), 184–185
Moonlight Sonata (*L. van Beethoven*), 30–33
Polonaise in A Flat (*F. Chopin*), 118–119
Rumanian Dance No. 5 from Rumanian Folk Dances (*B. Bartók*), 110–111
Souvenir d'Amerique (*H. Vieuxtemps*), 16–17
''Trout'' Quintet, Fourth Movement (*F. Schubert*), 14–15
Voiles from Preludes for Piano (*C. Debussy*), 56–57

Player Piano
Old Piano Roll Blues, The, (*C. Cohen*),118–119

Rauschfeiff, 40–41

Recorder, 40–41

Sanza, 40–41

Sitar, 40–41

Strings
''Trout'' Quintet, Fourth Movement (*F. Schubert*),14–15

Synthesizer
Bicycle Built for Two (*H. Dacre, arr. M. Matthews*), 20–21
Joyful (*A. Briggs*), 118–119

Tambourine, 40–41

Timpani, 40–41

Tom-Tom, 40–41

Violin
sound sources, 40–41
Souvenir d'Amerique (*H. Vieuxtemps*), 16–17

Water Drum, 40–41

Wind Ensemble
Lost Lady Found from Lincolnshire Posy (*P. Grainger*), 192–193
Shepherd's Hey (*P. Grainger*), 66–67

Xylophone, 40–41

LISTENING SKILLS
expressive elements, 32–35, 126, 145, 162, 203, 214, 234–239
following a call chart, 29, 192–195
harmonic elements, 100–101, 160
parallel and contrary motion, 100
recognizing form, 168, 205, 223, 246–247
recognizing a melody, 29, 43, 66, 96, 128, 172, 186, 199
recognizing instruments, 42–45, 64, 66–67, 96, 118, 129, 214
tonal elements, 70, 91

MELODY—K
based on scale, 52–53, 201, 220, 226–227, 248
high-low, 8
intervals, 142, 166–167
major scale, 52–54, 72, 116, 201, 248
melodic contour, 10, 21, 46, 49–50, 52, 78, 108, 138, 141, 164–165, 172, 188–189, 206, 208
melodic direction (up-down-same), 120, 145, 200, 220, 230, 250–251
melodic patterns, 74, 197, 225
minor scale, 69, 116–117, 190–191, 201, 230, 249
pentatonic scale, 173

step-skip-same, 26–28, 76, 116, 120, 142, 166, 188–189, 212, 220
tonal center, 8, 53–54, 66, 70–73, 83, 94, 100, 114, 116, 127, 139, 162, 182, 248
transposition, 53, 64, 70–72
whole-tone scale, 54–57, 204–205

MOVEMENT—O (SEE ALSO *CREATIVE ACTIVITIES*)
action songs, 18–19, 146–147, 168–169, 232
body as percussion instrument, 6, 18, 38, 222, 228
patterned dancing, 9, 75, 94–95, 103, 173, 180, 195

MUSIC DRAMA (SEE *CURRICULUM CORRELATION—LANGUAGE ARTS*)

NOTATING MUSIC
with ikons, 164, 230–231
with notation, 20, 181, 196

READING MUSIC
call charts, 29, 192–195
expressive elements, 48
harmonic elements, 160, 191
melodic ikons, 7, 12, 168–169, 202

musical maps, 44
musical notation, 20, 48–49, 62–64, 76, 139, 154, 170, 174–175, 190–191, 198, 215, 218, 228–229, 232, 242, 248
rhythmic ikons, 38, 168–169, 205
score, 15, 98–99, 141, 230–231
tablature, 150–155

RHYTHM—K
beat and accent, 10, 22, 24, 60, 62, 166, 190–191
even-uneven, 136, 233
longer-shorter-same, 181
meter, 22, 84, 102, 112–113, 134, 233, 248
mixed meter, 110–111
polymeter, 38, 156, 188–89
polyrhythms, 84–85
rhythmic patterns, 18, 22, 24, 38, 49, 64, 68–69, 82, 84–86, 104–105, 108, 112, 127, 136, 138, 174, 201, 222, 225, 233
shortest sounds, 22, 24, 36, 46, 102, 106, 136, 138, 181, 196, 242, 248
syncopation, 60–62, 84, 182
underlying pulse or beat, 46, 138

SINGING SKILLS—K
breath control and posture, 251

chanting, 22, 24, 46, 68, 82, 86, 104, 137, 182
choral speaking, 204, 224
diction, 231
difference between speaking and singing voices, 206
echoing, 8–9, 200, 218
sightreading, 28, 37, 250
singing and playing simultaneously, 122–123, 148–155
singing in parts, 6–9, 15, 37, 72–73, 77, 93, 115, 142–145, 170, 183, 186, 196–197, 199, 209, 218, 221, 226–228, 230, 232, 240–244, 249
singing with scale numbers, 8, 25, 28, 36, 66, 94, 105, 111, 141, 208, 244, 248
vocal inflections, 206, 250
vocal quality, 187, 241, 251
yodeling, 142–144

STRUCTURE (SEE *FORM*)

TEXTURE, 74–81, 188–189

TIMBRE, 32, 40–44, 85, 100, 118–119, 128–129, 199

Time and Place, 38–39, 98–99, 182–183, 208–209, 230, 233

Alphabetical Index of Music

Allegretto (*L.V. Beethoven*), 106, 172
Alleluia (*W.A. Mozart*), 141
Amahl and the Night Visitors (*G.C. Menotti*), 234
America, America, 116
Anyone Can Move a Mountain, 48
Autre Choral (*E. Satie*), 204

Battle Hymn of the Republic, three versions, 34
Bee and the Pup, The, 159
Bicycle Built for Two, 20
Black-Eyed Susie, 181
Blue Rondo à la Turk (*D. Brubeck*), 188
Blue Song, A, 188
Brandenburg Boogie (*L. Holloway*), 96
Brandenburg Concerto No. 2 (*J.S. Bach*), 98

Catch a Falling Star, 108
Christmas Is Coming, 232

Danse Macabre (*C. Saint-Saëns*), 44

Deep in the Heart of Texas, 160
Dobbin, Dobbin, 76
Dove, The (*B. Britten*), 202

Edelweiss, 178
El Yivne Ha Galil, 74
Elfin Dance (*E. Grieg*), 184
Ever Onward!, 220
Every Morning When I Wake Up, 200

Farewell My Own True Love, 215
Fifty Nifty United States, 86
Fossils (*C. Saint-Saëns*), 198
Found a Peanut, 152
Funkarello (*B. Evans*), 118

Galway Piper, 127
Garden Song, 106
Gerakina, 112
Glee Reigns in Galilee, 201
Groundhog, 151

Haleluyoh, 248
Happiness, 174
Harvest Time, 228
Hayride, 226

Here We Come A-Wassailing, 233
Hey Dum Diddeley Dum, 8
Hoe-Down (*A. Copland*), 194

I Believe, 52
I Believe in Music, 100
I Had a Dream, Dear, 242
In Dulci Jubilo (*J.S. Bach*), 118
Inchworm, The, 166
I'd Like to Teach the World to Sing (In Perfect Harmony), 62
I'm Going Crazy, 136

Johnny's My Boy, 170
Joyful (*A. Briggs*), 118

La Cucaracha, 26, 123
Let There Be Peace on Earth, 250
Let Us Sing Together, 146
Life in the Army, 83
Lift Every Voice and Sing, 50
Lion Sleeps Tonight, The, 92
Little Lamb, 222
Little Love Goes a Long Way, A, 208
Londonderry Air (*P. Grainger*), 126

Lonely Goatherd, The, 142
Look Down That Lonesome Road, 90
Lord, Lord, Lord, 60
Lost Lady Found, The, 190
Lost Lady Found, The (*P. Grainger*), 192

Magic Penny, 114
Maori Stick Game, 134
March (excerpts) (*P.I. Tchaikovsky*), 128
March (*P.I. Tchaikovsky*), 128
Mayo Nafwa, 38
Mockin' Bird Hill, 10
Moonlight Sonata (*L.V. Beethoven*), 32
Moonlight Sonata (*L.V. Beethoven*), 32
Morning Comes Early, 22
Music Goes 'Round and Around, The, 42
My Aunt Came Back, 18

No Need to Hurry, 37
Nocturne (*J. Ibert*), 214
Norwegian Mountain March, 102
Now Thank We All Our God (*J.S. Bach*), 229
Now Thank We All Our God, 229

Ode to a Washerwoman, 14
Oh, Dear, What Can the Matter Be?, 13
Oh, It's Great to Be Livin' This Morning, 196
Oh Susannah, 124

Old Dan Tucker, 173
Old Hound Dog Sally, 94
Old Piano Roll Blues, The, 119
Oleana, 27
On the Road Again, 6
On Top of Old Smoky, 25
One Bottle of Pop, 176

Pachycephalosaurus, 198
Pat-A-Pan, 230
Peace of the River, 145
Piano Quintet (*F. Schubert*), 15
Polonaise in A♭ (*F. Chopin*), 118
Pumpkin Song, 225
Put on a Happy Face, 168

Rock Island Line, 125
Rumanian Dance No. 5 (*B. Bartók*), 111

St. Louis Polka (*J. Biskart and F. Yankovic*), 180
Sarah the Whale, 24
Seven Limericks, 64
Shepherd's Hey (*P. Grainger*), 66
Silver Bells, 240
Sim Sa-La-Bim, 110
Simple Gifts, 28
Sinfonia (*G.F. Handel*), 118
Sing, 164
Skip To My Lou, 12
Slitheree Dee, The, 216
Smile Is a Frown Upside Down, A, 78
Soldier's Song (*L. Bernstein*), 162
Solomon Levi, 120
Solomon Levi and Spanish Cavalier, 156
Somebody Waiting, 245

Sound Categories, 40
Souvenir d'Amerique (*H. Vieuxtemps*), 16
Spider on the Floor, 70
Streets of Laredo, 155
Sunshine on My Shoulders, 138
Sweet Potatoes, 72
Symphony No. 6 (*L.V. Beethoven*), 202

Tallis's Canon, 248
There's a Hole in the Middle of the Sea, 46
There's Work to Be Done, 36
This Land Is Your Land, 123, 186
Tina Singu, 182
Toembaï, 68
Turn the Glasses Over, 104
Turtle's Song, The — "I Can Win!," 22
Tzena, Tzena, 212

Variations on a Shaker Tune (*A. Copland*), 28
Voiles (*C. Debussy*), 56

Wade in the Water, 17
Wade in the Water, 17
We Shall Overcome, 131
When the Saints Go Marching In, 154
Whippoorwill Round, 117

Yankee Doodle Boy, 84
Yellow Rose of Texas, 153
Yes Indeed, 218
You're a Grand Old Flag, 246

Zulu Warrior, 137

TEACHER'S NOTES

TEACHER'S NOTES

TEACHER'S NOTES